Debt Wish

Pitt Series in Policy and Institutional Studies

Bert A. Rockman, Editor

Alberta M. Sbragia

DEBT WISH

Entrepreneurial Cities,

U.S. Federalism, and

Economic Development

University of Pittsburgh Press

To my husband, Martin Staniland

Published by the University of Pittsburgh Press,
Pittsburgh, Pa. 15260

Copyright © 1996, University of Pittsburgh Press
All rights reserved
Eurospan, London
Manufactured in the United States of America
Printed on acid-free paper

Library of Congress Cataloging-in-Publication
Data

Sbragia, Alberta M.
    Debt wish : entrepreneurial cities, U.S. federalism,
and economic development / Alberta M. Sbragia.
        p.   cm. — (Pitt series in policy and
institutional science)
    Includes index.
    ISBN 0-8229-3942-8 (cloth : alk. paper). —
ISBN 0-8229-5599-7 (pbk. : alk. paper)
    1. Investment of public funds — United States.
    2. Intergovernmental fiscal relations — United States.
    3. Municipal finance — United States.   I. Title.
II. Series.
HJ3833.S26   1996
336.73 — dc20   95-51285

A CIP catalogue record for this book is available from
the British Library.

Contents

Preface

This book has taken a long time to write. I became interested in capital investment and the constraints imposed on governments by needing to borrow for such investment during my dissertation research on public housing in Milan, Italy. I then decided to carry out comparative research, thinking that I would probably write a comparative book. Yet as I delved more deeply into the topic, I realized that the American case was the most interesting. As my research progressed, I decided that the American case deserved a full-length in-depth analysis in its own right.

But, I then became aware, the American case was far more complex than I had realized when I was treating it in a comparative context. I became particularly aware of its complexity during the year I spent as a visitor at the Harvard Business School. Perhaps it takes a year at a first-rate business school to understand some of the constraints that influence the private sector. In any case, I came away from that year realizing that I needed to pay much more attention than I had anticipated to the legal system, the courts, and federal tax policy. Capital markets were not the autonomous actors that I had assumed, and I needed to understand how law and tax policy affected their operations. As I was beginning to understand that dimension (which had a very significant historical foundation), the Tax Reform Act of 1986 was passed by Congress, requiring that I spend more time than expected analyzing the contemporary federal role in shaping the system of public investment.

The final stage of research at least seemed straightforward enough. However, the Brookings Institution invited me to direct a project on policy making in the European Union (then known as the European Community). Given the historic processes of integration going on in Europe, and given my underlying interest in federalism and intergovernmental politics, I accepted. Little did I know how complex the process of European integration had become and how long it would take me (and the other members of the project) to make sense of it! That project, however, made me acutely aware of three factors that I underline in this study. The first is the importance of history. It became clear to me, as a student of "European history in the making," that if the experience in European integration succeeds, scholars a hundred years from now will miss a great deal if they ignore the historical foundation of the process by which an integrated Europe was created. Decisions are being made now in Brussels that will constrain the choices of future policy makers. Similarly, decisions made by American officials in the nineteenth century narrowed the choices available to their twentieth-century successors.

Second, my work on European integration highlighted the importance of politics between governments. The European experience helped to sharpen my argument (stated in the concluding chapter) that politics between governments operate in parallel with politics as traditionally defined. Electorates and interest groups — the traditional political actors — coexist with governments that in turn deal politically with each other. A comprehensive view of "politics" should then include both "state-society" and "intergovernmental" politics. Third, my work on Europe helped me to understand how governments can use the market as an ally. The role of the municipal bond market outlined in this study, while certainly having idiosyncratic elements, is not all that exotic after all.

Since my work on European urban and federal politics has deeply influenced the analysis presented here, my intellectual debts are necessarily wide-ranging. Innumerable conversations and writings on seemingly unrelated topics have shaped my argument. My acknowledgments cannot but be partial.

I do wish to thank the Harvard Business School for having provided me with an extraordinarily stimulating year during my stay there in 1983–1984, as well as for its generous financial support of my research during my visit. Thomas McCraw was particularly helpful during my stay. Without the school's influence, this book would have been out long ago, but it would have been much less ambitious. Richard Rose, director of the Centre for the Study of Public Policy at the University of Strathclyde in Glasgow, Scotland, also deserves special mention. His willingness to give me money to pursue my interest in the comparative politics of local borrowing was both materially and psychologically crucial in persuading me to continue work in what seemed a most arcane area to nearly everyone else. The University Center for International Studies at the University of Pittsburgh, for its part, helped me immeasurably in the final stages of the manuscript by giving me a semester-long faculty fellowship with research support. Both Burkart Holzner, the center's director, and Thomas Mc-Kechnie, the associate director, have been exceptionally accepting of the argument that research on the United States and Europe can be mutually supportive. The chairmen of my department have been consistently helpful. Guy Peters deserves special thanks.

Finally, I wish to thank with particular warmth three colleagues at the University of Pittsburgh. Morris Ogul patiently read and edited the first five chapters. Most important, however, he has been a source of constant encouragement and support. Morton Coleman has also been consistently encouraging; the classes we have taught together over the years have been an important stimulus to my thinking. Finally, Bert Rockman has been indefatigable in supporting this research, criticizing it, reading drafts, and pursuing this manuscript for his series. I particularly appreciate his early advice to follow my hunch that the politics of capital investment were worth investigating.

My husband, Martin Staniland, has played an unusual role. Given his general predisposition to shy away from all topics having to do with high finance, I have used him as my prototypical reader. I have tried to make this book as interesting — and as lucid — as possible, in the hope that, after reading the first chapter, he will not put the book down. I am also grateful to him for the sustained support he has given me over the years as I have done the research for this study. My children, Paul and Laura, constantly reminded me that politics and money are only a very small part of life after all.

Debt Wish

Chapter 1

Introduction

This book is about urban government as borrower and investor. Whether building infrastructure or supporting economic development, city officials historically have borrowed money and invested it. In fact, "the vital services at the heart of urban rule" depend on such capital investment.[1] Public power has mobilized private money for public purposes. Over time, such investment has become disconnected from the normal political and administrative processes of local policy making. A great deal of local government investment now takes place in an institutional world that differs significantly from the picture of urban politics and government presented in textbooks. This book addresses the question of why local government as borrower and investor differs from local government as we traditionally think of it.

The historical evolution of the American federal system provides an important explanation for the distinctiveness of those governmental institutions charged with local investment. This book consequently explores how local government's role as investor has been shaped both by the actions of higher levels of government and by local responses to such actions. It argues that intergovernmental politics have produced the distinctive institutional world within which much local public investment takes place.

A discussion of the politics of public investment must begin by recognizing the shrunken role of cities in the American system of government. As the federal system became institutionalized over two centuries, city government lost much of its formal autonomy. Major (and many minor) policy initiatives needed the approval of state legislatures. Cities also became limited informally. They began to compete for residents, employment, and tax revenue with the suburbs that provided an escape for citizens unhappy with the city. Although city officials themselves have long been aware of the limits within which they worked, scholars writing about urban politics in the 1960s and 1970s usually ignored these limits. Scholars regarded the policies of cities as originating in the political life of cities rather than as responses to forces outside. The debate over who governed in cities assumed that even if the "elite" was in fact several elites, urban political life was self-contained.[2]

Recent scholarship has challenged this assumption. Paul Peterson, for example, convincingly argued that cities are vulnerable to external forces and that such vulnerability creates limits on what they can do. In his view, cities are not like independent nation-states:

> Too often cities are treated as if they were nation-states. . . . It is the burden of my argument that local politics is not like national politics. On the contrary, by comparison with national politics local politics is most limited. There are crucial kinds of public policies that local governments simply cannot execute. They cannot make war or peace; they cannot issue passports or forbid outsiders from entering their territory; they cannot issue currency; and they cannot control imports or erect tariff walls. . . . [C]ity politics is limited politics. . . . The place of the city within the larger political economy of the nation fundamentally affects the policy choices that cities make.

Martin Shefter, for his part, notes that "cities lack autonomy juridically, economically, and politically," while Paul Kantor argues that "the modern city has become politically democratic but economically dependent."[3]

Seen in a historical context, the "limited politics" discussed by Peterson are a phenomenon particularly characteristic of the twentieth century. Although cities have never exercised the powers of national governments, they enjoyed far greater scope of action in the nineteenth century than they do now. Why and how, then, did cities' political and policy options eventually become more limited?

The conventional answer would emphasize "Dillon's rule," which rendered cities legally "creatures of the state." Yet Dillon's rule is often referred to in isolation, without recognition that Judge Dillon was writing in the midst of an important debate about the proper role of local governments in the economy.[4] Dillon's view of local government was shaped by the entrepreneurial role it had been playing for decades, a role that became increasingly controversial when state judges began to view cities' investment activities as moving beyond the proper boundaries of "public purpose." Dillon's rule, set in its own time, had as much to do with the political economy of the United States as with state-local relations.

An alternative answer to the question of why city politics are so limited might stress the limited reach of elected mayors and city councils within their own territorial boundaries. It might note the importance of independent authorities, which often cut across city/suburban boundaries. Peterson, for one, finds that developmental policies (those that benefit the economic position of a community) in cities are not controlled by elected city officials but rather "come under the direction of independent authorities." These authorities are self-financing rather than reliant on taxation, and this gives them enormous leverage and insulates them from normal political channels. (Such authorities differ from so-called special-district governments, which are typically elected, levy property taxes, and must submit their borrowing to the electorate in the form of referenda.) Annmarie Hauck Walsh notes that "the corporate form of public authorities permits jobs to be done and projects to be completed without the clamorous debates, recurring compromises, and delaying checks and counterchecks that characterize the rest of American government."[5]

These authorities or special-purpose governments do indeed weaken the control of elective institutions over capital investment and increase the power of those interest groups that are most closely affected by such investment decisions. The relatively insulated and closed nature of the politics surrounding public authorities allows economic-development activities under their control to proceed without much input from the electorate. This is important, because critics of Peterson's conclusion that "cities, like private firms, compete with one another so as to maximize their economic position," argue that he assumes "there tends to be a consensus in cities to promote 'rational' community economic goals."[6] No such consensus needs to exist, however, to the extent that authorities as opposed to elected officials are making the relevant economic-development decision. Given the closed nature of politics in authorities, they are often able to operate with little concern for the wishes of voters. Herman Leonard, in discussing the "quiet side" of public expenditure, points out that spending by authorities is deliberately insulated from legislative control:

> Spending by public authorities — like water and sewer commissions and port, turnpike, and public power authorities — could also be viewed as quiet

public spending. Public authorities annually spend billions of dollars raised through "user" fees. . . . [Yet such spending] is not supposed to be authorized through a legislative appropriations process. Public authorities have deliberately been sheltered from the appropriations process — excused from it by duly constituted legislative authority.[7]

Why do such authorities exist? Why did powerful mayors allow such obvious competitors for power to come into being? Why do they exist solely in those policy areas concerned with capital investment, and not in others such as social services? And why are they not elected or subject to legislative control?

The literature on urban politics is strangely silent about these non-elective institutions and the implications that their activities have for urban government and politics. Perhaps the very fact they are not perceived as part of the normal political landscape has shielded them from the scrutiny of political scientists. Whatever the reason, scholars have tended to focus on the governments that provide social welfare services and that levy taxes rather than on the governments that provide capital-intensive and economic-development services and that levy user fees. The literature on public administration, while giving some attention to these bodies, is also lacking.[8]

This book analyzes how city governments as borrowers and investors became subordinate to the state government; how and why they then gradually lost their role as investors to public authorities; and how the borrowing and lending activities of such authorities eventually put local capital investment on Washington's policy agenda. It argues that the use of public authorities represented an important way to circumvent the limitations on investment imposed on city governments by the state government. Given that the state attempted to limit city governments by empowering the electorate in the making of investment decisions, the dilution of state power has also led to the exclusion of the local electorate from the capital investment arena. General-purpose goverments (that is, city governments) created innovatively financed, non-elected, special-purpose governments in order to dilute state power and the power of local electorates. However, they have found that their own power has been diluted as well.

Once special-purpose governments became central to local capital investment, their activities moved far beyond the infrastructure-building typically associated with authorities. Local government capital finance then came under the scrutiny of Washington — of both the Supreme Court and Congress. The "politics of circumvention" that had maximized local governmental power while simultaneously fragmenting it and insulating it from electorates led ironically to an increased role for the federal government.

Governments as Actors

The analysis presented here treats local governments as unitary actors operating within a universe of other governments and governmental institutions such as courts. Its focus is not on those groups or individuals who have tried to influence decisions about which projects to fund. Briefly put, that part of the story is not surprising. Land speculators (eager for a railroad in order to increase their land values) and railroad investors (anxious for help with financing construction) certainly lobbied for the financing provided by local governments.[9] Certainly, too, the relationships between such owners and municipal officials were not always honest, and a substantial amount of corruption accompanied the entrepreneurial activities of state and local governments in the nineteenth century. More recently, firms specializing in the borrowing of funds for municipalities have been key campaign contributors. Candidates running for state and local office turn to such firms for campaign funds as a matter of course and steer business to them when borrowing.[10]

But this book is concerned more with the strategy adopted by governments — as institutions — to increase their power to borrow funds and thereby to invest. It is concerned with how local governments achieved their goal of being allowed to finance capital investment at levels they desired in the face of limits placed on them by state government and the courts. This analysis thus takes seriously the idea that local governments pursue their "institutional self-interest."[11] In the case of investment, such an interest has focused on maximizing local governments' ability to borrow and invest as much as they saw fit for activities of their own choosing.

Intergovernmental Politics

Although this book is concerned with the United States, its argument has been developed by the use of comparison. Both the questions asked and the answers provided by this analysis are rooted in a comparison between the United States and Great Britain. Although not a comparative study, this work has used comparison as a way of identifying those aspects of the American experience that differ enough to deserve extended analysis. In fact, it was a comparative habit of mind that first alerted me to the importance of the politics that take place among governments.

The lack of a "public sector" in the British sense has made American intergovernmental politics both more complicated and less visible than in Britain. Although it is difficult to discuss British urban politics without including central-local politics, for example, many analysts of American urban politics quite comfortably relegate intergovernmental "relations" to a separate subfield and pay it little heed. Many urban scholars ignore federalism except to make a token acknowledgment to Dillon's rule, which is seen as limiting the power of cities. Those political scientists who have analyzed federalism have tended to downplay both the role of judicial action and the behavior of governments acting in their own interest in the evolution of federalism. Instead, they have focused on the party system, social change, or intergovernmental relations as defined administratively, for example, as central variables in the evolution of federalism.[12]

Urban politics are typically not analyzed as intertwined with intergovernmental politics, although John Mollenkopf's *The Contested City* represents an important exception to this statement. Mollenkopf argues:

> The federal government . . . ceded a tremendous amount of discretion and control over its programs to local political actors who, in a sense, completed the construction of the intergovernmental program delivery system. The federal government provided some powerful tools, and designed them to achieve political as well as economic change at the local level, but in the final analysis local actors were the ones who put these tools to use. Their distinctive concerns and interests had considerable impact on the shape and effect of these programs. These local concerns led to outcomes which differed from those which national advocates of federal urban development programs had in mind.[13]

Politics in urban area are usually defined as involving *local* actors, whether these be community and neighborhood organizations, elected officials, corporate interests, those concerned with the development of real estate, or the local electorate. Debates among scholars of urban affairs have focused on the relative influence of economic interests vis-à-vis those of elected officials, community groups, or electoral coalitions.[14] Political activity is assumed to be about the representation of interests defined in societal terms. Elective officials, neighborhood organizations, and real estate owners, for example, pursue their interests in the political arena. In this view, government is the object of pressure from groups rather than an actor in its own right. Along the same lines, politics are defined as groups coming into conflict rather than as governments coming into conflict.

Yet if one examines the landscape of local government in any metropolitan area, one is struck by the number of governments — municipalities, counties, special districts, independent commissions, and public authorities — that exercise overlapping public authority in any given territory. Such governments are as likely to negotiate with other governments (as well as come into conflict with them) as are organized groups, for governments desire policy outputs from other governments just as groups do. In fact, Matthew Holden's notion of governments' conducting "diplomacy" with one another is apt. Samuel Beer too has noted this dynamic: "Government itself — the public sector — has become such a large proportion of the total society that it generates within itself powerful forces leading to further government action."[15] In the case of city governments, they must often negotiate with other units in order to be provided with capital-intensive services. They must do so partly because public authorities have been established and partly because much capital investment crosses territorial boundaries. City governments negotiate about the future with other governmental bodies whose primary function is to invest — and they also are forced to respond to the impacts of past decisions made by those same governmental investors.

Whereas "diplomacy" implies that the units bargaining are formally of equal status, "public-sector politics" often involves local officials' trying to influence governments (federal or state), which wield much greater power and authority. Beer has referred to public-sector politics as involving local governments in lobbying and negotiating in ways similar to those practiced by private organized groups.[16] Yet the participation of local governments in intergovernmental politics is not limited to the role of lobbyist. It is in their other roles that local governments have structurally changed the nature of local governance in the United States.

Politics between governments are central to explaining why capital investment takes place as it does at the local level. I use the term *politics* advisedly, rather than the more bland, conventionally used, term intergovernmental *relations*. Where there is an undoubtedly strong constitutive element to the distribution of power among different governmental units, that distribution is not so overwhelming as to eliminate the kinds of behavior we routinely classify as "political" when exhibited by representatives of societal interests such as interest groups. Governments bargain with each other as well as lobby, confront, ignore, threaten, circumvent, and sue one another. Furthermore, local governments are such important implementers of policy — even in such supposedly centralized countries as France and Italy in the 1960s — that they are able to modify national policy to fit their own objectives.[17]

This book analyzes three types of intergovernmental politics and argues that, in the case of local capital investment, the three are directly linked. The setting of limits, the circumvention of such limits, and intergovernmental lobbying are the three types of politics that have shaped the institutional world of local investment. The first two types are particularly important in explaining why the institutional world of local capital investment differs so significantly from that of municipal government as traditionally understood.

Governments set limits on the activities of subordinate governments. Politics between governments of unequal power often address the question of how much discretion the weaker government can exercise. The setting of such limits represents one of the key ways that governments interact with other governments. Limits, once established, set the parameters for future relations and are therefore of strategic importance.

In the investment arena, such limits have restricted the borrowing of those funds typically used for investment purposes. Borrowed capital is so central to investment that systems of public capital investment are primarily shaped by the locus of control over the opportunity to borrow. In the case of American local investment, the decision to shift the locus of control over borrowing from the local to the state level shaped the institutional world of local capital investment. When local governments were transformed from relatively autonomous borrowers to objects of state regulations on borrowing, the nature of state-local investment politics was profoundly affected.

This book argues that decisions about the locus of control over capital investment have played a key role in shaping the role of the city in both the federal and the metropolitan systems. City government lost the struggle to borrow and therefore invest as it saw fit, and that defeat became enshrined specifically in debt limitations and more generally in the law of municipal corporations. Not only were local investment activities strictly controlled but Dillon's rule ensured that the state became in all fields the city's legal master. City government inevitably played a subordinate role in a range of sectors unrelated to investment. Hendrik Hartog, for example, argues:

> In place of local autonomy and political decentralization, the new law of municipal corporations posed the absolute centrality of state power and the insignificance of local publics in the political order. In place of the distinctive chartered rights of cities and the particular customs of local communities — both of which earlier served to frustrate the designs of central authorities — the new "law" held localities to explicit delegations of legislative power.[18]

If the city in the nineteenth century had been allowed to maintain its autonomy in borrowing and investment, it is possible that the city's powers in the twentieth century would have been more expansive.[19] The defeat over capital investment was thus a strategic defeat and shaped the future role of cities in the federal system in the sense that subordination was to be the city's fate.

In contrast to the argument made here, most political scientists do not view the nineteenth-century experience as critical. Ester Fuchs, for example, notes in her important study that "The starting point for this analysis must be the 1930s, because the onset of the Great Depression was the formative period for modern city governments." That argument is certainly valid if one examines the non-investment-related activities of city government. In the area of capital investment, however, the legal foundations for aggressive public investment had been laid by the time of the Great Depression. Such foundations were critical, for public investment cannot proceed without a supportive legal framework.[20]

The Politics of Circumvention

A type of intergovernmental politics of particular importance to local capital investment involves circumventing limits imposed by higher levels of government. Circumvention can entail manipulating the organization of government itself. Such manipulation helps to circumvent regulations imposed by higher levels of government. Local governments, for example, have established public authorities in order to circumvent restrictions imposed by states.[21] Similarly, new instruments — such as the revenue bond — have been developed for use in the financial markets so as to circumvent state restrictions applicable to older instruments. Finally, public authorities and new financial instruments have been used to test the limits of federal subsidy of local investment. Local officials, then, have revamped or transformed both the institutions and the processes of investment in order to maximize their autonomy from both the state and the federal governments.

Public authorities, for their part, can be viewed as a type of government institution designed in the twentieth century to recapture the freedom localities had enjoyed as investors for much of the nineteenth century. Public authorities, created to ensure that local governments can invest with minimal restriction, are "pure" government investors — and distinctively American. They form a governmental strata largely ignored by scholars and citizens but crucial to understanding the political economy of both federalism and local capital investment in the United States.

The politics of circumvention have evolved incrementally, but the impact has been dramatic. By the early 1990s, the system of American local government had fragmented, with municipal government becoming ever less responsible for capital investment decisions. Non-elected public authorities were the dominant local public investors. Consequently, the link between electoral accountability and capital investment is tenuous. Although borrowing and investment in the 1970s and 1980s became increasingly directed toward economic development rather than toward the provision of capital infrastructure, the role of special-purpose government did not diminish. The definition of capital investment had changed — but the public authority was still one of the key institutions charged with borrowing and spending funds.[22]

Government-Market Relationships

Intergovernmental politics need financial resources — and the resources used in the field of investment are borrowed monies. Such borrowing takes place in the private capital market so that governments use "private" money to pursue their investment objectives — and, we shall argue, their own institutional self-interest. The argument made here is that, in the area of public capital investment, intergovernmental politics involved public authority using private finance capital to circumvent public restrictions. Private capital (in the form of the revenue bond) has been used by local governments to expand their own power vis-à-vis state governments. Private capital has been a tool used by public authority, an essential element of the politics of circumvention, which has helped define American federalism in the arena of capital investment.

Arguing this is not a conventional view. The conventional view is that capital calls the tune, that private interests use or constrain public authority. Capital plays a determinative role in structuring the relationship between public and private power in the United States. In the case of cities, both Marxist and non-Marxist analysts have identified "finance capital" or the "structure of capital markets" as crucial concepts in understanding urban political economy in the United States. In this view, the financial market "generally acts as a de facto 'outer boundary' for political choices made by city officials about service levels, tax rates, and economic development."[23] Local governments borrow funds from private lenders operating in the municipal bond market, which renders local governments vulnerable to the credit assessments made by such lenders. Therefore, local officials, in this view, are forced to be extremely responsive to business, whose locational decisions are critical for the fiscal health — and thus the credit rating — of any locality.

This school points out (rightly) that if business firms do not locate in a municipality, the latter's tax base deteriorates, which incurs a decline in creditworthiness and higher costs for borrowing. Stephen Elkin, for example, sees the reliance of municipalities on private credit markets as a crucial factor in relations between public officials and business. He continues:

> The effects on city politics are substantial and little appreciated by students of city political affairs. The shape of city public policy, the access of certain kinds of business to public officials and the latter's consuming interest in economic growth all are greatly affected by the city's reliance on private credit.

In a more historical vein, Steven Erie writes: "I join others in arguing that urban growth cannot be understood historically apart from the municipal bond market."[24]

Borrowing in the private capital market clearly renders local officials very sensitive to the credit ratings issued by *Moody's* and *Standard and Poor's*, ratings that can raise or lower the cost of borrowing.[25] Furthermore, if loan repayments cannot be made, cities may find their autonomy substantially reduced, as occurred in the case of New York City. Shefter

offers an excellent analysis of the changes imposed on New York City in
the period after March 1975 (the date when the city was denied access to
the capital markets). He writes:

> the most visible and enduring change in 1975 was the creation of a new set
> of institutions to supervise New York City's finances: the Municipal As-
> sistance Corporation (MAC) and the Emergency Financial Control Board
> (EFCB), . . . the Office of the Special Deputy Controller for New York City
> (OSDC), and the Office of New York City Finance in the U.S. Treasury
> Department. . . . To provide investors with an ironclad assurance that MAC
> would be able to meet the debt service payments on these bonds, the state
> legislature converted the city's sales and stock transfer taxes into state taxes.
> The proceeds from these taxes flowed directly into a special account, inac-
> cessible to city officials, from which MAC could withdraw funds to make
> interest and principal payments on its bonds.[26]

Given the costs borne by cities that do run afoul of the market, it may
not be surprising that the demands of the market for repayment have been
usually met. The experience of New York City is very atypical in the post–
World War II period. In general, even cities experiencing a fiscal crisis have
managed to avoid what Leeds terms the "financing crisis," which led to
the state's imposition of fiscal controls on New York City.[27]

Yet if we analyze the role of capital markets from a comparative perspective, we become more cautious about that role.[28] Private lenders
clearly do influence local officials a great deal in the United States; but
does this demonstrate the determinative force of capital markets or does
the explanation lie elsewhere? No system of investment is cost-free from
the point of view of local government. But the costs vary in different
countries. British local governments, for example, also borrow in the capital market, but the British and American systems of investment differ dramatically. Stephen Elkin points out that English local governments are less
worried than American governments about the judgments of the credit
markets. In his words, "English local authorities worry more about how
central authorities view them than they do about how prime lenders rate
their economic prospects. The result is that they have to be less dutiful in
seeking out and attending to the desires of local businessmen."[29] Each system imposes its own costs and offers its own benefits to local governments.

American localities are certainly more vulnerable than their British
counterparts to market criteria in terms of access to lenders and the cost of

borrowing. But they can borrow much more cheaply than either British local authorities or (perhaps most surprisingly) the American federal government itself. This does mean that British localities are insulated from certain market imperatives, but they seem to pay a relatively high price for such insulation. American localities are not insulated from these market imperatives, but they do enjoy important privileges not enjoyed by their British counterparts.

Could the sources of the power of capital markets identified by Elkin lie in the logic of the American federal system itself rather than in the influence of capitalists? Certainly, an explanation arguing that capital markets qua markets are the key variable in explaining the political economy of public investment is suspect. An alternative view (the view taken here) is that the system of public capital finance is driven by government rather than by the capital market. In the area of capital investment, higher levels of government — rather than the capital market — determine the relationship that local governments will have with that market. If such governments allow the market to be influential, then it will be. If they decide the opposite, the market will not be influential. In either case, the key decision maker is not the capital market but the public authority.

The subordination of the market to public authority goes much further, however. American local governments have used the market as a vehicle, or instrument, to circumvent legal restrictions on their borrowing. (British local governments also use the markets to circumvent restrictions on their borrowing, but these are restrictions having to do with the technicalities of borrowing rather than with the aggregate amounts they are allowed to borrow.)[30] Using the market in such a fashion is unexpected, especially since such restrictions were intended to minimize borrowing. Yet the market has created new financial instruments specifically designed to evade restrictions on local government borrowing. Such instruments have allowed American local governments to borrow a lot as opposed to a little. Local governments have been able to use the creativity of the financial market for their own purposes. The municipal bond market therefore is used to further subnational government's own political and economic interests.

If the city can be conceptualized as a firm struggling for wealth, it can also be thought of as struggling against other governments for autonomy. Just as certain business groups use government to gain an advantage over other business groups, subnational governments use markets to circumvent controls and constraints imposed by other political units. Government officials view other governments as more constraining to their autonomy than the imperatives of the private capital market that funds much of their capital investment. It is better to put up with the credit ratings demanded by private lenders — and the pressures for economic growth or fiscal austerity that credit ratings can promote — than it is to put up with the limits placed on capital investment by governments.

In the United States, the relevance of other governments is seen in the very birth of public capital investment. A strong federal role in investment was vetoed largely because of the fear of a too powerful federal government. State governments were more worried about the power of Washington than about the power of financiers. Laissez-faire ideology had little to do with the debate: the states went on to pursue public enterprises and other forms of extensive public economic activity. The relationship between subnational government and the market, therefore, was not determined by ideas about the proper role of the market — it was shaped by ideas about the proper role of the federal government.

The Role of Law

But the market alone cannot provide a mechanism for circumvention. The legal order must support the market's activity. The work of Willard Hurst in the field of legal history has had enormous impact on those studying the relationship between law and markets. Arthur McEvoy summarizes Hurst's overarching argument: " 'Law' and 'the market' . . . do not exist independently of one another but rather create each other. The law . . . creates and sustains the life of the market economy."[31]

Without law, the capital market cannot function. Local officials were able to develop a strategy of circumvention because the state courts legitimated the new financial instrument developed by the market. Ironically, it was the courts that allowed local officials to circumvent the laws designed to minimize their borrowing. The courts approved the "escape hatch" designed by the financial market, an approval that was absolutely critical.

The courts exacted a high price for their approval of circumvention, however. They encouraged the creation of a new form of government — the public authority. Authorities have gradually come to dominate the world of capital investment. They have diluted the power of general-purpose governments, have insulated themselves from the electorate, and have transformed taxpayers into ratepayers subject to user fees. The fragmentation of local government has been so great that the world of local government now looks very different from the way it did in the period before World War II. "Local" government is far from synonymous with "municipal" government, and the proliferation of public authorities helps explain that fact. In a sense, the courts both liberated local investment and transformed the structure of government responsible for it.

Local governments used both the market and the courts to evade laws designed to minimize their borrowing. Local governments used the financial market to evade restrictions on their access to that same market and they used the courts to legitimize evading the law. Finally, their pursuit of circumvention led them to create a new type of governmental entity, which over time minimized their own power and autonomy. The construction of the federal system in the area of public investment is thus rooted in a triple irony.

Given the fragmentation of public authority at the subnational level, the availability of the capital market as a provider of funds, and the legacy of history in the oldest domestic-policy sector in the United States, the federal government has faced the problem of how to channel subnational public investment activity in a way compatible with its own aims. Particularly problematic were state and local governments' activism in the area of economic development. Washington responded by using tax policy as an instrument with which to recast its relationship to the entrepreneurial activities of subnational governments. The Tax Reform Act of 1986, therefore, stands as a piece of landmark legislation in the reshaping of American federalism.

Tax policy allowed Washington to constrain both private and public actors in the public investment game, with the Internal Revenue Service acting to enforce the new rules written in Washington. By increasing the costs of borrowing for certain local activities but not others, tax law has allowed Washington to play a more influential role in local investment decisions than it had previously. Federal tax policy, therefore, does not only shape the activity of firms and individuals; it also constrains and limits the policy options open to local governments.

Politics among governments, therefore, involve the use of both law and market. Governments as political actors use resources from both public and private sectors in choosing their political strategies. The mobilization of such resources leads to unanticipated consequences over time. The institutionalization of federalism has not proceeded in a linear, straightforward fashion. The system is consequently full of counterintuitive surprises.

Plan of the Book

Given that nineteenth-century America was a developing country, its subnational governments acted, in Monkkonen's words, "as economic adventurers."[32] In some ways, they resembled the venture capitalists of the late twentieth century. Such activism shaped the way capital investment is undertaken today: it laid the foundation for the costs and benefits transmitted to contemporary local governments by the current system of investment. Furthermore, since most (civilian) public capital investment is undertaken at the local level, such activism has played a crucial role in the national system of capital investment in the United States.

This study argues that local government as investor can only be understood in light of its nineteenth-century interventionist and entrepreneurial role. As such, it differs from interpretations assuming that nineteenth-century America was the land of laissez-faire, and that markets (and the American economy) developed naturally and without extensive public intervention. In the nineteenth century, state and local governments took the risks that private entrepreneurs either could not or would not take. They mobilized financial resources for the building of infrastructure that was crucial for economic development.

The pathologies of such public entrepreneurship set off a chain reaction. Restrictions were imposed by state governments on both state and local investment. Subsequently, however, such restrictions were circumvented in order to provide the capital infrastructure necessary for public health and urbanized life. The "entrepreneurial state" (to use Peter Eisinger's term) reemerged after World War II, followed in the 1980s by restrictions imposed at the federal level.[33] The initial nineteenth-century sequence of activism, limitation, and circumvention was partially replicated when the Tax Reform Act of 1986 restricted the economic development activities of subnational governments.

The pattern of investment entrepreneurship, restriction, and circumvention constitutes a major theme of this analysis. The analysis traces this pattern by examining those investment activities of local government financed by borrowing in the municipal bond market. Activities that fall under this rubric include capital investment as traditionally defined (providing capital infrastructure) as well as those economic development activities funded by borrowed monies. The relationships discussed in this analysis characterize capital investment in all capital-intensive policy sectors in which local government plays a role. The aim is not to discuss the details of any one sector but rather to sketch the general contours of the system within which all American subnational capital investment takes place. Although my focus is primarily on local investment, I discuss "subnational" investment where it is appropriate to include an examination of the capital investment carried out by the states.

Chapters 2 and 3 explore the roots of the state-local relationship in the area of capital investment. The states are discussed in detail in chapter 2 because it was the reaction to their investment adventures that spurred local government to its period of intense entrepreneurial activism. These chapters analyze the roots of the symbiotic relationship that exists between state government and local government in the investment arena. That relationship is so fundamental that one can analyze "local" investment as local only if one is willing to ignore the importance of the structure, imposed by state government, within which local governments invest.

More specifically, chapter 2 examines the role of state governments as entrepreneurs and the legal reaction to such entrepreneurship. Chapter 3 discusses local governments' investment activism and analyzes the reasons behind that activism. Chapter 4 explores the second major function of local government — that of providing capital-intensive services. It discusses how such provision is intimately entangled with both debt and technological change, which in turn requires still more borrowing. The reaction to such active investment by state legislatures, state courts, and the Supreme Court is explored in chapter 5. The limits imposed by the states and the judiciary on the local borrowing that underpinned such entrepreneurialism are sketched.

Chapters 2, 3, 4, and 5 form a unit in the sense of (1) laying out the evolution of the legal and market structure within which twentieth-century local officials had to maneuver in order to borrow and (2) sketching the process whereby the role of local government within the American federal system came to be defined. In particular, these chapters highlight how contingent was the process whereby local government came to occupy the place it does in the governmental hierarchy. That process involved the experience of the states themselves, the consequences of the activities initiated by autonomous local governments, and the conflict between the state and federal courts. Taken as a whole, these chapters argue against the notion that laissez-faire ideology or the emphasis of

American culture on "privatism" adequately explains the division between state and market in the American system. The emphasis here is on the often contentious dialogue *between governments* concerning which government should do what and how much as an economic actor. The history of that dialogue has significantly shaped current relations among governments.

Chapters 6 and 7 form a unit for collectively they describe how local governments managed to avoid some of the most burdensome consequences of the limitations placed upon local borrowing by the states. They analyze the two-pronged strategy used by local officials to circumvent restrictions imposed on public investment, emphasizing the development of both law and the municipal bond market as instruments of circumvention. Chapter 6 examines the use of the market as a mechanism of circumvention, paying particular attention to the development of the revenue bond as the instrument that allowed the municipal bond market to play the role it did. Chapter 7 focuses on the creation of a new governmental unit — the public authority — as a means of circumventing debt limitations. Both chapters examine the role of the New Deal in facilitating the diffusion of instruments of circumvention. Both chapters stress the critical role that the courts played in the survival of the authority and of the revenue bond.

Chapters 8 and 9 examine the postwar period, and they too form a unit. Chapter 8 is concerned with the use of the public authority and the revenue bond in the area of economic development, exploring how the instruments of circumvention — developed and diffused in the period before World War II — came to be used by subnational governments in the 1960s and 1970s to help private firms and residential households. Chapter 9 focuses on the restrictions imposed by the federal government in the 1980s on the economic-development activities of state and local governments, paying particular attention to the impact of the Tax Reform Act of 1986, landmark legislation in the history of federalism.

Chapter 10 concludes by sketching some of the enduring characteristics of the American federal system suggested by this examination of capital investment. In particular, the chapter argues that the dimension of territorial politics — the politics among governments — needs to be recognized as coexisting in the American polity alongside politics as conventionally understood. Political parties and interest groups share the political arena with subnational governments pursuing their own interests as institutions.

Chapter 2

State Governments

as Entrepreneurs

Public capital investment in the United States, from a historical viewpoint, was distinctive both because it was locally rather than nationally driven and because it was entrepreneurial in ambition. The provision of canals and railroads—called "internal improvements" by nineteenth-century commentators—differed dramatically in the United States and Great Britain.[1] That difference helps explain why American local governments have been active both in economic development and in service provision whereas British localities have been primarily concerned with the latter.

The autonomous, entrepreneurial role played by American subnational governments in the provision of transportation networks crucial for the industrial and commercial development of the United States profoundly affected those governments' future as public investors. Unlike British local authorities, American state and local governments did not come on the scene after development had occurred. On the contrary, their viability and long-term health as governments depended on how well they accomplished the task of economic development.

The evolution of the American private sector was intertwined with public power, frequently exercised at the state and local level, much more directly than was the British private sector. Andrew Shonfield perceptively points out:

Historically, American capitalism in its formative period was much readier to accept intervention by public authority than British capitalism. The doctrines of *laissez-faire* bit very deep into the social and political life of England for a century and more. . . . In nineteenth-century America the attitudes towards public authority did not—at least until the last quarter of the century—acquire the ferocious doctrinal consistency which they assumed early on among the English.[2]

That difference was to help shape both the role subnational governments played in the process of economic development and the types of intergovernmental investment politics that characterize the British and American political systems.

The consequences of such public-private interaction in one historical period shaped the legal and institutional framework within which subnational governments would act in later periods. Government, economic development, and law all partially molded one another as they grew, so that in the twentieth century the system of public capital investment is profoundly conditioned by both political and economic history. It is striking that American state and local governments not only intervened forcefully in the economy but also borrowed and invested with complete autonomy from federal control. Such autonomy was unknown by subnational government in Britain or in much of Europe. Why did such autonomy exist for American state and local governments? How was that autonomy exercised?

In general, the answers to these two questions also help illuminate why especially state government intervened so forcefully in the private economy. More particularly, the answer to the first question takes us to national politics and the historical debate about the role and jurisdiction of the federal government. Politics, both domestic and international, determined that the federal government would play an investment role subordinate to that of state and local government. In particular, it would be very subordinate in mobilizing financial resources, whereas it would be more active in providing land for capital facilities.

The second question directs us to both the global and domestic economy of the nineteenth century. The literature on international political economy often describes Britain as the economic "hegemon" of the nineteenth century.[3] Such hegemony had a considerable impact on the development of the American system of investment. Britain's role as a capital-exporting country and the American need for foreign capital intersected in such a way that state governments took on an economic role far removed from the role that would have been prescribed by laissez-faire. State governments were the initiators, the activists, the borrowers of money necessary for investment. State governments became crucial actors in economic development at least partially because they alone were able to borrow money in the London markets for the building of canals and railroads. Such building was either carried on by states themselves in the form of public enterprise or carried out by private entrepreneurs who were, however, dependent upon the state's borrowing in their behalf.

This chapter examines state entrepreneurship in the areas of both borrowing and actual capital expenditure. It then outlines the limitations that states placed upon their own borrowing capabilities. Those restrictions represented the first step in the establishment of the state-local relationship in the field of capital investment.

Public Entrepreneurship in America

While the transportation network of Britain was built by private capital, its American counterpart received huge infusions of both public capital and public land. Whereas not even the central government in London was much involved with the British "transportation revolution," all levels of the American public sector were both intimately and rambunctiously involved with its birth and extension.[4] The United States needed to develop economically, and the development of basic capital infrastructure (or "internal improvements," in the terminology of the nineteenth century) was a central priority. In particular, the new country needed transportation in order to stimulate market activity.

Three factors help account for the extensive role of the public sector in the United States. First, the country was short of capital whereas Britain, as the economic superpower, was a capital exporter. Britain was able both to finance its system of inland transport from private capital that was domestically available and to lend funds overseas. The United States, by contrast, was forced to borrow capital from Britain. And British lenders, accustomed to lending to sovereign governments during the Napoleonic wars, strongly preferred lending to governments rather than to private firms.

Second, the United States had less experience with the private corporation as an organization capable of mobilizing the financial and administrative resources necessary to complete capital works of gigantic scale and cost. Britain had already had fairly extensive experience with this new form of organization, and both governmental and private-sector elites assumed that the corporation could handle the necessary tasks.[5] In the

United States, however, no such assumption was made, and government appeared to be the unit that logically should attempt capital investment.

Third, by the time the steam train became a commercially viable reality, Britain was essentially a settled, largely urbanized country. There was no "frontier" as such. A new railroad would simply connect channels of trade that previously had used other modes of transport. Although railway lines were fiercely competitive, potential profits were more certain than on American lines. By contrast, an American railroad would typically be opening up new, unsettled territory; traffic, rather than being instantaneous with the railroad's completion, was instead heavily dependent on any future settlement that occurred along the railway line. The *Times* (London) was partially correct when it characterized a typical American railroad as "running from 'Nowhere-in-Particular to Nowhere-at-all'" for although a railroad usually did begin at a particular town, it "ended at a point which was perhaps nowhere when the project started, but which was to become important as a result of the improvement itself."[6] In Britain, therefore, few arguments were made for the use of public capital. Building a railroad was not unduly risky, and private investors were happy to provide funds without the enticement of a public subsidy.

In the United States, on the other hand, domestic capital was wary of committing itself to railroads in what was known as "the West" in the 1820s and 1830s, and foreign investors were also often extremely cautious. In the United States, private investors were willing to finance railroads similar to the British railroads — that is, lines that connected well-established trade routes. But obviously, there were relatively few of these.[7] In William Seward's words: "a great and extensive country like this has need of roads and canals earlier than there is an accumulation of private capital within the state to construct them."[8]

The lack of capital provided a springboard for initiating government action. State and local governments in particular energetically pursued America's developmental agenda. In so doing, they helped set the stage within which economic-development activities, as well as the delivery of public services, took place in the post–World War II period of the twentieth century.

The Subordination of the Federal Government

Of particular significance for this study is that the federal government was less important in the provision of transportation than were state and municipal governments. The federal government's most important role was the granting of enormous quantities of public land to railway companies. It also loaned half the funds needed for building the first transcontinental railroad. Land grants became politically controversial and led to a protest movement when railroad companies came to be distrusted by the public. Nonetheless, the federal role in assisting transportation was a subordinate one. Alfred Chandler, the distinguished business historian, concludes

> Congress made lavish land grants to a number of Western roads. Although these grants became a major political issue and so still loom large in American history texts, federal aid assisted in the building of only 8 percent of the nation's railroad system. State, municipal, and county aid was in the long run more significant than federal assistance.[9]

State and local governments became, by default, the major public financial actors in the field of public investment. In the early years of the nineteenth century, it seemed as if the federal government would dominate the public effort to build turnpikes, canals, and railroads. The failure of the federal executive to muster support for a dominant federal role, however, left the door open for adventurous state and local officials who, once having taken the power to build, never yielded it.[10]

The so-called Gallatin Plan, calling for ten years of significant capital investment, represented the federal government's landmark attempt to control the field of internal improvements. Drafted by Albert Gallatin, Jefferson's secretary of the Treasury, the plan was presented to the Senate on April 4, 1808. The argument for national action rested on the scarcity of domestic capital, its reluctance to invest where returns were risky, and the difficulty that canal and turnpike companies would have in finding foreign lenders.[11]

The War of 1812, however, strained the federal budget and effectively killed the plan. Gallatin himself abandoned his support of internal improvements in order to maintain the ability of the United States to finance the war. After the end of the war, the movement for internal improvements regained momentum but was unable to overcome fierce sectional rivalries and fear on the part of some representatives that a strong federal role in capital investment might serve as a springboard for a similar role in other policy areas. The opposition of the southern states to a strong federal role in internal improvements was especially significant. The major projects proposed in the Gallatin Plan would facilitate trade between the

East and the West but would not help the South, especially the Lower South. Furthermore, internal improvements were to be paid for largely from tariffs established to protect the manufactures of the North. The South viewed internal improvements as helping to construct an East-West alliance in Congress, for internal improvements were particularly attractive to the West. Such an alliance would challenge the power of the southern states.[12]

Those who argued that the states were more than adequately equipped to handle the development of new infrastructure were given powerful ammunition by the construction of the Erie Canal. While the Gallatin Plan was being debated in Congress, one of its major components, the joining of the Hudson River with the Great Lakes, was accomplished by New York State. The first great example of public investment in the United States had been carried out by a state government.

The election of Andrew Jackson in 1828, a strong supporter of state rather than federal investment in internal improvements, sealed the fate of a national plan of investment. John Quincy Adams, writing in 1837, eloquently expressed the reaction of supporters of a strong federal role in investment to Jackson's victory in the presidential elections of 1828:

> I fell and with me fell, I fear never to rise again, . . . the system of internal improvement by means of national energies. . . . With this system in ten years from this day the surface of the whole Union would have been checkered over with railroads and canals. It may still be done half a century later and with the limping gait of State legislature and private adventure.

Washington would not dominate what the distinguished economic historian Carter Goodrich called "the most important and the most widely employed measures by which American governments attempted directly to promote economic growth."[13]

State Entrepreneurship

Economic historians in the past forty years have transformed our understanding of antebellum America. Rather than a nurturing home for laissez-faire policy and ideology, the United States — as represented in pioneering studies by Louis Hartz, Oscar and Mary Handlin, Milton S. Heath, and Carter Goodrich — was a country in which governments actively intervened in the economy in several crucial areas and in which public opinion supported such intervention.[14] Subsequent scholars have provided a wide range of evidence supporting the view that government, especially subnational government, acted as an entrepreneur in the antebellum period.

Furthermore, whereas the original studies such as those by Hartz and the Handlins assumed that laissez-faire ideology ruled after the Civil War, later scholarship has shown that many state and local governments maintained an active presence in the economy until the end of the nineteenth century. Fierce legal battles had to be fought before subnational governments would accept the role in the economy that twentieth-century analyses take as given. Overall, Robert Lively's summary of American economic history — written in 1955 in a review of the first wave of studies challenging the notion of the United States as a land of passive government and laissez-faire ideology — has been substantiated in its fundamentals by the scholarship appearing since 1955. Lively concluded that the new scholarship on the early history of American capitalism put forth

> a consistent report of economic endeavor in an almost unfamiliar land. There, the elected public official replaced the individual enterpriser as the key figure in the release of capitalist energy, the public treasury, rather than private saving became the major source of venture capital. . . . From Missouri to Maine, from the beginning to the end of the nineteenth century, governments were deeply involved in lending, borrowing, building, and regulating.

This new scholarship highlighted the role of state and local governments as investors, as risk-takers. In Lively's view, the authors of this new analysis "are united in their belief that the activities of state and local governments were of crucial importance in the stimulation of enterprise in the United States."[15]

Antebellum state governments were involved in economic development in a variety of ways. They established banks, granted corporate charters and franchises, established the legal right of eminent domain, and became actively involved in the building of internal improvements. Many states, in fact, borrowed funds with which to provide capital for banks. In some states — Indiana, Illinois, and Tennessee, for example — the profits earned by the state's banking investment helped pay the interest on the debts incurred for internal improvements. (In the South, banks funded primarily by state investments were established to lend monies to planters, whose demands for capital were high because of the need to maintain slaves while waiting for crops to be ready to market.) The establishment of the legal right of eminent domain and the building of internal improvements were of particular importance over the long-term. Overall, however, the degree of intervention in the private economy carried out by state governments was so great that Andrew Shonfield argues: "At times the degree of tutelage which state governments arrogated to themselves in Jacksonian America appears so extreme that it suggests the direct inspiration of Colbert, rather than anything that belongs to the Anglo-Saxon tradition."[16]

States were developing a legal system of crucial importance to economic development. Especially important to both public and private enterprise was the right of eminent domain.[17] It was crucial to the construction of internal improvements, just as today that power is essential for urban renewal, the building of infrastructure, and other activities of subnational government involving the use of land. State courts widely validated (in Harry Scheiber's words) "the requirement that a private owner involuntarily give up his property at an 'administered' price, appraised under procedures established by the state." State courts in effect extracted "involuntary subsidies for a public enterprise" by denying common-law remedies to discontented property owners. They also defined the "taking" of property very narrowly, so that private owners often had to absorb considerable losses without having the right to demand compensation. In general, their use of eminent domain law supported the use of "property 'as an institution of growth'" rather than "property as an institution 'merely of security.'"[18]

Furthermore, the right of eminent domain came to be delegated to private corporations chartered by state legislatures. Initially, such a right was delegated to private corporations providing transportation, railway companies in particular. (In many states, that delegation was accompanied by state regulation.) Without the right to acquire land, transport companies could have been paralyzed by property owners who were unwilling to sell. State courts firmly upheld the right of legislatures to delegate one of the most important and constitutive powers of government, and in fact until at least the middle of the 1800s the courts allowed legislatures to define almost any company as one exercising a public purpose and therefore able to exercise eminent domain.

When legislatures began to delegate this power to textile companies and other manufacturing companies, the courts still upheld them. The Supreme Court rarely intervened in cases involving the use of eminent domain until 1870 (the Court had decided in 1833 that the Fifth Amendment's provisions of "due process," "just compensation," and "public use" were not applicable to the states). When the Court did act, it supported the states. In 1848, for example, the Court ruled in the case of *West River Bridge v. Dix* that vested rights were subordinate to the power of eminent domain. The majority opinion made clear that the power of state government to exercise eminent domain was essential to the building of internal improvements:

> In fact, the whole policy of the country, relative to roads, mills, bridges, and canals, rests upon this single power, under which lands have always been condemned; and without the exertion of this power, not one of the improvements just mentioned could be constructed.[19]

It was not until after the ratification of the Fourteenth Amendment that the Supreme Court, assuming a dominant role in shaping the role of state governments in the economy, began to restrict what subnational governments could do in the pursuit of economic development.

Internal Improvements

The internal improvements that received the most sustained attention from state governments concerned transportation. Debates and decisions about transportation technology — as well as the financing, routes, and administration of the technology chosen — formed a large part of state policy making. Herbert Ershkowitz and William Shade, in examining legislative behavior in the 1830s, find that "discussion of railroads, canals, and turnpikes seemed at times almost the chief preoccupation of the period."[20]

Within the gambit of state involvement in development, the states' assistance to transport required the most comprehensive and sustained effort. Other economic activities required less fiscal and administrative capacity. For example, land grants, permissive water law, and banking laws did not require either funds or an administrative apparatus. But transportation was special: in Scheiber's words, "many states implemented policy aimed at what I shall term 'outright public enterprise,' by establishing public agencies to build and finance costly transport facilities such as canals."[21] The states went into business for themselves.

Twentieth-century scholars tend to treat the construction of infrastructure as a "traditional" use of public funds and as providing the "backdrop" necessary for private economic activity. It is seen as providing a service; it is not typically viewed as substituting for private enterprise. Antebellum policy makers did not, by and large, operate with such a paradigm. Infrastructure for transportation was not primarily a service but was essential for economic development. Furthermore, public and private action was not distinct and the proper role of government was not "supportive" to the exclusion of being initiatory, innovative, and entrepreneurial.

Economic development was viewed as a necessity, and the choice of public enterprise, publicly subsidized private firms, or "mixed corporations" was made on pragmatic rather than ideological grounds. "Americans did not feel themselves bound by any permanent and unalterable demarcation of the spheres of state action and private enterprise."[22] Nineteenth-century citizens saw government intervention in development as much less ideologically controversial than, for example, currency and banking issues or political and social reforms.

Interstate Rivalry

Although state governments became involved in the transportation revolution for a variety of reasons, the most compelling was that of the need to compete with neighboring states for control of the trade routes to the growing inland areas. To lose in the transportation race was, at best, to lose regional economic supremacy and, at worst, to suffer dramatic economic losses. The demonstrated feasibility of using steamboats on inland waters and the increasing importance of cotton in the Gulf region and of sugar in Louisiana all contributed to the commercial growth of the western states in the 1820s and 1830s. Both northern farmers and southern plantation owners became better able to buy goods manufactured in the East. Western farmers increasingly demanded better transportation facilities so that they could sell their produce in the East or export it to Europe, and the manufacturers along the seaboard saw the new inland settlements as a potentially lucrative market for their output. The state of New York was the first "to reach out to control the lucrative trade of the Western Country." In 1817 the state legislature, urged on by Governor Clinton, approved the building of the Erie Canal, and in 1825 its opening signified the most decisive "single event in the history of American transportation."[23]

The economic effect of the Erie Canal was immediate: the value of produce from western New York doubled, and towns and cities either sprang up along the canal route or became revitalized. Buffalo, Chicago, Detroit, and Cleveland began to grow rapidly and emerged as competitors to Pittsburgh, Cincinnati, St. Louis, and New Orleans. Utica, Syracuse, and Rochester flourished.[24] The canal was a resounding financial success, for the interest charges due on the loans that financed it were easily paid from the tolls collected. In fact, the surplus became so great that the Erie Canal Fund evolved into a development bank, whose monies influenced "the economy from one end of the state to the other." But, most significant of all from the point of view of neighboring states and cities, "New York City became the emporium of Western trade."[25]

The policy makers and elites of neighboring states and cities quickly realized that the Erie Canal threatened their own aspirations for commercial supremacy. The era of fierce interstate rivalry — and intercity rivalry (as we shall see in the next chapter) — that began with the completion of the canal in 1825 lasted until the end of the nineteenth century. Such competition is not surprising, for in 1820 over half of the American urban population (persons living in towns with populations of 2,500 or more) were found in America's six largest cities — New York, Philadelphia, Baltimore, Boston, New Orleans, and Charleston. Since New York and Philadelphia alone accounted for over one-third of all urban dwellers, and since in 1810 New York City had emerged as the most populous city and had widened its lead considerably by 1820, it is understandable that competition between New York State and Pennsylvania (as well as that between New York City and Philadelphia, of course) was particularly bitter.[26]

Pressure from Philadelphia encouraged the Pennsylvania state government to authorize, in February 1826, the Pennsylvania Canal, a canal that would link Philadelphia to Pittsburgh. Proponents of this canal argued that trade with the Ohio River Valley would bypass Pennsylvania, and Philadelphia especially, if a canal were not built. The competition with New York was serious. As Louis Hartz wrote: "It is hard for a later age, accustomed to a comparatively mild chamber-of-commerce mentality, to appreciate the intensity of the passions which the regional rivalries of this period evoked."[27]

The sense of competition was so keen that it affected Pennsylvania's choice of technology. In 1825, the Erie Canal was completed and the world's first railway (the Stockton and Darlington Railway) opened in England. The success of the latter raised the question of whether Pennsylvania should choose a canal or a railroad with which to compete with New York. Since the Stockton and Darlington was not a general-purpose railroad, choosing the railway option would require study and provoke delay.

The fear of New York encouraged supporters of the Philadelphia-Pittsburgh connection to choose the tried technology. The *United States Gazette,* an important Philadelphia daily, argued, for example, that the canal was "necessary to our prosperity, nay, almost to our existence, and every day that the work is delayed, is strengthening and multiplying the advantages that our gigantic neighbor has acquired over us." Thus, Julius Rubin, in comparing the New York and Pennsylvania experience, concludes that both states undertook expensive and complex public investment schemes. However, New York was able to plan and study her intervention. Pennsylvania, by contrast, "plunged into hers under extreme duress, bitterly aware of lost marches and of the need to overtake a powerful rival."[28]

But Pennsylvania was not the only state to respond to the Erie Canal. In 1825 Ohio began constructing a system of canals; in 1828 Maryland and Virginia broke ground for the Chesapeake and Ohio Canal Company; in 1827 South Carolina authorized the construction of the Charleston and Hamburg Railroad; in 1836 Indiana decided to supply the entire state with a network of canals and railroads; and in 1837 Illinois decided to construct its own system of improvements. Michigan's first constitution, written in 1835 when Michigan gained statehood, included the clause "that internal improvements shall be encouraged by the government of the state." It is not surprising that Scheiber characterizes the antebellum era as "one of rivalistic state Mercantilism."[29]

After the Civil War, the southern states during Reconstruction continued their extensive participation in providing internal improvements, railways in particular. Originally, the motive here was that of competition with the North, with the aim of creating a self-reliant South that could maintain its sectional identity. However, by the end of Reconstruction, it was clear that "states had striven for advantages over their neighbors, rather than for a New South."[30]

Politics of State Aid

Considering that national politics during the antebellum era emphasized disputes between the Whigs and Democrats on economic issues, it is noteworthy that state politics did not reflect fundamental disagreements over internal improvements. Politics in that area involved intrastate sectional conflict over where improvements should be built. However, the basic argument that the state should use improvements as an instrument of economic-development policy was not seriously nor widely challenged. At its inception, state intervention generally had bipartisan support. Ershkowitz and Shade have analyzed legislative behavior in New Hampshire, Pennsylvania, Ohio, New Jersey, Virginia, and Missouri between 1833 and 1843. Although they found significant differences in the voting patterns of Whigs and Democrats in the areas of incorporation of firms, banking, and currency, they conclude that the positions of the two parties were similar on the issue of internal improvement. Goodrich argues that the debate over internal improvements focused on concrete proposals rather than on broader issues of economic policy, probably because improvements did not highlight conflicting class interests the way debates over banking, currency, and the tariff did. Ronald Formisano argues that, in Michigan, internal improvements cannot be analyzed as either a class or interest-group issue. He concludes that "the Michigan parties never differed significantly on internal improvements and both generally favored them."[31]

During Reconstruction, the Radical Republicans tried to use the issue of railway aid to create a biracial coalition. It was the most important part of the Republicans' promise of economic development for a poverty-stricken, war-torn South. The desire to encourage the building of railways in the South, in fact, was so intense and widespread it has rightly been called "railroad mania." The Republican party, swept to power throughout the South in the 1868 elections for constitutional conventions, was so identified with railway aid that, in Arkansas, Republicans exhorted voters to "vote for railroads and the Republican Party." The political attractiveness of railway aid had to do with its appeal to numerous groups — the planter who hoped it would increase land value, the merchants who wanted to expand their penetration of their city's hinterland, and believers in a New South who hoped new people would immigrate to the South. Those who were more skeptical — such as the poor — never became a majority, and whenever railway aid was presented to the electorate it was approved.[32]

In sum, then, state aid to transportation was initiated with relatively little ideological controversy. Such aid did become controversial when actually implemented (as we shall see), but the fundamental idea that government should actively intervene to promote economic development was widespread and enjoyed strong support from numerous groups in the society. While state governments came to be criticized for how they tried to promote development, their assumption of the role of promoter of development was widely accepted as proper and legitimate.

States as Borrowers

The system of financing internal improvements involved state governments, foreign lenders (primarily British), and domestic investors. Regardless of whether the state government owned a system of transport outright, owned part of it, or lent or gave funds to a private firm chartered to build and operate a transport facility, funds had to be mobilized by the state government. And those funds needed to be borrowed. States therefore went heavily into debt to fund facilities of inland transportation. Whereas in 1820 the states owed merely $12.8 million, by 1830 the total debt was $26.5 million. By 1839 state debt had skyrocketed to over $170 million, and by 1841 roughly $193 million of state debt was outstanding. On January 1, 1843, states owed $231 million.[33] Borrowing for banks, canals, and railroads accounted for most of the debt. By 1838 the southern states alone had borrowed $54 million in order to supply working capital to chartered land banks, whereas total debt for canals amounted to $60 million and debt for railroads amounted to $43 million.[34] In contrast, the federal government was repaying its debt (the national debt was extinguished in 1836). In fact, the states were accumulating a total debt burden larger than any the federal government had had.[35]

The ability of governments and the inability of corporations to attract lenders encouraged state governments to play an activist role in the entire field of internal improvements. The vast amounts of capital needed for improvements could come either from domestic savings or from the savings of foreigners. After 1815 the United States had considerable savings available for investment in public works, but (at least before 1830) corporations were unable to induce even domestic investors to lend to them unless there was some form of government involvement with the corporation.

Lenders were much more likely to lend to a government than to an unknown firm, especially when that firm was proposing something as risky as building transportation facilities in a sparsely settled area. Few

American investors were willing to lend for projects that were risky and that would require years before a return could be expected. Most capital was held by small savers, who were usually unwilling to trade security for the possibility of a high return.[36]

The corporation, as an organization capable of mobilizing the resources necessary for large undertakings, was not familiar to American investors and therefore needed the "legitimacy" granted by government in order to attract capital. Callender argues that, before 1840,

> There was no body of private individuals in the country well enough known and with sufficient influence in the business world to establish the credit of a corporation so that it could command the confidence of . . . investors. The only securities that could do this were public securities, or the securities of corporations which were guaranteed or assisted by the government. American public credit had been raised to the highest pitch by the debt-paying policy of the federal government; and it was inevitable that the American people should turn to the only means in their power to provide for their needs.[37]

Foreign lenders, for their own reasons, were even more likely to avoid private borrowers. Furthermore, the state government was the only entity capable of issuing bonds in denominations large enough to obtain the vast amounts needed for internal improvements.[38]

The success of New York State in attracting investment capital to finance the Erie Canal encouraged other state governments both to view debt as a suitable financing mechanism and to view themselves as the most appropriate borrower.[39] One of the reasons that New York State had no difficulty in attracting lenders, however, was that the financing of the Erie Canal was carefully structured so as to reassure potential investors. The state was legally required to use earmarked revenues to repay debt, and in the early years, certain taxes were legally set aside to repay debt until toll charges would be collected. Other state governments, with projects for which the financing was much less carefully thought out, would find it far more difficult to attract lenders. Some states borrowed for their own public enterprises, while others borrowed on behalf of private railway companies that were supposed to actually build and run the railroad. In order to be able to sell bonds for railways, states found it necessary to pledge the "faith of the state"; that is, the state government promised to pay the interest and redeem the principal.[40]

Foreign Lenders

The self-financing nature of the Erie Canal encouraged British (and to a lesser extent Dutch) investors to lend to state governments that were borrowing to build canals and, subsequently, railroads. Foreign capital helped compensate for the risk-averse nature of domestic investors and helped lower the cost of borrowing for state governments.

A number of factors encouraged the high volume of British lending. First was the replacement of Amsterdam by London as the world's leading financial center after 1815 (it should be noted that the United States paid for the Louisiana Purchase in 1803 by raising a loan in Amsterdam). Whereas London lent funds to foreign governments in the first part of the eighteenth century and during the 1790s, its primary eighteenth-century role was to channel investors' funds toward the credit needs of the British government. Those needs, beginning with the war of the Austrian succession, were enormous. Riley points out that "although its resources equaled or exceeded those of any other market, London constituted a domestic rather than an international market."[41]

Second, after the end of the Napoleonic wars, British investors could no longer obtain the high interest rates to which they had become accustomed. Third, British investment in the First and Second United States Bank had been very profitable. Finally, the loans for internal improvements were being used for productive purposes at a time when investors began to think that loans for such purposes were safer than "political loans" to finance wars.[42]

In the foreign markets, the state guarantee that its "faith" was pledged was essential. "It was the guaranty of the state which alone made these stocks 'palatable to European capitalists' and the same statement is found constantly recurring in the correspondence of the bankers and in the columns of the press." Until the early 1850s, for example, Baring Brothers and Company, the major house in London dealing with American finance, would not even try to sell American railway bonds unless they were issued by a state or local government for a railway company.[43]

The fact that state governments were borrowing, rather than firms, allowed British investors to act on their desire to buy American securities, which paid anywhere from 5 to 10 percent interest as opposed to the interest as low as 1.5 percent paid in Britain.[44] And lend to state governments they did. Whereas in 1836 $50 million in bonds was held by foreigners (primarily Britons), in 1843 when the figure reached its pre–Civil War peak, it was $150 million.[45]

Debt Crises

The increase in state debt placed a strain on the states — construction of facilities took longer, cost more, and confronted more engineering problems than had been anticipated. Nonetheless, state debt increased by over $108 million between 1835 and 1838 alone, partially because the states were borrowing in order to repay old loans that they had initially expected to be able to repay from revenues. The Panic of 1837, although leading to a sharp contraction in economic activity, did not force the states to stop borrowing: the recession was viewed as temporary and the states felt it necessary to complete projects in progress so that they could eventually collect revenues necessary to repay debt.[46]

Significantly, however, the panic did affect the way state bonds were sold overseas. Until 1837, established banks in the United States served as agents for large European banks. These agents made recommendations for foreign investors, so that highly speculative securities were sold in the United States rather than abroad. However, in 1837, English firms handling many state bonds withdrew from the American market for a variety of reasons. Nicholas Biddle — the indefatigable president of the United States Bank of Pennsylvania (once the renewal of its charter was vetoed by President Jackson in 1832, the Second Bank of the United States was chartered as a state bank by Pennsylvania) — then began to sell state bonds in England. English bankers in turn unreservedly began to trust the endorsement of the United States Bank of Pennsylvania. Furthermore, states began to send their own agents to Europe to negotiate the sale of their bonds and stocks. The process of borrowing had so few controls that "some of the wildest schemes now appeared."[47]

The fact that the federal government had itself bought state securities was used by some to argue that all state bonds, even those issued by "unknown" states such as Arkansas, were deemed satisfactory by the federal government. Although the *Times* (London) was advising Britons not to purchase American state bonds, its advice was disregarded. In the summer of 1839, the London money market could offer an investor a choice from nearly $100 million of American securities.[48]

However, the good times for the borrowing states ended with the depression of 1839, the worst in American history up to that point. Biddle and his bank were ruined. Borrowers stopped borrowing. As the states began to struggle with their debt burden, the severe economic crisis, the intense public resistance to increased taxation, and the perception that state bonds had been illegally marketed created a climate conducive to default or, worse, repudiation.[49]

In 1840 and 1841, states tried in many different ways to find the funds to pay interest, including using trust funds earmarked for other purposes and liquidating financial assets. However, the political inability to raise taxes made default inevitable for some states and encouraged others to repudiate their debts altogether. Arkansas, Florida, Michigan, and Mississippi repudiated their debts, while Pennsylvania, Maryland, Illinois, Indiana, and Louisiana defaulted on their interest payments or otherwise adjusted their debt. Some acts of repudiation, such as Florida's and Mississippi's, were approved in popular referenda. Other adjustments were accompanied by drama: Illinois burned the bonds in question in a huge bonfire in front of the State House.[50]

The failure of state governments to pay interest on debt caused an uproar in the overseas financial community. Although the states that defaulted eventually repaid some or even all of their debt, the blow to the states' creditworthiness overseas was severe. In fact, all state credit was hurt by the default of others. The British could never understand the view that

> the defalcation of some of the states ought not to injure the credit of those who punctually met their obligation. To English bondholders this line of reasoning was totally foreign to their way of thinking. They could not understand why a citizen of New York did not consider it a reflection upon his state if some other state in the union defaulted or repudiated its debts.[51]

Pennsylvania's default was the most sensational — and the most distressing to foreign investors. Pennsylvania was one of the first states to engage in public construction and ownership of transportation facilities, but it did not construct a sound financing system for such improvements.[52] Nonetheless, Pennsylvania securities were regarded as particularly low in risk and therefore as appropriate investments for small investors because of Pennsylvania's status as one of the wealthiest of all the American states. The shock and outrage occasioned by the state's default in 1842 was well expressed by the Reverend Sydney Smith, Dean of St Paul's, in a series of widely discussed letters published in various newspapers. In one letter, written to the *Morning Chronicle* (London), he stated

> No conduct was ever more profligate than that of the State of Pennsylvania. . . . I never meet a Pennsylvanian at a London dinner without feeling a disposition to seize and divide him: to allot his beaver to one sufferer and his coat to another; to appropriate his pocket handkerchief to the orphan and to comfort the widow with his silver watch . . . he has no more right to eat with honest men than a leper has to eat with clean men.[53]

Six British banking houses hired an agent to orchestrate a nationwide press campaign to educate public opinion as to the need to regain creditworthiness for states by paying their debt. Pennsylvania was one of the campaign's chief targets. Coupled with skillful lobbying in the state legislature, the campaign succeeded in convincing the legislature to approve an earmarked tax to be used to pay debt interest.[54] Pennsylvania's resumption of interest payments on February 1, 1845 (followed by Maryland's in 1848), was viewed by foreigners as a sign that the defaulting states would eventually honor their debts. And such was the case, even though the terms of settlement were sometimes unfavorable to the investor.

Whereas the states that had experienced defaults and repudiation subsequently borrowed little, other states borrowed heavily after 1845. These latter were spurred on by continuing interstate rivalries and the general economic benefits they saw accruing to those states that had heavily funded transportation facilities in the 1830s. Domestic lenders were more important than foreign during this period of borrowing (which was more restrained than during the 1830s). European investors were now buying the securities issued by railway companies themselves, and "Eastern capital" was now willing to buy state and local securities (especially when issued to help railway companies). Further, state banks began buying state bonds to fulfill new state requirements that they hold collateral against the issuance of notes.[55] New York, Virginia, Missouri, Tennessee, and North Carolina borrowed a total of $90 million, primarily to finance railroads. South Carolina and Georgia also borrowed, although to a lesser extent.[56]

During the Civil War, both Union and Confederate states borrowed very heavily — but not for capital investment. Over $200 million was borrowed for the purpose of financing the war between 1861–1870. Generally, those Union states that had borrowed heavily in the antebellum period did not borrow a great deal, whereas by contrast, states such as

Delaware and New Jersey (which had not borrowed at all) borrowed heavily for the war effort. Monies borrowed during the Civil War were primarily used to pay bounties. Those bonds issued by the southern states before the Civil War that were held by northerners were repudiated. After the end of the war, the southern states were forced to repudiate all the debt they had accumulated during the war. Since many Confederate securities were held by banks, the repudiation ruined the banking system of the South.[57]

Despite various forms of debt limitation that were included in the constitutions written for the defeated states, many Reconstruction governments borrowed heavily in aid of railway companies. Such borrowing was accompanied by widespread fraud and corruption. Nonetheless, Summers argues that "lawmakers were not usually trying to defraud the state. They simply did not care whether the state was cheated or not — as long as the road was built." Whereas other historians have tended to focus on the corruption in debt financing as a major cause of the failure of railways to meet expectations, Summers argues that the failure of railway aid was much more complex. Commenting on the argument that corruption was responsible for the failure of railroads to be built or to reach their termini, he argues that although corruption certainly was important in the field of railway construction, especially in states east of the Appalachians, it was not the exclusive cause of the failure of railway aid. Rather he blames the "blind optimism of Southern businessmen and legislators," for both entrepreneurs and policy makers believed that the granting of public aid would cushion railway companies from the potentially harsh judgments of northern and overseas investors. However, many of the securities issued to help railway companies were not favorably received in the North, and those from states that had previously repudiated their debt never sold at par and sometimes could find no buyers at all. Cautious investors bought northern state bonds, and those seeking more risk chose western railroads rather than southern. Since most bonds sold below face value, the more bonds the railroad had to issue, the lower the price at which subsequent bonds were sellable, and the higher interest costs ran.[58]

Whatever was done with the funds, however, southern state debt increased roughly $100 million between 1868 and 1874. When the panic of 1873 began a depression in the South, over half the railroads in some states defaulted.[59] Railway aid lost support, as it became clear that even state aid could not ensure the completion of lines. Borrowing to aid railways practically ceased.

It was too late. The Republicans were blamed for the economic crisis. Along with the race issue, the economic issue was partially responsible for the defeat of the Republicans. Between 1874 and 1876, they lost control of every state government. Many Reconstruction bonds were repudiated shortly after Reconstruction governments were ousted and the Democrats put in control. Others were repaid only partially. In some states, voters actually forbade their state legislature to meet debt payments.[60] Alabama, Arkansas, Florida, Louisiana, North Carolina, South Carolina, and Tennessee repudiated some debts and scaled down others. Virginia did not settle the matter of its prewar debts until the twentieth century, because of its long-standing feud with West Virginia over the question of how much of the old state's debt West Virginia should assume. In Minnesota, prewar bonds were nearly repudiated in the 1870s. Voters favored repudiation, but by circumventing the need to acquire electoral approval for settling the question of the railway bonds, the legislature was able to avoid repudiation.[61]

Reaction

The prewar debt crises of the states provided the federal government with a second opportunity to play a major role in capital investment. After 1850, the federal government became much more active generally in assisting railways, primarily through the granting of federal lands. Whereas Washington had given land before 1850, after that the aid was much greater. In particular, the transcontinental railroad (completed in 1869) received a great deal of national assistance. Nonetheless, this federal aid supplemented the ongoing state and local aid; it did not channel or impose controls on subnational assistance. In fact, congressional assistance to the transcontinental railroad was made easier because so much of the route crossed territories rather than states.[62]

European investors expected the federal government to assume the states' debts, which would permit the investors to recoup their money. When the federal government showed no inclination to do so, investors refused to lend to the federal government, hoping thereby to pressure it into action. Consequently, the American federal government was closed out of the European money markets in 1842, although its own credit-worthiness was impeccable.[63]

Federal assumption had already become a political issue in the presidential election of 1840. After the inability of the federal government to receive a loan in the European markets and the state defaults of 1842, a congressional committee chaired by Representative Johnson was established to investigate that possibility. In the congressional debate of March 1843, some argued that the assumption of state debt would help the indebted states to the exclusion of the non-indebted states, whereas others argued that federal assumption would encourage the states to maintain their profligate ways.

The Johnson Committee Report made clear that since roughly $150 million of the state debt of $231.6 million was owed to overseas lenders, most of the debt would need to be paid in specie. The states' total interest payments amounted to roughly $12 million a year, roughly 14 percent of the value of the total exports of the United States. It became clear that repaying foreigners in specie would impoverish the United States.[64] The House tabled the Johnson Report. The federal government refused to assume state debts.

The failure of the Gallatin Plan followed by the failure to combine control over state borrowing with the assumption of state debts left the federal government playing a secondary role in capital investment. Control was asserted by state governments. The state rather than federal government became the primary regulator of subnational capital investment. This fact was to have enormous consequences for capital investment carried out by local government.

State Debt Limits

The spectacle of northern states defaulting in the 1840s and the defaults and repudiations of the southern states in the post–Civil War era led to a political reaction that institutionalized debt limits in all the states that were active in the era of internal improvements. Thus, the first limit on the use of state credit was imposed either by legislatures or by constitutional conventions as a response to the economic-development activities of nineteenth-century state governments.

The problems states had confronted in assisting canal and railroad development — problems including corruption, unsound or incompetent

companies, and unexpected engineering difficulties—led to what some
have termed a "revulsion" against internal improvements.[65] In particular,
it became clear that the selling of many bonds had not complied with state
laws. Although bonds were supposed to be sold at par, for example, they
often were not: Indiana, for example, sold bonds with a face value of
$14,057,000 for $12,303,989. Some of the argument about what constituted a "par sale" was due to the different ways Americans and Britons
used the term *par*. However, there were enough cases of outright illegali-
ties and corruption that McGrane concludes, "agents of the states violated
state statutes in negotiating the loans, and American bankers aided and
abetted them."[66]

In many cases, the same kind of consensus backed the imposition of
debt limits that had previously backed the use of public credit for the
promotion of internal improvement in the name of economic development and interstate competition. Louis Hartz, for example, concludes that
measures to restrict the use of public credit were popular in Pennsylvania:
"Public opinion was so widely in favor of these measures that their passage by the legislature and their ratification by the people met no important opposition." And legislative and popular vote majorities were lopsid-
edly in favor of measures restricting the use of state credit. The same high
degree of consensus seems to have prevailed during the Kentucky constitutional convention of 1849–1850. In Maryland and Virginia, whereas sectional and partisan conflict divided the delegates to the constitutional
conventions of 1850–1851, the provisions limiting the use of the state's
credit received wide support.[67]

The move to restrict state borrowing was widespread. Although before
1840 no constitutional limits existed on state debt, nineteen state constitutions were amended between 1842 and 1857 in the direction of credit
restriction. States admitted after 1864 usually wrote a debt limit into
their first constitution. In general, restrictions required electoral approval
for borrowing and did not permit the state's credit to be used for corporations.[68]

In the postbellum period, states that had begun borrowing relatively
late (such as Missouri) and the southern states adopted debt limits. Reconstruction governments in some states restricted the use of borrowing:
Florida, South Carolina, and Louisiana all passed constitutional amendments restricting state borrowing.[69] (Many of those limits were disregarded, however, and the Democrats repudiated many Reconstruction

bonds on the basis that they were illegal because limits had been ignored.) When those governments were ousted, the Democrats wrote new restrictions on state credit. They restricted the use of state credit for private corporations, and in general restricted borrowing for any reason.

The reaction to the crises in the use of state credit laid the first stone in the foundations of the state-local relationship in the area of capital investment. The limits had an effect. In the last quarter of the nineteenth century, most states gradually reduced their debts. The last decade of the nineteenth century saw the total net state debt reach $225 million, the lowest it had been since 1840.[70] However, the withdrawal of the states from the provision of transportation simply opened the doors wider for local government activism in economic development. The limits imposed by the states upon themselves did not apply to local governments. And so local governments began to borrow and build as furiously as the states had done before them.

Conclusion

The entrepreneurial activity of state governments followed by self-imposed limits on such entrepreneurialism were to have far-reaching effects. The restrictions not only established a model that would subsequently be imposed on local governments but also established a norm of limited rather than expansive public investment. The acceptance of restrictions preempted any potential federal role in regulating state investment. The states showed themselves able and willing to address the popular revulsion against state debt so that a federal role was not even to be considered.

This latter point is particularly important in understanding why the intergovernmental politics of capital investment would eventually involve Washington insofar as the cost of borrowing was concerned but would leave Washington out when it came to questions of investment levels. The irrelevance of Washington in deciding how much states can borrow strikes Europeans as surprising, for European systems generally have given national governments the right to regulate the levels of borrowing and investment incurred at the subnational level.

The acceptance of self-restraint on the part of state government helped institutionalize the autonomous nature of subnational capital investment by making such investment much less vulnerable to future federal

STATE GOVERNMENTS AS ENTREPRENEURS 43

intervention. State investment levels were not put on the national policy agenda but remained a state issue. The federal government would eventually appropriate federal monies for a variety of capital purposes, but it would not limit state decisions concerning state investment. No matter how big the percentage of total capital investment that would be represented by federal monies, the autonomy of state governments in determining their own investments would not be compromised. Whereas the national government in European systems determined the level and purposes of subnational investment, American states would be able to determine their own investment policy.

Chapter 3

Cities as Investors

The restriction of state borrowing was significant in that it removed the state from actively promoting transportation while it opened the door for local entrepreneurship. Local governments, which were unrestricted in their borrowing, emulated the earlier state activism. Economic development became a major priority for the local governments, just as it had been for the states. They too were spurred on by competition, and by the realization that to lose out in the transportation race could mean actual extinction. Nineteenth-century cities' investment activities in the area of economic development were an important building block in the construction of the system of local capital finance.

Cities, Competition, and Economic Development

Interstate competition for canals and railways in the antebellum era was often fueled by the wishes of urban elites to position their own city better within the emerging transportation network. Intense interstate rivalry was often promoted by cities that wished to use state resources to compete for trade with cities in neighboring states. Before the Panic of 1837, interstate and intercity rivalry were closely linked. Particularly in the canal era, when state governments were the major builders of large public works that profoundly affected trade flows, "urban and regional ambitions were directed largely toward manipulation and control of state policy."[1]

Cities became even more active after many state governments restricted their own development activities and as the canal was replaced by the new technology of the railroad. An extreme example of this tendency occurred in Wisconsin where the first state constitution of 1848 prohibited all state involvement in internal improvements but did not prohibit local government participation. Between 1848 and 1889, the state legislature consequently passed nearly two hundred laws authorizing local aid. While the state government was inactive, the city of Milwaukee in the 1850s was giving massive amounts of assistance to railways.[2]

Local government activism for economic development involved the borrowing of money to assist railway companies promising to build railway termini or branch lines. In contrast to state activism, which often involved public enterprise, cities (with the exception of Cincinnati) did not build their own railways. Nor did they borrow abroad as much as states had done. Local government aid was stimulated by local officials' belief that local government, on its own, could encourage the building of a railroad to serve local needs. In particular, they felt, local government could be catalytic if it gave financial help to private companies that were promising to build a railroad. The fact that the railroad could be built nearly anywhere was crucial, for canals had been far more dependent on geography than were railroads. Town elites realized that the railroad gave towns a second chance. Scheiber describes the process in the old Northwest:

> The new railroad technology reopened the critical question of which city would dominate trade in each region of the Old Northwest. As Chicago, Milwaukee, and St. Louis battled for control of the Mississippi valley trade in the most spectacular western urban rivalry, so too in every area of the West towns competed for positions on the new railroad and for hegemony in local trade areas.[3]

The process described by Scheiber, far from being unique to Ohio, Wisconsin, Illinois, Indiana, and Michigan in the 1850s, characterized the United States throughout the nineteenth century as the continent became settled, and population grouped and regrouped depending on the routes of the railways being constructed. Urban rivalry was just as fierce in the West in the late nineteenth century as it had been in the East in the early decades of the nineteenth century.[4]

The rivalry between Chicago and St. Louis in the period 1850–1880 was a classic case of big-city rivalry. Wyatt Belcher argues that both cities had a "supreme desire" to be the dominant midwestern city and each demonstrated "a driving ambition to surpass all rivals."[5] The railway gave Chicago the chance to overtake St. Louis, whose investors had put their money into steamboats. Complacent about the city's supremacy, they did not adjust quickly enough to the radical implications of the railroad, which allowed Chicago to attract trade from the Upper Mississippi Valley. River transport had made St. Louis the chief city of the Midwest, but railways allowed Chicago to overtake it.

Both Missouri state policy makers and St. Louis elites assumed that the railroad would always be secondary to river transport and, furthermore, did not realize how important it was to build railways quickly. Chicago elites, by contrast, did. Although its first railroad did not receive a charter until 1847, by 1860 Chicago was already the railway center of the United States. By 1875, Chicago no longer even viewed St. Louis as a competitor, and it turned its attention toward New York City.

Belcher argues that St. Louis elites lacked entrepreneurial drive, whereas those in Chicago were more open to innovation and were more dynamic. The attitude of elites provides only a partial explanation for St. Louis's lack of competitiveness, however. Christopher Schnell points out that the Missouri legislature was the only western legislature that did not aid transportation in the 1840s. The legislature — not wishing to borrow, being short of capital, and not wanting to raise taxes — did not pursue the active, interventionist type of policy necessary for St. Louis's competitive position until 1851 and then did not urge haste. Furthermore, Schnell argues that Chicago found it easier to obtain eastern capital whereas St. Louis was forced to rely on local monies. Finally, Chicago benefited from the Erie Canal and the fact that its railways could link up with an existing system of railways already built in the East.[6]

Like the interstate variety, rivalry between cities was sparked by the completion of the Erie Canal. The mercantile elites of Boston, Philadelphia, and Baltimore immediately recognized that the canal allowed New York City to control the trade of the expanding northern Midwest and to begin exercising influence over trade further south. Suddenly New York City, which had been disadvantaged in the turnpike era, now seemed to be in a position to dominate the settling of a continent. The rivals to New York City for national dominance, advantaged by the use of turnpikes, saw their position imperiled. Julius Rubin so aptly describes the feeling of rivalry and the reasons for it that it is worth quoting him at length:

> If New York's rivals did not get competing lines across their mountains, they would be shut out, it seemed forever, from the Western trade. This danger appeared precisely at the time when the center of economic interest was shifting from the ocean to the developing interior, from foreign to internal

commerce. A failure to achieve a line to the West, therefore, meant stagnation, even decline: this was the view of the advocates of internal improvement in all the rival cities. . . . Their agitation was unified with a sense of desperate urgency; to them it was a case of expand or die. . . . The achievement of a line to the West would bring with it enormous prizes; they would participate in the expansion of a continent.[7]

City elites developed different strategies of competition. Philadelphia successfully lobbied the state legislature for a state canal project, whereas businessmen in Baltimore exhibited an extraordinary tolerance for risk by investing their own funds in the Baltimore and Ohio Railroad as well as convincing the city government, state government, and small savers to invest. Merchants in Boston, by contrast, were reluctant to invest their own funds in any venture, were unsuccessful in lobbying the state legislature for either a state canal or a railway project, and had enormous difficulty attracting investors. When they were finally able to obtain state subsidies for a railway, they built a single-track road finished in 1842 whereas the merchants of Baltimore, acting in 1827, opted for a double-track railway.[8]

"Municipal mercantilism" (to use Rubin's term) had been launched. Cities competed fiercely for economic growth; the process of city-building was fundamentally one of competition with other towns that were also trying desperately to attract residents, capital, and transportation facilities. As Charles Glaab and Theodore Brown put it, "town rivalry was one of the great games of nineteenth century America." Furthermore, towns laid claim to overlapping hinterlands, leading Richard Wade to argue that cities engaged in "urban imperialism."[9]

Winners and Losers

Urban elites were convinced that to stop growing would mean economic stagnation. Acquiring good transportation links was essential to avoid stagnation. Attracting railroads was necessary for survival, but it was not sufficient for prominence. Jacksonville, Illinois, for example, was a town that between 1825–1870 perfectly confirmed Dykstra's argument that "most American small towns would be cities if they could." Don Harrison Doyle in a fascinating study traces the unsuccessful efforts of this small town to become a prominent city. As Doyle points out, most urban historians examine the history of a few towns that were successful in becoming major cities. "Yet for every Chicago, St. Louis, or even Springfield, there were hundreds of Jacksonvilles whose ambitions for urban prominence were betrayed by the conspiracies of nature, politics, and fate." Although by 1860 Jacksonville had five railroads connecting it to major cities such as Chicago and St. Louis (and deliberately avoiding its archrival Springfield), Jacksonville, for a variety of reasons, never attained even the modest prominence of its rival. Thus, whereas Park City did not receive a railway link and disappeared, Jacksonville acquired fairly good links but nonetheless, by 1870, had resigned itself to its fate as a small town.[10]

While towns competed for such prizes as the county seat, the most intense competition was for position in the transportation network that evolved during the nineteenth century, which drew the map of economic prosperity. In the West, for example, Albuquerque's ability to attract the Atchison, Topeka, and Santa Fe Railroad allowed Albuquerque rather than Santa Fe to become New Mexico's major city. For Western cities, connections to a transcontinental railroad were crucial. Omaha, Kansas City, Houston, San Antonio, Austin, Dallas, Denver, and Seattle all became important cities in their regions because of railway connections. Los Angeles voters were so anxious to obtain a connection to San Francisco and the East that they approved "a $602,000 bond subsidy — 5 percent of the county's assessed valuation — and control of the local railroad linking the city to San Pedro harbor" for the benefit of the Southern Pacific Railroad.[11]

In the case of small towns, competition for position along a canal — and later, especially, for railway links — was driven both by the desire to become a significant city and the simultaneous fear that failure to expand would lead to virtual extinction. Such analysis was not unreasonable, as the fates of Sandusky in Ohio, Leavenworth in Missouri, and Galena and Park City in Kansas all demonstrate. Of roughly equal economic importance in the 1820s, both Cleveland and Sandusky wanted to be chosen as the northern terminus of the Ohio Canal. After the Ohio state legislature chose Cleveland, its growth began to outpace that of Sandusky. Later, railroads chose Cleveland as a transfer point and bypassed Sandusky.[12] So Cleveland continued growing, and Sandusky disappeared as a competitor.

Along similar lines, postbellum Kansas City, Missouri, succeeded in becoming a regional center in competition against St. Joseph and, especially, Leavenworth. In 1863, a journalist, after visiting Kansas City and Leavenworth, wrote that the Kansas City–Leavenworth rivalry would soon be a thing of the past: "The world will soon speak of one of these places as one of the thriving cities of the country — and, the other, the world won't speak of at all."[13] Kansas City was more successful in positioning itself within the railway system — and clearly won that competition.

Perhaps the most extreme costs of losing the race for transportation links are found in the respective fates of Galena and Park City. Galena was not only a serious rival to Chicago, it was the more important city, and most observers assumed it would remain more important than Chicago. However, once Chicago developed superior railway links, Galena faded into obscurity.[14]

The politics of Park City's death, examined by Robert Dykstra, illuminates the intrigues city elites — backed by the electorate — would resort to in order to defeat a rival. Dykstra examines the conflict in the 1870s over railroads between Wichita (the county seat of Sedgwick County, Kansas) and Park City (its bitter rival), a conflict involving Wichita's alliance with Newton, another ambitious frontier town in Sedgwick County. His description gives the flavor that characterized much of the urbanization of America. After voters in Park City unanimously voted against railroad bonds that would help Wichita, Wichitans opened

> secret negotiations with the community leaders of Newton; the additional votes from Newton being enough to swing the (bond) election. . . . Newtonians would approve Wichita's railroad bonds. In return Wichitans pledged not to oppose a planned secession of Sedgwick's northern townships, which would go to . . . making up a new county with Newton as county seat. On August 11, 1871[,] the bond issue won a resounding majority. The vote sealed Park City's fate. Bypassed by the railroad, its businessmen lost all hope of urban importance. Soon they began packing up to find opportunities elsewhere, and within several years Park City had virtually returned to a state of nature.

Of the five major cattle towns in Kansas (Abilene, Dodge City, Ellsworth, Caldwell, and Wichita), only Wichita became a metropolitan center. And that status was largely due to the railway links it acquired.[15]

Cities already large and established enough that they could be assured of at least moderate economic growth competed just as fiercely as Wichita. The case of Milwaukee is illustrative. Milwaukee in 1850, then two-thirds the size of Chicago, hoped to obtain regional supremacy and correctly viewed the railroad as crucial. Although by 1860 it was clear Milwaukee was not going to overtake Chicago, both public and private elites pursued a vigorous policy of attracting railways. By 1873 the city was the terminus for four thousand miles of railroad and, although less important than Chicago, had nonetheless retained significance.[16] Milwaukee's competitive drive had been successful enough that it could view the history of urbanization not as a victim but as an assertive participant.

Most, if not all, of the nineteenth century saw towns and cities compete for survival and growth. Whereas the activities of boosters and businessmen are of importance in understanding the process of intercity competition and local economic-development activity, so too are elected officials at municipal and county levels.[17] Although many of these elected officials came from the groups most active in boosterism (journalists, businessmen, real estate developers, attorneys, and other professionals interested in economic growth), officials had powers that individuals in these groups, acting in a private capacity, did not. We now turn to a discussion of how the public purse was used in the competition among localities sketched above.

Local Government as Investor

Efforts to attract railroads involved many idiosyncratic factors. Kansas City businessmen, for example, convinced important stockholders in one railroad that a roadbed had been previously graded when in reality a surveyor had merely walked along it. It is important to remember that efforts to acquire railway links were often necessary but not sufficient for a town's emergence as a major city. Glaab's analysis of Kansas City's efforts to become a leading railway center is also applicable to the efforts of elites in other cities:

> The early history of Kansas City does not sustain the view that local leaders through heroic action created a city. Nor does it reveal the unfolding of a design whereby a wilderness community steadily and surely emerges as railroad center and metropolis. It shows instead a pattern of false starts, obvious turning points, and fortuitous combinations of circumstance.[18]

Nonetheless, nearly all communities offered financial aid to railway companies in their efforts to become a terminus for a line, to attract a branch line, or at least to become a stop on a line projected in the vicinity. During the nineteenth century, local governments in every single state financially aided railway companies. The attraction of railroads was generally the primary concern of town elites.[19]

State investment in transportation was clearly propelled by the inadequacy of private investment and not surprisingly accounted for a significant portion of all investment in transportation. Local investment, especially after the Civil War when it became particularly widespread, had a different function. It was not critical to nation-building in the way that state investment was. Rather it aided city-building.

States invested to build a transportation network that would help portions of the state's territory and that at the same time would begin developing a regional market. Cities invested when private capital was already heavily involved in shaping a national market. Cities invested to help their own economic growth, but (especially in the postbellum period) they were not critical to fashioning a national or regional market the way states had been. Statistics, although rough, indicate that government investment was much more important in the antebellum period, when states were most active as entrepreneurs and promoters, than in the postbellum period, when municipal aid was particularly widespread. At least after the Civil War, in many cases, local government needed the railroad more than the railway company needed local aid (see table 1).[20]

Although the total amounts of aid given by localities to improvements cannot be determined with any degree of accuracy, Carter Goodrich concludes that in the antebellum period, localities committed more than $125 million to internal improvements (compared to $300 million for state governments). In the postbellum period (1861–1890), by contrast, local governments probably committed more than $175 million (compared to the roughly $95 million of aid given primarily by Massachusetts and the nine states of the Reconstruction South). Goodrich concludes that total public aid in the period 1861–1890, although amounting to roughly $350 million (excluding land grants), "played a much smaller part than before the War in the increase of railroad construction."[21] Even before the Panic of 1873 (the period of most postbellum public aid), such aid was not crucial because private investment in railways had increased enormously. Local aid, therefore, was not critical to capital formation in the way that state/local aid had been before the Civil War.

Even though the proportion of total local aid to total investment in railroads was not high, the amounts were large for the towns that were giving the aid. Robert Fishlow — although arguing that antebellum local

Table 1. Government Investment as Percentage of Total Investment

U.S. Canals, 1815–1860	72.5
Public works	60.5
Mixed enterprise or aid to private enterprise	11.8
U.S. Railroads	
Mainly mixed enterprise or aid to private enterprise	
To 1860	25–30[a]
1861–1872	roughly 10[b]
1873–1890	roughly 1

Source: Carter Goodrich, "State In, State Out: A Pattern of Development Policy," *Journal of Economic Issues* 11, no. 4 (December 1968), p. 366.

Notes: [a]Plus federal grants.
   [b]Plus very large federal land grants.

aid was more reactive than that of state governments, which was more likely to be initiatory — goes on to describe why localities did give aid:

> it is true that the returns to municipalities from such local assistance, even if negligible financially, were often large. There were too many instances in which towns could be as easily avoided as traversed, and with eager competitors clamoring for relocation of the road, the chance could not be put to the test. Accordingly, the "social return" from the investment was almost infinite in opportunity cost terms; in the absence of aid there would likely be only a mournful history of municipal decay and decline.[22]

Local aid had to be legally authorized by state law.[23] Some laws authorized all counties and municipalities to give financial aid to any railroad. However, the majority were so-called special laws, and these identified the community that could give aid and/or the railroad that could receive it. Between 1830 and 1889, most states passed general authorizations; in addition, nearly twenty-two hundred special laws were passed by state legislatures. The most active period of local aid was between 1864 and the Panic of 1873. Roughly half of the general laws authorizing all localities to give aid, and over a third of the special laws, were passed in this period. Nonetheless, hundreds of special laws were passed in the 1880s; in 1890, fifteen states still authorized all local governments to assist railways.

By 1890 local aid had been given in every state of the Union, and aid was given until very late into the nineteenth century. In Illinois, the post-bellum period saw over fifty counties and nearly three hundred towns give financial aid. (Ironically, the reaction was extraordinarily intense in Illinois against *state* government ownership of transportation facilities.) In Kansas, towns gave substantial aid from 1870 until 1890. In Virginia, the Carolinas, and Mississippi, local aid was often given in the 1880s.[24]

It should be noted that neither Chicago nor New York City gave such aid. Private railway companies in Chicago found it relatively easy to raise money in the East. Chicago's role as a transportation center was assisted by the Illinois and Michigan Canal, completed in 1848. That canal, which received both state and federal aid, connected Chicago to the tributaries of the Illinois River.[25] Ultimately, however, Chicago's success may simply be due to its superb geographic position. Both New York City and Chicago (it should nonetheless be noted) were able to prosper at least partially because of the advantages gained from public works that had been paid for by state funds.

Policy makers in nearly all other cities, however, felt that municipal initiative was necessary in order to ensure good railway links. A key policy instrument in executing such initiative was the ability of local governments, when authorized by either general or specific state legislation, to borrow funds. (Other company aids that were used by localities included donations of land, bridges, and rights of way, as well as the encouraging of private investors to buy railway securities.) Those funds could then be used to make a cash donation to a company, to buy stock in the company, to buy bonds, or (as in the case of the Cincinnati Southern Railway and the Schenectady and Troy) to build a municipal railroad.

Cincinnati

Numerous cities that were not constitutionally prohibited from helping private railway companies did so. They viewed such companies as instruments in the city's competitive strategy. Cincinnati, however, was prohibited from offering such aid, but it was so desperate for railway links that it turned to municipal enterprise in the same spirit as other cities turned to public-private cooperation. The case of Cincinnati is illuminating, for it parallels the cases of state ownership of transport in Pennsylvania, New York, Indiana, and Ohio. Cincinnati's experience illuminates the imperatives that other cities also felt and the reasons behind their decisions to aid railways.

Cincinnati in 1860 was still considerably larger than Chicago, although changes in trade patterns threatened its economic dominance of the region. Although the city had celebrated in 1836 when the Kentucky legislature had granted a charter to the Cincinnati, Louisville, and Charleston Railway, onerous conditions imposed by Kentucky had delayed work until 1837, when the Panic of that year effectively killed the project. Although later attempts were made, no railway company succeeded in giving Cincinnati its much desired railway link with the South.

Meanwhile, both state and local governments were finding it difficult to repay the large loans they had incurred for internal improvements. Some counties even attempted to repudiate their debts, and as a consequence the state Constitutional Convention of 1850 completely prohibited state aid to public works. It also voted (78–16) to prohibit all local governments from aiding private transport companies in any way.

Cincinnati, therefore, could not hope to build a link with the South by aiding a private railway company. At the same time its competitive position weakened as railways linked New York City, Philadelphia, Baltimore, and Boston to the trade north of the Ohio River; as Chicago gained access in 1854 to the trade of the Dakotas, Nebraska, Minnesota, and Iowa; and as St. Louis increased its access to Indiana, Illinois, and Missouri. In 1859 Louisville, Cincinnati's most serious competition in the South, gained a direct railway link to Nashville, and by connections gained access to Knoxville, Chattanooga, Memphis, Augusta, and Charleston as well as to other important southern towns. Louisville therefore began to attract the river traffic that formerly had been claimed by Cincinnati.

The Civil War then solidified this emerging trade pattern. By 1868 St. Louis, Chicago, Cleveland, Toledo, and Indianapolis had attracted the trade from the North and West that formerly had converged on Cincinnati. In the South, Louisville continued to upstage Cincinnati. Since the railway connection Cincinnati had with the South was by using the river to Louisville and then the Louisville and Nashville Railroad, Louisville merchants deliberately set rail rates so that goods shipped from Cincinnati were at a disadvantage. Meanwhile, Southern merchants streamed into

Louisville to buy goods to sell to freed slaves who could now patronize stores and who demanded more varied goods than had been provided by plantation owners. By 1868, in Hollander's words:

> Cincinnati and Louisville were active competitors for southern trade. This trade was definitely established upon the basis of railroad transportation. Cincinnati possessed no direct railroad to the South; Louisville did. The advantages enjoyed by the former city in the era of water transportation were now held by the latter. Southern merchants dealing directly with the North were diverted from Cincinnati by the closer proximity of Louisville. Louisville, in a word, threatened to displace Cincinnati as the chief distributing point of Northern manufacturers to Southern consumers.[26]

When a constitutional lawyer proposed that Cincinnati itself should build a railroad, the city council agreed. The lawyer argued that the city, now losing the trade of Iowa, absolutely had to establish "an empire of trade; and that empire of trade was the South; that was the only place for Cincinnati trade."[27] On June 4, 1868, the council passed a resolution in favor of constructing the Cincinnati Southern Railway, linking Cincinnati to Chattanooga. The city borrowed $18 million to construct it, and the railroad was finished in February 1880.

A municipality therefore constructed a railroad hundreds of miles in length, borrowed and spent millions of dollars, negotiated with several state governments, and won several legal challenges to the constitutionality of the enterprise. Although the railroad was built too late for Cincinnati to maintain commercial supremacy (which might have been impossible no matter how many railroads it had built), it did allow the city to remain significant. In some sense, the experience of Cincinnati symbolizes the experience of all those cities in which both public and private elites felt desperate to acquire transportation links that would allow them to prosper as the economy of the United States underwent wrenching restructuring.

Investment in Other Private Enterprises

Although investment intended for economic development was typically directed toward transportation, city governments did expand their purview. When authorized by state law, cities invested in a wide range of manufacturing facilities. Although we do not have good historical information on this phenomenon, the information we do have indicates that municipalities in a fairly wide range of states assisted private firms other than railways. In Maine, Kansas, West Virginia, Illinois, Missouri, Nebraska, Ohio, New York, and Massachusetts, municipalities issued bonds for enterprises ranging from a furniture factory to iron- and steelworks.[28]

The information we have about local aid to milling companies or manufacturers comes primarily from defaults. It is very likely that such assistance was far more widespread than default data would indicate, but there is little historical record of this type of assistance. One exception is Don Harrison Doyle's study of the attempt by Jacksonville, Illinois, to become a major city. Doyle traces the efforts of town boosters, using bond monies approved by the electorate, to attract the machine shops of the St. Louis, Jacksonville, and Chicago Railroad.[29]

In Kansas, the state legislature expressly provided that certain municipalities should "have power to encourage the establishment of manufactories and such other enterprises as may tend to develop and improve such city." By 1874, in Kansas alone, local governments had issued over $2 million in bonds for enterprises ranging from hotels to manufacturing companies.[30]

Local Government as Borrower

Local borrowing increased dramatically between 1840 and 1880, although of course not all borrowing during that period was for canals and railways. Total municipal indebtedness was only $25 million in 1840, but by 1880 it had climbed to $821 million. Per capita local debt increased from $1.17 to $16.37. Meanwhile state indebtedness increased from $175 million to only $275 million, and per capita state debt was nearly halved in that period. In 1840 state debt was seven times larger than municipal debt, but forty years later, municipal debt was three times larger than state debt. The twenty cities with a population of 100,000 or more increased their debt (in the aggregate) by 176 percent between 1866 and 1876.[31]

Although not all debt incurred was for transportation facilities, a significant chunk of it was. Between 1840 and 1870, Hillhouse argues, "the larger portion of the rapidly rising municipal debt was for railroad aid." Furthermore, most of the bond repudiations and defaults that occurred after the Panic of 1873 involved railway-aid bonds. In New York, for example, localities before 1870 almost never defaulted, and when they did the bondholder eventually was repaid. Pierce states, "Yet, between 1870 and 1890, 57 towns and villages had repudiated securities. . . . With a

single exception, involving only $10,000 all of these bonds had been is-
sued to aid the construction of railroads."[32] New York's experience was
widespread.

The West (Montana, Idaho, Wyoming, Colorado, New Mexico, Arizona, Utah, Nevada, Washington, Oregon, and California) was an exception. Defaults were few, since most of these states wrote restrictions on
assistance to private firms into their constitutions when they gained statehood. Nonetheless, many localities even in the West lent monies to railway
companies. In California, by 1871, towns and counties had loaned over
$3 million to the Central Pacific and other railways. In the period 1835–
1930, railway-aid bonds "bulk large in total defaults." In the 1870s,
1880s, and 1890s, most defaults involved railway bonds.[33]

Much of the aid was given by borrowing money (that is, by selling a
municipal bond) and using it to buy railway stock, or else municipal
bonds were given to the railway in exchange for railway securities, and the
railway subsequently marketed the municipal bonds. Although local aid
often influenced the route of a projected railway rather than determining
whether the railway would be built, especially in the postbellum era, local
aid was significant. As Fishlow points out, "availability of such (local)
funds at an early stage of a project was an important asset when going to
the capital market in search of further private funds."[34] Railways usually
sold their stock or bonds to local governments on better terms than they
would have received from other buyers.

The municipal securities with which many towns bought railway stock
often sold at higher prices in the market than the companies' securities
would have done. In New York, "municipal railroad-aid bonds were almost invariably marketed at par or better" but "rare indeed was the company that could sell securities (at par)." In other areas of the country,
municipal railway-aid bonds sold considerably below par, but the companies' own securities would have sold for even less. The most secure
bonds were the so-called tax bonds, for they were secured by a pledge of
earmarked taxes and thus were extremely marketable.[35]

The fate of municipal securities issued in aid of railways varied, however, depending on their provenance. Bonds issued by municipalities in the
Reconstruction South did not easily attract buyers. Those issued in states
that had previously repudiated debt were almost impossible to sell in
the North. In fact, when Vicksburg gave a railway company $90,000 in
bonds, the company was unable to sell them at all.[36]

Although local railway-aid bonds could be used as collateral for loans from banks, this procedure was costly for the railway since a bank would want far more in securities than it would lend in cash. Thus, the $90,000 in bonds issued in Vicksburg, when used as collateral, only yielded $50,000 in cash in the form of a bank loan. Partially because local bonds were perceived as dubious investments, state aid was vital for railway construction in the Reconstruction South whereas it was often absent altogether in the North.

Politics of Borrowing

Unfortunately, urban historians have only recently begun analyzing the politics of taxing, spending, and borrowing in nineteenth-century towns. Similarly, they have only recently become interested in analyzing public policy. Therefore, while the data on electoral approval is consistent, it is fairly thin. Terrence J. McDonald and Sally K. Ward conclude that, although a great deal of urban history has been written, scholars have largely ignored "fiscal politics or, for that matter, politics at all." They argue:

> most historians of the politics of urban fiscal policy assume that once one has identified the social basis of support for an urban regime, one has identified the nature of the regime's fiscal policy. This follows because of the essentially functionalist notion that political and social institutions persist because they fulfill certain functions for their supporters. . . . However, because of the variety of variables intervening between them, there is no necessary connection between a political movement's social basis and the nature of its policy.

McDonald and Ward focus on Samuel P. Hays's pathbreaking work in the field of urban history. They argue that he "described a sea-change in the class basis of American urban politics" but avoided "the analysis of policy."[37]

Along similar lines, Jon Teaford in an important article has argued that historians have paid far too much attention to the role of the machine and its boss. He writes:

> The boss-reform synthesis has so dominated the study of urban politics and government that the actual holders of official power have receded into the shadows yielding the pages of history to party leaders and reform crusaders. . . . But the history of city government is not simply a story of

flamboyant political chieftains and juicy scandals. It is a story that must include the formal occupants of public office. Who were they? What did they do, and what were the consequences in terms of municipal policy? . . . Basic to all municipal policies, however, is the question of finance, and this topic is one of the most neglected. . . . [F]ew since the Progressive era have delved into the history of municipal expenditures, taxation, and debt. Historians have written blithely about waste, incompetence, and inefficiency in city government without ever testing these generalizations against the municipal ledgers.[38]

We do know that enthusiastic majorities typically approved the borrowing carried out by local governments to assist railway companies. Such borrowing often had to be approved in referenda, and the existing historical record indicates that the enthusiasm for using public credit in support of private companies was widespread. Again, precise figures are unavailable, but nearly every case study of local aid points out that the electorate was supportive.

Although railway aid was often challenged in the courts, such challenges were often brought by supporters of rival railway companies. In Kansas City, Glaab finds that nearly unanimous votes were cast for railway aid. In New York, Pierce finds that the electorate approved bonds in every community in which they were put to a public vote.[39] In spite of the opposition of other transportation (such as canal) interests, Pierce concludes:

> Prior to the panic of 1873, the opposition to municipal aid for railroads was numerically small and ineffectively organized. It was composed mainly of tax reformers, friends of rival railroads, conservative groups who raised the cry of socialism, and a number of well-meaning persons who deplored the use of public funds for the promotion of private enterprise.[40]

REPUDIATION

Borrowing was carried out with widespread approval, and so were the repudiation and defaults that plagued the railway-assistance bonds provided by such borrowing. In some cases, repudiation was approved by the electorate in referenda just as initial borrowing had been. The votes in favor of repudiation were lopsided.[41] Just as state governments had borrowed furiously and then defaulted or repudiated debt, so too did local governments.

Although the depression of 1873 began what Hillhouse terms "the era of repudiation," defaults on railroad bonds had begun in the antebellum era. Local governments in the nineteenth century either defaulted or sought judicial relief from their bondholders in twenty-five states. Technicalities were used shamelessly to avoid repayment; conflict between state courts and the Supreme Court flared in several states; and some towns even were eliminated as governmental jurisdictions and then reconstituted.[42] Some repudiations occurred because the promised railroad had never been built and the local citizens felt no obligation to repay bondholders. In other cases the railroad had been built but had not prospered. In other cases the locality felt it could not afford to repay the debt, and in others the citizenry felt they did not want to repay. Finally, gross fraud accompanied other efforts at municipal assistance.

Generally, a range of creative means were found by local officials to avoid repayment, and attempts to collect awards granted by courts led to drama. In some areas, local officials spent a good part of their office tenure in hiding. In others, officials only met in secret places and at secret times. The following episode gives a flavor of the lengths to which local officials went in their efforts to repudiate railroad bonds:

> In one Missouri county the officials customarily met only when the shiretown was carefully picketed against the approach of enemies and strangers, and service at the suit of bondholders was not obtained until a bailiff of the court, in the disguise of a drunken tramp, entered the place unchallenged and staggered into the presence of those against whom he held a writ.

In many cases, when local governments did settle with bondholders, the settlement was such that the lender was severely disadvantaged. However, local governments threatened that if their offer was not accepted, the debts would not be redeemed at all.[43] Often bondholders, worn out by years of litigation and resistance, finally agreed to settle on terms that ranged from unfavorable to disastrous.

Conclusion

Local elites used the public purse to pursue a variety of economic-development strategies, the attraction of railways being the most important. Their activism was an important part of the city-building process of the nineteenth century. As we shall see in chapter 5, the restrictions that followed such entrepreneurial energy laid another foundation stone in the system of capital finance.

Yet city elites did not borrow only to attract railways. They also borrowed to provide capital-intensive public services. The combination of borrowing both for economic development and for the provision of services led to rates of indebtedness that were judged to be threatening by state governments. It was in their dual role as service providers and economic-development activists that local governments became subject to debt limitations imposed by state government. In chapter 4, I shall sketch the evolution of the city as a service provider, whereas in chapter 5, I shall analyze the dynamics of the movement to limit the ability of cities to borrow.

The consequences of local assistance to private railway companies were such that a reaction to local activism set in. Just as local aid had been popular and then had been followed by popular repudiations and defaults, so too were proposals designed to restrict such aid in the future. State government had not managed to avoid being constrained in its future investment activities — and local governments met the same fate.

Chapter 4

The Provision of Services:

Municipal Government,

Technology, and Debt

T he American locality is distinctive because it has been active in both economic development and service provision. Capital finance is directed toward both activities, and the two have frequently been intertwined. In the nineteenth and early twentieth centuries, a symbiotic relationship existed in many cities between efforts at economic development and the provision of capital-intensive services. Debts incurred for economic development often constrained the provision of services in a subsequent period. Partially because of the debts Milwaukee incurred in its attempt to better Chicago as a railway center, for example, services were provided relatively slowly.[1]

Other cities provided a low level of services in the late nineteenth century because they had run up debts in an earlier period by providing expensive services rather than because of their economic-development activities (San Francisco is a case in point). In other cities, the provision of intercity and interregional transportation links were viewed as far more important than services. Only when transportation was taken care of did attention turn to intracity services (Houston, whose elites were obsessed with beating Galveston, fits in this category).[2]

In some cities, the provision of services connected particularly with public health were promoted by businessmen who felt these were essential for the city's economic well-being. In New Orleans, Atlanta, and Memphis (which all suffered from the effects of a devastating yellow fever epidemic in the Mississippi Valley in 1878), businessmen were critical in focusing attention on the provision of clean water and sewerage. In these three cities, "commercial men and industrialists thought of public works on sewerage and water supply as business investments in the projection of a favorable urban image."[3] In the case of Detroit, the city borrowed money in order to buy a privately owned waterworks and to provide sewers. Whereas the waterworks was indeed bought, the money that should have been used for sewers was used to buy stock in the Denver and St. Joseph Railroad Company instead. (The city defaulted on this debt in 1841.)[4]

This is not to say that service provision was always directly linked to economic development, at least if defined as local assistance to railways. Although this was true in some cities, it clearly was not so in others. Chicago and New York City, for example, were leaders in the provision of capital infrastructure but yet did not give any assistance to railways.

In San Francisco, similarly, the lack of service provision in the second half of the nineteenth century was not due to constraints imposed by economic-development debt. Rather, it was due to the political reaction against debt incurred for service provision in the period 1852–1856. Terrence McDonald argues that in the period 1852–1856 San Francisco understandably borrowed a great deal:

> The city and county governments were forced to pay gold rush prices for goods and services but were unable to collect gold rush taxes because of the transience of the population, resistance to taxation, and lack of legislation securing the tax base. The result was a revenue shortfall made up by short-term borrowing at very high interest rates. Moreover, most of the borrowing was done to pay local merchants, firms, and individuals, some of whom went to the state legislature to seek legislation forcing the city to pay them. In such a situation, it would have been remarkable if the city had remained debt-free.[5]

Nonetheless, such borrowing was interpreted as extravagant by the roughly 40 percent of the adult male population that qualified as voters. The political reaction to this period was such that the city did not borrow and provided low levels of service until the end of the nineteenth century.

In general, however, local officials in the nineteenth century were busy borrowing to assist railways but were also borrowing and investing capital for public facilities that were designed to provide amenities both to businesses and to households. And cities provided other types of services as well, such as police and fire protection. Monkkonen has found that:

> Cautious and fiscally conservative city officials and voters struggled for years to convince themselves and one another of the worthiness of establishing the earliest police and fire departments. Such innovations represented unprecedented and costly categories of fixed annual expenditures for local governments. . . . The new police and fire departments . . . were in fact early aspects of the new service governments that emerged more fully in the twentieth century.[6]

As fire fighting became "technology-intensive," debt was incurred for the capital-intensive portions of fire protection, but otherwise these services were funded by tax revenues. Public improvements such as waterworks and sewers, for their part, cost enormous amounts of money, involved huge debts, and initiated the professionalization of the city's bureaucracy. This chapter traces the process whereby municipal governments became major providers of capital-intensive services.

Municipal Government as Service Provider

Nineteenth-century local governments carried out huge capital projects, requiring sophisticated mobilization of financial, technical, and administrative resources. City governments, especially, carried out engineering projects that were breathtaking in their boldness and technical complexity. The increasingly professionalized urban bureaucracies (especially that of the civil engineer) applied technical expertise on a heretofore unimagined scale.

The sophistication and speed with which city government officials provided capital-intensive services allowed many American urban residents to enjoy public services far superior to those enjoyed by residents of even the major European cities. Jon Teaford terms the accomplishments of late nineteenth-century American cities an "unheralded triumph." He writes, for example, of Chicago's achievements:

> In a single lifetime Chicago residents had transformed a prairie into one of the greatest cities of the world, and during this short period the governmental authorities, with remarkable energy and daring, had provided migrants to the metropolis with a level of public services rarely equaled in the world

of the late nineteenth century. In the 1850s the city council had ordained that the level of the swampy city be raised ten feet, and it had been done. In later decades the municipal authorities had ordered that the flow of the Chicago river be reversed, and so it was reversed. The achievements of government in Chicago at times rivaled the feats of the Old Testament God.

The specifics of Chicago government's accomplishments are indeed impressive:

> In 1830 Chicago was a frontier trading post with a few log structures, a few muddy paths, and a few dozen inhabitants. Seventy years later it was a city of 1.5 million people, with a waterworks pumping 500 million gallons of water to its residents each day and a drainage system with over 1,500 miles of sewers. More than 1,400 miles of paved streets lighted by 38,000 street lamps crisscrossed the prairie, and 925 miles of street car lines carried hundreds of millions of passengers each year. A fleet of 129 fire engines protected lives and property, and over 2,200 acres of city parkland and a public library of 300,000 volumes offered recreation and a means for self-improvement.[7]

Teaford's argument is provocative, because earlier writings on nineteenth-century cities have focused on "machine politics" and painted a picture of corruption and policy incompetence. However, according to Teaford, it is important to view the American city's policy outcomes in comparative perspective. How were city governments in other advanced countries doing?

Teaford's answer is striking. In comparative terms, American cities provided a range of services that were unavailable to residents of London or Berlin. American cities had numerous shortcomings, as the critics of the machine constantly pointed out, but they also provided services that city governments in other advanced countries did not. Chicago was not alone. By the beginning of the twentieth century, American city governments "provided the most extensive, most advanced public services known to urban residents."[8] The figures on water supply in the United States, Britain, and Germany are indicative (as table 2 indicates).

Given these figures, it is perhaps not so surprising that in 1890, Berliners owned one bathtub for every seventy-nine residents, whereas the residents of the small town of Springfield, Massachusetts, enjoyed one bathtub for every nine residents. The figures for sewers and water mains, for miles of paved streets, for public parks, public libraries, and streetlighting were similar. The American city governments surveyed by Teaford far out-

Table 2. Per Capita Water Supply, 1895–1897

Cities	Daily Supply in U.S. Gallons
American Cities	
New York	100
Chicago	139
Philadelphia	162
Brooklyn	89
Boston	100
St. Louis	98
Baltimore	94
Cleveland	142
Buffalo	271
British Cities	
London	42
Glasgow	65
Liverpool	34
Manchester	40
Birmingham	28
Leeds	43
Sheffield	21
German Cities	
Berlin	18
Hamburg	52
Munich	38
Leipzig	16
Breslau	23
Dresden	24
Cologne	45

Source: Teaford, The Unheralded Triumph, p. 221.

invested their European counterparts. European city governments were much more likely to provide facilities for their poor and less likely to provide for their middle class than were American cities. "The comfortable majority was the focus of municipal endeavor and not the indigent minority. Chicago, Boston, and Baltimore readily spent fortunes on giant engineering projects for the convenience of the prosperous, but bathhouses for the uplift of the poor were an afterthought."[9] On the other hand, in the area of school buildings, where American investment lagged behind German and British investment, the schools that were built seem to have been more comfortable. Thus, that deficiency was somewhat ambiguous. Overall, American urban capital investment in many northern cities had, by the beginning of the twentieth century, provided a range of public facilities that were unequaled anywhere in the industrialized world.

The outlook, however, was different in much of the urban South. The rate of provision was undoubtedly slower in southern cities than northern, for southern local governments were more reluctant to spend public monies for services. However, the postbellum period saw a rapid extension of certain services even in the South. Whereas in 1860, there had been only two hundred waterworks in the South, the number had risen to five hundred in 1880, and many of them were privately owned. Houston, for example, had a private waterworks company. The city did not have the funds to build its own and therefore decided to encourage private investors to own and operate a waterworks. Later, the city engaged in a protracted struggle with the water company and finally bought it in 1906. Between 1880 and 1900 southern cities improved their park systems, installed sewers, paved streets, and built schools. (The services provided by southern cities in the 1880s and 1890s largely excluded black neighborhoods. Such neighborhoods did not receive water and sewer lines, had unpaved streets, and were generally far from fire stations.)[10]

Nonetheless, southern cities retained a strong interest in economic development whereas in northern cities the interest in direct assistance to private companies (such as had been given to railways) was replaced with an emphasis on the provision of services. In the early twentieth century, however, business elites in some southern cities began to view service provision as intimately linked to economic growth. In 1908, for example, one-third of Atlanta was without sewers or water mains, and "the Chamber of Commerce waged an all-out fight" for a bond issue proposed in 1910 to build waterworks and sewage-disposal plants.[11]

Infrastructure and Technology

The evolution of the city as a service provider (at least in the area of infrastructure) was often tied to technology. Much debt was incurred to cope with technological change, of which a great deal was unanticipated. The link between water and sewer systems is an example of one technological innovation — the provision of running water — with consequences that in turn led to a technological response. Another example has to do with the automobile. Local governments expanded the hard-surfaced road system, "because pavement was seen as having varied public utilities, most particularly in increasing the carrying capacity of horse-drawn vehicles."[12] This expansion facilitated the use of the automobile, which in turn caused more infrastructure development. New technologies were typically capital- rather than labor-intensive and therefore necessitated the spending of public monies, much of which was borrowed.

Waterworks were the first major capital projects to be built by American cities. In 1802 Philadelphia constructed the first water system, and by the late nineteenth century, hundreds of cities and towns had also built them. Water systems allowed local governments to obtain water outside their boundaries and to pipe it to the household tap, rather than obtain water from local wells or springs. When water became available at the tap, consumption skyrocketed. In Boston, for example, per capita water consumption increased so dramatically that the city had to build a second reservoir. Per capita consumption typically rose from between three and five gallons daily, before the building of a water system, to roughly a hundred gallons a day.[13]

In particular, running water allowed householders to install a new — and unanticipated — technology. The flush toilet followed quickly upon the availability of running water. Although attempts were made to encourage the use of the earth closet common in Europe, the new technology of the water closet became extraordinarily popular. Tarr and McMichael conclude that "by 1880, approximately one-third of urban households had water closets." By 1893 even 32 percent of the residents in Philadelphia's slums already had flush toilets.[14]

No city simultaneously built a water and a sewer system, however. Water systems were built first. The sixteen largest cities all built water systems before the Civil War, but only Brooklyn and Chicago built antebellum sewerage systems. Historians of environmental engineering, appropriately enough, refer to the period 1800–1880 as the "presewer period."[15] However, as flush toilets became widely used, the cesspools or privy vaults (typically cleaned by scavengers) that were used for the disposal of human waste overflowed.[16] They had to be cleaned out much more frequently, and the cost of keeping them operational increased.

Consequently, urban policy makers turned to another new technology — the sewer. Tarr and McMichael summarize well the impact of technological change on the infrastructure provided by local governments:

> The unanticipated result of the adoption of these technologies was to upset the existing system of waste disposal. . . . Increasingly . . . as more cities installed running water supplies and householders adopted water closets, urban policy makers became convinced that the only method to deal with the wastewater problem was to adopt another new technology — the installation of sewers that transported wastes by water carriage.

(The same decision in favor of sewerage was taken by policy makers in Britain, which provided leadership in all areas of sewage construction and design, and in France, where this new technology spread rather slowly from Paris to the provinces.)[17]

Whereas the previous method of cleaning cesspools and privy vaults had been labor-intensive, the new technology of water-carriage removal (sewerage) was capital-intensive and therefore required huge public works. The old technology had involved government to a minimal degree, whereas the new technology was to be implemented solely by government. Waterworks, on the other hand, were both publicly and privately owned. Between 1860 and 1890, municipal ownership of waterworks increased. By the beginning of the twentieth century, forty-two out of the fifty largest cities had municipally owned waterworks; and ten years later only 30 percent of cities with populations over 30,000 still had privately owned systems of water supply.[18]

Thus, local governments took on responsibility for a new technology that required both new and huge infusions of public capital. Sewers quickly became very popular, and despite extensive debates over the type of sewer to build, sewer lines were built throughout the United States. The number of miles of sewers increased dramatically in the space of fifteen years: "between 1890 and 1909, the total length of sewers in urban areas increased from 6,005 miles (9,664 km) to 24,972 (40,189km)."[19]

Sewerage systems conveniently disposed of human wastes, but the question then arose of what to do with raw sewage. This question was quickly answered, however, because of the notion then prevalent that streams were self-purifying. Thus, one town's sewage flowed into another town's water supply. The practice of dumping untreated sewage into water was so common that "in 1909, 88 percent of the wastewater of the sewered population was disposed of, without treatment, in bodies of water."[20] Chicago went to unusual engineering lengths to divert sewage from Lake Michigan, its water supply, but did not begin treating some of its sewage until 1922.[21] It then became one of the first cities to treat its own sewage.

Although proponents of sewers had argued that their adoption would benefit public health, the contrary seemed to be true. Atlanta, Pittsburgh, Trenton, and Toledo built sewer systems between 1880 and 1890, only to find that their typhoid death rates rose significantly. It became clear that when untreated sewage entered the water supplies, public health suffered. The irony was clear: anticipated health benefits had been a key factor in the adoption of water-carriage technology, but disposal practices generated serious hazards. However, because these hazards were often borne by second parties or users downstream, while the benefits accrued to communities upstream, municipalities continued to build sewer systems and to dump untreated sewage into the water.[22]

Cities were faced with several options in deciding how to avoid the problem of contaminated water. The first — adopted by some cities such as Newark and Jersey City, New Jersey — was to bring their water from remote areas, free of sewage. Another alternative was sewage treatment, which although costly nonetheless purified the water for downstream users. This option was often the choice of state boards of health, but they were unsuccessful in forcing municipalities to build sewage-treatment plants. The third option was the most widely adopted by local governments. Water filtration, a technology developed in the late 1800s, was adopted by many municipalities as an effective way of treating water contaminated by sewage. Although state boards of health (influenced by physicians) wanted local governments to use both filtration and sewage-treatment facilities, local governments (influenced by sanitary engineers) chose to filter their own water and let downstream users similarly deal with waterborne sewage by filtering their water. Filtration dramatically lessened the threat of typhoid.[23]

Water pollution per se was not viewed as a problem that municipalities wanted to use their money to prevent. Consequently, many streams became so polluted that they were suitable only to receive further waste. By 1930, while roughly one-quarter of the urban population had its sewage treated, nearly two-thirds of that same population drank filtered water. Not until 1931, for example, did New York City even have a plan for constructing sewage-treatment plants.[24]

It was not until the 1970s that local governments — under federal pressure stemming from the Federal Water Pollution Control Act Amendments of 1972 — would seriously begin preventing their sewage from flowing into others' water supplies. That effort, involving a "retrofit" of the system of technology already in place, has also been technology-intensive and expensive (although a significant share of the cost is paid by the federal government). In sum, contemporary sewage-treatment plants as a policy response have evolved from the intersection of several new, and often unanticipated, technologies spanning a century.

Services and the Metropolis

The provision of capital infrastructure gave impetus to annexation, incorporation, and the special district. The demand for the high level of services provided by the central city required that suburbanites joined the central city (annexation), incorporated as a municipality so that they could provide services for themselves (incorporation), or accepted participation in a district that furnished them a particular, desired service (special district). In some places, central cities expanded through the annexation of contiguous areas, whereas in other places, outlying areas that developed erratically along commuter rail lines incorporated and became legally distinct municipal governments.[25] And, often driven by the economies of scale intrinsic to large-scale capital-intensive public works, a new form of government was created that allowed for the provision of a particular service without raising the question of either annexation or incorporation.

Whatever the governmental result, the desire for the high level of service provided by the central city and the financing of large public works through locally assumed debt were powerful forces in the shaping of the metropolis. In the case of Los Angeles, areas that wished to receive water from the Los Angeles Aqueduct (funded through a $23 million bond issue approved by the electorate in 1907, which brought the city's debt up to its debt limit) had to agree to be annexed to the city. In Steven Erie's words:

> The aqueduct project had taught Mulholland (City Water Engineer) the importance of expanding the city's bonding capacity. Annexation would rapidly increase the city's assessed valuation and thus its debt ceiling, making other public water and power projects possible. . . . In 73 separate annexation elections held between 1906 and 1930, Los Angeles voters dramatically expanded the city's boundaries from 43 to 442 square miles.

The local government's ability to borrow gave many unincorporated areas a choice — they could join the central city, or they could incorporate and then borrow. In contrast to Britain, local governments were responsible for their level of capital investment within the parameters allowed by state law. Not only did they not receive approval from the center but they did not even inform Washington of their borrowing activities. It is not surprising, Monkkonen argues, that American municipalities possessed "a uniquely powerful local ability to raise capital."[26]

Although particularism and class distinctions were undoubtedly an important factor in encouraging the creation of new municipalities, Teaford argues, "perhaps the single most important motive was not separatism but the desire for improved public services."[27] In many cases, annexation was not feasible because the area was too far from the central city and geography made the construction of public works to such outlying areas too expensive or too difficult. In other cases, central cities did not wish to annex surrounding areas in need of services because of their burden on the tax base. Since city populations were expanding, local officials did not view annexation as necessarily desirable.

In cases where, for whatever reason, annexation to a central city was not likely, suburbanites naturally turned to incorporating themselves as a municipality. Services could not be obtained in any other way, since states did not allow counties to provide capital infrastructure. If an area incorporated, the new municipal corporation could borrow to finance the provision of services. Such incorporation was easy, for state legislatures in the nineteenth century passed general laws of incorporation. Any area with a minimum population could incorporate itself as a municipality if a certain percentage of its voters (stipulated by the state legislature) agreed in an election that they wished to incorporate. Citizens typically voted for incorporation because "dogs, desperados, sewage, and sanitation were all problems that confronted the unincorporated suburb, and municipal government was thought to be the panacea for these suburban ills."[28]

State legislatures withdrew so completely from the process of municipal incorporation that "local self-government was no longer bestowed by the state; it was assumed by the citizenry."[29] State legislatures certainly did not exercise the type of control over the formation of new political subdivisions that one might expect from the unitary relationship existing between American state governments and local governments. State capitals did not exercise any kind of central control or coordination as the metropolitan area gradually divided up into separate municipalities.

Permissive incorporation laws, combined with the indifference of the state legislature, were crucial in enabling a desire for improved services (as well as for separation) to fragment the metropolis. In Britain, by contrast, the desire for services was not allowed to randomly multiply the number of governments. There, central authorities had to approve incorporation: between 1888 and 1902, only thirty-five of fifty-five applications were approved. (Smaller communities were allowed to form urban districts, which in turn could provide capital-intensive services, but even these were generally larger than most American municipalities.) Similarly, central approval was also necessary for annexation. The boundaries of government were not considered the purview of the electorate — they were the purview of the center. Teaford concludes:

> lawmakers in London refused to yield responsibility for local governmental organization or decision-making authority to the local populace. . . . The destinies of metropolitan Britain did not rest in the hands of the suburban electorate but depended on the will of the nation's administrators and legislators.[30]

In the United States, the so-called special district was the third response to the demand for public services. The special district is a separate, corporate, independent unit of local government that has all the powers of local government — including the right to levy taxes, to borrow by issuing bonds, to sue, and to enter into contractual agreements. It often cuts across governmental boundaries, so that economies of scale can be realized. The first districts were set up for the provision of sewer and water services, for economies of scale are important in those areas. Since this governmental form did not raise issues of incorporation or annexation but nonetheless provided highly desired capital-intensive services, it became a popular governmental vehicle for the delivery of those services. This response also contributed to the fragmentation of the metropolitan area and to the erosion of the powers of municipal government (a theme we shall discuss at more length in chapter 6).

Infrastructure and Debt

Debt burdens rose sharply as cities began to borrow for the large public facilities needed to provide the amenities quickly becoming expected by American urban dwellers. Although a significant portion of the rapid increase in municipal debt from 1840 to 1870 was for assistance to railways, the next thirty years' rapid increase in local debt was largely for the provision of services. Between 1860 and 1875 the thirteen largest northern cities had their taxable valuation increase by 157 percent but their indebtedness rose by 271 percent.[31] Between 1866 and 1876, the twenty cities with more than a hundred thousand inhabitants increased their aggregate debt by 176 percent. Teaford concludes that net bonded debt soared in some of the nation's major cities:

> Between 1868 and 1873 the net bonded debt of New York City tripled, and between 1867 and 1871 the bonded indebtedness of Chicago likewise increased threefold. Boston experienced a tripling of its municipal debt during the years 1868 to 1874; Cincinnati's bonded obligations rose fivefold between 1868 and 1876; and Cleveland's net debt soared 1200 percent during the decade 1867 to 1877.[32]

By 1880, the per capita municipal debt was $14, but the regional variations are significant. Whereas the southern figure was an astonishingly low $4 and the western one $8, the per capita local debt in New England was over $31. Since local governments in the New England states had been almost absent from the move to assist railways, most of this debt was incurred for municipal services. New England debts rose 70 percent from 1870 to 1880.[33]

The depression of 1873 brought numerous cities to the brink of default because of the borrowing spree of the late 1860s and early 1870s. (Some, including Pittsburgh and Memphis, actually defaulted.) The combination of high debts, high interest rates, and plummeting prices characteristic of a severe deflation were lethal for city treasuries. The valuation of taxable property dropped sharply in city after city. Teaford concludes, "many comptrollers were kept busy devising financial maneuvers necessary to stave off default." Meanwhile, state legislatures were kept busy enacting restrictions on municipal borrowing (which we discuss in the following chapter). In spite of the depression of the 1870s and the defaults of that period, debt climbed by over $305 million between 1870 and 1880. In 1870, municipal debt totaled $516 million. Borrowing slowed in the next decade, however. New York City, Chicago, and Cleveland actually reduced their debt, while Boston, Baltimore, Cincinnati, and Saint Louis did not add to their debt burden.[34]

The burden of debt repayment lessened for these cities. Relatively low interest rates in the last two decades of the century, coupled with a stable or declining debt, freed up more monies for current expenditures. New York City's interest payments declined from 28 percent of the city's expenditures in 1880 to 7 percent in 1899; Baltimore in the same period enjoyed a reduction from 24 to 11 percent, while Cleveland's budget earmarked 21 percent for interest payments in 1880 but under 8 percent in 1899.[35] If we examine all municipalities, however, "by 1890 the demand for new improvements was so great that municipal borrowing began with feverish haste."[36] Nonetheless, municipalities fared rather well in the Panic of 1893 — in sharp contrast to that of twenty years before.

At the beginning of the twentieth century, municipalities owed well over a billion dollars. Debt kept rising, and after 1919 municipal borrowing expanded so rapidly that Hillhouse terms the period 1919–1932 "a new era of municipal borrowing, never before equalled."[37] Urban growth provided the impetus for the huge amounts borrowed. Almost half of all state and local debts were incurred by cities with a population of over 30,000. Borrowing financed water and sewer systems, airports, playgrounds, school buildings, and roads. Whereas the per capita local debt was $6.36 in 1860, it was $16.37 in 1880, $35.81 in 1912, and $123.06 in 1932.[38]

We have already discussed defaults on railway-aid bonds. However, cities also defaulted (although often only briefly) on bonds issued for improvements. Chicago, for example, borrowed to build a new courthouse and city hall, a city armory, waterworks, a high school, and a hospital — and then defaulted in 1857 during a financial panic. When the economic climate improved, the city resumed payment.[39]

In many cities, special-assessment bonds rather than general-improvement bonds were issued to provide streets and sewers to already settled areas. In these cases, assessment bonds were repaid by imposing a special tax on the owners of land abutting the improvements; those funds were kept separate from general-fund revenues. Whereas this system allowed public improvements to be provided more quickly than if such improvements had to rely on general-tax revenues, the system could, if it left discretion up to the property owners, easily discriminate against the poor. Property owners — especially big realty companies and industrial corporations that owned many rentals — could decide where improvements would be made. For example, in the case of Birmingham, Alabama, the use of special assessments led to the black quarters' not being provided with sanitary sewers or paved roads. Carl Harris analyzes the dynamics of this method of repaying bonds:

> In 1900 when Birmingham began its first major improvements in residential areas, only 13.6 percent of the heads of families owned their homes and had

a voice in decisions about when and where to pave streets and build sewers. The 86.2 percent who rented had no legal influence on such decisions, which lay entirely with their landlords, often large real estate companies. . . . The cheapest rent houses were unpainted Negro shacks packed into "quarters." There the realty companies and industries had no paving done. More important, under the special assessment system they could and did avoid building sanitary sewers in their Negro "quarters."

City health officials did not ratify this outcome. They constantly called for sewers to be built in these poor areas, which were major contributors to the typhoid that continually menaced Birmingham. The pleas of health officials were of no avail, however, for the system of financing did not put control in the hands of the city but rather in the hands of property owners. Harris concludes that "under the special assessment procedures the city simply did not force sewers onto owners who did not want to pay for them."[40] In many cases, defaults occurred on bonds issued to help finance improvements to areas being newly developed by real estate developers. Hillhouse argues that such defaults were analogous to railway-aid defaults and should be named "real estate aid bond defaults." In some cases, bonds that were initially issued as special-assessment bonds became transformed into general-obligation bonds, and default thus became a default by the city government. For example, officials in Elizabeth, New Jersey, were convinced that Elizabeth was meant to be central to the New York metropolis. They borrowed to provide pavement, "and gas lamps were installed, often into uninhabited wooded sections where favored promoters owned property." The hope that such improvements would lead to residential neighborhoods with taxable property was not realized. Although the bonds were special-assessment bonds, and therefore to be repaid from assessments on property benefiting from such improvements, a court decision transformed them into general-obligation bonds, which must be paid from the city's tax revenue. The city government defaulted, and it took over ten years to come to an agreement with bondholders.[41]

Generally, many defaults were on special-assessment bonds. By contrast, bonds issued for water systems have a very good safety record, as have bonds issued for school buildings. Nonetheless, all types of improvement bonds have defaulted over the past century and a half. Hillhouse concludes, "road, bridge, street improvement, courthouse, jail, town hall, school, fire equipment, armory, waterworks, gas, light and other public utility bonds — all have contributed to the total default history."[42]

Governance and Infrastructure

As debt increased, that increase was attributed by many observers to corruption and extravagance. Yet recent historical studies paint a more complex picture. The provision of capital infrastructure — and the borrowing that financed it — tended to be handled by professionals who were insulated from the partisan politics usually associated with the machine. On the whole, those areas of the urban bureaucracy concerned with capital infrastructure became professionalized earlier than other segments of the urban administrative apparatus. Professionals from the infrastructure . bureaucracies in turn became dominant when city bureaucracies became more generally professionalized during the Progressive Era.

The relationship between key urban officials and the machine deserves a great deal more study. Theodore Lowi argues that the machine allowed Frederick Law Olmsted to be superintendent of Central Park because the machine received benefits critical for its own constituencies:

> The political parties had a profound interest in the construction of public works and were even willing to permit an upper-class reformer to build a central park because what went in was less important to them than what came out. But Central Park was a great Tammany haven. Tammany leaders and their capitalist fellow travellers were the chief beneficiaries of honest graft, and Tammany followers got the jobs. The city at large was a beneficiary also, because public works made the city an employer of last resort.[43]

Two officials of particular importance to capital infrastructure came to occupy dominating positions within urban government. Whereas the (appointed) municipal engineer was in many ways in charge of the city's physical destiny, the (often elected) comptroller was in charge of the city's credit rating. Although both exercised pervasive influence, they typically were not subject either to the spoils system or to partisan interference with their judgments.

The city comptroller, charged with marketing the city's municipal bonds and acting as watchdog of the city's finances, was often not intensely involved in partisan politics and was usually a businessman rather than a ward politician. Furthermore, he was not tied to the political machine in any direct way. In 1896, for example, the New York City comptroller, who had been elected with Tammany support, called in twelve top financiers to help him choose a new deputy, and he ignored the name given him by Tammany chief Richard Croker.[44]

We know relatively little about the city comptroller; we know somewhat more about the city engineer, who emerged as a key urban official. Although the giving of contracts for the construction of public works was used by urban political machines to finance their operations, there are relatively few cases in which the recommendations of municipal engineers were not accepted. Machine politicians, by and large, did not interfere in technical decisions, even when those would affect the distribution of benefits for various property owners or would affect tax rates. The machine may even have insulated professionals, allowing them to make professional judgments. The fact that so many water and sewer systems built in the nineteenth century are still in use attests to the technical and construction competence with which they were built.

In Chicago, for example, Cain finds no evidence that "the potential for graft played any role in deciding among alternatives."[45] Furthermore, he finds that the advice of the municipal engineers concerning the sanitation policies that should be adopted by the city government was indeed followed in nearly all instances. Graft may have increased the cost of the alternative recommended by the engineers, but it did not influence the choice among alternatives recommended by the engineering professionals or accepted by the city's elective officials.

Perhaps the disastrous consequences of political interference in technical decisions deterred later politicians. The District of Columbia, for example, lost home rule partially because "the boss," Alexander Shepard, "wasted a $5,000,000 bond issue when contractors hired for political rather than engineering reasons built lateral sewers that ran uphill into the main sewers."[46] Even when politicians rejected their engineers' recommendations as being too expensive, they later regretted it. St. Louis had to rebuild the water system and Cincinnati had to rebuild the sewer system within a mere ten years because they had tried to cut costs, against their engineers' advice.

In general, however, politicians listened to the engineers. In many cities, engineers were the first officials to retain their jobs regardless of who won the election. High-ranking engineers in cities such as Boston, Providence, Chicago, New York City, New Haven, Philadelphia, Milwaukee, Minneapolis, Seattle, St. Louis, Baltimore, Cleveland, and Buffalo kept their positions for decades. Teaford finds that

Throughout the nation as a whole, a remarkable 23 percent of those who held the post of municipal waterworks superintendent in 1883 still occupied the same position in 1897. By contrast, in 1897 only one of the mayors of the nation's forty most populous cities was a veteran of five consecutive years in office and none could claim fourteen years of experience as municipal executive.[47]

The first to be given civil service status, well-known city engineers were also allowed to consult widely. The boss of the engineering department was not the same man as the boss of city hall, and in many cities the latter did not interfere in the former's territory. Engineers subsequently became important in two new professions, city planning and city management. By 1940, for example, nearly two-thirds of all city managers since 1915 had been engineers.[48]

Conclusion

Cities varied in the ways they handled the balancing act between economic development and service provision. Nonetheless, nearly all cities performed both functions very actively, so that urban government was interventionist, dynamic, and increasingly expert in the area of physical capital investment. The physical (often unseen) structures we take for granted today are the consequences of the city government's investing in capital-intensive services.

The combination of borrowing both for assistance to railways and for services led to a tremendous increase in debt, however. Cities became extraordinarily visible as borrowers. When macro-economic conditions became unfavorable for debtors in general, city governments came under severe fiscal stress. Their debt burdens became defined as a problem to which state governments should respond. State legislatures reacted by imposing restrictions on municipal borrowing. The courts added still further limits on the ability of municipal governments to borrow and to invest as they saw fit. Ironically, the Supreme Court used the issue of municipal borrowing for the benefit of railways to institutionalize the municipal bond market, the capital market that was to provide localities with an escape mechanism from the state restrictions. It is to those restrictions and the role of the Supreme Court in fashioning a role for the capital market in intergovernmental relations that we now turn.

Chapter 5

The Institutionalization

of Limits

The municipality, understood as borrower and investor, underwent
a definitive transformation in the last quarter of the nineteenth century.
How much could the municipality borrow? The state government answered that question. What was its legal status? The judicial system,
which viewed the private sector as needing protection and government as
needing to be restrained, decided the municipality was a public (as opposed to a private) corporation. Where did it fit in the government hierarchy? Judge Dillon answered that question. What could it borrow for?
The U.S. Supreme Court set those limits. By the end of the century local
government as investor was widely considered subordinate to state government, and marginal to economic development as had been understood
during the previous century. The city, understood as a legal and political
entity, had indeed become far less autonomous and far more subordinate.

The Subordination of the Municipality

The aid given to railways did not go unnoticed, either by state judges or by
the U.S. Supreme Court. The reaction to the borrowing, investing, and
repudiation by local governments was concentrated in two forums — the
judiciary (at both state and national levels) and the state legislature. State
policy makers responded to both local governments' economic adventur-
ism and their expansion of service provision by restricting local governments' future borrowing capacity. However, the Supreme Court's role was
more complex. The Court forced local governments to repay the debts

they had accumulated in their efforts to assist railways but, in so doing, provided the legal underpinning for a capital market that was to prove critical to local investment in the twentieth century.

State judges and legislators established the fundamental legal framework within which local governments would need to maneuver in order to borrow and invest. The Supreme Court, for its part, essentially provided the market that local officials would use as an instrument in this maneuvering. The Supreme Court's decisions hurt local governments in the short-term but provided them with access to private funds that, over the long-term, would allow local governments to circumvent the intent of the restrictions imposed by state judges and legislators.

State Limits on Local Debt

The debts accumulated by local governments were not ignored by state legislatures. State legislatures took responsibility for controlling local borrowing and investment and implemented such control through constitutional and statutory law. Although changes in law have subsequently occurred, such changes have essentially maintained the structure of control that the states imposed in the latter part of the nineteenth century.[1] Nineteenth-century laws underpin the legal foundation of the current system of local borrowing and investment.

State legislatures set out to limit the ability of municipalities both to borrow and to lend their credit to assist private corporations. Legislative action was driven more by a concern to limit capital expenditure — and, particularly, the debt that underlay such expenditure — than to protect bondholders. Since nearly all funds used to repay debt as well as interest came from the property tax, legislators wanted to protect future taxpayers from politically controversial tax rates. State legislators typically imposed state controls by amending the state constitution; in those cases where they did not, they used statutory law. (The states that did not change their constitutions so as to constitutionally restrict local borrowing were Connecticut, Delaware, Florida, Maryland, Massachusetts, Mississippi, New Hampshire, New Jersey, North Carolina, Rhode Island, Tennessee, and Vermont.)[2]

In Great Britain, by comparison, control over borrowing exercised by central government has taken the form of administrative control. That is, relevant central government ministries have to approve local borrowing.

No fixed limit on such borrowing exists, as the central government ministries maintain discretion. Thus, borrowing fluctuates depending on the policy objectives of the central government.[3] In the United States, on the other hand, law rather than administrative control was chosen as the mechanism for the control of debt. Such a choice, as we shall see, was to have significant repercussions in the twentieth century.

Critics of local borrowing felt that the initial error lay with the original authorization by the state legislature in allowing localities to borrow funds. Given the undeveloped nature of state administrative capacity, it seems that administrative controls analogous to those in Britain were never seriously considered. Lancaster argues,

> There existed almost nowhere an administrative organization competent to supervise local affairs. Assuming, as men did, that the very grant of borrowing powers was wrong, it is not strange that the only adequate remedy seemed to lie in so amending the organic law as to restrict this right within the narrowest compass and to make illegal its abuse.[4]

The constitutional restrictions on local debt were by and large written into state constitutions during the period from 1865 to 1880. The period between 1872 and 1879 was particularly important for restrictions. State governments reacted to the defaults (roughly one-fifth of all municipal bonds were in some form of default in the mid-1870s) and repudiations of local bonds brought on by the severe depression of the 1870s by restricting the borrowing autonomy of local government.[5]

Constitutional restrictions were typically directed toward both restricting aid to private corporations and to limiting the aggregate debt burden any one local government could be allowed to carry. Restricting aid to private corporations became very widespread. For example, between 1872 and 1879, Alabama, Arkansas, California, Colorado, Connecticut, Florida, Georgia, Illinois, Louisiana, Minnesota, Missouri, New Hampshire, New Jersey, New York, North Carolina, Pennsylvania, Tennessee, and Texas all changed their constitutions so as to restrict local assistance to private corporations (railways were the principal targets).[6]

The limits imposed on local governments, whether by statute or by constitutional provision, circumscribed a power that previously had generally been considered rather comprehensive. An opinion delivered by the Massachusetts Supreme Court in 1876 expresses well what state restrictions on municipal borrowing entailed for local governments:

The statute thus deprives cities and towns of the authority to contract debts for borrowed money, which they had previously possessed, whether derived from express grant, or held to exist as an implied power; and, instead of it, gives to these municipalities a limited power which can be lawfully exercised only in the mode specially pointed out. . . . It contains a positive prohibition of all debts contracted for borrowed money in any other mode. . . . All its provisions . . . establish a plain limit to the exercise of the power to borrow money.[7]

New York in 1853 was the first state to actually restrict the total size of the municipal debt. The limit was in the form of statute rather than constitutional law. Gradually the idea spread to limit local debt by tying it to a percentage of the assessed value of taxable property. In 1857 Iowa imposed constitutional restrictions on local debt using assessed value, and in 1870 Illinois followed suit. In the 1870s and 1880s numerous states, responding to the debt crises of the 1870s, followed their examples (in 1884, for example, the New York constitution was amended so as to tie debt limitation to assessed value). In those states where constitutions were not amended, statutes were passed to restrict municipal indebtedness. In either case, assessed valuation was the key referent in calculating permissible levels of debt. In Massachusetts, for example, the Municipal Indebtedness Act of 1875 set the limit at 3 percent of the assessed valuation of taxable property.[8]

Debt limits did in fact constrain local capital investment, in some cases even shortly after their imposition. After the great Chicago fire of 1871, for example, "the city had already reached its newly state-imposed debt ceiling, so it could not finance improvements by issuing municipal bonds." Since the city could borrow only 1 percent of its property valuation, it "often simply had to postpone undertaking improvements in municipal services because it had no money and no means for raising additional revenues." Although the city finally had its limit raised by the state legislature in 1919 (after having failed to achieve this in 1908), the fact that it had to expend the political resources necessary to do so constrained investment activity. Sanders finds that "Even with the adroit use of special assessment debt, the city could not legally manage a significantly greater long term debt. It took action by the Illinois state legislature to alter this limit before *any* substantial public works effort could be started."[9]

Los Angeles also, for its part, was limited by its debt limit, although California's limit was unusually generous. Steven Erie points out that, after the city had borrowed $24.5 million for its aqueduct, it "had reached the limits of its legal indebtedness. Private bids on the project approached $40 million, greatly exceeding the debt limit. As a result, Los Angeles was forced to use lower-cost municipal labor to construct the aqueduct." Subsequently, the city used annexation so as to "rapidly increase the city's assessed valuation and thus its debt ceiling."[10]

Debt limits were particularly constraining because they limited the use of the tax base with no offsetting provisions regarding need, and because they were imposed by law rather than by administrative supervision. Constitutional amendments restricting borrowing are especially difficult to modify and are certainly not as flexible as administrative control can be.

But debt limits expressed as a percentage of assessed value were not the only restriction applied to municipal debt. One of the most important was the requirement that the electorate approve bond issues; in some cases, a two-thirds or three-fifths majority was needed. In some states all bond issues had to be approved electorally, whereas in others only certain bond issues had to meet that requirement. In those states that did not have constitutional requirements, referenda were required by legislative statute. (Limits on the real estate tax rate were also viewed by some as "an adjunct remedy necessary to prevent an increase in taxes to pay for capital projects previously financed by public debt." Some states put such tax limits in their constitutions as well.)[11]

The requirement that bond issues be put to the electorate for their approval affected public investment in a noteworthy fashion. In Chicago, for example, the city was able to embark on a massive public-investment program between 1910 and 1927 because the state legislature raised its debt limit in 1919. However, bond issues still needed electoral approval. Such approval was largely forthcoming during a sixteen-year period. Although the state general assembly again raised the debt limit in 1927, the electorate turned decisively against large-scale public investment in 1928. Until the end of World War II, bond issues in Chicago were typically either defeated or not even placed on the ballot. In Cincinnati, voters were similarly negative when a convention hall–auditorium was proposed. They defeated the bond issue in 1939 and 1940. According to Sanders, "city officials did not even propose such a project again until 1962." In Los Angeles, voters in 1929 defeated a water bond isssue. The city then created a special district that required only a simple majority vote, rather than two-thirds approval, for borrowing to proceed.[12]

More recently, the requirement that electorates approve of municipal borrowing has encouraged local officials to turn to borrowing that does not require any approval — such as that carried out by public authorities. Borrowing that does fall under the state requirements becomes a political issue. Popular support needs to be mobilized. Such support is particularly important in cities that require a two-thirds majority vote in favor of capital borrowing. In San Francisco, for example, 89 percent of the bond propositions presented between 1944 and 1973 received a majority vote, but only 54 percent received the necessary two-thirds majority vote. And in 1962 and 1966, the majority of voters in St. Louis approved a bond issue for renovating Kiel Auditorium, but since a two-third majority is required the bond issues were defeated.[13]

The need to obtain electoral approval puts borrowing onto a city's political agenda. As one finance official put it during an interview: "We think of bonds as election campaigns, as political campaigns." The advisory opinions given about proposed bonds by individual representatives of major corporations and banks tend to be taken seriously, for such individuals are likely to be the major contributors to the political campaign. One official in an interview explained the importance of their verdict by pointing out that "you always need a little money for a campaign, someone to put an ad in the newspaper."

State-imposed limits on local borrowing can thus be very restrictive. Local borrowing is characterized by a more inflexible set of controls than other areas of local government activity. Although state governments gradually increased their administrative control over local policy activity, local governments nonetheless retained, at least in comparative terms, a significant degree of discretion in some policy areas. Finance, however, was not one of them.[14] Although city officials can at times convince state legislatures to raise debt limits, such efforts require the expenditure of political resources that can be mobilized only infrequently.

Judicial Limits on Local Debt

As state legislators responded to the borrowing of local governments, so did state judges. The municipality as a corporate entity gradually took shape. It was subordinate and its powers were limited; it was particularly limited in the area of local finance, borrowing included.

THE SUBORDINATE PUBLIC CORPORATION

The contemporary powers and limits of the municipal corporation are the consequence of the legal evolution of the municipality. This evolution, while complex, has had three critical turning points. The first was that which defined town government as a corporation. Neither state government nor the federal government is legally a corporation, but the municipality is, and this initial distinction between local and higher levels of government was significant (as we shall see). The second crucial point was that which defined the municipal corporation as a public rather than a private corporation. Such a definition subjected municipalities to numerous controls not applied to private corporations. The third and final crucial point is that which defined the municipal corporation as a creature of the state government.

The very structure of municipal government was shaped by these three decision points — and it is not surprising that the strategies of circumvention adopted by local officials in order to maximize their ability to invest (discussed in chapter 6) were often directed toward circumventing these three characteristics of local government.

How to classify the city in law has perplexed judges for centuries. As Gerald Frug argues,

> courts have for centuries wrestled with the question . . . whether to classify cities as an exercise of freedom by individuals or as a threat to freedom analogous to that posed by the state. . . . [T]he courts in effect had to decide whether cities, like the state, were a threat to freedom . . . or whether cities protected individual rights and thus needed protection from the state.[15]

The notion of the municipality as a corporate entity has medieval roots. The medieval town was neither part of the state nor legally an individual. It was neither public nor private. It was an association of merchants, "seeking protection against outsiders for the interests of the group as a whole." It was a "corporation" in that it was an "intermediate entity."[16] (The church and the university were among the other important medieval corporations.) Debates over its power were related to debates about the role of groups in society rather than the role of the state or of the individual. In the medieval town, the notion of individual rights was fused with the notion of group rights.

American law concerning cities is based on English law, and thus the experience of English towns is particularly relevant to understanding the American experience. Although English towns never achieved a degree of autonomy similar to that acquired by Italian and German towns, for example, they nonetheless were able to protect themselves against both the monarchy and individuals. They were also represented — as corporations — in the English Parliament. The relationships between the city and its residents and between the city and the king were institutionalized in the form of the city's charter. Although since the 1200s the king had claimed the right to revoke charters, the issue was not engaged until the time of Charles II.

In 1682, one of the most important cases in English legal history addressed the right of Charles II to revoke the charter of the City of London. If the monarchy won, the charters of English towns, private companies formed on the model of city corporations, and the charters of several American colonies would be vulnerable to central control. Although Charles II won the case, the decision was reversed after the Glorious Revolution had limited royal power. However, since that revolution had given Parliament power, it was unclear what the rights of charters would be if Parliament, rather than the king, wished to revoke them. What was the relationship to be between legislative power and corporate liberty? It was this issue that, in the nineteenth century, led to the distinction in the United States between public and private corporations.

In the United States, town governments were treated by the courts as corporations even though most towns were not formally incorporated and did not have charters. And since English law did not differentiate between municipal corporations and other types of corporations, post-revolutionary America had to deal with the question of how much power legislative bodies would exercise over all corporations, municipal ones included. American law in the early nineteenth century responded to this question by dividing the corporation: the public corporation became associated with the state whereas the private corporation became associated with the individual. "The very purpose of the distinction was to ensure that some corporations, called 'private', would be protected against domination by the state and that others, called 'public', would be subject to such domination."[17]

The city was therefore a "public" corporation, that is, limited in its exercise of corporate economic power. By contrast, the "private" corporation—especially after general laws of incorporation were adopted and incorporation was no longer a privilege allocated by the state legislature—was given a wide scope of activity as it was seen as needing protection from government. Kenneth Fox argues, "Being 'public' as opposed to 'private' corporations, city governments felt the ultimate impact of the doctrine of limited public power in a way exactly opposite to its effect on the business corporation."[18] The private corporation was liberated from public control whereas city governments became completely subordinate to it.

These legal complexities were not to have significance until the later part of the nineteenth century. In most states local government's legal status did not interfere with its entrepreneurship. At least until after 1850 local governments exercised a great deal of autonomy in most states.[19]

Local governments' extensive borrowing and repudiation of debt led state courts and state legislatures to circumscribe severely (and, most importantly, definitively) the policy latitude of local governments in the field of capital investment. Hartog points out that judges regarded the relationship between state and local governments as being outside their jurisdiction. Judges justified their limiting of municipal power because of

> the dangers municipal governments posed to the rights of private individuals and to the institution of private property. . . . In the conduct of the American city and of its agents, they saw a serious and significant challenge to the security of private estates. As taxpayers, property owners faced the prospect of being compelled by municipal extravagance to become involuntary contributors in enterprises in which they had no interest or which were actually contrary to their private interests.[20]

The power of the city was a question of political economy as opposed to a question of state-local relations understood in the traditional institutional sense. The economic activism of cities threatened the status of private property in the eyes of state judges. In response, state judges went so far as to decide "what a statute gave a city, and they would do so using formal legal categories that defined the legal rights of the municipality independently of any legislation."[21]

DILLON'S RULE

In the field of law, the earlier and often eclectic limits on municipal corporations came to be crystallized in a particularly definitive manner in the
last quarter of the nineteenth century. This was at least partially due to the
judicial evaluation of local government's economic interventionism, an
evaluation that (especially in the state and circuit courts) was negative.
Although railway assistance was often deemed to be legal, many judges
thought local governments had been imprudent and extravagant in giving
it. In this view, although local officials may have acted legally, they had not
acted prudently.

Local government's experience as an investor in economic enterprises
was certainly a factor in the rationale used by judges such as Judge Dillon
when circumscribing the latitude of local officials. Dillon had been chief
justice of the Iowa Supreme Court during a period of turmoil over municipal railway bonds, and as a subsequent U.S. circuit judge he confronted
numerous cases involving municipal assistance to various private enterprises, both railway and non-railway. For example, as a circuit judge he
ruled that towns in Kansas could not assist manufacturing companies because they did not fulfill a "public purpose" (a decision subsequently upheld by the U.S. Supreme Court in *Loan Association v. Topeka* [1875]).[22]

Dillon, therefore, was not writing in a vacuum when he argued for state
supremacy over municipal government — the so-called Dillon's Rule — in
his *Treatise on the Law of Municipal Corporations* published in 1872. He
argued that municipalities had been profligate in their investments in private enterprises and had intervened in economic affairs that were "better
left to private enterprise."[23] Dillon concluded that because state governments were completely "public," state control of municipal government
(finance in particular) would minimize the mingling of public and private
functions, which he saw as detrimental in the operations of municipalities.
Thus, the entrepreneurship and economic interventionism of local governments were an important catalyst in the formulation of the legal doctrine
that was to subject them to stringent state control in the area of finance.
This was a doctrine promulgated and enforced by the state judiciary.

Dillon's Rule — that local governments are "creatures of the state" —
rather quickly obtained widespread acknowledgment by state judges. In
the twentieth century, it was not even questioned. The alternative conception of municipal government — as an exercise in self-government — was

not to make much headway once state judges began to use Dillon's conception as their basic referent in dealing with issues of state-local relations.

Dillon's interpretation was so influential that, ironically, even though he personally became convinced that local government needed more latitude and autonomy, the state courts diluted the effectiveness of the "home rule" movement Dillon supported at the end of the century.[24]

"Home rule" — the constitutional granting to municipalities of the power to write and amend their own charters — was viewed by many reformers and political scientists as enabling city governments to avoid being subjected to detailed state intervention in their affairs. Recent historical scholarship argues that the content of "state interference" was usually determined by the representatives of the city in the state legislature. Jon Teaford concludes that

> early advocates of municipal home rule sought to liberate the city not from an unresponsive legislature but from one that was all-too-responsive, that granted too much with too little thought. . . . [They] endeavored to curb the interfering authority of the state legislature as exercised by the local legislative delegation.[25]

In this view, then, arguments over "state" interference were actually based on disagreements among various constituencies within the city. Those constituencies (reformers particularly) that were in conflict with the constituencies controlling the city's legislative delegation would favor either home rule or administrative supervision by the state, increasingly dominated as the latter was by professionals.

Even though home rule became accepted by legislators in major states in the first two decades of the twentieth century, its impact was blunted by the state judiciary. Writing in 1935, Albert Lepawsky concluded that home rule

> has not come up to expectations primarily because the courts, particularly the state supreme courts, in interpreting the constitutional or legislative or charter provisions respecting home rule, tend to construe narrowly the general grant of power made to the city. . . . The courts have in some cases narrowed . . . general grants down to a point where the powers which can actually be exercised are but little wider than those permitted under the Cities and Villages Act in Illinois, where general home rule does not exist.[26]

The subordination of the city to the state was so complete that it was difficult to later give the city back some of the autonomy it had lost.

The Supreme Court and Local Government as Borrower

While state judges were critical in defining the role of the city within the state, the U.S. Supreme Court was the key actor in shaping the capital market that provided the funds borrowed by local governments for capital investment. The Court also defined the kinds of activities for which local officials could borrow. The evolution of the municipal bond market was affected very directly by the Court's decisions on railway-aid bonds and on bonds for other private companies. Although the municipal bond market as we know it is anchored in the decisions made by the Court in the last few decades of the nineteenth century, the Court's role vis-à-vis that market has been ignored. Charles Fairman terms the topic "a wilderness — trackless even to knowledgeable students of the Supreme Court."[27]

Such a lack of analysis is surprising because the defaults and repudiations of railway bonds consumed a great deal of the Supreme Court's attention. In the 1875–1876 term, cases related to such defaults were actually the single largest category of cases heard by the Court. Between 1864 and 1888, the Court heard one hundred cases dealing with railway-assistance securities. Justice Field, who served thirty-four years (from 1863 to 1897), heard over three hundred municipal bond cases.[28] During that period, the Court heard more municipal bond cases than any other type. Charles Warren writes:

> Judge Davis said in *Thomson v. Lee County*, 3 Wall. 327, in 1866: "There is hardly any question connected with this species of securities that has not been discussed and decided by the Court." This statement showed curiously little appreciation of the troubles that were to face the Court, since in succeeding years the Court had before it about three hundred cases involving such bonds. Of these cases, sixty-five arose in Illinois; fifty in Missouri; twenty-five in Iowa; twenty-two in Kansas; eighteen in Wisconsin; fourteen in New York; eleven in Indiana; six each in Kentucky and Tennessee; the others being scattered over eighteen states; none, however, arising in New England.[29]

The problems incurred by local governments as venture capitalists became linked to the general question of how far government could intervene in the economy. In particular, when local governments repudiated their debts and bondholders sought relief in the courts, the courts had to decide if the original government intervention had been constitutional. If railroads were in some sense public (as had been argued by both public officials and state courts when advocating or upholding municipal assistance), then local governments were obligated to repay the holders of railway bonds. Local officials had acted legally when assisting railways if the railways were indeed performing some kind of public purpose.

However, local governments now justified their repudiation of bonds by arguing that railways were in fact private. Following on this argument, state legislatures had not had the authority to authorize aid and therefore the obligation to repay did not exist. Furthermore, some local governments were also subsidizing private manufacturing companies — and repudiating some of those bonds as well. However, holders of such bonds argued that, just like the holders of railway bonds, they also had the right to be repaid.

To complicate matters, the role of local government as borrower and investor was intimately entangled with the postbellum debates about regulation of the railways. Proponents of regulation argued that regulation was justified precisely because railways had a public purpose, as demonstrated by the privileges given them by public officials. Charles W. McCurdy argues:

> Regulatory agitation emerged at the very time that state and local governments were also repudiating internal-improvement bonds. . . . [T]he convergence of litigation . . . was especially important in that common law regulatory and promotional legislation were part of a single doctrinal continuum. Private businesses that had been granted special privileges by state and local governments did not hold their property by "common right" and were therefore subject to regulation. As a result, litigation resulting from regulatory statutes involved a reconsideration of governmental interventions on the promotional side, and vice versa.[30]

The U.S. Supreme Court, in its 1875–1876 term, heard a large number of bond cases as well as the so-called *Granger* cases, in which state governments claimed the right to regulate railways. In *Munn v. Illinois,* the Supreme Court upheld the states' right to regulate, arguing that "when property had become clothed with a public interest, the owner must submit to be controlled by the public for the common good." (The Court reversed itself in 1886, when it ruled that only the federal government could regulate interstate commerce.) The rulings in the *Granger* cases recognized the railways as corporations "affected with a public interest."[31]

The railway-bond cases raised the same broad question as the *Granger* cases. The specific issue was whether bondholders had the right to be paid by the local governments that had issued these municipal bonds. The bondholders claimed the bonds had been legally issued; the repudiating communities disagreed, and the Court, therefore, had to decide if the issuance of the bonds had been legal. To answer that question, the Court had to decide how far local intervention in the economy could proceed, that is, which types of private enterprises could be said to be "clothed with a public interest." Did all companies have some public purpose and therefore qualify for municipal assistance? did just the railways? or did none of the private companies?

The Court's opinion consistently upheld the holders of railway bonds and argued against "judicial repudiation." As Charles McCurdy has written, "The court ruled that the public's interest in railroad expansion was undeniable . . . railroads were 'public highways' even when constructed and owned by private persons." The direction to be taken by the Court was indicated in 1859, when the Court ruled on *Knox County v. Aspinwall,* fundamentally deciding that "whenever the governing body of a city or county issued bonds reciting that they had authority, then true or false, the municipality was bound as against a bona fide purchaser." Evidence of gross fraud involved in the obtaining or the issuance of bonds was not to be taken into account by the Court.[32]

Federal-State Conflict

The Court upheld the rights of bondholders so strongly and did so by such a strong assertion of federal power that it came into direct conflict with various state courts. (The reason the Court exercised jurisdiction was because of the diversity of citizenship of the various bondholders, that is, they lived in a variety of states.) Typically, the Court would have followed the state supreme court's ruling on the meaning of "public purpose" — the clause that authorized state legislatures to grant aid. However, the Court was so determined to uphold bondholders that it construed "State statutes — on the powers of municipal officers, on debt limits, on the privileges of railroad corporation, etc. — contrary to the construction given them by the State courts."[33]

The state courts had upheld local aid to railways, although often reluctantly. One of the most influential early rulings was made by the Pennsylvania Supreme Court. In *Sharpless v. Mayor of Philadelphia* (1853) the state court had, in a 3–2 vote, upheld municipal aid to railways. The majority argued that "a railroad is a public highway for the public benefit."[34] Land could be taken by eminent domain for railways whereas it could not for other types of enterprises (such as a mill, for example); because of the precedents recognizing the public ends served by railways, three justices upheld the constitutionality of the railway bonds issued in Pennsylvania. Similarly, in 1858 the Illinois Supreme Court upheld aid. In both cases, however, the state courts expressed grave concern about the likely consequences of widespread local aid.

Nonetheless, state courts upheld the constitutionality of railway aid during the period when it was very popular. Later, when local governments began defending repudiation on the grounds that railways did not have a public purpose and therefore they were not obligated to pay, most state courts upheld the bondholders by ruling that state legislatures had acted in accordance with state constitutions. In over twenty states, the state courts ruled against the repudiating communities.[35]

In an early decision concerning repudiation, Iowa was an exception, however. The state courts in Iowa upheld municipal railway aid from 1837 until 1859, in which year the state supreme court ruled that "municipalities had no power to aid in railroad construction, and that the legislature could not confer such power." The state supreme court overturned its own earlier decisions in so ruling against railway aid, and in a subsequent decision maintained its pro-repudiation stance. Essentially, the Iowa Supreme Court "held that under the State constitution the citizen could not be taxed to aid a railroad."[36]

Within that context, Gelpcke — a New York banker representing German bondholders — brought a case in federal court asking that interest on railway bonds be paid and the case went to the U.S. Supreme Court. In 1864, the Supreme Court ruled in the landmark *Gelpcke v. Dubuque* case that bondholders must be repaid. The case attracted widespread attention because the Court had overruled a state court on a matter of state law. Gelpcke had gone to the Court because the federal court in which he brought suit had accepted the Iowa Supreme Court's pro-repudiation interpretation and had held that Gelpcke's bonds (issued to the Dubuque Western Railroad) were not redeemable. The U.S. Supreme Court, however, upheld Gelpcke.[37]

The response in Iowa for the next five years was one of fairly widespread resistance to federal court orders to levy taxes to repay the bonds. In 1869, for example, a state judge discharged local county supervisors who had been arrested by a federal marshal for refusing to levy a railroad tax. A federal judge ordered the marshal to "summon a posse and bring the supervisors, by force if need be." But no one would agree to join the posse, and so the state judge's discharge order was carried out. However, the Iowa Supreme Court by then was unwilling to further challenge the U.S. Supreme Court, and when a letter from President Grant in 1870 stated that he was determined to carry out federal court orders, resistance melted.[38]

The supreme courts in Michigan, Wisconsin, and New York also upheld repudiating communities. They too were overruled by the U.S. Supreme Court. When it came to upholding bondholders, the state courts were not allowed to have the final word on state law.[39]

Doctrine of Public Purpose

Underlying all the bond cases was the conflict over how to define the term *public purpose,* and the question of what is or is not a public purpose has been central to the judicial determination of what is permissible capital investment. The first explicit articulation of the doctrine of public purpose was made by Chief Justice Black of the Pennsylvania Supreme Court in the case *Sharpless v. Mayor of Philadelphia,* mentioned above. Black argued that the state legislature did not possess the constitutional right

> to create a public debt, or to lay a tax, or to authorize any municipal corporation to do it, in order to raise funds for a mere *private* purpose. . . . Taxation is a mode of raising revenue for *public* purposes. When it is prostituted to objects in no way connected with the public interests or welfare, it ceases to be taxation, and becomes plunder.[40]

The notion that public monies or powers should not be used for private purposes came to be widely accepted. And (as we have just seen) the conflict over state intervention in the operations of the railways focused on whether railways were public or private.

The most impressive argument made for railways' being private was made by Judge Cooley of the Michigan Supreme Court (also the first chairman of the Interstate Commerce Commission). The conventional argument — made by Justice Black and innumerable judges afterward — was that, since railway corporations were permitted to exercise eminent domain and had to submit to state regulatory policy, they were corporations with a public purpose. Cooley, however, argued that "an object may be *public* in one sense and for one purpose, when in a general sense and for other purposes, it would be idle and misleading to apply the same term."[41] Cooley's reasoning was not accepted, however, and the conventional notion of railways' being public stood.

A new dilemma appeared when local governments began to issue municipal bonds for manufacturing companies rather than for railway corporations. Some industries refused to locate within a town unless they were offered municipal monies. Local governments, therefore, began to use public funds to keep local industries and to attract new ones. In Maine, the state supreme court ruled against a state authorization of a loan by the town of Jay to a private firm that promised to build a steam sawmill and a box factory. The court recognized that the company would increase employment and tax revenue, but the chief justice considered such aid as "communism incipient, if not perfected." Other state courts in states such as California, Michigan, Nevada, New York, Massachusetts, and Tennessee argued along roughly similar lines.[42]

State court judges were often vociferous in their opposition to an expansive definition of public purpose. For example, when Justice David Josiah Brewer was on the bench of the Kansas Supreme Court, he ruled against an 1875 Kansas law that allowed local governments to borrow in order to help farmers who were suffering from drought. Sidney Fine concludes that Brewer

> rejected the contention that such legislation was necessary lest those "temporarily embarrassed" might otherwise become actual paupers. "Let the doorways of taxation be opened," he declared, "not merely to the relief of present and actual distress, but in anticipation of and to guard against future want, and who can declare the result."

When Brewer joined the U.S. Supreme Court, he wrote opinions along similar lines. The thrust of judicial thinking between 1865–1901 was very important for the definition of what state governments could do or allow their local governments to do. Fine summarizes the period thus:

> during the period 1865–1901 laissez faire was read into state and federal constitutions and . . . judicial formulas were devised to limit the scope of state social and economic legislation. In effect, the courts set themselves up as the special guardians of the negative state. . . . Since in most cases coming

before the courts during this period, judges were compelled to strike a balance between the claims of individual rights as embodied in the Fourteenth
Amendment and the claims of the state governments as subsumed under the
police power, the general effect of the broadening of the former concept and
of the narrowing of the latter was to play havoc with the ability of the states
to act on behalf of the general welfare.

Fine rightly concludes that "Laissez faire might be overthrown in the state
legislature, but it was still to have its day in court."[43]

The U.S. Supreme Court, for its part, ensured that municipal bonds
would *not* be allowed to assist private, non-railway, corporations. The
bondholders holding repudiated bonds issued by the city of Topeka for the
King Wrought-Iron Bridge Manufactory asked the Court to order repayment. The bondholders pointed out that the state legislature had authorized cities "to encourage the establishment of manufactories and such
other enterprises as may tend to develop and improve such city."[44] Municipalities in Kansas alone had already issued over $2 million in bonds to
attract factories and other types of establishments.

However, the Court ruled in *Loan Association v. Topeka* in 1875 that
the bondholders had no rights. Justice Miller wrote the opinion that "no
line can be drawn in favor of the manufacturer which would not open the
coffers of the public treasury to the importunities of two-thirds of the
business men of the city or town."[45] Helping a clearly private manufacturing company was deemed different from helping a privately owned railway company, for the latter was viewed as shrouded with a public purpose. Later, the ruling that tax revenue could be applied only for a public
as opposed to a private purpose was linked to the Fourteenth Amendment
protection of "due process."[46]

Consequences for the Municipal Bond Market

The majority of the Court was so consistently in favor of the bondholders
and opposed to the repudiating municipalities that Justice Miller, a consistent dissenter, termed the anti-repudiation stance taken by the Court a
"mania." Writing to his brother-in-law in 1878, he complained:

the feeling which has control of the court against all municipalities who
contract any asserted obligation in [bonds] amounts to a mania. If I were a
practicing lawyer today, my self respect, knowing what I do of the force of

that feeling, would forbid me to argue in this court any case whatever against the validity of a contract with a county, city or town under any circumstances whatever. It is the most painful matter connected with my judicial life that I am compelled to take part in a farce whose result is invariably the same.

Along similar lines, Justice Miller wrote that "If there is a written instrument its validity is a foregone conclusion."[47]

The anti-repudiation stance taken by the U.S. Supreme Court, with its dismissal of issues concerning fraud, was extremely important for the institutionalization of the municipal bond market. Charles Fairman argues that the Court "made new law peculiar to municipal bonds. From the outset, these became a specially indulged category." The Court's decisions were such that municipal bonds became privileged within the securities market. For example, New York State courts were prevented from continuing to treat municipal bonds as ordinary negotiable securities. In 1876, a federal judge concluded that "the adjudications of the Supreme Court of the United States have invested municipal bonds . . . with anomalous and peculiar immunities, and it is now too late to apply the ordinary doctrines of the law of commercial paper."[48]

Municipal bonds were special. Local borrowers had unlimited obligations to their lenders, whereas private borrowers could limit their obligations by going into bankruptcy and selling their assets. So municipal bonds began to be viewed as carrying less risk than securities issued by private borrowers (such as corporations). Private commercial paper did not have the Supreme Court acting as "a nationwide collection agency."[49]

The overriding interest of the Court was in ensuring the marketability of the bonds, and its decision could not have been more effective in achieving the Court's objective of marketability. By the late 1880s, experts could claim that "It is especially to the Supreme Court of the United States that is due the present importance, stability, and value of the municipal bond as an investment security."[50] By the last decade of the nineteenth century, "no investment was as sound as a municipal bond."[51] The Court was certainly aware that by emphasizing the rights of bondholders and protecting the negotiability of bonds, it was making them attractive to investors. In 1858, Justice Nelson wrote that if the Court did not protect the bonds' negotiability, the bonds would no longer provide funds "for the accomplishment of many of the greatest and most useful enterprises of the day."[52]

In summary, then, the courts consistently upheld the right of bond-holders when the bonds had been issued to assist railways. However, bonds issued to assist other types of corporations were not valid. Tax monies had to be used to repay bonds issued for railways but could not be used to repay bonds issued to other private enterprises. Financial markets are shaped by the way in which law enforces contracts. The justices were aware that their rulings were regularizing a market. They overruled state supreme courts and forced local governments to retract repudiation even when gross irregularities and fraud had accompanied the issuance and sale of the railway bonds. The municipal bond market would have been very different—if it were to exist at all—had the U.S. Supreme Court been more ambivalent in its rulings. The Court, in consistently ruling for the bondholders in the railway-bond cases, played a crucial role in establishing the municipal bond market as a market.

These decisions established the parameters within which most local governments were to borrow until after World War II. The concept of public purpose was limited. Local governments, even when authorized by their state legislature, were not to be allowed to act as economic adventurers. The courts closed off that option—for the time being. As it was, local governments entered the last quarter of the nineteenth century having been restricted in what they could borrow for but also having access to a specialized and fairly regularized financial market. In the twentieth century, they would use that market to achieve some of the autonomy the courts had taken away.

Conclusion

The U.S. Supreme Court, especially, found that broad questions of government-business relations were interwoven with the specific facts of particular municipal bonds. The basis upon which questions related to municipal issues were decided was relevant in the simultaneous ongoing national debate about the role of government regulation in the economy, especially as related to railway regulation. Government promotion and government regulation of railways were closely linked in judicial logic. Furthermore, the Court—ruling on bond issues sold to assist railway companies—provided the foundations for the municipal bond market and established the boundaries within which local governments could borrow within that market. The Court ruled on the notion of public purpose and thereby delineated the future role of local governments as investors. This framework simultaneously gave life to the municipal bond market as a financial market, limited the role of local governments, and opened the way for regulation of the railroads.

Thus, the seemingly arcane issues related to municipal bonds opened a Pandora's box, for they allowed the Court to make the distinction between "public" and "private." This distinction is crucial in American federal law and politics, and maintenance of this distinction is a mechanism of federal control (as we shall see in chapter 9). Conversely, state and local governments seek to erode and circumvent the distinction, in order to maximize subnational autonomy. In the 1990s, local governments are still engaged in the battle not to let such definitions restrict them from economic development policies. Whereas Washington seeks to narrow "public purpose," local governments seek to enlarge it.

Along similar lines, the relationship between local government and the state became formalized in the late nineteenth century. Judge Dillon, in his famous writings, ruled that local governments were "creatures of the state." Again, that decision was intimately bound up with municipal bonds — that is, with the economic intervention local governments had been carrying out.

In sum, the courts (1) ruled on the purposes for which local governments could borrow, (2) secured the marketability of municipal bonds and thus provided the underpinnings of a special financial market, and (3) institutionalized the general state-local relationship. For their part, state legislatures were also busy establishing controls on local investment that were similar to the ones the states had adopted on their own borrowing and investing. Debt limits and other forms of constraint on local government were passed into statutory or constitutional law.

By the turn of the century, the basic structures of the system of local capital finance were in place. Local governments had been adventurous and interventionist but had failed to manage their activities in a financially successful fashion. The imposition of state controls on local borrowing (as well as on local taxation) at the end of the last quarter of the nineteenth century — coupled with the Supreme Court's delineation of what constitutes a "public purpose" — established the basic framework within which local governments were to invest throughout the next century.

In the forthcoming chapters I argue that local officials in the twentieth century have had to maneuver within that basic framework in order to invest both for service provision and for economic development activities. Local government capital investment in the late twentieth century is very much a consequence of nineteenth-century decision making — decision making vis-à-vis both government structure and the municipal bond market. Such maneuvering has entailed circumventing the restrictions placed by both court and legislature on local capital investment. American city governments have used both the law and the market to maximize their autonomy and to insulate themselves from both state and national government. It is to those strategies of circumvention that we now turn.

Chapter 6

Circumvention by

Law and Market

Local governments in the twentieth century faced the task of investing within a complex framework of limitations constructed by state government, state courts, and the Supreme Court. Their response was to develop mechanisms — legal, financial, and organizational — that would allow them to circumvent these limitations. Given that these restrictions were intended to restrain local borrowing, local officials who wished to borrow at higher levels than those permitted had to find ways to honor the letter of the law while violating its spirit. This chapter analyzes one strategy devised by officials, and chapter 7 analyzes a complementary strategy. The combination of the two form the substance of the "politics of circumvention" that have characterized intergovernmental politics in the area of local capital investment.

Debt Limits

The debt limits imposed by state action in the last quarter of the nineteenth century varied widely from state to state so that local governments differed in their borrowing discretion. C. Dickerman Williams and Peter Nehemkis Jr. argue that "the wide variation in state constitutional percentage limitations indicates that the lawmakers had little in the nature of a scientific criterion as a guide in the selection of a particular figure." Nonetheless, after the imposition of debt limits, local borrowing typically could increase to the extent that the taxable base increased. Such an increase could be achieved by annexation, population growth, or rising prices (the latter being particularly important after 1919). In fact, increases in the taxable base could be very large. For example, Baltimore's outstanding debts increased by 56.9 percent in the period 1919–1926. Yet Baltimore remained within its debt limit (in Baltimore's case, such a limit was imposed by banks that bought securities rather than by direct state-imposed limits).[1] Indeed, local borrowing continued to rise.

Increased borrowing was not due solely to increases in the taxable base. Other ways were also used to expand borrowing while respecting state limits. In particular, state legislatures granted exemptions from limits in specific cases. In New York, so many exemptions were granted by constitutional amendment that the New York State Tax Commission reported:

> The result of all this is a veritable hodge-podge of cumbersome exemptions and exceptions, one sentence alone containing more than 400 words. Furthermore, many of these new provisions were inserted without recasting the other clauses, thus complicating the whole structure so that it is difficult to read and more difficult to understand.[2]

All classes of municipalities increased their debt burden. In the period 1902–1912, they borrowed roughly $1,700 million. In the 146 cities with more than thirty thousand residents, per capita net debt was $53.08 in 1903 but $77.78 in 1917, whereas per capita interest payments had climbed from $2.06 to $3.57 in the same period. Although local borrowing largely ceased between the spring of 1917 and 1919, borrowing resumed in 1920 at a particularly heavy pace.[3] Interest payments correspondingly increased: in 1915 cities' net debt per capita was $75.56; in 1929 it was $138.32; in 1933 it was $169.70. Cities were paying $129 million in interest in 1915 whereas such payments had climbed to $366 million in 1929.[4]

Nonetheless, debt limits did begin to bite. They began to constrain local capital investment, in some cases even shortly after their imposition. After the great Chicago fire of 1871, for example, "the city had already reached its newly state-imposed debt ceiling, so it could not finance improvements by issuing municipal bonds."[5]

In many municipalities, demands for capital-intensive services continued even though debt limits had been reached. Although cities were successful in having their debt limits raised, such an effort was politically costly and always uncertain. Reconciling the provision of services with the constraints of debt limits meant that the debt limits imposed by the state government had to be circumvented. Ways had to be found to continue borrowing.

Such circumvention took many forms. The City of New York, for example, managed to continue borrowing huge amounts while remaining within its state-imposed financial limits. The Report of the Joint Legislative Committee to Investigate the Affairs of the City of New York, a committee established in 1921, reported that

> the city has run in debt approximately a hundred thousand dollars a day since the Greater City was incorporated. The funded debt has fluctuated around the constitutional debt limit for ten years. The tax rate has risen until it has reached, if not passed[,] the constitutional tax limit. All other means of raising funds having been exhausted, resort has been had to various devices including . . . increasing and making permanent the floating debt. These devices proving inadequate, the power of assessment has been resorted to by the city administration . . . until the assessment has reached approximately 94 per cent of the actual value, a rate much larger than the rest of the state.[6]

Furthermore, legislatures used special legislation to exempt borrowing for selected purposes from the state-imposed limits. Such exemptions were very important, for example, in the state of New York. Williams and Nehemkis find that

> water bonds of New York City issued subsequent to January 1, 1904, were excluded from computations of the debt of that city; thereafter, in quick succession, amendments followed for the exclusion of other water debts, first of second-class cities and then of third-class cities, and additional provisions concerning tax anticipation notes and debt subsequently to be incurred for revenue-producing public improvements, and previously incurred for rapid transit and dock improvements in New York City. In 1917 permission was obtained by another amendment to exclude certain water debts of Buffalo and Rochester; finally, in 1927, appeared amendments exempting a limited amount of assessment bonds of Buffalo, Rochester and Syracuse, $300,000 of debt for new subways in New York City and all water debt.[7]

However, two strategies evolved that had structural consequences for the very organization of local government itself. It is these structural impacts that are of interest, for they help to explain why local government in the United States is fragmented and so frequently specialized. Circumvention did not merely involve using techniques that affected individual municipalities in idiosyncratic ways. Rather, it also included strategies that changed the very meaning of the term *municipal government,* changed its structure, and helped change the kinds of public services that entered the public domain. These strategies, coupled with the lack of federal control, help explain why the American structure of local capital finance is so much more fragmented and decentralized than, for example, the British.

Both strategies circumvented debt limits by neutralizing them in some fashion.[8] Each strategy was based on a pivotal mechanism that acted to neutralize the limits set forth by state constitutional conventions or state legislatures. One strategy was based on municipal governments' using the capital market for circumvention whereas the other strategy focused on the creation of new governments. One involved the development of a new financial instrument — the revenue bond; and the other led to new types of local government units — the special district and the public authority.

Both instruments of circumvention have been shaped by the state judiciary. Judges have ultimately decided — state by state — how difficult circumvention would be. Indeed, the role of the state judiciary has been so influential in shaping the system of local capital investment that the state courts can almost be said to be a constitutive element of the system.[9]

In brief, my argument in this and the following chapter is that local officials developed two structurally significant ways of circumventing state debt limits. One used a new financial instrument (developed by investment bankers) and the courts.[10] The second created new governmental units as permitted by the courts. This chapter analyzes circumvention based on the capital market, and chapter 7 analyzes the creation of new governments. The state judiciary acts as the bedrock of both strategies of circumvention.

Financial Innovation

Capital markets are creative. That is, new financial instruments periodically appear. (The fashioning of the "junk bond" is a recent example.) The design of a new financial instrument is one of the ways in which funds are mobilized either for new purposes, from different categories of investors, or at lower cost for the borrower. Such innovation is typically analyzed in isolation and is of interest primarily to those who actually design the instrument (and often thereby become very rich), investors, and users of the funds thus mobilized. Of more general significance, however, is that a new debt instrument often allows a borrower to borrow for purposes that more orthodox debt instruments do not permit.

Innovation in financial markets is often tied to larger changes either in the sectors that the financial markets serve or in which they attract funds. It is also linked to the legal system, for the new financial instrument must be recognized as a valid call on resources by the judiciary. An instrument that does not have legal standing will not be used by either lenders or borrowers, for the contractual relationship that lies at the heart of the lender-borrower relationship would therefore be void. The link between financial instrument, borrowers and lenders, and the legal system is operative within both the public and private sectors.

The late nineteenth century was a time of innovation in capital markets serving both public and private borrowers. The American economy underwent massive restructuring in the last years of the nineteenth century and the first decade of the twentieth century. Both mergers and vertical integration occurred within critical industrial sectors, leading to the emergence of "big business" or the large corporation.[11] Within the public sector, various changes were made as well. Typically grouped under the rubric of "Progressive-era reforms" such changes involved the restructuring of city government so that increased centralization occurred.[12]

The restructuring of both public and private sectors was accompanied by the introduction of new debt instruments. In fact, some historians argue that the changes in the capital market as they affected private firms greatly facilitated the restructuring that occurred.[13] In the public sector such innovation, although occurring alongside governmental centralization, actually laid the groundwork for the consequent decentralization and fragmentation of local government.

The Evolution of Capital Markets

Capital markets in the nineteenth century developed rather episodically. The Civil War marked a turning point, for the huge borrowing carried out by the Union restructured the way funds were lent and borrowed in the United States. In particular, the link to foreign lenders was substantially weakened and investment bankers began to emerge. Richard Bensel points out:

> the American Civil War promoted the development of an autonomous capital market by first, encouraging a repatriation of securities from Europe and a subsequent domestic funding of the war effort; second, forcing the nation

off of the gold standard and, in that way, insulating the financial system from the influence of foreign markets; and, last, abetting the emergence of a largely new class of financiers who, upon the withdrawal of the Treasury from the capital market in the postbellum period, moved easily into a dominant position in the coordination and financing of industrial expansion.

Not only did the Treasury stop borrowing after the Civil War, but the federal government began to repay its huge debt at a rapid pace. James Savage argues that such rapid debt repayment was tied to the politics of the tariff. He concludes:

> the Republicans were obsessed with protecting the tariff wall, and the best way to justify the tariff, they reasoned, was to spend the government's accumulated surplus revenues. Besides increasing federal expenditures, however, the Republicans legitimized their tariffs by their efforts to reduce the national debt.[14]

Until 1873, securities markets dealt almost exclusively with the bonds of governments (including municipalities) and railroads. After the Panic of 1873, however, corporate shares gradually became an ever more important component of the securities market. Furthermore, a new corporate debt instrument was developed—the corporate bond secured by the corporate mortgage. After 1910 industrial corporations and public utility companies became more important actors in the capital market than the railroads.[15]

The Private Sector and the Law

As the capital markets became both more institutionalized and larger, so the legal arena in which private firms (railroads, utilities, or industrials) acquired funds also changed. Securities depend on the legal system for their legitimacy—that is, for the ability to be transformed into cash—and such a dependence exists for public and private borrowers equally.

Martin Sklar argues that in the case of private borrowers in the period 1886–1914 the impact of the Supreme Court—and the judiciary in general—was to allow the emergence of a capital market in industrial securities, a market that included the trading of shares. Such a phenomenon was fundamentally dependent on a recasting of the legal notion of property. He concludes that the Court "defined property to include the pursuit, and therefore the legal protection of intangible value, or earning power. . . .

Property . . . embraced both the use value of physical things and the exchange value of tangibles and intangibles." Such a redefinition underlay the emergence of the corporate securities market, that of industrial securities in particular. Since shares of stock are claims upon future earnings, and such earnings are dependent on intangibles, the redefinition of property as carried out by the Supreme Court was critical:

> the Court's redefinition of property solidified the legal ground for the liquidification of property, the transferability or negotiability of titles-to-ownership, and hence of titles to earnings or gains, through the conversion of capital from fixed tangibles into fluid intangibles. In short, it provided a secure legal environment for the capital market in industrials.[16]

Sklar's more general argument that the emergence of such a market was significant in permitting the transition from competitive to corporate capitalism does not concern us here. What is of relevance is the deep impact that extra-legislative (that is, judicial) decisions had upon the relationship between the corporation and "the state, its management, and its investors."[17]

Such an impact is analogous to that exercised by the judiciary on the relationship between municipal governments and their external environment. Just as the legal recasting of "property" was pivotal for the operation of the corporate sector, so was the reconceptualization of "debt" critical for the operation of the public sector.

The Municipal Bond Market

Local governments had been borrowing since the early days of the American republic. Although the date of the first municipal bond issue is unknown, we do know that bond issues were issued after 1812. Typically, those businessmen who dealt in securities dealt with municipal bonds, along with railroad securities.[18]

Very little is known as to who bought municipals and about the history of the municipal bond market. As Barrie Wigmore of Goldman and Sachs concluded: "The municipal market is ignored by all but those who participate in it. Scholars ignore it; there are virtually no studies on its history or mechanics. . . . Even the newspapers barely touch it." Wigmore's conclusion is supported by others on Wall Street. In 1983, the editors introduced a major study of the market by arguing that "over the past 15 years the buying and selling of tax-exempt debt has become a major activity on Wall Street. Yet, unlike corporate bonds, U.S. governments, and common stock, little has been written about this industry."[19]

The buyers of antebellum municipals, whoever they might be, had found a secure investment. In the antebellum period, municipal defaults were rare. Mobile, Detroit, Chicago, and Philadelphia defaulted on bonds, but in general, municipal finance was not problematic. Defaults after the Panic of 1873 led to state-imposed debt limits, and municipalities also defaulted after the Panic of 1893. However, from 1893 until 1926 municipal defaults were not common. According to George Edwards:

> There was also a marked drop in municipal defaults arising out of acts of invalidity due to technical legal irregularities. In the seventies and even eighties many municipalities took advantage of some small irregularity in the issuing of their bonds subsequently to declare their obligations void. However, these acts in time decreased and by the beginning of the century the practice was negligible.

Estimates are that the municipal bond market was very large by 1929. Municipal borrowers had accumulated nearly as much outstanding debt as the federal government (the former had borrowed $15.7 billion whereas the federal government had $16 billion outstanding). Various types of corporate borrowers trailed behind, for, as Wigmore put it, "utilities, railroads, and industrials each had $10–$12 billion outstanding."[20]

The record on defaulted bonds does indicate that banks bought bonds as did insurance companies and wealthy individuals.[21] In 1932, an estimate made by the executive director of the Municipal Finance Officers Association indicated that wealthy individuals were the largest buyers of municipals (see table 3).

Federal Tax Exemption

The Supreme Court gave municipal bonds a secure legal environment by ruling in favor of lenders in the railway-bond cases (see chapter 5). Municipals, however, acquired a status different from that enjoyed by corporate bonds once the Sixteenth Amendment to the Constitution, passed in 1913, allowed a national income tax to be levied. The interest on municipals was tax-exempt, whereas the interest on corporate bonds was not. The effects of tax exemption were immediately felt in the municipal bond market.

Table 3. Owners of Municipal Bonds

Individuals with annual incomes exceeding $5,000	$4,500,000,000
Corporations, except banks and insurance companies	$4,000,000,000
Sinking funds, public trust funds, and investment funds of states and their political subdivisions and districts	$3,380,000,000
Banks	$2,800,000,000
Life, fire, and casualty insurance companies	$1,000,000,000
Fraternal insurance companies	$500,000,000
Individual investors — annual incomes under $5,000	$900,000,000
All others, including charitable and educational institutions, endowment funds, foreign holders, private trusts, estates, etc.	$1,420,000,000
Total	$18,500,000,000

Source: An estimate by Carl H. Chatters, as of December 31, 1932. Carl H. Chatters, *Municipal Debt Defaults: Their Prevention and Adjustment: A Report to the Executive Committee of the Municipal Finance Officers Association of the United States and Canada* (Chicago: Public Administration Service, 1933), p. 2.

Although municipal and corporate borrowers had paid roughly the same interest rate before 1913, municipal borrowers began to pay significantly lower interest rates after 1913.[22]

The tax exemption allows state and local governments to borrow at interest costs substantially lower than private borrowers or the federal government. The federal government loses money by not collecting taxes on the interest paid, but lenders can obtain a desirable yield while charging less interest than they do on federal and private borrowing. The non-taxed interest rate on municipals competes with the after-tax yield on corporate and federal government bonds. The higher the income tax rate paid by a lender, the more attractive becomes lending in the municipal bond market rather than the corporate bond market or the Treasury securities market. It is for that reason that higher-income investors find the municipal bond market an attractive investment opportunity. Even though the local government borrower pays a lender less interest than other borrowers do, the lender retains as much or more of the interest paid because of the lack of federal taxation on interest paid by local governments.

Tax exemption on interest from municipals was secured after the Six-teenth Amendment, at least partially because an earlier attempt at impos-ing an income tax had been declared unconstitutional. An income tax had been passed in 1894 (as one component of the Wilson-Gorman Tariff Act) but was immediately challenged in the Supreme Court.[23] The Court was asked to rule on whether the federal government could constitutionally impose a tax on interest from municipal bonds. (The law exempted inter-est on federal bonds.) The Court in *Pollock v. Farmers' Loan and Trust Co.*, in 1895,

> ruled that a tax on the interest on state and local government bonds was ultimately a tax on the state that issued the bonds and was unconstitutional under the doctrine of intergovernmental tax immunity because such taxa-tion would restrict the state's borrowing powers, and therefore its ability to operate.

Since the Sixteenth Amendment explicitly states that the federal govern-ment can tax income "from whatever source derived," the debate over the amendment raised the question of whether the tax exemption would ap-ply. Congress argued that the exemption would indeed be applicable, and "members of both the Senate and the House went on record denying that the amendment affected the immunity of state obligations from federal taxation."[24]

The tax exemption for interest earned on municipal bonds has been maintained. (However, the Court substantially weakened the constitu-tional foundation of the tax exemption in 1988, and the Tax Reform Act of 1986 eroded the universal application of the exemption [see chapter 8].) The exemption's statutory basis is found in the Internal Revenue Code, which has, since its original formulation, recognized the interest on municipal bonds as free from income tax. However, the Internal Revenue Code has never specified whether the exemption was based on a constitu-tional right of exemption or on the decision of Congress to grant such exemption.[25]

Because the exemption costs the federal government in forgone tax revenue, the Treasury has consistently opposed it and has even actively attempted several times to have it eliminated. Secretary of the Treasury Andrew J. Mellon opposed it vigorously. A constitutional amendment removing the exemption was actually approved in the House but was stopped in the Senate.[26]

During the Depression, two major efforts were made to make municipal bonds taxable. Tax exemption of both municipal and federal bonds was proposed under a Senate bill introduced in February 1933 by Senator Cordell Hull (later secretary of state). The elimination of the tax exemption became part of the National Industrial Recovery Act, as passed by the Senate, but was killed during conference committee. The salvation of the tax exemption for municipals seems to have been incidental to concern for saving it for federal securities, for the Roosevelt administration opposed the elimination of the tax exemption "for the short-term goal of not disturbing a large U.S. Treasury financing when the market was still weak from the Bank Holiday." In 1938, the Treasury convinced the Roosevelt administration to support the elimination of the exemption. Congress did not support the Treasury, but the Treasury nonetheless attempted to have the Supreme Court terminate the exemption. In 1945 the Court refused to hear the government's case, and the tax exemption persisted.[27]

The tax exemption created a distinctive market for municipal issues, the so-called tax-exempt market. Even before the Sixteenth Amendment, municipal issues had become differentiated from each other. Once the tax exemption came into play, all municipals were tax-exempt but continued to differ. All bonds issued and traded in the municipal bond market, therefore, share the feature of tax exemption but differ along other dimensions. It is precisely those differences that are critical to the strategy of circumvention analyzed in this chapter.

The Evolution of Debt Instruments

The fashioning of a new debt instrument within the municipal bond market opened up to municipal officials the technical possibility of changing the financing of capital investment. A new type of debt instrument — the revenue bond — allowed them to move from borrowing backed by taxes to borrowing backed by self-liquidating projects that generated their own funds for bond repayment. The courts, in turn, allowed municipalities to use the revenue bond to circumvent debt limits.

The use of the new instrument was linked to a substantial increase in the so-called proprietary activities of local government. The courts began to make a distinction between "municipalities as business proprietors rather than as units of government."[28] Whereas local government had performed so-called governmental functions typically financed by property taxes, it now was increasingly able to develop its own self-financing enterprises. In so doing local government transformed its taxpayers into ratepayers.

General-Obligation Bond

The typical municipal bond in the nineteenth century and in the pre–World War II period pledged the "full faith and credit" (that is, the taxing authority) of the issuing municipality. A bond that will be repaid by taxes (that is, a bond backed by the borrowing government's full faith and credit) is known as a general-obligation bond. Writing in 1949, Maxine Virtue defined the essential characteristics of the general-obligation bond:

> The general obligation bond is the typical, and by far the most widely used, kind of municipal security. The language of the official act which creates the bond, as well as recitals in the bond itself, pledge the full faith and credit of the municipality to the discharge of the obligation. Such general obligation bonds are payable from the general property tax collections.[29]

Given the commitment made by taxpayers to repay the bond, borrowing by issuing a general-obligation bond uses up debt-incurring capacity unless the state legislature explicitly exempts the bond from the state's debt restrictions. Generally, therefore, debt limits are held to apply to all borrowing carried out through the instrument of a general-obligation bond.

Two bonds in particular were developed that differed from the general-obligation bond: the special-assessment bond and the revenue bond. The assessment bond was developed for reasons other than the circumvention of debt limits but became used as a circumvention device once limits were imposed. Perhaps most important, the assessment bond set the precedent used by state courts in permitting the development of the revenue bond.

Special-Assessment Bond

The use of special assessments — taxes levied on property owners whose property would be benefited by such actions as the opening up of streets or their subsequent paving or other improvements — had been imported to the United States from England. Special assessment as a financing mechanism was first extensively used in New York and gradually spread to other states. It was vigorously attacked in the courts, which, however, consistently ruled that special assessment was both constitutional and different from taxation in the more general sense.[30]

Assessment bonds became widely used and were important in the provision of services. They were distinguished from general-obligation bonds (which are backed by the general taxing power) because they were backed by an earmarked tax, that is, the special-assessment tax. The courts ruled that, since the general credit of the issuer was not involved, such bonds did not incur "debt" as understood by debt restrictions.[31]

Numerous special-assessment bonds defaulted, however. In such cases, bondholders attempted to obtain judicial rulings that interpreted the bonds in question as general-obligation bonds. Bondholders were successful in some cases but not in others. In the former, the courts typically ruled that city officials had not played a proper role in the administration of the assessment taxes or that the law authorizing their issuance had been unconstitutional.[32]

For our purposes, the most relevant feature of assessment bonds was that they were treated by the courts as different from general-obligation bonds. Just as assessment taxes were not treated as general taxes, so borrowing for improvements that would then be subjected to such assessment taxes was not the same as borrowing for "general" purposes. In other words, borrowing for such improvements did not involve the full faith and credit of the issuing municipality (unless, as in Florida, a statute explicitly specified otherwise under certain conditions or unless the court found that the municipality's role was such that a general obligation had been incurred).

The important point is that borrowing carried out by special-assessment bonds did not fall under the debt restrictions passed by the states. Since the full faith and credit of the municipality was not involved and since (according to the courts) neither state legislators nor delegates to constitutional conventions had that kind of debt in mind when they imposed debt limits, the courts reasoned that assessment debt was not "debt" under the meaning of the states' debt restrictions. It was largely because of this precedent that revenue bonds were easily considered as *not* adding to a city's debt burden.[33]

The Special-Obligation or Revenue Bond

The term *revenue bond* is now popularly used to indicate any bond that is backed by a specific revenue stream from a revenue-producing service, or rather, any bond that does not commit the municipality's full faith and credit and therefore does not entail a commitment by taxpayers. As their use spread, however, a great deal of confusion arose concerning what to call a bond that was issued by a "general-purpose" municipality (as opposed to a special district or an authority) backed by a specific non-tax-revenue stream rather than by general taxes. The term *special-obligation bond* was therefore often used as a general rubric to encompass bonds that were not backed by general taxes — regardless of whether the issuing government was a general-purpose government or a specialized district or authority. John Fowler used a threefold classification in order to distinguish between different types of borrowers. He differentiated between state-revenue bonds (issued by a state government); municipal-revenue bonds (issued by all those units of governments with the power to tax such as cities, counties, and special districts); and agency-revenue bonds (issued by units of government without the power to tax such as boards, commissions, and authorities). The term *special-obligation bond* covers all three types of revenue bonds.[34]

The special-obligation or revenue bond represented a major technical innovation within the municipal bond market. Although the courts treated it as somehow analogous to assessment bonds, in reality the revenue bond was a fundamentally different type of debt instrument within the municipal bond market. (The first time it was used, by the city of Spokane, its novelty was such that it was officially termed a warrant rather than a bond.) It was, in fact, an adaptation of securities used in the corporate market. Knappen concludes that "revenue bonds are more akin to private corporation bonds than they are to the standard municipal bond."[35] In a similar vein, some states allowed local borrowers to accompany revenue bonds with indentures, which set out precise relationships between borrower and lender, patterned on those used in the corporate bond market.

In brief, the revenue bond represented a debt instrument inspired by those instruments used by private borrowers. It is not surprising that the very format of a revenue bond was very different from that used by general-obligation bonds. Knappen describes the differences:

the revenue bond resolution, instead of being as brief and perfunctory as it often is in the case of full faith and credit obligations, is likely to be extensive and detailed. It customarily sets forth, in addition to the usual items found in general obligation resolutions[,] . . . provisions relating to the establishment of separate funds into which the proceeds of the loans, and the revenues resulting from the project, are to be deposited, and provisions relating to the management and operation of the enterprise. It is also apt to include covenants dealing with the beginning rates to be charged; the changes of rates to be made, if necessary; the collection of the bills rendered; the insuring of the property; and the keeping of separate books of account for the project. Such matters in the past have been found more often in private corporation covenants than in municipal bond resolutions.

Since the revenue bond was a new debt instrument, relatively few investment banking firms knew how to set up such a bond. At one point, only six investment banking houses possessed the technical expertise needed to issue a revenue bond. At the end of the 1930s, the expertise required continued to be so scarce that one of these original firms was often still involved in formulating a bond issue.[36]

The Use of Revenue Bonds

The city of Spokane, Washington, was the first issuer of a revenue bond to be recognized as such. Cities in the western United States generally made the first (successful) use of this new debt instrument, and eastern cities were typically the slowest to move to such financing. John Fowler concluded that "western municipalities . . . served as experimental laboratories for the nation in the development of revenue bonds." Since principles of home rule were particularly strong in the western states, western cities were consequently more likely to issue a revenue bond in the absence of state-enabling legislation. Fowler argues that the principles underlying home rule

> not only pervaded the written law of the western states but was a potent influence upon the decisions of judges in the molding of legal doctrine. The western cities accordingly found it possible to engage, upon their own initiative, in new fields of municipal enterprise and often to issue revenue bonds without asking for permission from the state legislature.[37]

In the case of Spokane, the city could not issue general-obligation bonds to finance a waterworks system because it had used up its taxing and borrowing powers. Both tax and debt limits had been reached. It therefore decided to borrow, using the revenue from the waterworks system as the source of repayment. Litigation ensued, but the state supreme court in

Winston v. City of Spokane upheld the right of the city to issue warrants backed by the revenue of its waterworks system. The Court gave its approval by using an analogy to the practice of issuing assessment bonds.[38]

However, city officials subsequently felt that the interest rate on the warrants (8 percent) was too high. So they issued serial revenue bonds that would pay a lower interest rate, and the money from this bond issue would be used to repay the warrants. Although the bond issue was composed, it did not sell because of the uncertainties "of the legal and economic status" of this new type of security. The city was again taken to court, and the Washington Supreme Court in *Kenyon v. City of Spokane* upheld the right of the city to issue the revenue bond and to use that money to repay the warrants. Because of the novelty of the financing procedure, "the obligations, in the end, were termed warrants, upon the advice of legal counsel, but it was stated at the time that the obligations were 'bonds in every essential having definite dates for payment of both interest and principal.' "[39] Spokane's experiment led to attempts by other cities to borrow by pledging revenue rather than taxes — by issuing a self-liquidating loan.[40]

In the period before World War I, the practice of issuing revenue bonds was restricted largely to cities in Washington, with Tacoma, Spokane, Seattle, Aberdeen, Centralia, Everett, and Walla Walla borrowing through the use of revenue bonds. During and immediately after the war, Seattle in particular used revenue bonds to develop its publicly owned utility systems. Revenue bonds began to be more widely used after the end of World War I. Numerous cities issued them and usage spread, from Seattle, "eastward and southward, the local communities in Illinois and Indiana being particularly active in revenue-bond financing." Cities such as St. Louis, San Antonio, Bowling Green, and Louisville issued revenue bonds, typically either for the purposes of expanding waterworks or to build bridges.[41]

In 1926 the Port Authority of New York offered two issues (totaling $34 million), which are considered "a landmark in the history of revenue-bond financing." Not only were the bonds for amounts larger than ever before but they were also for a new type of project — toll bridges — and they were issued by an "authority" rather than a city, town, or district. Although authority financing was to increase dramatically (see the next chapter), cities continued to issue revenue bonds as well. In the period leading to the Depression, cities such as Seattle, Chicago, Tacoma, and St.

Louis continued to use revenue bonds, but cities in states with no record of revenue bond usage continued to issue general-obligation rather than revenue bonds.[42]

In the pre-Depression period, some states either amended their constitutions or passed laws authorizing localities to issue revenue bonds. Washington and Illinois allowed revenue bonds to be issued before the turn of the century, and Michigan amended its constitution in 1909, Ohio in 1912, and Pennsylvania in 1913. By 1930, in addition to those five states, Texas, Louisiana, Wisconsin, Missouri, Indiana, Kentucky, Nebraska, North Dakota, Alabama, Iowa, and South Dakota had changed their legal provisions so that local governments could issue revenue bonds. In most cases, state laws allowed revenue bonds for the purpose of either acquiring or expanding water systems. By the beginning of FDR's presidency, then, "the revenue bond had ceased to be an unknown quantity."[43]

The Road to Circumvention: Revenue Bonds and the Courts

The link between the development of the special-obligation or revenue bond and the desire to circumvent debt limits was widely recognized. A classic article on municipal bonds by Williams and Nehemkis, published in 1937, argued that "the prevailing method of avoiding debt restrictions in the acquisition of needed public improvements has . . . been by means of the 'special obligation.'" And John Fowler argued that "revenue-bond financing has proved to be the most satisfactory all-round solution of the debt-limit problem." This is not to say, however, that only communities facing debt-limit thresholds issued revenue bonds. Many issuers could have issued general-obligation bonds but chose not to. Fowler argues that one of the reasons communities not facing debt limits have chosen revenue-bond financing is because that "method of financing assures a more equitable distribution of the costs of a public enterprise among the persons benefited than any other plan of financing which has been devised." He goes on to discuss how revenue bonds address the tensions between taxpayers and users:

> Revenue-bond financing eliminates latent controversy between the taxpayers and the users of a service. If the service was financed by general-obligation bonds, it may be in the interests of the taxpayers to establish higher rates for the service in order to reduce or avoid a deficit which

must be met by taxation, whereas the eternal desire of the users is that the rates be kept at a minimum.[44]

Nonetheless, the innovative self-liquidating loan was of value to officials primarily because they saw it as a way of borrowing more than they could if they continued to rely exclusively on borrowing backed by taxes. Furthermore, officials in those sixteen states where the constitution required the levying of a tax simultaneous with the incurring of debt viewed the use of revenue bonds as a way of avoiding the hazards of amending the constitution, an often complex and politically fraught procedure that local officials would just as soon avoid.[45]

However, revenue bonds would permit governments to borrow more than allowed by debt limits only if the monies borrowed did not qualify as debt, as understood by state constitutions or statutes. If the same definition of *debt* — and therefore the same restrictions on debt — were applied equally to general-obligation and revenue financing, revenue financing would indeed have changed the nature of the groups from whom money was collected to repay the loan (changing from property taxpayers to users of the service). In that case, however, revenue-bond financing would not have allowed the expansion of borrowing beyond that permitted by debt limits. It is vital to point out that revenue bonds could be used to circumvent debt restrictions only if the courts granted the debt incurred by revenue bonds a *legal* status different from that granted to debt incurred by general-obligation financing.

Should self-liquidating loans be given a distinctive status vis-à-vis debt restrictions? If so, how differently should revenue-bond debt be treated? Should borrowing governments issuing revenue bonds be permitted to ignore debt restrictions such as referenda requirements? Should self-liquidating loans be allowed to increase the amount of borrowing for which a given population is responsible far beyond that outlined by debt limits? It was up to the state courts to decide. Their answer rested on the definition they gave to the term *debt*.

What Is Debt?

The notion of debt — and a debt limit — seems straightforward enough. A debt is a sum of money that needs to be repaid, usually with interest. Borrowing produces debt. The imposition of a debt limit signifies that a government can only borrow up to a certain limit. That limit may be defined in a variety of ways, but the limit was often expressed as a percentage of the assessed value of property.[46] Furthermore, a requirement that the electorate approve any borrowing carried out within the debt limit provided another dimension to such restriction. State legislators and delegates to state constitutional conventions reasonably thought that the debt limit would be clear and effective.[47]

Local officials, however, found that they could borrow without having such borrowing count as debt (as recognized by the courts) by using financial instruments that moved the risk of default from the taxpayer to the bondholder, and the onus of repayment from the taxpayer to the actual end user (in the form of user fees). This shift became very important when the distinction between taxpayers and ratepayers blurred (see chapter 8). As publicly owned utilities providing water, sewer and sewage treatment, and electric power (sometimes generated by nuclear plants) came to be required of all residents in an area, the distinction between taxes and user fees came to be more one of form than substance — particularly in those cities where usage was not well correlated to the price structure of the service being granted. Yet this difference in form permitted capital investment to proceed by allowing the circumvention of debt limits.[48]

State limits were viewed as restricting borrowing in order to protect the taxpayers from the high tax bills resulting from heavy borrowing. So, officials argued, borrowing that did not require the taxpayer to pay taxes to repay the loan did not qualify as debt, as understood by the states' debt limits. And the courts agreed with this reconceptualization of what constitutes debt.

The link between debt, defined as such within the judicial arena, and the imposition of tax levies needs to be emphasized. The courts interpreted debt limits as protecting the interests of future taxpayers. The courts — as well as economists — have argued that capital investments should not be paid for by taxpayers who do not make use of that investment. That is, a borrowing generation should not be allowed to borrow as much as it wishes and simply pay the interest on the loans while future taxpayers have to repay the principal even though they do not enjoy the benefits of the investment. David Gelfand argues:

> the real beneficiaries of debt ceilings were the taxpayers of the future, who would not have to pay inordinate debt service on capital projects producing

no tangible benefits for them. . . . Contemporary economists label this concept "intergenerational equity." This principle requires each generation of taxpayers to pay, through debt service or otherwise, for its "stream of use" of government structures and services.[49]

The fact that the courts interpreted the debt limits as primarily protecting future taxpayers was to have sweeping implications for the system of local capital finance. If the courts had interpreted debt limits as indicating a "spirit of economy," they would have been far less amenable to the circumvention of such limits.[50] They would probably have dealt differently with debt incurred for municipal utilities (nuclear generating plants included). In general, they would have been more sensitive to the aggregation of debt within a given territorial area, debt that is often all supported by the same population in the guise either of taxpayers repaying debt through property taxes or of customers paying user fees to repay the debt.

Special Fund Doctrine

The state courts developed a conceptual framework that gradually allowed them to approve financing techniques that increased the aggregate debt of a given territorial area while nonetheless allowing an individual government to remain within the debt limits expressed in constitutions or statutes. The special fund doctrine was used by local officials to increase debt and capital investment, while seeming not to violate state-imposed restrictions. This doctrine in essence allowed debt instruments to be used that satisfied both the demands of bondholders for repayment and the demands of local officials who were searching for funds to be used for increased capital investment.

The doctrine was developed by analogy to an earlier taxing and borrowing procedure that had consistently been approved by the courts — the procedure of imposing special taxes on property that benefited from improvements financed by borrowed monies. Special assessments had a long history during which such taxation was distinguished from "general" taxation (see chapter 4). Special-assessment taxes were levied and used to repay the bonds that had been issued to carry out the improvements. Judges consistently approved of both borrowing and taxing for improvements to property and just as consistently differentiated them from general taxing and borrowing activity.

The special fund doctrine was first articulated by the Washington Supreme Court in the case already mentioned of *Winston v. City of Spokane*. The city of Spokane, having incurred all the debt allowed it, nonetheless wished to finance a water system. The city could not pledge its full faith and credit, that is, it could not finance the system by issuing general-obligation bonds and exceeding its debt limit. It therefore tried the novel technique of issuing bonds that were to be repaid by a special fund composed of the water system's revenues. When the city's right to issue such a bond without incurring debt was challenged, the state court held

> the transaction . . . equivalent to an issue of warrants payable out of a fund created by an assessment upon property benefited by a local improvement. In *Winston*, the Washington Court implicitly defined the word "debt," within the context of its constitutional prohibitions, to mean the general credit or general revenues of a city.[51]

A major precedent and referent had been established. A city could now issue a bond for a self-liquidating project, not secured by the city's full faith and credit, which was not secured by its general revenues. A city could increase its debt financially without using up its debt-incurring capacity, if such borrowing did not involve a commitment by present or future taxpayers. Bondholders rather than taxpayers bore the burden of the project's risk while users rather than taxpayers bore the cost of repayment. The road to circumvention was open.

After the *Winston* decision, supreme courts in other states took a variety of positions on when debt (as understood in the debt-limitation provisions) was incurred. Some courts developed the restricted special fund doctrine by arguing that debt limits were irrelevant only if the particular facility being constructed — or the expansion of an existing facility — was completely self-financing. In those states in which the courts argued that improvements or expansions to an existing system had to be self-financing in order not to constitute debt, local governments found it particularly difficult to borrow outside the debt limits. When the Utah Supreme Court adopted that position, local governments found that self-liquidating loans for expansions or improvements to existing utilities became almost impossible to obtain. Revenue bonds were difficult to use within these constraints. Ogden City, Utah, was turned down three times by the supreme court when it tried to sell revenue bonds for improving its water system. During the Depression, the Public Works Administration found it impossible to grant self-liquidating loans to Utah municipalities unless the municipality followed the procedure of holding a referendum, just as it would have to for general-obligation debt.[52]

However, the restricted special fund doctrine declined in popularity as state courts came to accept the "broad special fund doctrine." The Illinois Supreme Court, for example, was the initial author of the restricted special fund (which it first articulated in 1902 in the case of *City of Joliet v. Alexander*). The court reversed its position in 1930, however. The broad special fund doctrine allows the special fund to be fed by the revenues of existing facilities as well as by those of the facility for which the borrowing takes place. Today, the term *special fund doctrine* typically is synonymous with the "broad" version of the concept, although every state supreme court has interpreted it in a slightly different way.[53]

The courts have come to the general position that local governments — although not necessarily general-purpose municipal governments (as we shall see in chapter 7) — could borrow for self-liquidating projects without being subject to debt restrictions, as long as those loans were repaid with other than tax monies. Over time, the courts accepted the idea that borrowing and the general taxing power of the governmental borrower were no longer inextricably linked.[54] The special fund doctrine, as enunciated by the state judiciary, provided the legal base both for the creation of new debt instruments and for the creation of new governmental units (see chapter 7). It formed a critical component of the two strategies of circumvention that are of interest to us.

With respect specifically to financing and to the use of the bond market, the doctrine allowed the creation of debt as defined by financiers to be divorced from debt as defined by debt limits. It greatly facilititated the use of the revenue bond, which by the late twentieth century had come to be the major financial instrument used by local governments in the bond market. It encouraged governments to begin providing services to users who paid user fees or rates as opposed to providing services to taxpayers who paid taxes for the delivery of services. In essence, the doctrine allowed the gradual transformation of taxpayers into customers, as well as the public sector's move into proprietary activities and away from strictly governmental functions. Above all, however, the special fund doctrine allowed local governments to borrow far more than the authors of debt limits would have dreamed possible. In that sense, the special fund doctrine and its various permutations allowed a system of capital finance to evolve that could cope with technological change, rapid urbanization, and demands for higher levels of service provision as well as for economic development activity.

The Special-Obligation Bond and Municipal Ownership of Utilities

The system of local capital finance that evolved also facilitated the municipalization of various utilities. It is not surprising that the first court case involving a bond issued for a self-liquidating project concerned a utility; special obligations were issued primarily in relation to utility financing.[55] They became an integral part of one of the fiercest political conflicts in urban politics, the conflict over municipal ownership of utilities.

In many cities, attitudes toward public ownership of various utilities were sharply polarized and became symbolic of positions on numerous issues related to business-government relations. Many contemporary scholars think of utilities as involving primarily transit and public power utilities. Since municipal ownership did not become the norm in those areas, the extent of municipal enterprise is often overlooked. For example, although Harold Platt analyzes how Houston officials after a bitter struggle municipalized the water system, his general conclusions are based on utilities such as the electric utility in which municipal ownership was not obtained:

> Twenty years of municipal reform helped to steer the United States between full-fledged socialism and unbridled competition onto a middle route of regulated capitalism. . . . In the battle over public utility franchises, the progressive compromise meant the defeat of municipal ownership and an acceptance of privately owned "natural" monopolies. . . . At base, the rapid modernization of the city's transit, gas, communications, and electrical services under private management defused discontent with . . . the utility corporation.[56]

Yet the advance of municipal ownership was more extensive than Platt's analysis would suggest. Water systems, for example, came to be primarily publicly owned (often after bitter conflicts). Whereas in 1880, 49 percent of waterworks were municipally owned, by 1915, 69 percent were in public ownership. By 1932, 73 percent of all waterworks were municipally owned. Municipal ownership also made significant inroads in the area of electric power. By 1922, roughly 41 percent of all electric light plants were municipally owned. (In terms of total output, however, private ownership dominated. Municipal plants tended to be built in smaller cities, and large cities tended to have privately owned electric light plants.)[57] By 1934, 1,808 municipally owned power plants were in operation. (Some utilities systems passed into municipal ownership only after bitter court battles with their private owners.) And "private sewer companies practically disappeared." In the 1920s, most privately owned sewer systems were found in Texas.[58]

Water and sewer services have become transformed into traditional "governmental" functions, so much so that it is often overlooked that they once often belonged to the private sector. For their part, municipal power plants are rarely noticed, although they are now huge borrowers in the municipal bond market and involved in controversial activities such as nuclear power generation. Although the term *regulated capitalism* certainly describes a great deal of the political economy of local public services, such a characterization should not be allowed to obscure the proprietary activities that local governments gradually took on in the pre–World War II period.

The expansion of their proprietary activities was inextricably tied to both the bond market and the courts. Utilities — whether providing water, sewage, transit, or power — often used special-obligation bonds either to build new facilities or to expand or improve existing facilities. Utilities were the principal self-liquidating projects to which the special fund doctrine was applied and for which special obligations were issued.[59] Municipal utilities directly benefited from the redefinition of debt as stated by state courts.

The courts often ultimately decided the fate of municipal ownership. In those cases in which they agreed that utility financing by a special obligation did not constitute debt, such financing went ahead. But the reverse was also true. For example, Rosen finds that

> despite the passage of a series of referendums in which Chicagoans authorized the city to municipalize the streetcar lines, the Court prevented the city from carrying out this plan of action by disallowing a state law that would have permitted the city to finance municipalization by issuing special debt certifications that would have skirted its restrictive municipal debt ceiling.[60]

In general, however, the courts allowed municipal ownership to proceed by allowing debts incurred for self-supporting utilities to not count toward the state-imposed debt limit. They sharply distinguished between the user of a service and the payer of taxes — even though the two would often be identical. They helped transform the taxpayer into a ratepayer, who in the arena of capital finance enjoyed a different judicial status from the taxpayer. Critics of such an approach have argued that "many courts have been unwilling to recognize that the ratepayers and taxpayers are in substance the same group, and that constitutional provisions limiting municipal indebtedness do not serve their fundamental purpose unless they are construed so as to protect the individual in both capacities."[61]

The case of sewage systems illustrates the trend to divorce the role of ratepayer from that of taxpayer. Sewage systems had been financed by either general-obligation bonds or assessment bonds, both repaid by levying a tax. Although a city could charge for the service, the city could also subsidize the service through tax monies if it so wished. However, in the pre–World War II period, such systems gradually came to be financed by revenue bonds, which in turn were repaid out of user fees tied to some standard of water consumption. Users now pay fees, or rates, rather than having their sewage provided (either wholly or partially) as part of the package of services financed by their property taxes. Although users have some control over how much they use the system, such control is only very partial. Fowler points out: "the fact that the residents are bound by hygienic regulations to make use of the sewage-disposal facilities places the service charge of these projects in the category of an involuntary payment."[62]

The range of services for which "taxes" were paid changed. Municipal officials were able to expand their capital-intensive service delivery while not having such expansion perceived as a burden on citizens' taxes. Municipal ownership of utilities could occur while still permitting tax monies to be used for other purposes. Although rates were charged regardless of whether general-obligation or revenue-bond financing had been used, the use of revenue bonds both institutionalized the use of rates and limited the maneuverability of the municipal government. It could neither subsidize rates nor (as easily) make a large profit from them.

The use of rates was an important choice for local officials. It effectively took capital-intensive services out of the tax economy. If utility users had been given water, sewage, and power "free" — that is, paid for from property taxes — the service profile of the American locality would have evolved differently. The widespread acceptance of rates and the transformation of the taxpayer into a ratepayer has been critical for the contours of public services in the United States. The revenue bond was not the cause of such a transformation but it did strongly reinforce the drawing of a tight link between the use of a public service and the need to pay the cost of that service.

It is a paradox that, although the courts had limited municipalities by not allowing them to engage in certain "private" purposes, they subsequently did allow the municipalities' proprietary activities to expand by allowing them to use special-obligation bonds to circumvent debt limits. The notion of public purpose expanded to include a range of utility services, and the permissive attitude toward debt circumvention allowed such an expansion to take on operational reality. Municipal officials would also experience a different paradox. They would find that such expansion of their proprietary activities led to a fragmentation of control and authority over the metropolitan territory. The special-obligation bond initially allowed municipalities to obtain control over certain services, but the bond — in conjunction with the courts — also laid the groundwork for the general-purpose municipality's subsequent loss of such control.

The Federal Role

The Depression changed the picture of local capital finance by bringing the federal government in as an actor. Its activities were numerous. It encouraged the use of revenue bonds (as well as authorities), lent large sums to local governments, passed federal bankruptcy legislation to cope with municipal-bond defaults, and tried to remove the tax exemption from municipal bonds. It also spent huge sums on public works in the form of grants. Its role in promoting the use of revenue bonds is of particular interest to us here.

Background

Municipalities had borrowed heavily in the 1920s. They spent on capital improvements, 60–70 percent of which were financed by borrowing (these figures are for cities with a population of 30,000 or more). Nonetheless, there were wide variations in the amounts of debt incurred. For example, municipalities in Florida increased their per capita debt by 426 percent between 1922 and 1932 and those in Illinois increased theirs by 210 percent, whereas municipalities in Minnesota actually cut their per capita debt and those in Utah increased their per capita debt by only 0.6

percent. Per capita net debt also varied widely within a single state. In New Jersey, for example, some municipalities in 1929 had a per capita net debt of $2,540 whereas the state average was only $216.51.[63]

The Depression profoundly affected the general finances of local governments in that assessed valuation dropped in many areas as did tax revenue. In the 1920s cities' interest payments had typically been around 10 percent of their total expenditures (the equivalent figure for state governments was only 4 percent), but by 1933 that figure had risen to 14.4 percent. Defaults on bonds occurred and the ability to borrow was severely diminished. By 1934, thirty-seven defaults had occurred in cities with populations over 30,000. If coterminous school district defaults are also included, "38 percent of the gross debt of all cities and school districts in that population group" was in default. Nonetheless, municipalities were not as badly hurt by the depression of the 1930s as they had been by the depression of the 1870s. Hillhouse concluded that "about 10 per cent of municipals have been affected now, as compared with about 20 per cent in the earlier depression."[64]

The municipal bond market hit rock bottom in May 1933, but even before then many big cities were in terrible financial trouble. Their plight was dramatized by "a Detroit-sponsored bill in the House of Representatives which would have given the courts the power to delay municipal debt payments up to ten years." The bill was defeated, and many cities to keep financially afloat had to use methods that qualify as technical defaults (such as using sinking fund monies to pay current operating expenses).[65]

Their financial situation was made especially difficult because relief expenditures were the responsibility of the cities rather than of the states and state governments did very little to assist city governments financially, in spite of increasing state revenue through new taxes (sales taxes in particular). In some industrial states, therefore, state government bonds sold while offering low interest rates, whereas large cities in those same states found it almost impossible to find buyers for their bonds regardless of how high an interest rate they offered.[66]

Bonds issued by cities in 1933 fared differently depending on the borrowing government's "outstanding debt, tax base, business conditions, social harmony, and administrative skill." At the end of 1933, New York State was paying 3.30 percent on its bonds, whereas Binghamton was paying 3.85 percent, Buffalo 4.2 percent, New York City 5.73 percent, and Mamaroneck 7.50 percent.[67]

Detroit was the most hard-pressed. Half its revenues were allocated to debt service in the 1933–1934 budget but it was unable to meet interest payments on February 1933. Detroit's default symbolized the plight of many cities. Cook County, Cleveland, Mobile, Miami, St. Petersburg, Toledo, and Atlantic City (among others) defaulted, and cities such as New York City (unable to sell bonds for a time) faced tough constraints. Four states had more than fifty defaulting general-purpose governments, and nine states had more than fifty defaulters if special districts are included.[68]

Although Miami's and Detroit's disastrous fiscal and debt woes were in the minority, many big-city mayors felt that something had to be done about the large-scale unemployment that afflicted their residents. Even though they did not undertake the large-scale relief efforts (financed by borrowing) begun by Mayor Frank Murphy in Detroit, they did support federal government intervention to help cities cope with the demands of unemployment. Mayor Murphy called a national conference of mayors in the spring of 1932, which subsequently convened in June. The conference "endorsed resolutions . . . requesting $5 billions in federal works expenditures, a national relief program big enough to 'satisfy all needs', and federal loans to municipalities to enable them to refund their maturing obligations."[69]

The Federal Response

The federal government's response to the problems of unemployment was the Emergency Relief and Construction Act, signed by President Hoover on July 21, 1932. The mayors received far less than they wanted. The act did take the Reconstruction Finance Corporation (RFC) into the business of helping state and local governments. States were to receive $300 million in relief loans from the RFC (which were never repaid), and $1.5 billion were to be lent by the RFC only for public works that would pay for themselves through user fees.[70] The act did not address municipal debts at all.

The emphasis on self-liquidating projects was viewed as a setback by the mayors who had conceived of public works monies as primarily concerned with relieving unemployment. Hoover, however, divided public works into those that were productive (that is, self-supporting) and those that were unproductive (that is, not self-supporting). He was vehemently opposed to federal financing of unproductive works, arguing that the jobs they created were not worth the cost.[71]

The provision for loans for self-liquidating public works set off an explosion of requests. A Self-Liquidating Division was established within the RFC and quickly found itself overwhelmed. However, spending for the kind of infrastructure that generated revenue cannot be turned on like a faucet, as the RFC quickly found out:

> time-consuming delays were inherent in the self-liquidating approach. Projects capable of producing a revenue involved complex planning. Bridges, toll roads, hydroelectric plants, electric power distribution lines, slum clearance and low-income housing, and urban sewer systems required detailed engineering studies before actual construction could begin.[72]

The kinds of bonds that the RFC accepted included general-obligation bonds, if the projects funded by such bonds charged user fees; special-obligation and general-obligation bonds, which relied primarily on user charges but which backed up these fees with the power of taxation; and revenue bonds. Roughly one-third of the loans made by the RFC involved revenue bonds. The division had actually spent only $20 million when Roosevelt became president in March 1933. Overall, the program was viewed as ineffective, both because projects had to be self-liquidating and because the RFC charged interest rates close to those of the market.[73]

Roosevelt, who emphasized public works expenditures in his recovery program as a way of addressing unemployment, transferred the responsibility for these revenue-producing public works to the Public Works Administration (PWA), officially known as the Federal Emergency Administration of Public Works, which became effective on June 26, 1933. Roosevelt seems to have been particularly struck by the possibility of civil disorder in Chicago, a city whose fiscal problems were widely acknowledged to be caused by mismanagement and corruption. (Detroit's problems, in contrast, were largely due to its attempts to address the needs of the unemployed.) Mark Gelfand argues: "it was Chicago's wretched condition that broke the back of conservative opposition to federal aid in the summer of 1932." Roosevelt therefore began what was to become a series of programs dealing with relief for the unemployed, most of which involved direct grants rather than loans.[74]

Further, the National Industrial Recovery Act, which effected the transfer, eliminated the requirement that projects be self-supporting, provided grants to complement loans (grants ranged from 30 to 45 percent of the cost of a project), lowered interest costs, and relaxed the requirements needed to qualify for a loan.[75]

The PWA lent funds to local governments by buying their bonds, selling them to the RFC, and using the funds from the RFC to make new loans. According to Olson, Harold Ickes, Secretary of the Interior and responsible for the PWA,

> worried about the liquidity of the bonds [the PWA] acquired from local governments. . . . The last thing Ickes wanted was for the PWA to become saddled with a huge volume of unmarketable assets. He complained to the president about the problem, and Roosevelt had the RFC assist the PWA by purchasing the bonds it accepted from local political agencies. By 1936 the RFC had purchased $700 million in PWA bonds.[76]

Since many projects funded by the PWA were federal, the PWA loaned only about $434 million to state and local governments out of the $2 billion originally allocated it under the National Industrial Recovery Act. Later, as grants became more important and as its interest rates were relatively high, its importance as a lender diminished even further.[77]

The PWA's attractiveness as a lender from a mayor's point of view was severely tarnished by the interest charges it imposed on all loans. In fact, the interest rate charged by the PWA was a source of constant tension between the PWA and city mayors. The PWA charged 4 percent interest, roughly the market rate. Mayors were infuriated by the idea of paying market rates when they were already facing extraordinary financial troubles. They made their views known, but to no avail.

In 1934, "the mayors demanded that the Federal Government supply money at no charge or at most, at the rate of ⅛ per cent."[78] Although Roosevelt agreed to increase the ratio of grant to loan monies, he listened to Secretary of the Treasury Henry Morgenthau's counter-arguments and kept the interest rate at 4 percent. And there it stayed, even though it meant that some PWA monies available for lending to local governments were never borrowed.

Revenue Bonds

Although the PWA was not required to lend only to self-liquidating projects, it nonetheless lent a great deal of its money for precisely such projects. The PWA strongly encouraged the use of revenue bonds: revenue bonds made up roughly 40 percent of all the municipal bonds bought by the PWA. As of August 1937, the PWA had bought 1,494 general obligation bonds worth $225.3 million and 1,051 revenue bonds worth $166 million.[79] Although most revenue bonds were issued by general-purpose municipalities, the actual dollar amounts of revenue bonds issued by districts or authorities was larger.[80]

PWA officials liked the revenue bond for the same reason local officials did: loans incurred through its usage did not count as debt, and its usage thus circumvented debt limits. The PWA quickly found that many local governments could not borrow from the federal government using general-obligation bonds because they had already reached their debt limits. Frequently, "municipalities had no power to issue bonds without concurrently levying a tax for their payment." In the case of Georgia, neither the state nor its municipalities were able to take advantage of the PWA programs because of the extreme restrictiveness of its debt limits.[81]

The PWA, therefore, encouraged states to pass legislation that authorized the issuance of revenue bonds. Whereas in 1931 only fifteen or sixteen states had laws permitting revenue bond issuance, by 1936 forty states had laws that allowed local general-purpose government to issue revenue bonds. In 1937, Fowler finds that "sixteen states passed laws authorizing the financing of water services, sewage systems, electric plants, airports, levees, docks, river terminals or toll bridges by revenue bonds."[82] Some states passed laws that authorized their use for a wide variety of purposes. In some states, courts that had previously applied the restricted special fund doctrine began to loosen their interpretation of what did and did not constitute debt. By 1937, revenue bonds had been used to fund a wide variety of functions, including a health resort, a hygienic laboratory, tunnels, sanitariums, ferries, armories, and parking facilities.[83]

By 1937, state and local governments owed approximately $19 billion, of which $1 billion was in revenue bonds. Roughly a quarter of that billion was owed by general-purpose local governments, while roughly a half was owed by specialized agencies/authorities. Regional variations emerged. In the South and West, general-purpose governments tended to use revenue bonds for "domestic services" (that is, water, electricity, gas, and sewage disposal). In the Northeast, revenue bonds tended to be used by authorities responsible for bridges and tunnels. The lack of use of revenue bonds for domestic services in the Northeast is striking. Fowler found that, "in the entire group of northern Atlantic states, the only important issue of revenue bonds for domestic services has been that of the Buffalo Sewer Authority."[84]

The PWA was undoubtedly a major stimulus in the adoption of the revenue bond by local officials. Its officials, for example, personally helped state legislators draft legislation that facilitated the use of revenue bonds. Writing in 1935, the director of the PWA's Legal Division concluded:

> The broadened field of social service that the modern municipality will accord to citizens will be due, in no small measure, to the use of devices like revenue bonds, the sustained development of which will be traceable to the present period. In the past two or three years, greater strides have been made than ever before in the law relating to financing public improvements through the issuance of revenue obligations.[85]

The encouragement of the revenue bond instrument was to be one of the most important (often ignored) long-term impacts with which the PWA can be credited. Its grants-in-aid have rightly received more attention than its loans, for the latter were less important than the monies given as grants. However, the loans did encourage the use of a debt instrument that was still considered unorthodox in many parts of the country and that even investment bankers did not always understand. By 1940, the revenue bond was much more widely known, accepted, and understood. That may well be the strongest legacy of the PWA as lender.

Conclusion

The development of the revenue bond — legitimated by the courts — allowed debt to be shaped and used in ways very different from those that had characterized the general-obligation bond. Debt became more malleable as it became distanced from taxes. It also became more divorced from the electorate. It could be defined and redefined so as to increase the discretion of local government and increase the aggregate amounts of borrowing. Such redefinition gradually created an institutional world responsible for capital investment, which looks significantly different from its counterpart responsible for expenditures financed by taxes.

The revenue bond helped compartmentalize those services paid for by taxes from those services paid for by user fees. Capital-intensive services became different from social services or police services, for example. They were financed by user fees, which became an invisible part of the governmental landscape so that most studies of local finance focus simply on tax burdens and revenue and pay little heed to the fee structure of those services financed by revenue bonds.

The federal government encouraged the use of the revenue bond so as to circumvent state debt restrictions. But the government went further. It also encouraged the creation of a new governmental body that could also evade those same state limits. The federal government, in fact, facilitated the development of two complementary strategies that allowed local governments to expand their investment activities in spite of the states' desire to limit such activities. It is to the second of these two strategies — the creation of the public authority — that we now turn.

Chapter 7

Circumvention by Law

and Government

Circumventing state limits, however, required more than the development of the revenue bond. It also required the construction of a new governmental entity. Whereas the special district had been a nineteenth-century mechanism for evading state debt limits, the public authority was to prove to be a favorite of the twentieth century. The debt restrictions that state governments had placed on municipal governments could be evaded by creating self-financing special-purpose governments whose debt was treated differently from the debt incurred by general-purpose governments. The creation of such governments was a critical part of the two-pronged strategy that made up the intergovernmental politics of circumvention.

The revenue bond provided one instrument to use to escape from debt limits, and the creation of a new governmental unit — the public authority — constituted a second instrument. The two instruments — the authority and the revenue bond — were to have a symbiotic relationship. In Robert Smith's words, "basic to any definition of a public authority is its reliance on the revenue-bond method of finance."[1] The authority is inseparable from the revenue bond. Whereas many general-purpose governments now can issue both general-obligation and revenue bonds, authorities typically can only issue revenue bonds. The Council of State Governments, in one of the earliest studies of authorities, defined authorities in relation to revenue bonds and chose two characteristics as defining an authority:

First is the power to issue revenue bonds, payable solely from charges against consumer use of the agency's facilities, and the lack of dependence on taxes or power to levy them. . . . The second criterion is that the reliance on revenue bonds, not taxes, is a *basic pattern* of the agency in question, not a characteristic only of certain of its secondary activities. Many departments and agencies have revenue bonding powers for specific aspects of their central function. Agencies whose *primary* responsibility is the administration of a regulatory activity or a tax-supported service, and which are only incidentally concerned with revenue bonds and user charges, are not regarded as Authorities for purposes of this study.[2]

The revenue bond and the authority, typically joined together, enabled state and municipal governments to borrow in spite of debt limits, referenda requirements, and the other restrictions on the issuance of general-obligation bonds that were imposed by states in the late nineteenth century. Many general-purpose governments now also have the right to issue revenue bonds, and in many cases issuing such bonds for self-financing projects does not increase the government's legal debt burden.[3] Therefore, the use of the revenue bond is probably a more important component of the current strategy of circumvention than is the creation of public authorities. In the period when state law limited municipal debt more stringently than it does now, however, the creation of authorities was an essential factor in the circumvention of such limits.

Many general-purpose governments, even after being empowered to issue revenue bonds without incurring a debt as legally defined, have chosen to create authorities to issue revenue bonds instead. The causes of such a choice have scarcely been researched. However, in at least some cases, the issuance of revenue bonds by municipal governments is more burdensome than their issuance by authorities. (Interest rate limits may be placed on a municipality's revenue bonds but not on an authority's, for example.) Furthermore, their issuance by an authority may make the project more defensible legally. The rating agencies may also count a municipality's revenue-bond debt as contributing to the debt burden even if such debt is not a legal debt. And finally, authorities are also thought to be more "businesslike" and "efficient," an argument that would make them attractive even when not absolutely necessary.[4]

Because they allowed so much flexibility in the area of finance, one observer, Harry B. Strickland, identified revenue-bond authorities as "a lazy official's approach to the problem of government." George Sause and

Andrew Bullis, in comparing municipalities with authorities, also noted the latter's flexibility: "an Authority is restricted as to the functions it may perform and is relatively free as to the methods it may use. A municipality, on the other hand, is relatively free with regard to services rendered but it is restricted as to the methods employed."[5]

The prototypical authority is a semi-independent single-purpose functional agency with corporate status; a board that is appointed rather than elected; the power to issue revenue bonds; and a budget that relies on revenues in the form of user fees from its projects rather than on taxes. Its inability to tax makes it dependent on self-financing projects and the authority is thus typically found in those functional areas characterized by the construction of physical facilities or by the lending of funds, which are then repaid by the borrower. There are now so many public authorities that they

> touch the lives of millions of Americans. They may provide the electricity and the water that produces the morning coffee. They may have subsidized the mortgage on the family home, built the airport the family flies from, financed the office park where the parents work and the campus dormitories where the children study. They finance hospitals, nursing homes, apartment buildings. They run race tracks, ports, turnpikes, bridges, tunnels, subways, buses, public beaches, sports stadiums. Only the rare American can make it through a day without encountering the work of some public authority.

It is not surprising, then, that when Atlanta was selected as the site of the 1996 Summer Olympics, the state legislature promptly formed the Metropolitan Atlanta Olympic Games Authority to raise funds and supervise the construction needed for the Games.[6]

Given their importance to the provision of capital-intensive and credit-based services at the state and local level, authorities have been surprisingly little studied. In particular, we have few histories detailing why specific authorities were originally created or analyzing the political calculations and conflicts involved. The politics of authority creation is an area waiting to be explored. The Committee on Home Rule and Local Government of the 1938 Constitutional Convention in New York pointed out that, in Edelstein's words, "authorities . . . have come into being with comparatively little of the excitement usually attending the creation of any additional governmental unit, much less the creation of a new kind of governmental unit." The lack of public notice of authority creation helps explain why scholars have not pursued its study.[7]

Historians have ignored the authority, and so have political scientists, in the most part. The authority as an actor is sometimes included in studies of urban politics and of selected developmental policies such as urban renewal and transportation.[8] However, it is far from becoming an integral part of political scientists' mental map of subnational government or of the American federal system. Whereas many studies do not mention authorities except in passing or as one actor among many, those that put the spotlight on these special-purpose governments tend to view them as akin to an "underground government."[9]

Authorities elicit divided judgments even from specialists. For example, Jameson Doig's study of transportation politics in the New York region found that "opinion is probably more sharply divided on the impact of the authority than on the role of any other government institution in the metropolis."[10] The same characteristics — financial independence, insulation from a wide array of constituencies, a narrow functional focus, distance from elected officials, a dependence on user fees rather than on taxes, and an administrative structure devoid of many of the regulations and restrictions applicable to state and local line agencies — are viewed by supporters as allowing the authority to function effectively, flexibly, and quickly, while being identified by critics as leading to a lack of accountability and oversight that encourages corruption, anti-democratic tendencies, and the evasion of constitutional and statutory limits applicable to general-purpose governments.

To their supporters, public authorities represent competence, professionalism, and the ability to get things done, across municipal, county, or state jurisdictions when necessary. The multi-county authority seems to be an important new variant of authorities in metropolitan areas. It may be particularly important in the area of transportation. Such authorities combine the use of user fees and taxation. For example, the Regional Transportation Authority in Illinois provides public transportation for six counties in northeastern Illinois and, since 1983, has been able to levy a sales tax (higher in Cook County than in the other five) and to issue revenue bonds.[11]

During the state's 1938 constitutional convention, former governor of New York Alfred Smith referred to authorities as "the one method we have discovered of getting work done expeditiously and without overtaxing our people to get it done." One of the governor's adversaries at that same convention argued that most authorities "were established simply to evade limitations imposed in the Constitution."[12]

Other critics point to the semi-independence of authorities from their parent governments and worry about authorities' financial independence, their lack of accountability, and the loss of electoral control over authority operations. Many critics worry that the operations of the authority, narrowly defined as they are, drive the decisions of general-purpose governments in directions they might otherwise not take. Jerome Shestack gave the following example:

> A few years ago the parking authority of a large eastern city selected a particular area for construction of a parking garage. Plans were prepared for submission to the city's planning commission. . . . The commission's ideas for that area were hardly in a formative stage. . . . But now the planning commission was faced with the necessity of an immediate decision. In dealing with regular city departments, this commission had the assurance that its decisions would be enforced by the city's chief executive. But dealing with an independent public body was a different matter. The authority considered itself on an equal governmental level. With due subtlety the authority indicated that if the commission's decision was delayed or unfavorable, the commission faced a battle with the authority. . . . Had the planning commission resisted . . . it would have been a rare act indeed. The garage was authorized. A few years later, when it was too late, the garage proved to be an obstacle rather than an aid to the solution of the city's problems.

Many critics would agree with the thrust of William Quirk and Leon Wein's conclusion that "authorities are created only for antidemocratic purposes — the evasion of rules that apply to government itself."[13]

Robert Moses — whom Robert Caro calls "America's greatest builder" — is undoubtedly the best-known person associated with the public authority. Moses, as the architect of numerous New York City authorities, has come to personify the entrepreneurial quality often attributed to public authorities. His enormous influence has sometimes also been projected onto the public authority as a form of government. In Robert Caro's words:

> Moses was able to shape a city and to build an empire because [his] supple mind . . . had focused on the possibilities of an institution still in its infancy as an urban force when he came to it in 1934: the public authority. [It] became the force through which he shaped New York and its suburbs in the image he personally conceived.

As Michael Danielson and Jameson Doig rightly point out, Caro underestimates the demographic and economic forces that shaped New York City, its suburbs, and cities and suburbs all across the United States. Although Danielson and Doig have a more measured view of the influence of both Moses and the authority, they do conclude that "the independent authority structure, and the motivations of its leaders, were crucial to the timing of development in the New York region."[14]

Authorities exercised such power in the New York region because they share an important power with general-purpose governments — the right of eminent domain. In some cases, redevelopment authorities may even have stronger powers of eminent domain than their parent governments. That right gives them the power to acquire land for their various capital-intensive projects in areas such as transportation, housing, urban redevelopment, or environmental protection. In this respect they differ from many nonprofit corporations, which resemble authorities in some respects but typically are unable to exercise the right of eminent domain.[15]

Authorities now are usually permanent structures in the public sector. But they were not originally conceived as such. Robert Moses' first authorities were originally structured so that they would go out of existence once the bonds that financed each authority's single project had been retired. In that sense, they resembled all the other authorities in the United States (with the Port Authority being an exception). Authorities were originally conceived by both mayors and the state legislators who authorized them as "mere creatures of the sovereign city," with a lifespan limited to that of the bonds that financed them.[16] Their properties, it was assumed, would be turned over to the parent municipal government once the authority was terminated.

Moses' genius lay in realizing that the authority could be far more than a creature of the city, that it could become a separate component of urban government. According to Caro, Moses "had glimpsed in the institution called 'public authority' a potentiality for power whose implications no one else — no one in City Hall or the Albany State-house for certain and, so far as research can determine, no one anywhere in the United States — had noticed."[17] But in order to make the authority a government with its own institutional power, he had to find a way to institutionalize it beyond the life of its founding bond.

Moses solved this problem by slipping permission to refund bonds into amendments to the Triborough Bridge Authority Act. The drafter of the original act, which had required the authority to go out of existence when its original bonds were paid off, explained the significance of refunding:

> "He had figured out a gimmick. . . . [H]e had power to issue forty-year bonds and every thirty-nine years he could call them in and issue new bonds, for another forty years. La Guardia had thought that authorities . . . would be temporary creations that would build something and then turn it over to the city and go out of existence as soon as it was paid off. But with that gimmick in there, it would never be paid off."

Moses needed a gimmick because he faced a political dilemma in obtaining approval for the institutionalization of his authorities, a dilemma illuminating the issue that presumably faces all elected officials when they approve the establishment of an authority:

> [The public officials] who were thinking men would realize that if they gave it [their approval] they would be adding, without sufficient thought and consideration[,] . . . a whole new layer to urban government in America. The rest of them, concerned with power and patronage, would realize that to the extent they gave away power, they would be diminishing their own power.[18]

Although we do not know what political stratagems other authorities used to extend their lives politically, by 1962 authorities in Pennsylvania, for example, had the right to issue new bonds "as the need for improvements and additions to projects arises."[19]

Although authorities are similar to general-purpose governments in many of their powers (taxation being the key exception), they operate in a way very different from general-purpose governments. Given their narrow functional perspective, leaders of authorities do not confront the array of conflicting constituency pressures that elected officials do. Their processes of decision making are also different. Authorities' financial independence allows them to escape from the budgetary politics and the attention to legislative desires that continually confront line agencies. They operate outside many of the political and administrative routines typically associated with the public sector. Danielson and Doig's analysis of functional agencies is accurate with particular force for public authorities:

> the activities of functional agencies tend to be characterized by narrowly focused rationality rather than responsiveness to a broad range of constituency interests. While the general political leadership of the . . . city, a state, or the nation must be sensitive to a wide variety of demands, the program

agency enjoys a substantial degree of isolation from these pressures. Statutory and financial insulation are joined with skilled leadership and specific yardsticks of success to permit the functional organization to calculate its future goals and current strategies more clearly, and with greater likelihood of success than is true for hard-pressed mayors, governors, or members of Congress.[20]

The authorities' detachment from the normal political processes helps explain why they have been overlooked by analysts. Their operations are rarely "politicized," that is, angry citizens may make speeches at the city council meeting but only infrequently would they even know of an authority's existence. Authorities have tended to become embroiled in controversy when the values of development that many of them embody have come into conflict either with environmental groups or with groups of citizens who will be displaced by the authority's activities. Danielson and Doig point out that authorities are vulnerable to challenge once new and hostile constituencies become involved in the politics of the functional area concerned. The demands of new constituencies can change the intergovernmental dynamic within the sector. In the area of transportation, "the rise of the environmentalists and the new power of other anti-highway forces meant that state leaders could act — indeed had to act — to undermine the influence of public works alliances that earlier governors had helped to build and to insulate from direct public accountability."[21]

One reason why scholars interested in urban pro-growth coalitions have included authorities in their analyses is because of the enormous controversy engendered by urban renewal projects, typically carried out by urban redevelopment authorities. Such authorities were at the center of a great deal of the political conflict in cities during the 1960s and 1970s.[22] Typically, however, authorities can operate for decades with very little controversy surrounding them. Financing authorities that issue the bonds discussed in the next chapter (rather than build sewers or tunnels) are almost never visible to the public.

Walsh notes that authorities do not typically operate under the same constraints as general-purpose governments. Their corporate status insulates them from much of the conflict to which local officials in general-purpose governments are subject. In her words, "the corporate form of public authorities permits jobs to be done and projects to be completed without the clamorous debates, recurring compromises, and delaying checks and counterchecks that characterize the rest of American government."[23]

The structure of authorities is not accidental. That structure is strongly shaped by the reason they were created in the first place. In many instances, authorities were established in order to help state and local officials evade the debt restrictions discussed in chapter 5. In this chapter I first discuss the problems of analyzing authorities and then go into the historical reasons for their creation and widespread adoption. I argue that the creation of the authority was the second prong of a strategy of circumvention that developed in order to evade the restrictions on state borrowing imposed in the late nineteenth century. This two-pronged strategy laid the foundations for a new round of subnational entrepreneurialism in the period 1960–1987 (as we shall see in chapters 8 and 9).

Identifying Public Authorities

Authorities do not constitute part of the apparatus of municipal or state government as traditionally defined; they are different from the agencies that make up municipal, county, or state government. They do not, for example, typically need to follow civil service regulations in the hiring of their personnel. Above all, however, authorities do not depend on tax revenue. They are typically financially self-contained and independent because they depend on ratepayers and user fees rather than on taxpayers. In her seminal study, Annmarie Hauck Walsh concluded:

> A distinguishing feature of public authorities . . . is that they raise capital from private investors through the money and capital markets to invest in public facilities and services. . . . These corporations engage in activities that produce revenues. . . . Public authorities do not levy taxes but retain their own earnings, borrow funds for investment by issuing . . . long-term bonds, and receive government loans and grants. These ways of getting and spending financial resources make public authorities distinctly different from normal government agencies, which must request funds from annual government budgets.[24]

Having said that, however, we cannot identify the number of authorities currently existing in the United States. To put it simply, no one keeps track. The exact number of public authorities that are primarily reliant on revenue-bond financing (and thus are of interest in this study) is simply currently unknown. Walsh found that "none of the available sources of nationwide data precisely defines public authorities . . . or provides counts of them." For his part, Jerry Mitchell concludes that

> The number of public authorities in the United States has been difficult to estimate. . . . State and local governments do not compile inclusive rosters of authorities. There are few state or local agencies required to regulate authorities or to keep up-to-date records about their operations. Many large authorities are often not listed in annual guides to state and local officials. Even phone companies neglect to list authorities in the governmental pages of their telephone books. . . . Most important, the United States Census Bureau — the source of government statistics — fails to separate public authorities from special districts.

And Dennis Zimmerman writes: "So who are the organizations that issue the revenue bonds? The answer is that they are an unknown number of authorities."[25]

The exact legal status of many special-purpose governments is extraordinarily complex and the given name of a body does not necessarily clarify its actual status. Bodies that we would consider a public authority for analytic purposes in this study — that is, they have a separate corporate status, are governed by an appointed board, rely primarily on revenue-bond financing and user fees, and can borrow without holding a referendum — could be referred to as "special municipal corporations, special districts, public authorities, public corporations, commissions, boards, and the like."[26] The Pennsylvania Turnpike Commission, for example, would be classified as an authority but yet does not include "authority" in its title. Estimates of the number of state and local authorities range from six to seven thousand.[27] Some states rely far more heavily than others on authorities, but, given the degree of uncertainty in this area, no definitive list is available.

The actual finances of many authorities are intricate and rely on a combination of revenues. For our purposes, however, it is sufficient to make a basic distinction between governments that rely on their full faith and credit and on their taxing power for their financial status, on the one hand, and those that rely on revenue bonds and non-tax revenue for their financial health on the other. General-purpose governments and many special districts fall into the first category whereas authorities fall into the second.

In general, a special district refers to a local government that often charges fees, may levy property taxes, and is generally governed by an elected (rather than appointed) board.[28] Such governments typically have the right to issue general-obligation bonds (and may have the right to issue revenue bonds) but may not be subject to the same debt limits as municipal governments. In the case of bond referenda, for example, a special district may need to obtain a simple majority whereas the municipal government may need to obtain approval from two-thirds of the electorate.[29]

Public authorities, by contrast, are primarily dependent on revenues from their projects rather than taxes and therefore rely on revenue-bond financing. They are typically not governed by a directly elected board although their board may well include elected officials from other jurisdictions. They are therefore considered semi-independent, with a lower degree of autonomy from other governments than that characteristic of special districts. Their debt does not qualify as such under debt-limitation laws. Given their lack of taxing power, authorities raise funds in capital market only by issuing revenue bonds. Some authorities need to have the issuance of their bonds approved by, say, the city council. Most, however, do not need any approval for such issuance.[30] They do not need electoral approval of their borrowing.

Since many local governments that are primarily reliant on revenue-bond financing now also have some authority to tax, the term *authority-district* is also found. Robert G. Smith uses this term, arguing that those governments categorized by the Bureau of the Census as special districts are, in fact, three kinds of special-purpose governments — special districts, public authorities, and authority-districts. Smith suggests that

the differentiation among the three categories, regardless of what they are called, be thought of as the financial sources of income for their capital and operational needs, which has determined their degree of independence. The special district is understood to be a unit of government, operating outside the normal scope of conventional government, to accomplish a single function, or closely related functions, relying primarily on a special tax levy, often on property. The public authority, again is a special purpose government, but differs from the special district in that it must finance itself without taxation, which it does primarily by the issuance of revenue bonds ... , in its own name, usually without the support of the "full faith and credit" of any general-purpose government. The authority-district is the newest type of ad hoc government ... to appear in metropolitan centers of America. It combines certain features of the special district and the special public authority. The authority-district . . . relies, where possible, on the collection of user charges, but in order to incorporate deficit modes with profitable ones, the powers of the authority-district extend as well to the use of special means of taxation.[31]

For the sake of clarity, however, this chapter will use the term *public authority* for those units that are primarily reliant on revenue-bond financing and user fees (including those that do rely to some extent on taxation) and whose borrowing is not subject to approval by referendum.

The Creation of Authorities

The public authority as a governmental form has been used for a variety of reasons. State courts have ruled that its debt does not constitute "debt" as legally defined. Its resemblance to a business has intrinsic attractiveness to Americans who often feel that such a structure will be more insulated from politics and freer from red tape than general-purpose governments. Its reliance on the revenue bond, its self-financing nature, and its appointed rather than elected board reinforce its image as a business rather than a government.[32] Finally, it is able to cut across jurisdictional lines so that authorities may have jurisdiction in their functional area over a territory otherwise governed by a number of municipalities.[33] Some authorities are created by a number of governments. Port and transportation authorities are particularly important examples of regional authorities.

Many analysts have been puzzled by the unwillingness of municipalities to issue revenue bonds, even when they were empowered to do so without adding to their debt as legally defined. Why do elected officials prefer to establish an authority to issue revenue bonds rather than doing it themselves? It has been argued that the image of the authority as an efficient organization, run like a business and detached from politics, helps explain why municipal officials made such a choice; the uncertainty with which municipal revenue bond borrowing was treated by the state courts is another reason. The influence of attorneys and investment banks who stand to profit more from a permanent authority than from a single issue of a revenue bond has also been suggested.

It is probably an underlying political reason, however, that also makes the authority attractive, a reason that harks back to our discussion in the last chapter about transforming taxpayers into ratepayers. It is easier to do this if elected officials distance themselves. There is likely to be less resistance to transforming a service once funded by general taxes into a service funded by users if the municipal government is not directly involved. Elected officials can then argue that they cannot control the rate hikes and other economic measures necessary to making a service self-financing:

> The direct imposition of user charges by State and local governments is not likely to be as well received as is the indirect imposition by a public authority. For a long period of time the concept of paying for all government services and improvements from general tax revenues was so well advocated and so widely practiced that general charges for particular services are not likely to be well received when imposed by local government or even by the State itself. This is especially true when user charges are to be imposed for traditional services which have been paid for previously out of general revenues.[34]

This dynamic was played out after Pittsburgh created a Water and Sewer Authority in 1984 to finance a major capital improvement program. Although water users had to pay a fee for use when water provision was a city responsibility, the authority raised user fees dramatically. The authority raised fees by 14 percent in May 1984, by 4 percent in August 1985, by 14 percent in January 1986, by 19 percent in January 1987, and by 18 percent in January 1988. In February 1987, a city councilman railed against what he termed "outrageous water tax increases." He stated: "The mayor brags, 'No tax increases in the last two years.' What the hell does he call water tax increases?" The councilman argued that his own quarterly water bill had "risen from $14 to $20 two years ago to nearly $75."[35]

Whereas a political logic may underlay the creation of an authority, its very structure, once chosen, is likely to channel and screen the political pressures that will be successfully brought to bear on the authority as well as to shape the authority's definition of its mission. The structure of an authority determines to a great extent who will be heard and what functions the authority will think of as legitimately its own. The issues presented by the design of structure were illuminated by the conflict over the purpose and governance structure of a proposed new authority for the expanded Greater Pittsburgh International Airport. When the airport's capacity was to be expanded by building a new terminal, the question arose how to cope with the economic growth (involving primarily four towns) that was expected to occur in the area around the airport.

Consultants recommended that an authority (the Greater Pittsburgh International Airport Area Development Authority) be created to "market county and private land, coordinate activities with the four towns and act as a 'one-stop shop' for developers seeking information and assistance." Since the county was responsible for the airport, the county commissioners would have to decide whether to establish such an authority. However, Tom Foerster — the key commissioner — argued that an existing county authority would be preferable to the creation of an authority with more limited jurisdiction: "There's a lot to be said in using an existing county authority, because benefits would be derived all over the county. I want to make sure every citizen in the county benefits from the airport." Opposed to such a view was the executive director of the Airport Area Chamber of Commerce. In her view, "If there is one authority for all of Allegheny County, I'm not sure it will be able to give that much attention to our own area."[36]

The differences in the recommended structure of the board of the authority said much about the different conceptions of the new authority's proper role. The consultants' report recommended that the eleven-member board should "include representatives from the four towns, the Airport Area Chamber of Commerce and high-profile business, professional, university and airport area leaders. The study does not call for the city of Pittsburgh to be represented."[37] County Commissioner Foerster, on the other hand, argued that if a new authority was in fact created, the city and the Mon Valley (an area devastated by the dramatic decline of the steel industry in the Pittsburgh region) should be represented. The city government (backed by neighborhood leaders) as well as representatives of the Mon Valley viewed representation on the board as allowing them to influence the authority's decisions so as to benefit their respective areas. The consultants' report, on the other hand, considered the airport's impact to be of concern to the governments of the areas directly affected by growth as well to the region's private/nonprofit sector, but to be of no concern to the governments in the region whose territory lay outside the airport area. If the city and the Mon Valley gained representation, there was at least the possibility that the authority would be sensitive to its role in the regional economy; if they did not, the authority was likely to define its mission in ways that might only incidentally benefit the city (its neighborhoods especially) and the Mon Valley.

The Authority as Different

Whereas the special district, with its elected board and acceptance of taxation, has not been viewed as a fundamentally different type of local government from that embodied by general-purpose governments, authorities have been viewed as quintessentially different. In Smith's words, special districts "do not disturb the democratic pattern of local government." By contrast, the public authority in the 1930s represented "an entirely new frame of reference for special government." In Smith's analysis:

> The . . . public authority lacked all the normal assurances of governments: it could not rely on property taxation; it was not governed by a group of persons elected within its fixed-boundary jurisdiction by citizens living therein; it could not borrow money by pledging the value of the property within its area; and it could take on only selected functions each of which would have to return a surplus to be paid by those persons who were to use its facilities. Nothing like this form of government had been known in America. It clashed with the traditional concepts of fixed boundaries, real-property assessments and tax collections, [and] elected representatives selected by the residents.[38]

Public authorities are different because they are designed to reconcile public power with the power of the capital market. They attempt to harness the logic of investment for the fulfillment of public purposes. The revenue bond, as interpreted by state courts, represents the bridge between these two types of power. And tax exemption is the underpinning of that bridge. The triangular relationship between the revenue bond, the public authority, and tax exemption was to represent an important component of both infrastructure provision and economic development in the postwar period.

The role the authority came to play in American politics and policy is rooted in its historical development. Its role is particularly tied to the reason the authority was adopted so quickly across the country. The birth of the public authority was linked to (1) the limits imposed by states on the incurring of general-obligation debt and (2) the federal government's encouragement of the authority and the revenue bond as two mechanisms of circumventing such debt, so that federal monies could be sent to help state and local governments during the Depression.

Debt Limits

Authorities are widely viewed as having been created to evade debt limits and other types of restrictions (such as the need for voter approval) that were imposed on the incurring of debt backed by the issuing government's full faith and credit.[39] (The Port Authority of New York was an exception.) Of particular significance has been their insulation from the bond referendum. Municipal governments, by contrast, have had to submit their plans to borrow to the voters for scrutiny:

> American local governments are generally required to submit general obligation bonds . . . to the voters for their approval. In many cities, a two-thirds majority is necessary for passage. . . . The impact of such a ⅔ requirement can be rather heavy: in San Francisco, for example, of bond propositions presented since 1944, 89 percent have received a majority vote, 74 percent have garnered a 60 percent vote of acceptance, but only 54 percent have received the necessary two-thirds majority vote.[40]

Debt limits had initially been evaded by the creation of special districts, many of which had the power to levy property taxes. Writing in 1936, Foley found that "until the present decade state legislatures hesitated to create new forms of public corporations for public purposes . . . and were content to create special districts. . . . Rarely was one of these districts dependent for its existence solely upon its income-producing ability." Foley mentioned the case of Cook County, which had numerous special districts with the right to levy taxes.[41]

Although the special districts did not contribute to their parent government's debt burden, they borrowed too, using their own credit and creating their own debt. Special districts' debt was also limited by state laws but less stringently than municipal debt. Bollens found that districts were infrequently limited as to the amount they could borrow. Rather, their limits had more to do with interest rate limits on the bonds they issued. Typically, when they issued general-obligation bonds, they too needed a two-thirds majority but often a simple majority was all that was required for the issuance of revenue bonds.[42]

The authority, using revenue bonds, could issue debt that was not so legally defined as it relied on user charges. The courts ruled that debt that would not be repaid from taxes did not constitute debt as defined in state limits (see chapter 6). Authorities' ability to borrow without creating debt was so important that early observers termed them "borrowing machines."[43] Their financial attractiveness—coupled with the arguments that they would be more efficient because their corporate status allowed them to be run like a business, with customers who paid for their services—made public authorities an attractive option for officials who were searching for ways to organize the delivery of capital-intensive services.[44]

The general idea of the authority was borrowed from the Port of London Authority, founded in 1908, and was first applied to the Port Authority of New York, established in 1921. The Port Authority was formed by an interstate compact between New York and New Jersey. It financed its own activities and was governed by an appointed board. Although the Port Authority "was the star that the coming galaxy of authorities sought to emulate," the reasons that led to the creation of authorities in the 1930s were rather different from those that had led to the establishment of the Port Authority.[45]

Authorities, initially often established in order to circumvent debt limits, represented circumvention by government rather than by market. Such circumvention was stimulated by the Depression, which forced a reduction in borrowing power due to the lowered assessed valuation of property. Authorities provided local officials with a mechanism that allowed them to borrow in spite of debt limits that prohibited such borrowing.

Circumventing debt restrictions was clearly the primary reason for the creation of public authorities in Pennsylvania, the state that still leads the country in the number of state and local authorities and that served as a pioneer in their use. In 1935, Pennsylvania passed legislation permitting the creation of local authorities (Alabama and South Dakota also passed similar legislation). From 1935 to 1939, 24 local authorities were established, and in the 1940s, 165 were created. Between 1950 and 1959, 1,103 local authorities were incorporated. Municipalities in Pennsylvania were subject to very restrictive debt ceilings in the 1930s. (These limits were eased a great deal in 1972 but Philadelphia's limit was made more stringent than that of other Pennsylvania municipalities.) Although provisions for municipal debt have been modified, the circumvention of debt limits is still given as a reason for the creation of new authorities. The

Pennsylvania Economy League in 1989, for example, concluded that "Philadelphia does use authorities to circumvent debt limits." The League described the city's options regarding debt in the following manner:

> The state constitution limits city tax-supported debt to 13.5 percent of the ten year average of the assessed value of taxable real estate. In FY89, the city's debt limit was $818 million; the amount of net tax-supported debt applicable to this limit was $766 million. Because of the small debt margin allowed by the state constitution, the city has had to resort to lease agreements with the Municipal Authority in order to construct several important projects, including court-mandated expansion of prison facilities and a new detention/court center.

Although Pennsylvania law allowed municipalities to issue revenue bonds, court decisions had been such that the bonds were not marketable (it was not until 1959 that the Pennsylvania Supreme Court in *Beam v. Ephrata Borough* first upheld the right of municipalities to issue revenue bonds that would not count as legally defined debt).[46]

Whereas the issuing of non-debt revenue bonds by municipalities was clouded with legal uncertainty, their issuance by authorities was given judicial blessing. Furthermore, until 1961, the so-called non-debt revenue bonds of municipalities were more restricted by state law than were revenue bonds issued by municipalities. Even after action taken by the 1961 legislature allowed authorities "to issue non-debt revenue bonds with terms and conditions comparable to those of Authority bonds, municipal non-debt revenue bonds . . . could not be issued for as many purposes as Authority bonds."[47]

At the state level, it is not surprising that the state government created authorities. Until 1969, the state itself could typically only borrow through a constitutional amendment. The amendment had to be approved by two successive legislatures and then a referendum had to be held. In the words of the Bureau of Municipal Research of Philadelphia:

> Since the Legislature meets only once in two years, considerable delay is inevitable; moreover, a proposal that is approved by one Legislature may be defeated by the next Legislature or by the voters themselves. In contrast, if the debt is to be created through an authority, the enabling act needs to be passed by only one Legislature, and no proposal has to be submitted to the voters.[48]

The process for changing a city's debt limit can be equally burdensome. In Philadelphia's case, it would "require a change to the state constitution, which would require passage of the amendment by two successive sessions of the legislature and then approval in a statewide referendum."[49] Given the politics of the state legislature, getting the amendment through the legislature would involve so many bargains and negotiations that it is not surprising Philadelphia, and cities in similar positions, would rather use authorities than try to change their limits at the state level.

Given that debt limits for many cities have been eased in the last twenty years or so and that non-debt revenue bonds have become more widely used by municipal government, state restrictions on local debt now are presumably less likely to be the major reason that state or local officials create authorities.[50] It is unclear how uniform the easing of debt limits has been, however. For example, even though debt limits have been eased in Pennsylvania, Philadelphia's have not. Partially due to property assessments that did not reflect increased market values, in 1988, "Philadelphia's debt limit per capita is less than one-third the limit per capita of Pittsburgh, Erie or Allentown."[51]

For its part, the ratings process, in at least selected cases, probably encourages the issuance of revenue bonds by authorities rather than by municipalities, even when municipalities operate under permissive debt limits or when municipalities themselves are able to issue revenue bonds. Ratings are "report cards" used by investors to assess the likelihood that the borrower will repay incurred debt; the lower the rating, the higher the interest rate the borrower must pay to the lender. The two major rating firms — Moody's Investor Service and Standard and Poor's — both examine the burden of all debt incurred by the borrower (whether legally defined as debt or not) in rating any particular bond. Revenue bonds issued by a municipality, therefore, may not count as debt, as defined by state statutes, but would constitute part of the municipality's debt burden as defined by the rating agencies. The rating agencies' position is clearly spelled out in a newsletter published by Moody's:

> There are many ways a municipality has of issuing debt. Some avenues require voter approval, others do not. When an issuer approaches the public markets with a financing instrument — whether it is legally considered debt or not — it is putting its own credit on the line with a promise to repay. The willingness to honor that commitment is a key factor in the rating evaluation

and in the investment community's comfort with investing in similar projects or other projects of the same issuer — no matter what the instrument securing the obligation.[52]

Although debt limits have declined in importance, they have played a key role in encouraging the formation of public authorities in the past. They affected the creation of authorities directly, as in the case of Pennsylvania. Furthermore, they affected such creation somewhat more indirectly. Debt restrictions caused the federal government to encourage state and local governments to establish authorities and use revenue bonds in order to qualify for federal funds flowing from the New Deal. Franklin Delano Roosevelt needed debt limits to be circumvented in order to deliver aid to nearly bankrupt states and cities. It is to an analysis of the intersection between state debt limits and the New Deal that we now turn.

The Federal Role

The federal government became a major player on the American political scene when authorities were still relatively new. Its role was critical in encouraging state legislatures and governors to adopt this new form of special-purpose government. Yet, while it was encouraging authorities, it was also challenging the idea of tax exemption for municipal bonds. It is fitting, perhaps, that one of the key leaders of the opposition to that proposal was to become the head of the first American authority. The very institution that provided a model for the New Deal's reshaping of local government was to play a significant role in defeating a proposal that would have devastated the foundation stone of the authority's power in the postwar period.

The Federal Encouragement of Authorities

Washington, D.C., encouraged the creation of authorities to such an extent during the Depression that they were sometimes referred to as "depression babies."[53] As president, Roosevelt drew on the experience with authorities that he had gained as governor of New York and turned to the public corporation as an instrument of governmental intervention. In 1933 he asked Congress to establish the Tennessee Valley Authority, and in December 1934 he wrote to the forty-eight governors asking them to consider the use of public corporations at the state and local levels. According to the Council of State Governments, the letter suggested

> that in formulating programs for the coming legislative sessions they might consider proposing legislation that would enable states and municipalities to participate more fully in federal public works. The President suggested two possible approaches: One was to enact legislation authorizing existing governmental agencies to issue revenue bonds to finance revenue-producing improvements; the other was the adoption of legislation providing for the creation of new public corporations empowered to exercise similar functions.[54]

Roosevelt wanted to engage in capital spending as a way to put people to work. Yet he had found that when loans were offered to local governments, they had to refuse them because of legal barriers to borrowing. In his letter, therefore, Roosevelt strongly urged the governors to circumvent the debt restrictions imposed by their own state laws. (More than twenty years later, Eisenhower was to do the same.) In effect, Roosevelt

> was recommending that the governors use the carrot of federal funds . . . to encourage the state legislatures to create ad hoc agencies to circumvent the normal restrictions that the states had come over the years to impose on borrowing by local governments. . . . The federal government was proposing that the states either overlook their . . . restrictions, or enable the federal government to run around them and work with new special-purpose governments down in the towns and counties that would not be bound by these provisions that apply to the general-purpose governments only.[55]

Roosevelt even offered the governors the assistance of the Legal Divison of the Public Works Administration to help draft the appropriate legislation.

He suggested the public authority as one alternative, while the second involved giving further powers to municipalities. Although many states did give their municipalities more power to incur debt, in general the governors felt that the second alternative would lead to extended conflicts in the state courts. The creation of authorities was relatively quick and easy, and that choice was widely made.[56] (Another reason authorities became more active in issuing revenue bonds even when municipalities were so empowered is that municipal officials have traditionally linked the revenue bond with earmarked taxes, of which they disapprove.)

In the years between 1933 and 1936, nineteen states created authorities, and by 1951 nearly all states had approved legislation authorizing state-level authorities. Local authorities were also authorized in at least half the states. Pennsylvania responded to the call for authorities with particular alacrity: by 1947, it already had sixty-three municipal authorities, and by 1953 that number had grown to three hundred.[57]

The Public Works Administration was very much involved in this proliferation of authorities. After 1935, its legal division "crafted more than five hundred proposals to state legislatures for creating . . . authorities." It was particularly active in the area of housing.[58] Once the courts stopped the PWA from engaging in slum clearance, Washington encouraged the establishment of local housing authorities. Again, its legal division sent governors drafts of laws establishing housing authorities. The U.S. Housing Act of 1937 provided funds to local governments willing to take responsibility for housing. In Bollens's words:

> This congressional action served as a catalytic agent for local housing authorities. Additional states passed laws permitting the creation of authorities; others revised their original acts. . . . In the single year of 1938 the number of local housing authorities quadrupled. . . . Vitalization of a new governmental unit had materialized through the device of financial aid from the national government.[59]

The public housing program established by the Lanham Act during the war encouraged still more authorities, and the Housing Act of 1949 led to another surge in the number of housing authorities.[60] Bonds issued by housing authorities are guaranteed, whereas most others are not. According to Greenberg:

> Public housing authority bonds are used to raise funds for public housing projects and are backed by an agreement between the local housing authority and the Department of Housing and Urban Development (HUD). HUD guarantees unconditionally to lend the local housing authority sufficient funds to pay the principal and interest on the bonds until maturity. Because the federal government has sought to encourage the construction of low income housing projects these bonds are federally guaranteed. These bonds differ from properly termed revenue bonds because debt service is typically dependent on grants from federal, state, and municipal governments.[61]

Later, federal monies stimulated the creation of urban renewal authorities, which eventually became the center of a great deal of political conflict in the 1960s. Mark Gelfand concludes:

The initiative for urban renewal usually rested with business-dominated redevelopment authorities . . . Rarely did the local agencies let the public know what they were doing. They kept the general populace in the dark about their operations for as long as they could, because they feared, as one city official admitted, that the voters "would not like it if they understood it."

This conflict arose because the authorities ignored the relocation requirement approved by Congress. In Gelfand's words: "In case after case, cities filed in Washington the necessary and bulky forms that detailed how they would take care of the unhoused and then went ahead and, as one federal official described it, 'gave the families a few dollars and told them to get lost.' "[62]

The creation of public authorities therefore was much facilitated by the New Deal's desire to spend money on capital projects quickly. The use of federal credit encouraged the use· of the revenue bond (see chapter 6). Similarly, the use of loans made the circumvention of borrowing limits an imperative. Authorities, as governmental institutions that could borrow and not be constrained by the state courts, emerged as an important part of the local government sector.

Federal funds were clearly crucial catalysts to the creation of the early authorities. In New York, for example, eleven state authorities "borrowed money from either the R.F.C. (Reconstruction Finance Corporation), the P.W.A. (Public Works Administration), or both, and seven authorities received P.W.A. grants for public works."[63] Mollenkopf points out:

> Between 1933 and 1939, the PWA spent $4.8 billion building highways, bridges, dams, airports, public buildings, sewer and water projects, and other public works. . . . The PWA made grants and loans to local jurisdictions for large, durable public works built at "prevailing rate" union wages. These included . . . 16,700 state and local projects costing $2.4 billion, representing an unprecedented federal contribution to local infrastructure. . . . The PWA often established these ties by working with a local "authority" which could condemn property, borrow money, and build its own staff while operating beyond the control of local party machines.[64]

Throughout the 1930s and 1940s, federal funds nurtured these new governments with loans and grants. They allowed the national government to pursue its goals by circumventing state controls. Governors and mayors were often eager to do whatever was needed to ensure that desperately needed federal funds and credit were spent in their jurisdictions.

The relationship between federal funds and the public authority as an institution began to change in the 1950s. The turnpike authorities were the first to venture successfully into the capital market to such an extent that federal aid became less important than private capital from investors. Whereas the Pennsylvania Turnpike went into operation in 1937 and began with a federal grant received in 1932 from the RFC, the New Jersey Turnpike Authority, in 1950, borrowed more than half of its capital from private lenders.[65] Subsequently, although federal aid was to remain important for most authorities, bondholders provided the largest part of their capital and the users provided most of their revenue. (Public housing authorities are an exception.) Although many authorities do receive aid from a variety of general-purpose governments, such aid is typically less important than the funds borrowed from the capital market.

Tax Exemption

In April 1938, and again in January 1939, FDR asked Congress for a "short and simple statute" ending the tax exemption that municipal bonds had enjoyed since 1913. His case against the tax exemption was to be repeated in 1986 by the Treasury: the existence of the tax exemption that allows interest to remain untaxed is unfair. In FDR's words: "a fair and effective income tax and a huge perpetual reserve of tax-exempt bonds cannot exist side by side."[66] Furthermore, the Treasury estimated that the elimination of the exemption would yield roughly $150 million for the federal government.

The Conference on State Defense—composed of forty-two state attorneys general—immediately replied that it would oppose the proposal on both economic and constitutional grounds. That group was to lead the fight in Congress against FDR's proposal. The Conference on State Defense had been formed largely under the leadership of Austin Tobin, then the assistant general counsel for the Port of New York Authority.[67] After a special committee had been formed in the Senate, charged with examining the issue of tax exemption, Tobin had approached the attorneys general of New York and New Jersey, the two states represented in the Port Authority, who at his suggestion called a meeting of attorneys general. There they agreed to form a Conference on State Defense to oppose the loss of tax exemption. Tobin became the conference's secretary and developed the group's political strategy.

The opposition was organized, informed, and energized by Tobin. The opposition expressed in the testimony given at the Senate hearing had been carefully organized by Tobin and his associates. He focused on the House committee, with its fifteen Democrats who were expected to support FDR. According to Doig, Tobin and his aide Daniel Goldberg went to each Democrat's district:

> With them they carried information on the tax rate and debt of each city and town in each district; they met with the mayor and city council . . . and they explained the impact that Roosevelt's bill would have on the town's debt. And they got results: resolutions from towns across the country landed on the doorsteps of the Democratic committee members.[68]

Although FDR's bill was approved — barely — in the special Senate committee, it was rejected by the Senate in 1940.

The man who would be chosen as the Port Authority's executive director in June 1942 had played a key role in defeating a proposal made by FDR in the name of tax fairness. FDR and the Treasury analyzed tax exemption through the prism of the debates about tax policy, whereas Tobin viewed the exemption as directly affecting the "Authority's ability to sell bonds and carry forward its program."[69] To authority officials, the exemption had nothing to do with fairness and everything to do with their ability to get done the things they wanted to do. Tax exemption is one of the pillars (albeit typically one taken for granted and thereby invisible) of the public authority's power.

A New Role for the Revenue Bond: The Building Authority

The authority, in the New Deal framework, was designed to provide projects that would be self-financing at some point in time. (Housing authorities were again an exception.) Yet it quickly became adapted to the need of local governments to provide public facilities that were not revenue-generating and that would traditionally have been funded by general-obligation debt. We now turn to the so-called building or lease-back authority, an adaption of the authority, which allows local governments to transform traditional infrastructure into a revenue-generating business.

The 1960 and 1970s were to see the proliferation of authorities that —

rather than operating a service such as a toll road or an airport—engaged in the financing of activities carried out by others (see the next chapter). Whereas in the 1960s such authorities began to be used for the benefit of firms in the name of economic development and therefore attracted criticism, their cousins, which financed activities carried out by general-purpose governments, quietly went on financing through revenue bonds many public facilities that traditionally had been financed by general-obligation debt.

These latter—known as building authorities—were explicitly established to allow general-purpose governments to evade debt restrictions so as to construct non–revenue generating public facilities. They were the first manifestation of the so-called financing authority, an authority that did not operate an enterprise but rather acted as a "conduit" for tax-exempt borrowed monies. Financing authorities are different from operating authorities and serve a different function within the public sector. Operating authorities are a "publicly owned business . . . which earn commercial revenue from private users."[70] The authorities that were financed by the PWA and that were authorized in the 1930s and 1940s were of this type.

Building authorities are also known as lease-back authorities, for they typically build a facility, with money borrowed through a revenue bond sold in the municipal bond market, and then lease the facility to a municipal, state, or county government, using the rent as the revenue that repays the bondholders. They were clearly established to evade debt restrictions. Writing in 1958, Morris concluded that "evasive devices and fine distinctions are employed to escape debt limitations. Building authorities are the most recent of these devices."[71]

Again, Pennsylvania was a pioneer in the use of lease-back authorities. Both the state supreme court and the state legislature acted to facilitate their use by agreeing to the notion that lease-back financing was renting rather than borrowing. And thus only the annual rent counts as debt, rather than the cumulative cost of the lease. The underlying rationale has to do with how rent is treated in law:

> At common law, rent to fall due beyond the current rent period is not a present debt. Therefore, if a public body has someone build the facility, and then rents it, the indebtedness of the body is increased only by the annual rent, and not by the full cost, even though the public body takes title when

the cumulative "rents" have equalled the full capital costs. Thus the public body gets the benefit and eventual ownership of the facility without exceeding debt limits.[72]

Thus, any public facility (such as a jail or school) that does not generate revenue from users, which would traditionally have been financed by general-obligation debt, can now be financed using a revenue bond issued by a building authority. Since the debt is considered non-debt by the courts, the debt limit has not been breached. In the case of Pennsylvania school districts, lease-back financing operates thus:

> the school authority, after selling its school revenue bonds, uses these monies to construct school buildings, and the premises are then leased to the sponsoring school district. . . . The lease rentals are then paid out of the current revenues of the school district which are derived from local taxes and Commonwealth [state] revenues which have accrued to the district as part of the state's appropriation for education. The lease rental funds . . . are used for the debt service requirements of the school authorities' revenue bonds.[73]

Strickland points out that, whereas "there can be little doubt that these municipal school authorities have operated in the best interest of the public and have provided needed school construction, the fact still remains that they have done it in a subverted, although legal, manner." Subverted it may have been, but President Eisenhower encouraged the use of such school authorities by proposing that the federal government help states establish and maintain state school-building authorities.[74]

The proliferation of lease-back authorities in Pennsylvania has contributed to the large number of authorities in that state. It has also benefited a large number of firms involved in the issuance of bonds. Walsh found that "Pennsylvania has more legal firms with municipal bond business and more underwriters' *local* offices than does any other state. Local and regional attorneys, banks, and underwriters encourage local officials to create authorities." Furthermore, since 1954 when the courts ruled that a referendum was not required for lease-back financing, the creation and operation of such authorities has been nearly invisible to the public.[75]

The use of lease-back financing allows local governments to build public facilities even if their debt burden is at the limit. In the case of Philadelphia, which was close to its limit in 1989, the Pennsylvania Economy League found that the city had used a lease-back authority to finance a court-ordered expansion of its jail and a new detention center as well as solid waste management facilities. Without such a device, the city could not have acquired those facilities. Further, it could not afford to dissolve the lease-back authority that built the city's facilities (a dissolution the League favored) because it would be unable to issue general-obligation debt. The League concluded that "under the current debt ceiling, authority management is a necessity for the amount of existing long-term debt."[76]

The public authority, therefore, emerged from the Depression and the war years as a strong contender in the local government arena. By 1960, both operating and financing authorities had been developed and received approval in the courts (the former more than the latter). The revenue bond — even when legally permitted as issued by general-purpose governments — was viewed as the authority's financing instrument. This form of public corporation was ready to both provide infrastructure (a "traditional" activity) and to finance "non-traditional" activities. The latter would be particularly important as local governments gave more attention to economic development and therefore began to use the authority and the municipal bond market to help private actors. Their activism, in turn, was to set off a new round of restrictions on their borrowing — but this time the restrictions came from Washington, D.C., rather than from their state capitals. And it is to that story that we now turn.

Chapter 8

Local Entrepreneurship

via Tax Exemption

The combination of the revenue bond and the public authority created new options for local officials. The municipal government could use general-obligation debt for those capital-intensive services that did not generate revenue, while creating authorities financed by revenue bonds to deliver revenue-producing services. The intent of state debt limits could successfully be evaded by pyramiding debt across different local governments. Local officials began to take up their new options with particular vigor in the 1970s. The use of traditional general-obligation debt declined, and the role of the municipality as an investor also diminished. The institutional world of capital investment gradually began to differ significantly from the world concerned with expenditures financed by taxation and used to pay operating costs. Although investment financed by general-obligation debt remained in the hands of mayors, city councillors, and voters, the preponderance of debt was not under their control. The local governments that took control of much capital investment were non-elected and increasingly engaged in non-traditional activities. Rather than investing in infrastructure, they began to focus on economic development.

Overview

State and local governments in the post–World War II period combined the instruments of circumvention developed in the previous half-century and vigorously used them to pursue the goal of economic development. Simply put, state and local officials created public authorities dependent on tax-exempt revenue bonds. Such authorities provided funds borrowed at tax-exempt rates to private users, both household and commercial. The triangular relationship between revenue bonds, public authorities, and the tax exemption showed its power. It undergirded the economic activism of state and particularly local governments in the 1960s, 1970s, and early to mid-1980s. It allowed local governments to use their access to tax-exempt credit for purposes other than those of providing infrastructure.

The aggressive pursuit of economic-development objectives, significantly dependent on local government's privileged position within the capital market, was resisted by Congress. It saw forgone tax revenue and inappropriate assistance to the private sector where subnational government saw the opportunity to help develop possibilities for economic growth. Local government looked at a world characterized by "an intensely competitive interjurisdictional environment," in which the maximization of local access to low-cost capital might produce at least some of the rewards of economic growth and revitalization.[1] By contrast, Washington viewed such maximization as increasing its own financial burden at a time of increasing federal deficits, as well as challenging the assumptions (crystallized in the late nineteenth century) of the proper role of subnational government in the nation's political economy. Federalism as a structure — as an institution — confronted the issue of economic development for the first time. That confrontation illuminated the limits within which both cities and markets operate.

Congressional limitations, begun in 1968, gradually became more frequent, culminating in the Tax Reform Act of 1986. That act significantly reshaped the arena of capital investment at the subnational level by restricting the uses tax-exempt financing could be put to.[2]

Washington increased its power, therefore, not by taking on the responsibility of capital investment or economic development itself, but rather by narrowing the advantages enjoyed by state and local governments in the capital market. The federal relationship in the area of public investment was altered, with Washington becoming a focal point for the relationship.

By the early 1990s, the construction of the federal relationship in the area of capital investment was nearly complete. The federal government had exercised a power given it by the Sixteenth Amendment — the power to tax income — in such a way as to shape the activities of state and local governments. Whereas states had restrained themselves, and then local governments, from acting as economic adventurers in the nineteenth century, it was Washington (more specifically Congress backed by the U.S. Supreme Court) that restrained state and local governments' economic initiatives in the late twentieth century. It is ironic that such initiatives were dependent on the mechanisms devised to circumvent the earlier state restrictions. Washington restricted the purposes to which tax exemption could be put and in so doing shaped the federal relationship in the area of capital investment and economic development. Whereas states and localities had been able to use the capital market and the state courts so as to circumvent nineteenth-century restrictions, circumventing federal restrictions while retaining the advantages of tax exemption was going to be difficult in the post-1986 era.

Thus, state and local government officials began to organize politically, both to roll back some of the limitations and to protect those areas of maneuverability that remained to them. The federal relationship became politicized in a way that state-local relations had not. Local officials had not organized to try and convince state legislatures to undo debt limitations and referendum requirements. It was easier to use the revenue bond and public authorities to accomplish one's investment objectives. It was also easier to present arguments to state courts than to state legislatures. However, given the centrality of tax policy in this policy area, given that the whole institutional structure of the sector was organized around the tax exemption, and given that the Supreme Court in 1988 ruled that the tax exemption was not constitutionally protected but rather was under congressional jurisdiction, organizations representing state and local officials began to realize that they must lobby to protect their interests. Intergovernmental lobbying became much more important than it had been.

This chapter analyzes the growth of revenue-bond financing carried out primarily by special-purpose governments such as authorities for so-called private purposes in the pre-1986 period. Chapter 9 discusses the impact of the Tax Reform Act of 1986 and examines the political reactions of local governments to that impact.

Public Authorities

Public authorities began to be accepted during the years of the Depression (see chapter 7). At the state level, authorities were used in the fields of housing, toll-bridge operation, public power development, and the development of ports. Some states allowed municipalities to establish authorities to operate various utilities. In the post–World War II period, their use spread. Local housing authorities, for example, increased in number as a result of the Housing Act of 1949. States created new authorities to build and operate toll roads and ports, and they gradually became responsible for an extensive array of activities and for large budgets. Further, subnational governments (when allowed to by state courts) began using the lease-back authority, thereby transforming government-owned facilities such as schools and courthouses into ostensibly revenue-generating organizations.[3] These types of authorities often did not operate the facilities but rather borrowed the capital necessary to finance them. They were the first examples of financing or conduit authorities, which do not have operating responsibility but simply mobilize tax-exempt capital for another party.

The purposes for which authorities were created gradually expanded from those of infrastructure provision; and conduit authorities became more important as borrowing expanded for economic development, and therefore for private actors. Such conduit authorities essentially borrowed tax-exempt monies and then loaned such funds to private actors, whether these were firms or households. By 1981, John Petersen concluded that the acquisition of financial assets was replacing the acquisition of physical infrastructure. Subnational governments, often in the form of authorities, were acting as brokers in the borrowing and lending of funds. In Petersen's words, government "acts as a financial intermediary . . . a conduit for supplying funds to private sectors in the economy."[4]

The use of such conduit authorities spread quickly. For example, when Industrial Development Agencies (IDAs) were formed in New York State in the late 1960s, forty-five states had already established similar bodies. By 1975, there were at least seventy-nine authorities in thirty states that were essentially "financial intermediaries." Such authorities tend to be called state bond banks, industrial-development agencies, pollution-control investment authorities, hospital authorities, and housing finance agencies.[5] By 1980, public authorities were borrowing for "purposes not traditionally associated with local government. These quasi-public purposes include hospitals, public power projects, private sector housing, industrial pollution control, convention and sports centers, and various types of private sector development."[6]

Thus, governmental entities dependent on revenue-bond financing have been established to provide a wide range of infrastructure and non-infrastructure-related services. These include low-income housing, low-interest mortgages, financial aid to undergraduate and graduate college students, economic-development incentives, public school buildings, ferry services, subways, auditoriums, heliports, college buildings (including dormitories), terminals, bridges, tunnels, flood-control projects, highways, parkways, traffic-distribution centers, parking spaces, stadiums, convention centers, canals, shipyards, golf courses, playgrounds, public beaches, botanical gardens, museums, zoos, parks, ports, wharves, terminals, buses, trains, airports, parks, recreation grounds and facilities, sewers, sewer systems, sewage-treatment works, water systems, industrial-development projects, steam-heating plants, incinerator plants, swimming pools, hospitals, nursing homes, clinics, and homes for the aged.[7] Given the range of activities for which public authorities are now responsible, it is not surprising that they gradually become more important issuers of debt than general-purpose governments such as municipalities and counties.[8]

The Government Finance Officers Association (GFOA) found that "as of 1975, revenue bonds issued by public authorities and special districts represented the largest single source of new state and local government security sales." In 1986 authorities borrowed 50 percent of all long-term funds borrowed in the municipal bond market. In 1960 they issued only 18 percent of all bonds, whereas in 1976 they issued 36 percent and in 1983 they issued 55 percent of total tax-exempt bond sales.[9]

By contrast, state governments, which had issued 15 percent of tax-exempt bonds in 1960, issued only 8 percent in 1983; the equivalent figures for municipalities were 30 percent and 19 percent. The Public Securities Association concluded that "the relative importance of statutory authorities as issuers of municipal securities has increased dramatically during the 1970s and 1980s."[10] The General Accounting Office also confirmed this trend. It found that in 1982, authorities and special districts borrowed 57 percent of all funds borrowed at tax-exempt rates. It pointed out that such forms of government "generally have appointed decisionmakers and have the authority to sell revenue bonds."[11]

As authorities became more important as borrowers, voters became less important. The 1970s witnessed a sharp increase in bond issuance without referendum. In 1975–1977, only 10–15 percent of municipal bonds received voter approval; by contrast, in 1968, more than half of the money borrowed on the municipal bond market had been subjected to a referendum.[12]

The ACIR concluded that one of the reasons for the importance of statutory authorities in the issuance of debt had to do with the avoidance of
"constitutional and statutory debt limitations." In relation to debt backed
by the full faith and credit of government, Zimmerman found that "in
1986, 40 states limited state borrowing in some manner beyond requiring
that each bond issue receive legislative approval, and every state imposed
some restriction on local government." Another reason had to do with
"the large number of industrial development authorities empowered to
issue tax-exempt bonds."[13] Those authorities were central to the entrepreneurial activities of local government, and their activities triggered the
congressional reaction that reshaped the arena of public investment in the
United States.

Revenue Bonds: The Underpinning of Entrepreneurialism

The revenue bond is the postwar twin of the authority. John Petersen
concluded that "the factors leading to the dominance of the revenue bond
are many, but generally track with those fostering the growth of the statutory authority — the desirability or necessity to finance activities without
pledging the power to tax."[14] As special-purpose governments dependent
on revenue-bond financing (including industrial-development authorities)
became more important, revenue bonds became a more important part of
the municipal bond market and helped fuel its expansion.[15] As the Public
Securities Association pointed out:

> the most far-reaching change in the municipal marketplace has been the rise
> and eventual domination of the market by revenue bonds. . . . By the end of
> the 1970s, the volume of new revenue bonds was outpacing traditional
> general obligation debt by almost a two-to-one margin, a trend which ex-
> tended into the first half of the 1980s. Only a decade earlier, general obliga-
> tion debt comprised some 65 percent of annual new issues.

By the mid-1980s, general-obligation debt represented only 25 percent of
the tax-exempt market.[16]
    The use of revenue bonds expanded the scope of what local govern-
ment did: they became much more involved in non-traditional activity. In
particular, local governments became much more involved in economic-
development efforts. Generally, the major purposes for which so-called
private-purpose bonds were issued included housing, industrial develop-

ment, and pollution control (along with hospitals and student loans). The revenue bond allowed local officials to expand into non-traditional activities without going through the procedures designed by state legislatures to make borrowing difficult. As the Public Securities Association pointed out, "the advent of revenue bonds alone gives state and local governments a range of alternative financing methods that neither require a voter referendum nor will add any debt to the community's balance sheet."[17]

While revenue bonds are local government's chief instrument for evading state debt limits, they are not the only instrument used. For example, using tax-exempt leasing also allows local governments to circumvent state laws restricting local debt. As John Illyes of Nuveen Research put it:

> Leases have been called the chameleons of municipal finance vehicles because they can be adapted easily. . . . Leases finance everything from convention centers and courthouses to police cars and fire trucks. Leasing gives immense flexibility to tax-exempt borrowers by providing an alternative to the traditional bond issue as a way to acquire property. . . . Technically, [leases] are not debt, and so are not subject to voter requirements or debt limits. But leases are considered borrowing for federal tax purposes, creating interest which is federally tax-exempt.[18]

So-called Certificates of Participation (COPs) are secured by leases. COPs have been used widely in California since Proposition 13 effectively eliminated the possibility of issuing general-obligation bonds. Illyes argues that "COP's allowed California issuers to again access the capital market."[19]

Local officials used their newfound autonomy and discretion to act entrepreneurially. In ways reminiscent of the postbellum period, they began to pursue firms — and later single-family homebuyers — as fervently as they once had pursued the railways. In linking their use of borrowing to the goal of economic development, local officials changed the mission of subnational government in the United States. They were no longer primarily interested in the provision of traditional infrastructure; rather, they saw themselves as responsible for supporting the economic health of their communities. Officials acted entrepreneurially in that they used available financial instruments to compete with other localities in the attraction of both businesses and households as well as to assist those firms and households already in place.

Whereas the interdependence between the public and private sectors is taken for granted by European officials, it raised controversy in the United States, partially because the public subsidy of private activity is viewed with much greater suspicion in the United States than abroad. Given the unusually adversarial business-government relationship at the federal level in the United States, it is not surprising that Congress viewed the subsidies granted to private business by local governments with suspicion — especially since it was Washington that was forgoing tax revenue. Once deficits became a preoccupation, that revenue loss was to loom ever larger. Finally, given the emphasis on defining the term *public purpose* in the nineteenth century, the question of whether helping a private actor actually helped the public was rooted in the American political system.

Yet, even taking several considerations into account — the inefficiency intrinsic to using tax exemption to help industry; the haphazard fashion in which local governments tried to help business; the straightforward links between the granting of such aid and the political benefits received from it; and the forces of "competitive federalism," which drove local governments to assist business firms — it can be argued that local officials in their guise as economic-development officials living in a competitive world foreshadowed the debate about national economic development in the 1980s and 1990s.[20] The national debate about the appropriateness of the government's helping business in a competitive international economy in many ways echoed the themes developed in the debate over subnational economic-development activity.[21] The tension between service provision and economic development that emerged at the state and local level was to be replicated at the federal level.

State and local governments do not enjoy the same array of policy options in addressing issues of economic development as does Washington, however. They do not control the levers of macro-economic policy. The municipal bond market was the institution that could most easily allow them to play a role in economic development, for it allowed them to offer private actors capital at below-market cost. (The federal government also lends funds to private actors as well as guaranteeing loans. Such activity, however, has not come under the same scrutiny as lending by state and local governments, partially because no tax exemption is involved.)[22]

Municipal bonds thus permitted local officials to take the initiative in economic-development policy. Industrial-development bonds (known both as IDBs and as IRBs), mortgage-revenue bonds (MRBs), and pollution-control bonds (PCIDBs) are of particular interest to us here. Private-

activity bonds, not surprisingly, were linked to the growth of public authorities—the key governmental form involved in economic-development
activities. The General Accounting Office found that "among the fastest
growing types of districts and authorities are those that issue bonds for
non-traditional purposes, such as housing and economic development."[23]

Local governments (as well as some state governments) began to borrow for three purposes not traditionally associated with subnational capital finance that are of particular interest to us. They began to subsidize the
capital costs of private business, began to subsidize the interest costs of
individual homebuyers, and began to assist businesses with pollution-
control efforts. All these efforts were marked by the use of the revenue
bond—typically issued for a public authority. Each of these efforts was
also an attempt to shore up the economic and tax base on which local
government's financial health depends.

Private-Activity Bonds

The growth of so-called private-activity bonds for non-traditional uses
accelerated in the late 1970s. (I am using the term *private-activity bond*
to indicate a bond that finances non-traditional activity. It is not meant
to be legally accurate relative to the Internal Revenue Code.) In general,
private-activity bonds have been distinguished from bonds sold for "governmental" purposes. John Petersen defines bonds for "nongovernmen-
tal" purposes loosely as "bond proceeds that are used directly or indirectly in any trade or business of a private firm (including loans to private
individuals)."[24]

Private-activity bonds can be seen as indicators of local governments'
redefinition of their mission. Rather than concentrate on providing roads,
for example, local governments were lending funds borrowed at tax-
exempt rates to single-family homebuyers (using MRBs) or to firms to
help them construct plants (using IRBs) or meet new environmental standards (using pollution-control IRBs). Rather than borrowing for public
facilities, local governments were borrowing for private facilities, or for
facilities that involved public-private partnerships.

By 1983, the volume of revenue bonds issued for so-called private
purposes had skyrocketed. In 1970, less than a billion dollars of tax-
exempt bonds were issued for non-traditional purposes, whereas in 1975,
roughly $5 billion in tax-exempt bonds (one-sixth of the municipal bonds

issued) were issued for purposes other than those traditionally associated with local government. By 1982, the figure had climbed to at least $41 billion, about one-half of the long-term tax-exempt bonds issued by state and local governments for all purposes.[25] Herman Leonard found that private-use tax-exempt borrowing in 1983 accounted for 58 percent of all borrowing in the tax-exempt market: "[I]ssues of private purpose tax-exempt debt first exceeded those for public purposes in 1978 — and have never looked back." John Petersen concluded that, "by the mid-1980s, traditional borrowing constituted less than half of that undertaken by governments."[26]

Borrowing for private purposes became so important that the traditional link between state-local borrowing and state-local capital investment (that is, infrastructure provision) was significantly weakened. Local officials became so involved in the area of economic development that, writing in 1981, knowledgeable scholars concluded:

> the traditional link between capital spending on public works by state and local governments and their borrowing has been greatly attenuated. The bricks-and-mortar rationale has given way to new motivations as governments . . . have found new missions as suppliers of capital funds to those outside of the public sector.[27]

Local borrowing had typically financed roughly one-half of state and local capital investment, but in 1977 borrowing financed only 32 percent of state and local capital expenditures (43 percent of such expenditures were financed by federal aid). Peterson found that "long-term tax-exempt bond issues in 1977 *exceeded* total sectoral capital investment by almost 20 percent, but a good share of the bond proceeds were used outside the public sector." The U.S. General Accounting Office (GAO) found that "in 1970, over 95 percent of the $18.1 billion in municipal bond issues was used to finance traditional public infrastructure. By 1982, such use dropped to only 48 percent of new issues. In the past decade, the tax-exempt market was increasingly used to finance non-traditional endeavors."[28] The GAO defined traditional public infrastructure as including highways, bridges, buildings, mass transit systems, and public utilities (water, sewer, power). Non-traditional uses included multiple and single-family housing, industrial development, private hospitals, acquisition of pollution-control equipment by private industry, and student loans.

In 1983, the Treasury Department concluded that 68 percent of all tax-exempt borrowing was in the form of private-purpose bonds.[29] It is important to note that the category "private-purpose bonds" used by the Treasury includes bonds that conventionally would be thought of as having a public purpose, although private users benefit. The legal definition of IDBs contributes to the confusion. Although it is not the purpose of this study to delve into the technicalities, it is worth quoting from a letter written to Senator D'Amato by the Government Finance Officers Association (GFOA):

> Our association has taken the position that the present definition of IDBs needs to be revised because it includes not only bonds issued by state and local governments for the sole benefit of private users, but also bonds issued to finance *public* facilities where private users employ the facilities in a trade or business. Included in this category are bonds issued to finance airports, docks and wharves, parking garages, water systems, sewers and other public facilities.[30]

Although the category overstates the use of tax-exempt funds for truly private purposes, the trend suggested by the data collected in this category is accurate. In 1983, using actual data rather than estimates, Clark and Neubig found that "the largest volume of private activity bonds was for private businesses under the small issue industrial development bond exemption."[31] The data indicated, for example, that while $13.6 billion of new issues were sold as small-issue IDBs, only $5 billion were for multifamily rental housing and $1.2 billion for sewage and waste-disposal facilities. In 1985, only 37 percent of the borrowing for new capital was for traditional purposes, that is, for publicly owned facilities.[32] Borrowing, therefore, did not automatically translate into infrastructure provision.

Borrowing, in fact, was financing the non-traditional activities that defined local officials' economic-development agenda. In particular, it was helping to subsidize the interest costs of monies borrowed by private firms and by individual homebuyers. And it is to those activities that we now turn.

Industrial-Development Bonds

Industrial-development bonds have been widely used by local governments to help attract private firms to their jurisdictions because these bonds are tax-exempt and thereby offer "lower costs than would be incurred through traditional methods of corporate bond financing."[33] Technically, industrial-development bonds can be used to borrow funds for purposes that most would accept as public (such as publicly owned airports), as well as funds that benefit private industry only. Political and policy discourse concerning industrial-development bonds typically refers to those bonds that finance private activity, including small-issue and pollution-control industrial-development bonds. Whereas in the 1930s the bonds issued for economic-development purposes had been general-obligation bonds, revenue bonds began to be used subsequently. By 1954, the Internal Revenue Service had approved the tax-exempt status of revenue bonds that were sold to provide funds to private businesses.[34]

An IRB allows a government issuer (that is, a government borrower) to "transfer its tax-exempt status to a private borrower."[35] However, since IRBs were backed by corporations (not governments), problems encountered by such corporations were reflected in the fate met by their IRBs in the secondary market. For example, IRBs issued for corporations that became involved in buyouts or takeover battles dropped in price:

> Recently, . . . Kroger Co. bonds were downgraded by Moody's Investors Service Inc. and Standard & Poor's Corp. as a result of Kroger's restructuring plan. The downgrading also affected $125 million of Kroger-backed tax-exempt bonds. . . . Before the downgrading, investors holding a $10,000 Kroger-backed . . . bond could have sold it for $12,200. . . . [N]ow those bonds are trading around $11,422.[36]

Private business firms are given access to the tax-exempt market, thereby lowering the cost of capital for the private firm. An IRB requires the private borrower to repay the bond and the bondholder bears the risk if the firm defaults:

> Typically, a local government agency issues an IRB and uses the proceeds to buy or build a facility or to purchase equipment that a private enterprise will then buy on installment or lease for a period that may range from five to 30 years. The borrowing company pays a rent that is equal to the amount necessary to meet the interest and principal payments on the bonds. Once the bonds are retired, the company will either renew the lease or buy the facility for a nominal sum. In general, the only security for the bonds is the revenue from the lease payments or the facility itself.[37]

A firm using an IDB would pay anywhere from 2 to 7 percent less interest than it would if it issued its own corporate bonds. (Pollution-control bonds, discussed later, have similar characteristics.) Lamb and Rappaport conclude that

> industrial development bonds and pollution control bonds are really corporate bonds disguised to look like municipal bonds. Although each is officially a type of municipal revenue bond, they differ from all other types of bonds . . . which have a direct backing of a municipality or public authority. . . . In contrast, pollution control bonds and industrial development bonds are backed solely by the corporation (not by any governmental unit at all) and as such are actually corporate credits.[38]

Although IDBs were first used in Mississippi and subsequently in southern states, they began to be widely used in the North in the 1960s. The use of the IDB was still concentrated in the southern states as late as 1965, though. Arkansas, Mississippi, Alabama, and Kentucky "accounted for 80 percent of total industrial-development bond financing accomplished during 1964, and 90 percent of the total in the first half of 1965."[39] By 1963, twenty-three states had given their local governments permission to issue IDBs, and thirty states had been authorized to issue such bonds at either the local or state level, or both. Forty states were using IRBs by 1968, and whereas the volume of IRBs had been $100 million in 1960 it reached $1.8 billion in 1968.[40] Large corporations were often the beneficiaries of such financing, which often involved large sums. For example, "one port authority in Oregon borrowed $140 million to construct facilities for a Japanese-owned aluminum company. That figure exceeded the total net debt of all Oregon municipalities." Peter Eisinger points out that such financing is "generally not employed to nurture new business formation . . . because bond buyers are wary of purchasing obligations backed only by the future business performance of companies without a track record in the marketplace."[41]

The fact that IDBs were corporate bonds "disguised to look like municipal bonds" (as Lamb and Rappaport put it) helped make them controversial, with some subnational government groups like the Government Finance Officers Association opposing their use except in special circumstances. Where was the public purpose for which tax exemption is given if indeed these were corporate credits? The criticism was fueled by the fact that large corporations were often the beneficiaries of such tax-exempt financing.

Congress restricted the use of IRBs through the Revenue Expenditure and Control Act of 1968 by limiting tax-exempt issues to $1 million or less (the amount was later increased). Walsh analyzes the politics of the act thus:

> In 1968, the volume of new IDB financing was $2 billion. . . . The game had been overplayed, and even some of the fans deserted. Objections to runaway IDB financing came from some of the groups that had previously fought any limits on tax exemption: the Investment Bankers Association, the municipal law section of the American Bar Association, and the Municipal Finance Officers Association. . . . [T]he bond market participants lost their cohesiveness. Underwriters that specialized in IDBs were reaping huge profits. Other underwriters and financial advisers specializing in traditional state and local government financing were finding it harder to attract investors. . . . Representatives from various states, including New York, Massachusetts, and Illinois complained that they were losing jobs in a "second war of the states." Several trade union organizations protested the shift in jobs to nonunion states.[42]

They then became known as small-issue IDBs. In the hearings that led to the act, Congressman Byrnes summed up much of the criticism they were to face in the next twenty-five years and called for the end of the tax exemption, a call repeated in the 1980s. He argued that industrial-development bonds

> pervert the tax-exemption privilege enjoyed by state and municipal governments. The exemption privilege . . . was never intended as a means whereby private corporation could borrow money at low interest rates using the governmental unit as an "umbrella." . . . This practice . . . makes a mockery of our tax laws. The tax-exempt status of interest on [IDBs] must be limited to legitimate governmental functions where it is the credit of the municipality that supports the bond, not the credit of some second party beneficiary.

(The Advisory Commission on Intergovernmental Relations by 1963 had already decided that the industrial-development bond was "a device which the Commission does not endorse or recommend.")[43]

As of 1981, such bonds could no longer be issued for amounts larger than $10 million. IDBs were not restricted if they were to be used for pollution control, airports, convention centers, hospitals, residential investment, housing, docks, wharves, industrial parks, parking garages, and sports stadiums. (At the time of passage, the activities excepted from the limit on small-issue IRBs represented a small amount of total IRB borrowing. By 1979, however, the exceptions — including housing and pollution control — had grown so much that 40 percent of tax-exempt borrowing was for such purposes.)[44] Congressional restrictions on the size of IDBs seemed to have little impact on their popularity. The Congressional Budget Office (CBO) in 1981 reported:

> As of 1970, most states used small issues only for manufacturing and closely related facilities. But by the mid-1970s, state and local officials, brokers, bankers, and businessmen realized that federal law made virtually any enterprise eligible for small issue IRB financing. . . . Although small issues still finance industrial plants, their use for less traditional purposes is growing rapidly. Today, small issues finance all manner of ventures, from shopping centers to grocery stores to private sports clubs.[45]

By 1980, small-issue IRBs accounted for 15 percent of all long-term tax-exempt bonds. (In 1975, small-issue IRBs had accounted for only 4 percent of the long-term tax-exempt market.) Although the CBO concluded that precise data on the volume of small-issue sales were impossible to obtain, it estimated that, whereas $1.3 billion of small-issue IRBs had been sold in 1975, the figure had skyrocketed to $8.4 billion in 1980.[46] In 1983, using data available for collection because of the reporting requirements instituted by the Tax Equity and Fiscal Responsibility Act of 1982 (TEFRA), Clark and Neubig found that publicly reported small-issue IDBs were only a small portion of total small-issue sales: "In 1983, publicly-reported small-issue IDB's constituted only one-third of the $14.4 billion total volume."[47]

The use of the small-issue IRBs has been closely tied to the public authority. Such a body can be named a local industrial-development authority, an industrial-development board, or an economic-development commission, but whatever its name it can issue a revenue bond without a referendum. In twenty-three states, local authorities issue IRBs. In many states, the authority to issue such a bond is held simultaneously by authorities and by general-purpose governments; however, the authority issues many more bonds because it does not need to subject its issuance to a referendum whereas the general-purpose government often would need to.[48]

IDBs have been subjected to a great deal of criticism. The stories about them are nearly endless. The CBO study pointed out:

> the use of small issue IRBs has no relationship to local planning processes. . . . In a much publicized case, a local industrial development authority in outly-

ing Chester County, Pennsylvania, issued a $400,000 tax-free IRB to purchase a seven-story building that housed an "adult" bookstore and a topless go-go bar in downtown Philadelphia. The Philadelphia Industrial Development Commission had refused to issue the bonds. In this instance, the Pennsylvania Commerce Department approved the transaction on grounds that it conformed to state law, and the local IDA collected a fee for its services.[49]

Moore and Squires concluded that "industrial revenue bonds (IRBs) have become one of the most popular, expensive, and controversial programs in the urban economic development arena."[50] Critics have argued that they do not provide public benefits and that they provide undesirable competition (that is, leading to higher interest rates) for those municipal bonds that finance more traditional capital-intensive government services such as bridges, roads, and sewers. Many have argued that infrastructure provision suffered because of the proliferation of IDBs, which in turn provided benefits only to a few private parties. During congressional hearings in 1983 Congressman Rostenkowski, chair of the Committee on Ways and Means, pointed out that he was "concerned that bonds are being issued without any sense of public priorities. For example, in my own city of Chicago, IDB's were recently approved for a liquor store and luxury boxes for a sports stadium." K-Mart, for example, in the period 1975–1980 "used $220.5 million of IRBs to open some 96 stores in 19 states," which particularly infuriated critics, not to mention the Treasury, which was concerned with the forgone tax revenue represented by the booming small-issues market.[51]

For its part, the Council of Industrial Development Bond Issuers commissioned a study, which concluded that the overwhelming users of IDBs were small and medium-sized businesses, that small-issue IDBs did not compete with other tax-exempts because the former were bought by banks whereas the latter were bought by individuals, and that nearly two-thirds of these types of bonds had been used in areas of high unemployment. It argued finally that IDBs were not often used to steal firms from other jurisdictions and that two out of five small-issue users were affected by exports.[52]

Whatever the merits of the debate, IDBs were clearly popular with local government officials, who thought of them as an important tool of economic development. Given the importance of the economic-development agenda for state and local officials in the 1970s, it is not surprising that this tool—relatively costless to local government—became widely used.

After all, industrial-development bonds had striking similarities to the debts that state and local governments had undertaken in the nineteenth century to finance "internal improvements" — many of those projects (as we have discussed earlier) were privately rather than publicly owned.[53]

After the 1968 restrictions, relatively minor regulations were imposed by Washington until 1982. The Tax Equity and Fiscal Responsibility Act of 1982 (TEFRA) removed the tax exemption from those IRBs any portion of which would finance massage parlors, racetracks, tennis clubs, country clubs, skating rinks, suntan facilities, hot tubs, and golf courses — and restricted their use for restaurants and automobile dealerships. Reporting requirements were instituted so that Washington could develop a better idea of the extent of small-issue IRB financing. To aid in such reporting, TEFRA required that, in order to retain the tax exemption, a municipal bond must be issued in fully registered form. (As we shall see, this requirement led to the 1988 landmark U.S. Supreme Court decision in *State of South Carolina vs. Baker,* discussed later.) Finally, all small-issue IRBs were to be eliminated at the end of 1986.[54]

TEFRA, however, was only the beginning of the restrictions to emanate from Washington. The Deficit Reduction Act of 1984 (DEFRA) foreshadowed the restrictions of the Tax Reform Act of 1986 and should be viewed as an important part of the movement to restrict the discretion of subnational officials in the area of tax-exempt borrowing. DEFRA limited the issuance of small-issue IDBs and pollution-control and student-loan bonds by imposing a state-by-state ceiling. Such bonds were subject to a ceiling, set at $150 per person with a minimum of $200 million, a ceiling that, after the lower limits set in 1986, was to seem generous only in retrospect. However, many types of revenue bonds — for airports and docks, for instance — were not placed under the cap. Furthermore, the life of those small-issue IRBs that financed manufacturing facilities (that is, manufacturing IRBs) was extended. They could be issued through December 31, 1988.[55]

Pollution-Control Bonds

Pollution-control industrial-development bonds (PCIDBs) were nearly unknown in the early 1970s, but by the early 1980s they accounted for $4–5 billion of tax-exempt borrowing annually. As put by Lamb and Rappaport, these bonds were "really corporate bonds disguised to look like municipal bonds." These types of revenue bonds — created because of the environmental laws passed in the 1970s — granted private firms faced with complying with federal environmental regulations "a substantial subsidy from taxpayers at large in carrying out their pollution-control investment programs."[56]

Pollution control was one of the activities that were exempted from the regulations imposed by the Revenue and Expenditure Control Act of 1968. Pollution control was viewed as being in the public interest and not terribly important financially. Only after the major environmental laws were passed did the exception become important. But after pollution-control bonds began to be used, they quickly became important. No such bonds were issued in 1969 and 1970.[57] However, investment bankers who had seen their business cut by the restrictions on IDBs moved quickly into the pollution-control bond business. By mid-1972, a vice-president of Eastman Dillon stated, "We've been responsible for changing laws in fifteen to twenty states." Walsh found that

> the leading underwriters, by volume, of pre-1968 industrial development bonds were among the leaders in pollution control (or "environmental") industrial revenue bonds. . . . In 1976, six major investment banking firms were managers of an incredible 96.9 percent of the pollution control revenue bond volume underwritten nationwide.[58]

By 1973, "pollution control bonds raised . . . approximately 8 percent of total corporate long-term borrowing." By 1976 they accounted for $2.6 billion of tax-exempt borrowing, reaching $6.6 billion in 1982. They became so important that, in the early 1980s, tax-exempt pollution-control bonds "financed approximately 40 percent of all private investment in pollution control equipment."[59]

Pollution control was one of the major reasons for the issuance of industrial-development bonds. Between 1976 and 1979, roughly $14 billion of IDBs were issued. Of that amount, roughly $9.3 billion of industrial-aid bonds were pollution-control bonds. By 1974, such bonds had been issued by localities in forty-three states.[60] Public authorities issued them in most states. The growth of pollution-control bonds had a great deal to do with the availability of the authority as a governmental body that could act as a conduit of tax-exempt monies to the private firm. The industrial-development authority, the firm being assisted, and the investment-banking firm involved in the bond sale acted in partnership. However, the industrial development authority is the least active of the partners in this three-way arrangement. The government corporations that issue industrial revenue bonds are little more than conduits. First, an investment banking promoter working with a private industrial firm devises the financing arrangement. He then brings the proposal to an industrial development authority. The security that backs the public authority bonds in these deals is a lease calling for rental payments by the industrial firm.[61]

Pollution-control financing became so important in the 1970s that it came to be seen as a major loophole in the restrictions imposed by the 1968 act. That act had wanted to restrict public borrowing for private firms, but the pollution-control exception permitted local governments (and investment bankers) to use authorities to continue assisting the private sector. In 1981, pollution-control bonds represented the single largest segment of the market for industrial-development bonds. That assistance continued into the 1980s. Whereas in 1976, $2 billion were borrowed through pollution-control bonds, that figure rose to $5.9 billion in 1982, roughly $8 billion in 1984, and $7.4 billion in 1985.[62]

IDBs (including the small-issue and pollution-control bond) were widely viewed as politically strong. Although the small-issue bond was placed under a volume cap in 1984, IDBs were thought to be entrenched. Writing in the mid-1980s, Herman Leonard concluded:

> the IDB program has evolved . . . into an almost impregnable political niche. It finances activities that are strongly supported even though they may not have much impact on development. It provides visible, and considerable, benefits to businesses, which can be counted on for grateful and vociferous support. Benefits flow through a politically supportive network of local administrators. State and local government officials can take advantage of IDBs to appear to produce economic development benefits without having to pay for them. Local taxpayers, who face only a small slice of the cost, have little say in IDB decisions. . . . When the bill does arrive, it is paid for out of less visible, uncollected federal tax revenues. It is difficult to conceive of a structure better insulated from the political and fiscal accountability of the annual appropriations process.[63]

Mortgage-Revenue Bonds

The mortgage-revenue bond is another example of a conduit bond, in which tax-exempt monies are borrowed and then lent to a private user. It is an important component of private-purpose tax-exempt borrowing.

Whereas an IRB passes the proceeds of a tax-exempt loan to a private firm, an MRB passes the proceeds of such a loan to a homebuyer:

> Mortgage bonds are intended to secure for housing investment the cost savings associated with tax-exemption. A municipality or other local government unit issues tax-exempt long-term bonds. The proceeds are used to finance mortgages through local thrift institutions. . . . The sponsoring governmental unit has no involvement in the operation of the program; it merely lends its authority for tax-exempt purposes and establishes guidelines regarding mortgage recipients.[64]

Prior to 1978, mortgage-revenue bonds were issued by state housing finance agencies primarily for low-income multifamily rental housing. When industrial-development bonds were restricted in 1968, the permission to use such bonds for "residential real property for family units" was added in conference committee. The CBO suggested that the conferees may not have realized that the tax exemption could be used for single-family homebuyers, "since state housing finance agencies did not begin to finance single-family housing with tax-exempt bonds until 1970."[65] In 1978, such agencies began to shift their attention to the single-family homebuyer: whereas in 1977, 34 percent of housing agencies' borrowing was for single-family homes, that percentage dramatically increased to 62 percent in 1978. In the first four months of 1979 it reached 84 percent.[66] State housing agencies, therefore, set the stage for the local mortgage-revenue bond by shifting their focus from multifamily rentals to single-family homebuyers.

In 1978, local governments also began to issue single-family MRBs, initially as a way to retain middle- and higher-income single-family homebuyers within the city limits and thereby to strengthen the property tax base on which municipalities depend. "The local programs were often aimed at a higher-income group than were state programs, and they focused on homeownership rather than on rentals." Again, MRBs were not subject to referenda and were only rarely subject to debt limits.[67]

Using the tax-exempt market to help households buy single-family dwellings was viewed as a facet of economic development, for although it did not create jobs it did strengthen the tax base. In conjunction with the shift of focus by state housing agencies, the efforts by local housing finance agencies rendered the homebuyer (rather than the renter) the prime beneficiary of state and local intervention in the housing market. Peterson and Cooper conclude:

The history of tax exempt financing of housing shows a substantial shift in recent years from support of low and moderate income multifamily housing provided in conjunction with federal subsidy programs, to single family housing targeted to middle income households. This shift is apparent both within the volume of housing financed by state Housing Finance Agencies and in the growing importance of veterans' housing bonds and local mortgage-backed bonds in the total mix of tax exempt financing. Both of these latter programs provide exclusively for subsidizing owner-occupied housing, often without income limitation or with generous income ceilings.[68]

Many of the beneficiaries were also more affluent than previous beneficiaries of tax-exempt housing finance. Chicago set an income limit of $40,000, which included 90 percent of the homebuyers in Chicago. Denver targeted its money more narrowly, but even so, its program "appears to be helping those who would have bought homes without it." The CBO found that most programs included about 85 percent of all households and 75 percent of all homebuyers.[69]

Large cities led the way in using MRBs. Chicago, Denver, Albuquerque, Anchorage, Little Rock, Minneapolis, New Orleans, St. Paul, and Wichita all issued local MRBs. Although smaller communities would seem to be advantaged when raising tax-exempt funds (they had more single-family housing and more stable housing markets), they lacked the experience enjoyed by large cities in using the capital markets. Peterson and Cooper conclude that "the presence of experienced revenue bond authorities accounts in large part for the greater borrowing activity to date of large cities." However, they also point to the strong possibility that municipalities in a given metropolitan area might begin competing with each other. The experience of Pueblo, Colorado, rang a warning bell:

> In response to the city of Pueblo's tax exempt borrowing for support of home mortgages, both the county of Pueblo and the state housing authority launched comparable programs for the rest of the urban region. The amount of tax exempt mortgage funding available from the three authorities now exceeds the *total* annual level of mortgage financing in the area. Although the greater part of tax exempt financing to date has been undertaken by relatively large cities, this difference is likely to disappear as local mortgage bonds become a familiar financing device and the institutions are created to administer them in smaller communities.[70]

The popularity of local MRBs stunned analysts and members of Congress alike. Writing in 1979, George Peterson concluded that "tax exempt housing bonds have become the fastest growing instrument of U.S. capital markets." In July 1978, the city of Chicago sold the first local MRB. Denver followed suit, and by the end of 1978, numerous municipalities, often acting through newly established special-purpose governments, had also issued MRBs. In 1979, $12 billion of MRBs were sold, an extraordinary increase from the $5.5 billion of the year before. In 1979 MRBs accounted for nearly 30 percent of all long-term tax-exempt issues (in dollar volume). In 1980, $10.8 billion of MRBs for single-family home-buyers were issued, compared to only $2.2 billion for multifamily rental housing.[71]

MRBs issued by local governments became so popular so quickly that they became the first revenue bonds to be restricted by Congress since it had restricted IRBs in 1968. The direction of congressional intervention in the tax-exempt market was first indicated by congressional action in this market. The first major restriction of MRBs came in the Mortgage Subsidy Bond Tax Act of 1980. Indeed, the type of restrictions introduced then specifically for MRBs foreshadowed the restrictions Congress was to impose in 1984 and 1986.

The act restricted MRBs in a variety of ways. First, Congress set limits on the volume of bonds that could be issued in any state. The formula allowed states to choose between a limit of $200 million in bond volume and a limit of 9 percent of its annual mortgage originations averaged over the past three years (states could choose the higher). The formula favored relatively unpopulated states: Alaska, for example, had a much higher per capita bonding authority ($500) than did New York State (which received on a per capita basis only $24 of bonding authority under the formula). The CBO pointed out that many states had given the allocation to the state housing agency:

> Although the act specifies a formula for allocating a state's total bonding authority among political jurisdictions within the state, it also gives governors and state legislatures authority to prescribe a different intrastate allocation. Many governors and legislatures have used this authority, most typically to allocate all of the state's authority to a state housing agency. The California legislature enacted a complicated formula allocating bonds within California: one-third to be divided among four state agencies, one-third to local agencies with programs restricted to low- and moderate-income families, and one-third to local agencies for a broader range of housing programs.[72]

Second, only first-time homebuyers could be assisted with MRB funds and a limit was set on the purchase price of homes that buyers could choose. Third, all MRBs had to be issued in registered form so that the Internal Revenue Service could keep track of bondholders. (MRBs became the only form of tax-exempt bond that could not be issued in bearer form and therefore could be tracked by the IRS.)[73]

Although the act provided for the elimination of MRBs in December 31, 1983, they were so popular that their termination kept being postponed. In the end Congress permanently extended their life in the deficit-reduction bill that passed in August 1993.[74] The MRBs proved impossible to kill, although they are subject to the volume caps imposed in 1986. State and local officials have tenaciously fought for extensions. Such devotion is not surprising. For example, as of March 1988, the use of MRBs was credited with helping forty thousand Pennsylvanians to become homeowners.[75]

Whether these homeowners have become so primarily because of MRBs is a matter of controversy. Although MRBs are popular with many local officials and have been saved from extinction by Congress (albeit placed under the volume cap), they have been criticized by many analysts. The General Accounting Office (GAO), for example, concluded that most of the buyers benefiting from MRBs would have obtained mortgages anyway. Its criticism summarizes the critique that has often been directed against the program by policy analysts:

> GAO believes that qualified mortgage bonds are an inefficient and costly way to provide assistance to first-time home buyers, serve mostly buyers who could afford homes anyway, and have done little to increase home affordability for low- and moderate-income people. For these reasons, and because these bonds cost the federal government $150 million in foregone tax revenues for each $1 billion in bonds issued, GAO questions whether bond issuance authority should be extended.[76]

Many state and local officials began to view private-purpose bonds as hurting those bonds issued for more traditional purposes (such as infrastructure) and as leading to self-destructive competition among local governments. For example, the cochair of the Municipal Bond Task Force of the National League of Cities, testified to the House of Representatives Committee on Ways and Means that his task force supported eliminating IRBs.[77] Furthermore, the Municipal Finance Officers Association supported congressional efforts to limit IDBs. The association supported IRBs only if they were targeted: "The MFOA has a longstanding policy supporting federal restrictions on small-issue IDBs with one exception carved out. The Association believes that small-issue IDBs could be used as an effective economic development tool if they are restricted to areas of serious economic deprivation."[78]

Yet many other state and local officials — although admitting that abuses had occurred and that some restrictions might be useful — felt that, generally, private-purpose bonds were essential instruments for state and local governments as they struggled to increase economic growth. The disputes between Congress and state/local officials on the proper use of private-purpose bonds illuminates the "cleavage that exists between many local officials and many national officials, regardless of partisan identification or general ideological predisposition, when it comes to conceptualizing the relationship between the public sector and economic growth."[79]

State and local officials themselves were divided, therefore, on the appropriateness of congressional intervention in this area. It must be made clear, however, that even those officials who favored congressional restrictions on the issuance of private-activity bonds vehemently supported the tax exemption for public-purpose activities. Although the exemption was viewed by the Treasury as allowing the wealthy to escape taxation, subnational governments viewed its loss as inevitably leading to higher costs for subnational governments. State and local officials rejected the notion that the tax exemption should be replaced by federal interest subsidies. As the then executive vice-president of the National League of Cities put it in arguing against such a proposal,

> [It] would not be unreasonable for a Congressman or a budget director to question the rationale for continuing a very costly subsidy programme. . . . From the cold, hard logic of experience, city officials doubt that they would continue to receive from Congress a direct automatic unrestricted subsidy of the necessary magnitude for state and local bond issues. This is further borne out by the unhappy experience of local governments abroad whose capital projects depend upon the permission of the central government.[80]

Although controversial, private-use tax-exempt borrowing — insulated as it was from voters and debt limits, and popular among business leaders and many state and local officials — seemed to be politically protected. The Tax Reform Act of 1986, therefore, surprised nearly everyone with its restrictions on tax-exempt private-activity borrowing. It is to a discussion of that act that we now turn.

Conclusion

By the mid-1980s, the world of local government was far more complicated than that of a municipality governed by a city manager or by a mayor and a city council. In the area of capital investment, the institutions that borrowed and spent money were often authorities. Special-purpose government had taken over a significant chunk of the responsibility for local capital investment. Such investment, however, was no longer concentrated on the provision of capital infrastructure. Rather, it was directed toward assisting both firms and homebuyers. The redirection of local capital investment from the provision of infrastructure to the aiding of economic actors mobilized Congress to intervene. Its instrument of intervention was tax law and the object of that law was the municipal bond market. Just as local governments had used law and the market to circumvent state restrictions, so did Congress use law and the market to impose new federally determined limits on local investment.

Chapter 9

Washington Takes Control

People think taxation is a terribly mundane
subject. But what makes it fascinating is that
taxation, in reality, is life. If you know the
position a person takes on taxes, you can tell their
whole philosophy. The tax code, once you get to
know it, embodies all the essence of life: greed,
politics, power, goodness, charity. Everything's in
there. That's why it's so hard to get a simplified
tax code. Life just isn't simple.

The explosion of tax-exempt borrowing for purposes not linked to
the provision of infrastructure in the 1970s and the early 1980s put the
issue of local government borrowing on the congressional agenda.[1] Congress worried about the loss of federal tax revenue as well as the purposes
for which tax-exempt borrowing was being used. It responded by passing
the Tax Reform Act of 1986 (TRA), which significantly reshaped the
system of local capital investment. Washington became more important as
a political actor because it intervened to restrict local initiative — and because the Supreme Court ruled that the tax exemption was a political
rather than a constitutional question. Once Congress became so central,
state and local officials responded by creating a coalition of intergovernmental lobbies. Intergovernmental politics had now become central to the
ability of local governments to carry out local investment.

Tax Exemption and Public Purpose

The federal debate about the proper role of subnational government in
economic development — symbolized by the issuance of private-purpose

bonds — addressed the issue that divided local officials themselves. How much discretion should state and local officials enjoy in the area of economic development when such discretion often benefited private actors and led to foregone federal tax revenues? Private-activity tax-exempt borrowing benefited many business firms, as well as law firms and investment bankers involved in the market, so that the issue aroused interest from both public-sector officials and representatives of the private sector.

The debate addressed the issues of federalism by focusing on the specific issue of tax exemption: which activities should benefit from tax-exempt financing? (This specific question foreshadowed a more far-reaching debate about the appropriate role of government in the economy.) Although most theorists of federalism do not spend much time analyzing the American tax code, the imposition of taxes — or lack thereof — is a core issue in the areas of public investment and economic development and is central to the politics of federalism in both areas. Federal tax policy does not shape the behavior of only households and corporations, it shapes the behavior of state and local governments as well. It directs the relationship between state and local governments, on the one hand, and the private capital market on the other, making it a powerful lever in constructing the political economy of local government.

It is impossible to overstate the importance of the tax exemption for the municipal bond market. The municipal bond market is so dependent on the existence of the tax exemption that it would be fundamentally transformed by its elimination. During the negotiations leading to the Tax Reform Act of 1986 (TRA), a proposal was made by Senator Packwood, chairman of the Senate Finance Committee, to institute a new minimum tax that would include the interest received on municipal bonds by high-income taxpayers with low tax burdens. The *Washington Post* reported:

> the multimillion-dollar municipal bond market virtually collapsed yesterday when investors panicked. . . . "For all practical purposes, the market ground to a halt," said Thomas Opdycke, vice president and manager of Bank of America's municipal securities and public finance department . . . almost no one was willing to buy or sell municipal bonds yesterday.[2]

It is this exemption that separates municipal securities from those issued by corporations or the federal government. The doctrine of reciprocal immunity, which had been established before the passage of the federal income tax in 1913, influenced the income tax law. Consequently, "a clause was written into the Internal Revenue Code clearly stating that interest on municipal securities was exempt."[3] Whereas corporate and municipal bonds carried roughly the same interest rates before the income tax law, the rates on municipal securities fell after 1913 and remained lower than taxable corporate-bond interest rates. In the 1970s, for example, interest rates on municipal bonds were roughly one-third lower than those on corporate bonds. If issuers in Ohio, for example, had had to borrow at taxable rates the funds they borrowed in 1987 and 1988, they would have had to pay $1.6 billion more in interest through the year 2000 than they paid using tax-exempt bonds.[4]

It is therefore the tax-exempt status of bonds that allows local governments to provide assistance to private firms or households (in the form of relatively low-cost capital) and that gives Washington a powerful lever with which to control local government borrowing. The status of tax exemption is dealt with in income-tax legislation: of the seventeen tax laws passed by Congress in the period between 1968 and 1989, fifteen had an effect on municipal bonds and eleven of those seventeen had effects that are of concern here (that is, they addressed the questions of public purpose and volume caps).[5]

Whereas the Revenue and Expenditure Control Act of 1968 restricted IDBs but nonetheless allowed local governments to continue borrowing for a great many purposes apart from the provision of traditional infrastructure, the legislation passed in the 1980s significantly constrained local government's use of the tax exemption. John E. Petersen, writing in 1987, concluded:

> The last seven years have seen a procession of congressional actions designed to clamp down on the use of tax-exempt borrowing, especially that for private-activity purposes. In 1980, the Mortgage Subsidy Bond Act restricted the issuance of owner-occupied housing and, most significantly, placed a cap on the volume that could be issued in each state. The Tax Equity and Fiscal Responsibility Act of 1982 (TEFRA) placed several restrictions on IDBs. . . . More sweeping were the limitations placed on private-activity bonds by the 1984 Deficit Reduction Act (DEFRA). Following the lead of the Earlier Mortgage Subsidy Bond Act, it placed state-by-state caps on the dollar borrowings for IDBs and student loan bonds. . . . DEFRA further reduced the share of interest expense that banks deduct, from the cost of funds used to finance tax-exempt purchases of tax-exempt securities, from the 85 percent established in TEFRA to 80 percent.[6]

Congress has also passed legislation restricting the ability of state and local governments to reap so-called arbitrage profits — profits gained from borrowing at tax-exempt rates and reinvesting those funds at taxable rates. Such restrictions have also constrained the autonomy of local officials.[7] The TRA was the most important law of the 1980s because it restructured the federal relationship. It generalized the restrictions introduced by previous narrower legislation and eliminated some forms of tax-exempt borrowing altogether.

In 1980, as already mentioned, MRBs were restricted in the Mortgage Subsidy Bond Tax Act of 1980 (enacted as part of the Omnibus Reconciliation Act of 1980) so as to target first-time homebuyers of modest means. Whereas MRBs were subjected to volume caps, the tax exemption was selectively expanded. The Crude Oil Windfall Profit Tax Act of 1980, for example, allowed tax-exempt bonds to finance solid waste disposal plants that produced electricity or steam. However, Congress became increasingly aware that, after 1979, state and local borrowing for nontraditional private purposes surpassed tax-exempt borrowing for traditional purposes.[8] TEFRA further restricted the use of IDBs and set the sunset date of 1986 for the elimination of small-issue IDBs. In 1984, DEFRA continued the process of restriction, primarily by instituting volume caps on IDBs and student-loan bonds as well as by imposing new restrictions on their issuance.

But it was in 1986 that Congress passed the public law that, for the municipal bond market, represented "the biggest change of its life." Petersen characterized the Tax Reform Act of 1986 (TRA) as embodying "major changes for issuers and investors in tax-exempt securities, in part as a response to the rapid expansion in tax-exempt borrowing, particularly that done for purposes other than the traditional financing of state and local projects."[9]

The TRA generalized the restrictions that had previously been imposed on state and local borrowing for specific private purposes. The act is extraordinarily complex. Along with the related Technical Corrections and Miscellaneous Revenue Act of 1988 (TAMRA), it "instituted a new comprehensive tax system for all aspects of the American economy. Among the changes affecting the tax-exempt market were extensive adjustments in the regulation of arbitrage, private activity bonds, and the issuance and recordkeeping of bonds in general."[10] It also changed the incentives for various types of investors to buy municipal bonds, such that individual investors, often acting through mutual funds, dominated the market by the late 1980s.

The act was, of course, important for many issues other than tax-exempt bonds. It changed most aspects of the U.S. tax code, which is now referred to as the Internal Revenue Code of 1986. A leading study argues that the TRA

> altered so many provisions of the U.S. tax code as to stagger the imagination and vocabulary. As one leading accounting firm later cautioned its clients: "Describing (the TRA) and suggesting ways to tackle and master its stunning breadth and depth are tasks that will challenge the taxpayer and tax adviser. The legislation begs for superlatives and epithets. . . . The magnitude of change cannot be overstated."[11]

The TRA addressed the question of what constituted borrowing for the public purpose in comprehensive fashion.[12] Congress narrowed the definition it had previously used and thereby restricted the use of the tax exemption by state and local governments.

The act restricted a good deal of private-purpose tax-exempt borrowing by establishing a unified volume cap for such borrowing and eliminated some forms of private-purpose borrowing altogether. In 1989, state and local officials were allowed to borrow roughly $14.4 billion in the tax-exempt market for private purposes; by comparison in 1984, such borrowing accounted for $66 billion.[13] The borrowing allocation available to any state changes with census results. After the 1988 population estimates published by the Bureau of the Census, Florida, Georgia, Arizona, and Maryland gained borrowing authority whereas Colorado, Illinois, Kentucky, Louisiana, Oklahoma, and Texas lost authority.[14] State and local officials were significantly restricted in the discretionary use of the tax exemption that they had enjoyed since 1913. The act

> divided all new government securities into two categories — "essential function government activities", the traditional government bonds, and "private activity" bonds. . . . With the exception of certain designated "qualified exempt activities", all bonds whose proceeds are primarily used to benefit private persons or corporations are taxable.[15]

Those municipal bonds that finance traditional facilities owned and operated by government are "governmental purpose" bonds. Less than 10 percent of the bond can be used for private benefit if the bond is to retain its tax exemption. These bonds were not capped by Congress. Such bonds accounted for roughly 40 percent of the municipal bond market's volume in 1984.

John Petersen classifies bonds as now belonging to one of four categories: (1) governmental purpose, (2) private activity: taxable, (3) private activity: capped, and (4) private activity: uncapped.[16] Certain private-activity bonds lost their tax exemption altogether and became taxable. Except for those projects that were specifically protected in the transition rules, various projects — industrial parks, sports stadiums, convention centers, non–government office buildings, and most parking facilities, for example — could no longer be financed by tax-exempt bonds. Industrial pollution control bonds would no longer be allowed to claim the tax exemption either. These "private activity: taxable" bonds accounted for 16 percent of the market in 1984.

"Private activity: capped" bonds are those subject to the unified volume cap. MRBs, manufacturing small-issue IDBs, student-loan bonds, local electric and gas facilities, some hazardous waste facilities, mass transit facilities, and multifamily housing, for example, retained the tax exemption but had to compete with one another under the cap. This category had accounted for 32 percent of the market in 1984.

Finally, the "private activity: uncapped" bonds retain the tax exemption and are not subject to any volume limitation. These bonds include bonds issued by universities and hospitals and for governmentally owned airports, docks, wharves, and solid waste facilities. This group of activities had represented about 13 percent of the market in 1984.

The "private-activity: capped" bonds (also referred to as "qualified exempt activity bonds") were placed under a unified volume cap, which was more restrictive than the one that had been imposed solely on MRBs in 1980. The uniform volume cap had consolidated three volume caps that previously had been used to restrict the issuance of MRBs, student-loan bonds, and IDBs. "The intention of Congress in creating the cap in 1986 was to bring all the acceptable private uses of tax-exempt funds under one volume limitation. Thus, if a state wanted to stress one private use over another, that would be its option."[17]

As of January 1, 1988, each state was granted borrowing authority of $50 per capita or $150 million annually (states could choose the higher figure). Thus, all private-activity bonds that retained their tax exemption — small-issue manufacturing IDBs and MRBs, in particular — were subject to the cap. Other private-activity bonds that retained their tax-exempt status but were included under the volume cap were student-loan bonds and nonprofit-organization bonds.[18] Further, a series of tests were imposed to ensure that "all tax-exempt bond issues are used for the benefit of the general public instead of individual profits or ancillary 'economic development' uses."[19] Whereas certain types of infrastructure financing (such as that for privately owned solid waste facilities) were allowed to retain the tax exemption, even if it did benefit a private firm, such borrowing would be subject to the unified volume cap.

The TRA also significantly increased the involvement of elected officials and/or the electorate. All tax-exempt private-activity bonds had to be discussed in a public hearing before being issued, and public approval had to be obtained either by voter referendum or by receiving approval from an elected official.[20] The law therefore addressed both the lack of accountability to elected officials of private-purpose borrowing and the widespread use of the tax exemption. Although authorities charged with providing infrastructure retained their traditional independence vis-à-vis selected officials and Washington, those concerned with economic development lost much of theirs.

The Politics of Tax Exemption

Congressman Rostenkowski had targeted private-activity bonds in the early 1980s. Worried about the growing federal deficit, searching for revenue (in 1983, the estimated loss to the Treasury from all tax-exempt bonds was nearly $14 billion), and suspicious of their public purpose, he had tried to restrict them several times with limited success.[21] In 1983, he laid out the issues as he saw them:

> The volume of tax-exempt bonds issued by State and local governments to finance private activities has increased at an explosive rate during the last few years. As recently as 1975, the volume of long-term issues for private purposes was about $5 billion. Last year, the volume was at least $41 billion and represented about one-half of the long-term tax-exempt bonds issued by State and local governments for all purposes. In 1975, private activity bonds represented only one-sixth of all tax-exempt bonds issued. The use of tax-exempt bonds to finance private activities has been an issue of Congressional concern in recent years because of their impact on the ability of State and local governments to finance traditional public purpose projects such as

schools, streets and highways, sewer systems and transit facilities. In view of the massive deficits confronting the country, Congress has also been concerned about the erosion of Treasury receipts. Moreover, questions have been raised about the appropriateness of specific uses of tax-exempt bonds, whether any significant public purpose is served when subsidized financing is provided. . . . At a time when our States, cities, counties and school districts need to rebuild highways, expand and modernize sewer systems and rehabilitate older buildings, the committee is concerned that the market for tax-exempt bonds will be swamped by private activity issues to benefit firms that have adequate access to capital markets, commercial activities that take jobs away from established businesses, and projects that merely move jobs from one area to another.[22]

Given that the TRA had to be revenue neutral, taxes had to be raised somewhere to offset the overall lowering of tax rates that made the TRA distinctive. It is not surprising, given the criticisms addressed to private-purpose bonds and Chairman Rostenkowski's own suspicions about them, that the use of private-purpose bonds was limited by the act.

In spite of the restrictions imposed by DEFRA in 1984, private-purpose borrowing continued to grow. Where governors and mayors saw a valuable instrument for economic development — one that was politically valuable for it allowed them to help businesses and households at no cost to state/local taxpayers — reformers viewed private-purpose tax-exempt borrowing "as a rip-off of the taxpayer under the guise of civic do-goodism. 'It's pretty straightforward,' said Bob McIntrye, of Citizen for Tax Justice. 'The Federal government puts up the money in the form of interest subsidies, and corporate executives spend the cash.' "[23]

The Treasury had tried for many decades to eliminate the tax exemption on all municipal bonds (even when they were used almost exclusively for infrastructure provision). It argued that the exemption allowed the wealthy to escape taxation, and that the federal government lost revenue which by rights belonged in its coffers. Williams and Saltzman conclude: "studies have estimated that every $1 billion of tax-exempt bonds issued cost the federal government between $20 and $30 million annually in lost tax revenues."[24] The Treasury had not been successful, however, in significantly restricting the tax exemption. For instance, President Franklin Roosevelt in January 1939 asked Congress to end the tax exemption on state and local securities, but that effort failed, as did subsequent attempts (see chapter 7). The Conference on State Defense, made up of state attorneys general, announced "that it would fight the proposal to the last ditch on economic and constitutional grounds."[25] The Treasury had not changed its position by 1985. It viewed tax exemption "as just an outmoded vestige of American federalism."[26]

Given the impact of the TRA on all aspects of the American economy, it is significant that Birnbaum and Murray concluded "the taxation of municipal bonds was one of the most intensely lobbied parts of the tax bill."[27] Indeed, the determination of which activities would be spared restraint altogether, which would be placed under the unified volume cap, and which would be eliminated had much to do with the politics of putting together a majority to back the improbable effort at tax reform that finally culminated in the act. Rostenkowski's need to gain a majority on the House Ways and Means Committee and Senator Packwood's need to follow suit on the Senate Finance Committee, for example, help explain why governmentally owned solid waste facilities were treated well but municipal bus facilities were not.

In the House (in which the Democrats were the majority party), Rostenkowski found the working group on tax-exempt bonds to be one of his most difficult. Even his allies found it difficult to restrict the issuance of tax-exempt bonds that were important to their individual districts. Congressman Flippo, "who was supposed to be one of the chairman's allies in trying to limit tax-exempt bonds, voted instead to retain the use of the bonds to finance ports, which were important to his state of Alabama."[28] Congressman Coyne of Pittsburgh, who owed his place on Ways and Means to Rostenkowsi, voted against the chairman's position until Rostenkowski telephoned him and pressured him to change his position. In the end, Rostenkowski offered tax exemption to those activities of special importance to members of the working group:

> Fowler won an exemption for airport facilities. McGrath was able to keep a break for bonds used to build solid-waste disposal facilities, and Flippo and Coyne were allowed to revive some so-called small-issue industrial development bonds, the type of bonds used most often to benefit companies directly.[29]

Nonetheless, the changes made by the committee were estimated to eventually raise $4.2 billion more in federal revenue than the pre-1986 laws would have generated.[30]

In the Republican-controlled Senate the chairman of the Senate Finance Committee, Robert Packwood, followed a similar pattern. In his case, those senators who supported tax reform and formed part of the inner core were able to protect their favored private-activity bonds while opponents saw their favored bonds restricted or eliminated. Those who seek to find a straightforward public-policy rationale in the changes made to the TRA are bound to be disappointed:

> The first tax breaks to go were those favored only by committee members *not* in the core group. Those who had not embraced Packwood's plans were made to suffer for their reluctance. . . . A scheme providing tax-free bonds to finance municipal bus service, favored by John Heinz of Pennsylvania, was . . . excised. . . . Even Bradley [a Democrat] got a special deal: Limits were removed from the amount of tax-free bonds that could be used to finance the construction of government-owned solid-waste disposal facilities.[31]

The transition rules agreed upon exempted specific private-activity bonds from the general restrictions contained in the act. Convention centers and sports stadiums in certain cities (the New Orleans Superdome was one), for example, were allowed to proceed with tax-exempt financing even though such financing would be prohibited in the future. Even Senator Metzenbaum of Ohio, who crusaded against many of the provisions of the transition rules, "personally advocated transition rules for the Cleveland Dome stadium and convention centers in Columbus and Akron."[32]

Impact of Congressional Restrictions

Bonds for traditional purposes replaced private-purpose bonds in the market after the TRA. Borrowing came to be related much more closely to capital spending, a return to the period before local governments had begun to pursue economic development with zeal. Whereas in 1985 borrowing for non-traditional purposes had accounted for over half of tax-exempt borrowing, by the end of the 1980s private-activity bonds subject to volume caps accounted for less than 20 percent of all bond sales and all private-activity bonds represented about one-third of state and local government's tax-exempt borrowing.[33]

With regard to IDBs specifically, their use declined sharply after being limited to small manufacturers and to being placed under the volume cap. Whereas IDB volume had averaged roughly $13.6 billion in 1984–1986, it reached only $3.2 billion in 1989.[34]

The decline in tax-exempt borrowing for uses defined by Congress as "private" helped focus tax-exempt borrowing on infrastructure provision.

By 1990, "if an investor is going to buy a tax-exempt security, an infra-structure bond is one of the few options available; this is the reverse of the case pre-1986 when the tax-exempt market appeared to be overrun with mortgage instruments."[35] The role of revenue bonds within the tax-exempt market remained strong. Whereas tax-supported (general-obligation) debt equaled 8 percent of GNP in 1970, it had fallen to 4.4 percent in 1989.[36]

The TRA had the impact desired by Congress. Infrastructure financing seems to have improved. Municipal bonds financed 54 percent of infrastructure expenses in 1989 (they had financed only 38 percent in 1981 with federal grants providing 42 percent).[37] As federal grants fell, municipal-bond financing picked up the slack. The years 1990 and 1991 were years of "record financing for infrastructure" in the market: $40 billion in 1990 and $55 billion in 1991.[38] In 1991, roughly $125 billion (in new long-term issues) was borrowed in the market; 73 percent of the market was owned by individuals (including mutual funds and money market funds).

State and local borrowing for purposes considered by Congress to be private declined significantly. Graham and Shinn found that borrowing for parking facilities, civic centers, sports stadiums, and convention centers had dropped sharply. Although it is not yet clear how public facilities that would previously have enjoyed tax-exempt status are currently being financed, Graham and Shinn conclude that "in many cases, the projects have simply been abandoned."[39] The data is not yet in, but it is likely that those infrastructure projects that relied on joint financing from governments and private firms have been particularly hurt. Although such projects would conventionally have been thought of as fulfilling a public purpose, their method of financing, which relied heavily on private sources, made them unsuitable for tax-exempt financing under the TRA's restrictions. Such joint financing had been particularly important in financing water supply, wastewater treatment plants, and solid waste disposal facilities.[40]

However, it is likely that local officials and investment bankers will still manage to push ahead with at least some projects. In building convention centers, for example, "local issuers must navigate a legal minefield to sell tax-exempt bonds." Since private-activity bonds issued for convention centers are now taxable, local officials must issue a "governmental" bond in order to finance a convention center at tax-exempt rates. To qualify as a governmental bond, the convention center must involve little use other than that available to the general public. For example, no more than 5 percent of the center's space could be leased to, say, clothing stores. In spite of the difficulties involved, Pierce found that at least some local governments had been able to go ahead with tax-exempt convention-center financing.[41]

For its part, the volume cap has begun to restrict private-purpose borrowing for those purposes that are subject to its discipline. Its impact is especially felt by the more populated states. The activities receiving most of the borrowing allocations under the cap are MRBs, small-issue IRBs, and student loans (accounting for almost 75 percent of the borrowing in this category). Twenty-seven of the fifty states routinely borrow as much as the cap allows, whereas the other, mostly less populated states do not take up their full borrowing allocation.[42]

Although Congress set the level of the cap, it was up to the state governments to decide how to allocate borrowing authority. The state decided the delineation between state and local borrowing and the purposes for which borrowing allowed by the cap would be used.[43] States have differed widely in their choices: some have kept control with the governor, others have given it to departments such as the Department of Commerce, Department of the Treasury, or the Department of Economic Development. Most states "have either established priorities among activities or have allocated the cap among competing projects according to some set of economic criteria, most often the number of jobs created or number of low-income persons benefited." Nearly every state has identified the stimulation of economic growth and employment as the prime objective of the bonds issued under the cap. MRBs and small-issue IDBs tend to be the types of bonds favored by the states' allocation systems.[44]

The establishment of the uniform volume cap allowed Congress to restrict the issuance of bonds for activities that did not have a public purpose sufficiently compelling to allow untrammeled borrowing for them. It also allowed the state governments to exercise much more control over local borrowing for activities covered by the cap. Prior to 1986, local governments typically issued IRBs without being subject to state-level regulation. Now, even in those states that give borrowing permission on a first-come first-served basis or that have agreed to local set-asides, the potential for tighter state control exists.

The use of the revenue bond and public authorities allows the circumvention of state debt limits but does not allow the circumvention of volume caps, which are determined by Congress and allocated by state government. Whereas the TRA strengthened the role of Washington significantly in the determination of those activities likely to be financed by subnational governments because of their tax-exempt status, it also reshaped the state-local relationship in important ways. Whereas local economic-development activity had been largely under the control of local governments, in 1986 such activity came under the control of both Washington and the state capitals.

Tax policy served as the instrument that reshaped the federal-state and state-local relationships in this area. The debates over tax policy vis-à-vis subnational government were based on decisions and themes harking back to the nineteenth century. In a similar vein, the activities of state and government that provoked Washington's intervention also harked back to the nineteenth century. The entrepreneurialism of state and local governments that angered Congress has deep historical roots, as do the institutions and financial instruments that have evolved to facilitate such entrepreneurial efforts.

Political Response to TRA by State and Local Governments

The reaction to the TRA was mixed on the part of subnational governments. Transition rules helped many large, visible projects (such as stadiums) proceed so that the real effects of the restrictions would not be felt for some time. Furthermore, those officials who favored greater attention to infrastructure provision felt that the TRA would improve the market for infrastructure-related bonds (which proved to be true). Although the TRA had limited the use of the tax exemption for economic-development purposes, many state and local officials thought Congress had acted appropriately to restrict abuse of the tax exemption.

Such ambivalence, however, disappeared in 1988, when the very existence of the tax exemption came to be seen as vulnerable. State and local officials worried that such vulnerability, coupled with the willingness to impose restrictions on local borrowing recently shown by Congress, threatened the future of all tax-exempt borrowing, including that related to infrastructure financing.

South Carolina v. Baker

The Supreme Court opened the door to congressional action by its decision in 1988 that state and local governments had no constitutional right to borrow at tax-exempt rates. The decision in *South Carolina v. Baker* significantly strengthened the regulatory power of the federal government over subnational governments. American federalism had moved a step closer to a system in which the center was strong indeed. In Margaret Wrightson's words, the Court ruled that "the Constitution contains no substantive protections against national regulatory powers *vis-à-vis* state and local governments."[45]

The case arose from the Tax Equity and Fiscal Responsibility Act of 1982 (TEFRA), which required states and localities to issue municipal bonds in "registered" rather than "bearer" form. South Carolina, backed by the National Governors Association, took the requirement to the U.S. Supreme Court in 1983 and the case was decided in 1988. South Carolina argued that the registration provision violated the doctrine of reciprocal tax immunity, founded on the Tenth Amendment. The GFOA, for its part, argued that the legislative history of the Sixteenth Amendment protected the tax exemption. The GFOA's argument in its amicus curiae brief laid out the conceptual importance of the case in the evolution of American federalism:

> The historical development of tax immunity is rooted in the very foundation of the federal system and, as such, cannot and should not be dismissed lightly. The power to tax can indeed be the power to destroy. If our system of federalism is to mean anything, neither the legislature nor the courts should tamper with the vital immunity of the States and their instrumentalities from the potentially coercive and destructive taxing power of the Federal government.[46]

In *South Carolina v. Baker,* the Supreme Court essentially confirmed that it meant what it said. In *Garcia v. San Antonio Metropolitan Transit Authority* (1985), the Supreme Court had ruled that Congress had the power to impose the Fair Labor Standards Act on subnational governments. Further, Wrightson points out, the Court had stated, "State sovereign interests . . . are more properly protected by procedural safeguards inherent in the structure of the federal system than by judicially created limitations on federal power." Wrightson concludes that, in *Garcia*, "the safeguards the Court identified are 'structural,' that is, they are derived from state and local government participation in the national political process. These safeguards include, for example, state involvement in national electoral processes as well as political pressure and lobbying activity."[47]

Much to the dismay of state and local officials, the court in *South Carolina v. Baker* not only ruled against South Carolina but did so in an expansive fashion. The Court did not issue a narrowly based ruling, but rather, on April 20, 1988, it overruled *Pollock v. Farmers' Loan and Trust Co.* (1895) altogether and in so doing established a new doctrine of reciprocal tax immunity. *Pollock* had served as the case upon which state and local governments based the assumption that the tax exemption was constitutionally protected. In *Pollock*

> the Court . . . had ruled that a tax on the interest was ultimately a tax on the state that issued the bond and so was unconstitutional under the doctrine of intergovernmental tax immunity. Over the years the court has rejected the rationale of *Pollock* in a number of cases involving contracts with state governments. In these cases the Court ruled the federal government could tax state employees' income, or the income of state contractors, and it was not a tax on the government itself. Justice William Brennan, who wrote the *South Carolina* decision, saw overturning *Pollock* as the logical extension of these cases, finding that there is no constitutional reason for bondholders to be treated differently than others with government contracts. . . . Brennan's opinion also pointed out that the sources for the federal and state immunity doctrines are not the same.[48]

Wrightson concludes:

> it seems clear that *South Carolina* established a new doctrine of reciprocal tax immunity, one which is wholly consistent with a philosophy of a supremely powerful national government and semi-sovereign states. Whereas the old doctrine implied a measure of equal treatment, the Court's new interpretation makes it official — national tax sovereignty is always greater. . . . The most obvious lesson of *South Carolina* is a general one: American federalism has been construed by the Court as a political and administrative relationship rather than a constitutional one.[49]

The Political Response

The message was clear. In essence, the Supreme Court had told state and local governments that they had to depend on their political skills to defend their institutional self-interests in the American federal system. The constitutional protection that subnational governments had long taken for granted had been eliminated. In a sense, they were to come to Washington primarily as political actors à la lobbyists rather than as governments.

State and local governments heard the message and responded accordingly. It was not only the *South Carolina* case that prompted a political response. By 1988, protests and complaints about the TRA had become very loud. The TRA was viewed as far too burdensome by even those state and local officials who wanted to restrict private-purpose bonds. Many of the TRA's provisions had to do with various technical issues, such as arbitrage. (Although these provisions are not discussed here, they are viewed by subnational officials as reducing their maneuverability in the capital markets and as requiring inordinately complex and often very expensive procedures. They are fiercely resented. A comprehensive analysis of changes that have occurred in American federalism would require a thorough discussion of these technical changes, for they represent a penetration of federal regulation into the very routines of subnational government operations.)[50]

The political response to the TRA and the Court's decision in *South Carolina* had two components. The first involved a congressional reaction. The second involved the mobilization of state and local government associations into a lobbying group focused on protecting the tax exemption and rolling back some of the more burdensome technical restrictions on local borrowing imposed by the TRA.

On the congressional side, Congressman Beryl F. Anthony Jr. (Arkansas) on the House Ways and Means Committee created a commission to examine the role of tax-exempt financing. Six of the twenty-one members of the Anthony Commission on Public Finance were state and local officials: Governor Campbell Jr. of South Carolina; Governor Clinton of Arkansas; Mayor Latimer of St. Paul, Minnesota; Mayor Abramson of Louisville, Kentucky; County Supervisor Shipnuck of Monterey County, California; and Utah State Treasurer Alter. The Anthony Commission, formed in January 1988, presented its report *Preserving the Federal-State-Local Partnership: The Role of Tax-Exempt Financing*, distributed by the GFOA, in October 1989. That report became a benchmark for future congressional debates and recommended changes to the tax code, changes that state and local officials viewed as more compatible with their own interests.

The Anthony Commission was most unusual in that it was appointed by a single member of Congress rather than by the president or congressional leaders. It held hearings and commissioned studies and thus was viewed as a serious foundation stone for further legislative efforts to enhance tax exemption on Congressman Anthony's part. It made the argument that whereas tax exemption does involve revenue loss, eliminating the exemption would impose real costs on subnational governments. Yet Anthony himself realized that the revenue loss to the Treasury that is intrinsic to municipal bonds will always present problems. In his words, "You can't get away from the revenue question."[51]

The Anthony Commission report helped Congressman Anthony emerge as a congressional leader in the area of tax-exempt financing. In presenting the report, Anthony made the link between the tax-exempt status of municipal bonds and the critical role of such bonds in financing infrastructure. In November 1991, Anthony — along with Senator Bob Graham, Senator Christopher Bond, and Congressman Don Sundquist — formed the Congressional Infrastructure and Public Finance Caucus. The caucus's mission was "to educate members of Congress on the infrastructure problems facing the country and [on] the need to ease restrictions on the state and local financing tools necessary to ensure increased investment in the nation's future."[52] State and local officials had found a champion in Congress, and tax exemption was thus likely to receive at least some of the institutional support necessary to protect the tax-exempt status of municipal bonds.

Anthony emerged as a key representative for the general area of tax-exempt financing, and other members defended particular types of tax-exempt bonds (mortgage-revenue bonds and industrial-development bonds in particular). Congressman William J. Coyne of Pittsburgh, for example, continued to defend the use of IDBs, and they gradually began to acquire more supporters in the House. When Coyne introduced legislation in 1991 (H.R. 1186) to extend IDBs, he was able to attract 171 cosponsors. In 1992 the sunset provision that had applied to them was permanently eliminated. IDBs were saved.

An important instrument for local economic development had been protected in Congress, partially due to Coyne's own commitment to their use. Nonetheless, the post-1986 IDB was quite different from the IDB of 1980. It could be used only for smaller manufacturing companies and it was subject to the volume cap. It thus had to compete with other tax-exempt private-activity bonds.

The problems posed for environmental infrastructure by the TRA's restrictions were taken up by Democratic Congressman Guarini and by

Republican Senator Domenici. Local officials had used IDBs for the construction of environmental facilities, such as resource-recovery plants. Given the restrictive definition of the term *public purpose* as proposed by the Treasury, both businessmen and officials had worried about how expensive environmental facilities were to be paid for, given that public-private partnerships were often a key component in the construction of such facilities.[53] They proposed so-called infrastructure bonds for environmental facilities that would be private-activity bonds exempt from the TRA's restrictions on such bonds and not subject to the volume cap.[54]

Thus, by 1992, individual members of Congress, particularly on the House Ways and Means Committee, had taken up the issue of tax exemption in some form or other as a major concern. From the point of view of state and local officials, such champions were critical. The Supreme Court had given Congress the upper hand, and subnational government officials therefore had to worry about finding allies in Congress and developing coalitions there. It was to help state and local governments develop such allies and coalitions that the Public Finance Network (PFN) was formed.

The Public Finance Network: A Politicized Response

State and local officials—acknowledging that the intergovernmental game in the area of tax exemption was a political game—realized they had to organize a broad grassroots constituency to help protect the tax-exempt status of municipal bonds. State and local governments had already successfully lobbied in Congress to reduce the impact of the Court's decision in *Garcia,* which would have forced them to pay overtime wages. Elser points out:

> the affected governments quickly made clear to Congress the financial implications of the decision. As a result, Congress amended the law so that states and local governments had a one-year grace period in which to comply with the FLSA (Fair Labor Standards Act), traditional volunteer labor was allowed in certain circumstances, and employees could take compensatory time rather than extra wages for overtime.[55]

As the executive director of the GFOA put it:

> In the post-Watergate era the Washington, D.C., establishment has relegated state and local governments to special interests. We need to convey the message that state and local governments are not some special interest group

with a PAC (political action committee) fundraising arm, but rather we are a part of the system of federalism and a vital part of government in this country. . . . We must demonstrate that tax exemption is in the national interest and build support for that policy beginning at the grassroots level, including the citizen beneficiaries and business and civic leaders.[56]

The possibility that all municipal bonds could have their tax-exempt status removed by Congress galvanized state and local government officials. Such an event would harm not only the private-purpose bonds used for economic-development initiatives but would also increase the cost to subnational government of providing traditional infrastructure. That infrastructure provision began to receive more attention in the 1980s.[57] And given this, the mere possibility that the tax exemption might be removed from all subnational government activities frightened local officials.

Given the increasing pressures within Congress to find revenue, as the federal deficit kept growing, officials feared that the tax exemption for even the most traditional purposes would gradually be eroded. H.R. 1552 was an example of what they feared. The bill, introduced in 1991 by Congressman Brian Donnelly of Massachusetts, proposed penalizing taxpayers who earn tax-exempt interest by reducing their itemized deductions. "In other words, tax-exempt interest would not be fully tax-exempt."[58]

State and local government associations thus organized into the Public Finance Network, a broadly based coalition of groups based in the public sector with an interest in preserving the tax exemption. By January 1992, the PFN had grown to include forty-two state and local government interest groups.[59] It sponsored workshops around the country on the issue of tax exemption, organized local and state government officials by state, produced a newsletter and material useful for lobbying, and generally tried to ensure that state and local officials got the message to Congress that tax-exempt financing is critical for state and local finance and the provision of public facilities.

The PFN defined its mission as "protecting state and local borrowing from federal taxation and unnecessary regulation."[60] It was formed in the summer of 1988 by the GFOA, the American Public Power Association, and the National League of Cities. In December 1988, more than two hundred state and local government officials from Ohio, Michigan, Indiana, Pennsylvania, and Illinois met in Cleveland for a one-day summit. In this first regional workshop, officials discussed how to develop a strategy by which state and local governments could use grassroots lobbying to protect the tax-exempt status of local borrowing. Attendees were given basic lessons in how to lobby, techniques for conducting meetings with members of Congress and their staffs, including the suggestion that they meet with members of Congress in their home district office rather than in Washington.[61] State and local officials were being socialized to think of themselves as lobbyists, a role many of them had not considered compelling before the *South Carolina* decision.

The deficit makes their worries about tax exemption much sharper than they would be otherwise. As Congressman Donald Pease, a member of the House of Representatives Ways and Means Committee, put it: "the price of municipal tax-exempt bonds is eternal vigilance."[62] He warned that the need to raise revenue would certainly put pressure on the tax exemption:

> The federal budget deficit must be dealt with and spending cuts or restraints will not be enough. Some revenues must be raised. Although there is no single member of the committee who is hostile to tax-exempt bonds, the need for revenue will force members to look at every market sector for possible ways to raise tax revenues.[63]

Congressman Pease warned that state and local officials will need to constantly remind members of Congress how important tax exemption is to subnational governments.

The PFN has been trying to follow his advice, holding regional workshops across the country and sending out staff to help various states organize a state-level affiliated organization. States such as Michigan, Missouri, Minnesota, and New Jersey were organized relatively quickly. California State Treasurer Kathleen Brown decided to organize the PFN in California in 1991, for in her words, "with no network there is no communication to the local representatives in Congress."[64]

The PFN in each state coordinated the activities of a large number of state and local government organizations in the area of tax-exempt financing. In Florida, for example, the PFN's steering committee was composed of the State Treasurer and Insurance Commissioner, Office of the Governor, Florida Association of Counties, Florida League of Cities, Florida Government Finance Officers Association, Florida Association of Court Clerks, Florida Municipal Electric Association, and the Florida School Boards Association.[65] The range of participants indicates how widely the tax exemption is used in the state and local government sector. The PFN deliberately decided to include organizations for which the issue of tax-exempt financing is a secondary but nonetheless important one.

Prodded by various officials, state legislatures began to pass resolutions urging Congress to protect the tax exemption by passing a constitutional amendment. Utah called for a constitutional convention. Legislatures in Indiana and Nebraska urged Congress to maintain the tax-exempt status of municipal bonds.[66] In general, PFN activists tried, in a variety of ways, to make the issue of tax exemption salient to their respective members of Congress.

The PFN deliberately chose to include state and local government officials in their lobbying effort — and to exclude investment bankers and bond counsel. They felt that the bankers and bond counsel had done the bulk of the lobbying in Congress to defend the tax exemption, to the detriment of the cause. Bankers and lawyers were likely to be viewed as self-interested, whereas officials were more likely to focus congressional minds on the purposes for which tax-exempt borrowing was carried out. And the PFN seems to be having an impact. Congress is now more likely to link tax exemption with facilities such as schools, water treatment plants, or drug treatment centers. The lobbyist for the National League of Cities argued that, before the PFN was formed, Congress thought of the tax exemption as helping rich bankers and lawyers or rich old ladies: "We felt that the last thing Congress seemed to think about was jails, drug treatment centers, elementary schools, water treatment plants and the like."[67]

During the debates on tax law changes in the mid-1980s, the lobbyists on tax exemption had come from the world of finance; by the late 1980s, the lobbyists were local officials from the Congress members' own districts. Congressman Robert Matsui of the House Ways and Means Committee laid out the difference:

> When we were drafting tax bills in 1985 and 1986, we weren't hearing from mayors or statewide office holders on municipal bond issues. Investment bankers, public securities people, private university and hospital officials were very active in the process. But people here [in Congress] were not necessarily sympathetic to them. . . . This year . . . we're hearing much more from local officials. They've been very, very active.[68]

Four years after the Supreme Court decision, state and local government officials had managed to put together a lobbying effort that had at least begun to alert members of Congress as to the importance of the tax exemption for subnational government finance. They had taken seriously the Supreme Court's admonition that federalism was largely political rather than constitutional.

Conclusion

The fact that the issue of tax exemption was so linked to the politics of tax policy and deficit reduction was a guarantee for state and local officials that tax exemption would never be addressed as a straightforward issue of federalism in the old, traditional sense. Given the power of tax policy, the use of tax exemption raises questions about equity among taxpayers and about the efficiency of exemption. And the pressures of the deficit give the federal government the incentive to use the power it has over other governments for its own financial advantage.

The need for state and local government officials to organize as a lobby to protect tax exemption indicated that the intergovernmental politics of public investment could no longer rely on the politics of circumvention. Using the revenue bond and public authorities had allowed local investment to go beyond state limits, but these two complementary strategies both relied on the availability of the tax exemption. Once that was called into question, intergovernmental politics — understood as intergovernmental lobbying — came to the fore. The politics of circumvention were sufficient as long as the federal government played a passive role. However, once Congress (supported by the Supreme Court) intervened in ways designed to limit local discretion, state and local officials had to develop a coalition among themselves so as to bring political pressure to bear in Congress.

Chapter 10

Conclusion

Each American government moves through a universe made up of tens of thousands of other governments. Each of these governments has, in Fritz Scharpf's term, an "institutional self-interest" that is defended, enhanced, and pursued vis-à-vis other governments.[1] When governments pursue their institutional self-interests, they are engaging in politics. They are political actors in that universe.

The interest of a government as an institution can be pursued in various ways, each of which has its own appeal. In financing public works and economic development, local governments have used the strategy of circumvention to increase their discretion and flexibility. The price of this strategy is clear: discretion now is bought by narrowing discretion in the future.

The politics of circumvention—and the cost of that type of politics—have shaped the way that local public investment occurs within the American federal system. Judges, the bond market, and the actions of both federal and subnational governments have molded federalism throughout the past two centuries. In the nineteenth century, economic entrepreneurship was dominant. State and local governments took their turn as entrepreneurs until they were stopped. They then began establishing the legal and financial channels that would let them resume activist policies. The process sketched out in the preceding chapters, therefore, is one of entrepreneurship, restriction, and circumvention (which in turn allowed a renewal of entrepreneurship followed most recently by restriction).

State governments, local governments, and state courts have been central players: the federal government has permitted, and ultimately redirected, this process in the twentieth century through granting tax exemption. In the nineteenth century, the federal government in general played a secondary role, but the Supreme Court made rulings that helped to establish the municipal bond market. Subnational governments subsequently used this market as a pawn in their chess game.

Such a historical view is not always taken, however. Scholars usually stress the independence of the municipal bond market, relative to the capital investment sponsored by states and cities. The market for these scholars is a privileged player. They attribute the bond market's influence to a general phenomenon — the power of markets over public authority. My argument is that, looked at historically, the relationship between public authority and private money has been such that governments have actually shaped the investment system. The reason for the bond market's influence over the finances of American cities has little to do with the imperatives of capital markets or the notion that money talks. It has a great deal to do with the historical choices made by public authorities, including the courts.

The municipal bond market, subnational governments, and Washington, D.C., form a triangle. Although market judgments about the creditworthiness of local borrowers do affect what borrowers can borrow and at what terms, the market's power derives from the public investment system itself — a system that has moved through the pattern of entrepreneurship, restriction, and circumvention described in earlier chapters. A capital market operating within a different investment system would not have the same kind of influence as the American municipal bond market.

The American market has power over subnational borrowers partly because the federal government does not guarantee debt. Risk concentrates the mind and calls for measured judgments about local government borrowers as much as about corporate borrowers. The market's power also derives from its legal status under tax law. Tax law and the municipal bond market are inextricably intertwined. Tax law controls access to the municipal bond market and is therefore an instrument with profound implications for American federalism. To assert its control over state and local entrepreneurship in the 1980s, in fact, Congress found it necessary to change tax law. Washington — not bankers or lenders — ultimately determines how much power the municipal bond market has over cities. Conversely, the cities' access to the bond market is also controlled by Washington, not by bankers or lenders.

Within the federal system, however, the importance of the bond market has lain primarily in the possibilities for evasion offered to local governments. The market allows subnational governments to circumvent the numerous restrictions imposed by state law on their borrowing. In other words, the municipal bond market allows local governments to evade state governmental constraints. The market allows local officials to "push the limits." It is the instrument that allows the politics of circumvention to proceed — as long as state rather than federal law is being circumvented.

The market's role in the strategy of circumvention shows how public-private institutional networks undergird the system of public investment in the United States. The private sector facilitates the political strategy pursued by local governments, while imposing its own costs and demands (such as credit ratings) on local borrowers. The market was an integral part of the strategy developed by governments trying to cope with the present under the constraints imposed by the past.

Interactions between governments, courts, and capital markets changed the options and opportunities available to each actor in the system. And this interaction led to the creation of a new actor in the system — the public authority. The creation of the authority represented an essential tactic in the strategy of circumvention. It was an act of intergovernmental politics. Once in place, public authorities then became important actors in the next phase of intergovernmental politics. The odyssey of public authorities in the American system is instructive in that it shows how intergovernmental politics in one period shape such politics in a subsequent phase.

Historical analysis also shows that the opportunities open to officials at any level of government are neither fixed nor infinite. Any equilibrium reached within the federal system is transient. Governments — local governments in particular — have used both law-based and market-based strategies to achieve greater maneuverability in a particular system. Yet the cost of obtaining such maneuverability was often paid by local officials in subsequent generations.

Once cities had been definitively subordinated to the states, they could not overcome their status. However, they did try to maintain an aggregate level of investment activity that was greater than was permitted by the state's limitations. Debt limits (including the requirement of electoral approval) were viewed as constraints on desired investment and were therefore circumvented. In many states, the creation of a new institution — the public authority — provided one answer to local government's dilemma.

The authority diluted the power of city government, but it also allowed the provision of badly needed public services. In the postwar period, it allowed local governments to engage once again in economic development. The elected government had been the investor and entrepreneur in the nineteenth century, whereas the public authority, in many states, played that role in the postwar period. Given the tenuous relationship between many elected municipal governments and the public authorities that control significant investment in the cities' territorial boundaries, this might be viewed as a problematic bargain. Nonetheless, that bargain is essential to understanding the fragmentation of the metropolitan area and to understanding the compartmentalized nature of politics in capital-intensive sectors.

Entrepreneurship has thus occurred twice at the subnational level — in the nineteenth century and in the 1970s and 1980s. In these periods, state and local governments used public capital investment extensively for purposes of economic development. Entrepreneurship has in turn been followed by measures designed to restrict local government activism.

The creation of authorities relied heavily on local governments' being able to use the financial market to their own ends. Governments and markets, depend on — and use — one another over time. But using the market as an instrument can only occur as the law permits it. Capital markets are profoundly dependent on the legal order, for it is that order that structures the contours of markets. It is ironic, then, that state courts were critical actors in the fashioning of the strategy of circumvention. State judges ultimately decided whether the law could be evaded by local government borrowers. The market was there to be used by governments, but it could be used only if the state courts so permitted.

Once the authority was in place, the competition between local governments to attract industry and to promote economic development generally led to an expansion of borrowing. Economic development efforts boomed during the 1970s and early 1980s as authorities used their powers in creative ways. The federal government then moved to restrict such entrepreneurial activity in the mid-1980s by using tax policy to make local borrowing more expensive.

Subnational governments have not reacted to economic or social forces impinging upon them within a political/administrative vacuum. Their entrepreneurship in the nineteenth century was certainly inspired by technological change, as well as by the desire for economic growth. But politicians invent and manufacture within their own realm. In this case, their entrepreneurship involved positioning themselves in both the federal system and the economy as it evolved over time. Their response to economic change is so shaped by the federal system that they could not address such change without simultaneously thinking about how to manipulate or work around the federal system. The concepts of "urban political economy" and "political economy of federalism" are interwoven.

The resulting system is an extraordinarily complex one. Governments are far from acting simply as the forum for interest-group competition or as access points or veto points for contending interest groups. Yet neither are government officials autonomous actors choosing from a portfolio of policy choices that are unconstrained by the legacy of previous choices. Strategies and choices in the public investment portfolio vary with context; they are different in the 1830s, the 1960s, and the 1990s.

Subnational officials in the United States work within a system in which their predecessors have made Faustian bargains. In order to circumvent state restrictions, while benefiting from the federal tax exemption on local borrowing, they created new governmental entities that qualified for the tax exemption. However, in so doing, they fragmented their own power. The landscape of local government in the United States, therefore, looks far different from the one portrayed in most textbooks. General-purpose governments have become surrounded by special-purpose entities, which are often insulated from the pressures of decision making that are intrinsic to general-purpose governments accountable to electorates. In a political landscape where taxes are transformed into user fees and citizens into users, the electorates are more remote.

The contemporary pattern of policy making in American public investment is the unanticipated consequence of a process that began with the earliest debates over the appropriate national role in the provision of internal improvements. The range of choices that contemporary policy makers face are not those they would necessarily prefer. It is a range that historical forces have handed them.

Elected officials who wish to improve their chances of reelection, build coalitions, and reward political friends must work within relatively narrow limits. In the capital investment arena, many potential choices are simply not available. Elected officials need to address constituency demands and simultaneously maneuver within the constraints and opportunities provided by the legal system that regulates both their behavior and the market within which they borrow.

That market, however, is hypersensitive to law and politics, for it is founded on property rights as defined by courts and on tax law set by the Supreme Court and Congress. Officials, therefore, are affected by law both directly (as it affects their maneuverability) and indirectly (as it shapes the market from which they borrow). Whether investing for infrastructure or for economic development, local officials are operating within an elaborate legal framework. The legal order lies at the heart of the investment system.

Public authorities, unaccountable to electorates, play a different game, one that is neither acknowledged nor understood by either citizens or scholars. Given how little scholarly research there is on these entities, it is difficult to analyze their role in the evolution of the federal system. Their very existence, however, constrains the choices available to elected officials.

Public authority officials also need to maneuver within legal and market constraints, but their insulation from the electorate and their relative invisibility gives them a privileged position. This study has examined the foundation of the public authority system, but future work on federalism, urban politics, metropolitan politics, and state and local government will need to develop our analytic understanding of the role of public authorities.

The American system is characterized by a loose-jointedness that, perhaps paradoxically, makes it difficult to "erase history." It is difficult to mobilize the political resources necessary to change restrictions and laws; circumvention is an easier strategy than a frontal assault on a constitutional provision or statute. The powerful role of the judiciary facilitates that circumvention.

The loose-jointed nature of the American system also binds the public and private sectors together in a symbiotic relationship. Public-sector officials can use private-sector resources to maneuver within a system that is not well articulated administratively. Maneuverability and the capacity for discretion within the public sector, however, is paid for by dependence on private-sector resources. A more centralized system in the United Kingdom gives local officials much less flexibility but also eases their dependence on private-sector resources. A lack of centralization may well correlate with high levels of public-private cooperation and dependency.

Historical analysis of public investment reveals an enduring characteristic of the American federal and policy-making systems. Circumvention is cheaper than change, even though its outcomes may well be far from ideal. The complexity of the system increases over time: when new circumventory mechanisms are invented, the mechanisms of the past are retained rather than eliminated.

It is in this context that the municipal bond market was important. It has allowed local governments to fashion a strategy of circumvention that has tempered the need to attack anachronistic state restrictions directly. The use of the private sector allowed the public sector to create public authorities and thereby to become ever more Byzantine in structure. The state courts acted as the bond market's allies. Without the bond market, the revenue bond would not have been born, but without the state courts' validation, the revenue bond would not have survived. Thus, the state courts, the municipal bond market, and the general strategy of circumvention were inextricably bound together — with the result that the system of state and local capital investment became ever more convoluted as the creation of public authorities added a final touch.

But the strategy of circumvention shaped state-local relations only. The intervention of the federal government in the 1980s added another dimension to the intergovernmental politics of local capital investment. Washington did not change state restriction or the fragmentation of local government. Rather, it added new restrictions, which could not be circumvented as state limits had been. Local governments could not use the market to circumvent federal limits, for those same limits shaped the market itself. The municipal bond market, based as it is on the federal tax exemption of local borrowing, can provide an escape from state limits but not from their federal counterparts.

Washington's intervention was an example of intergovernmental politics at its most visible. The use of tax reform to limit the maneuverability of subnational officials was not primarily an example of partisan politics, but it is still politics, in that national legislators imposed on subnational officials their idea of the proper way to carry out economic development.

Governments act politically toward each other. Much public policy making involves politics between governments, as well as more traditional politics rooted in state-society relations and expressed through interest groups and political parties.

Democracy and Territorial Politics

The conventional view of politics involves elected officials and interest groups; the picture of politics sketched here involves judges' allowing governments to circumvent other levels of government as well as national legislators' forcing state and local borrowers to change their ways. Governments are politicians in their dealings with other governments.

This view of politics requires us to treat intergovernmental politics as seriously as politics that involve social groups. Politics based on the interests of governments as institutions coexist with politics based on the organization and representation of societal interests. To treat federalism as a structural characteristic — as a static feature — of the American political system rather than viewing it as a political dynamic is to diminish the complexity of American politics and policy making.

The intergovernmental form of politics is a less democratic version of politics than that rooted in state-society relations. Electorates are often simply uninvolved and unaware. Some of the governments involved — public authorities in particular — are not elected governments. Even when elected officials engage in intergovernmental politics, they may not be responding to pressures from citizens or (societally based) interest groups. In fact, so-called technical policy areas — which typically do not interest the participants in electorally based politics — are generally those most likely to be the object of intergovernmental politics.

Technical matters are precisely those that are likely to affect the institutional self-interest of governments. Government operations — widely viewed as technical — can be marginal to politics as conceived according to the state-society model but at the very core of intergovernmental relations as discussed in this analysis. The use of the revenue bond, the legitimation of that bond by state courts, and the creation of public authorities are not, and have not been, important to political discourse as traditionally defined in any city or state government. They are invisible on the political map as conventionally drawn. Yet they have changed the face of American subnational government and the system of financing and have transformed taxpayers into ratepayers.

Further, the channels through which action and conflict take place are not those specified in democratic theory. The role of the courts in this form of political dialogue is particularly difficult to analyze using traditional categories. And the use of the market as an instrument does not fit into our categories of politically relevant action. Yet, simply because the activities identified within the general realm of intergovernmental politics do not fit within our notions of how the exercise of political action is linked to the exercise of democracy does not justify ruling out intergovernmental politics as an important part of the American political dynamic.

Conflict between governments is sometimes viewed as being of more relevance to students of public administration than to students of political science. Relations between governments are not viewed as "politics" because they are not rooted in state-society relations; that is, social or economic or racial groups are not involved in influencing the government. Yet, the outcomes of intergovernmental politics set the parameters of choice for traditional political actors.

If we generalize from the sector of public investment, it seems that intergovernmental politics in the United States have at least three important features. The first has to do with "horizontal politics." This element manifests the competitiveness that is intrinsic to American federalism. American state and local governments have been competing with each other for over two centuries now, and this competition has been ferociously intensified by the ease of incorporation in the United States. As new states entered the union and as local governments proliferated within both new and existing states, the number of competitors constantly increased. It is this competitive element that drives a great deal of intergovernmental politics at the subnational level and that dominates the pursuit of economic development. Whereas German federalism has developed rules that are designed to minimize competition among territorial units, the history of American federalism — and of horizontal relationships among states and among local governments — has been based on competition for economic growth.

Second, intergovernmental politics in the area of economic policy (especially in the post–World War II period) are driven by two different views of the American economy and of economic growth. Washington tends to think in macro-economic terms, and more recently micro-economic views (those focusing on specific industrial sectors) have become more prominent. Yet subnational officials view the economy spatially; they think territorially. Seen from Washington, D.C., it does not matter where a business firm locates, pays taxes, and hires workers (as long as it does not move abroad), but in the dynamic of territorial politics that locational decision is all-important. It is the collision between views of the economy viewed through the lens of macro-economic indicators (including federal revenues) on the one hand and through the lens of territory on the other, which leads to such disparate positions of what is appropriate policy in the area of economic development.

Third, this conflict will encourage the development of strategies that are intended to increase the discretion of local officials, even as the structural limits that impinge upon them become more stringent. Such strategies will use private-sector institutions and "non-political" institutions such as courts to stretch the bounds of the restrictions that state and local officials find themselves facing. At their end, federal officials will continue to use a variety of mechanisms — including tax laws, mandates, and a wide variety of regulatory measures — to assert control.

Conclusion

American federalism is not a static feature of American politics and policy making. It shapes a territorially based politics, which coexists with that socially based dynamic traditionally defined as "politics." Governments are central actors in the "politics of federalism." Indeed, governments act toward other governments much as interest groups relate to government. Governments drive a political process that involves shifting coalitions, changes in the importance of the main actors, the introduction of new actors, the development of strategies, the use of unexpected instruments such as tax law, the creation and sustenance of public-private networks, judicial intervention, and the erosion of the influence of the electorate and electorally based politics. Intergovernmental politics in the United States are not marginal to politics and policy but, rather, form part of the very fabric of American governance.

The opportunities and constraints that confront a government are not constant over time. The opportunity structure that faces local governments in the present has evolved over nearly two centuries and is deeply rooted in the historical legacy of governmental intervention in the American economy. The development of that structure has been driven by governments' jostling and competing for position, authority, jurisdiction, and finance. The creation of the structure we now find in situ has been fraught with intergovernmental conflict, and its shape has been defined by the winners and losers of those battles. In many cases, the arbiter of such conflict has been the judiciary — both the state courts and the U.S. Supreme Court.

In a federal system, roles and responsibilities can never be completely fixed or defined. They are constantly being challenged by one governmental unit or another. The options available to any single government are typically unclear enough so that officials from any unit may find it worthwhile to push against the boundaries. Federalism, far from being a static property of the American political system, packages the conflict between governments. It lays some of the ground rules and provides the ammunition for all participants in the never-ending game of intergovernmental politics.

Intergovernmental politics coexist with the kinds of politics that are grouped under the rubric "state-society" relations. Governments qua institutions must be thought of as political actors — as politicians — in their own right. They do not simply respond to interest-group pressures or provide the incentives for individual officeholders or administrators. They also act within a universe of other governments, peers if you will. They maneuver within that universe over time, using strategies that are designed to increase the range of discretion and the number of vantage points suitable for action.

It matters whether one uses the prism of intergovernmental politics or the prism of state-society relations to analyze politics and policy. The two models emphasize different actors, different motives, different time frames, and different channels of action. This study argues, for example, that the politics of circumvention played a key role in the intergovernmental politics of local capital investment. Governments are viewed as purposive, capable of using the legal and financial system to achieve their institutional ends. Territorial units rather than functionally organized interests are central to the analysis. A wide range of institutions — including the judiciary — play important and interdependent roles. Rather than focusing on specific investment decisions, this type of analysis focuses on the constraints and opportunity structure within which any individual decision is taken. The focus is on understanding the parameters within which political choices, as traditionally understood, are made.

By contrast, a study of local public investment based on the state-society model would focus on the local political coalitions that affected local choices about investment. Local officials would be seen as responding to certain pressures rather than others, and the focus would be on elections and electorates, mayors, campaign contributors, organized interests, and the imperatives of the municipal bond market. In this type of analysis, the existence of the revenue bond and the public authority would be taken as givens, as would the fact that capital-intensive services charge user fees.

Intergovernmental politics enjoy an ironic quality. They are invisible, yet they are entrenched in the American political system. They can seem bloodless, when compared to politics as conventionally understood. In short, intergovernmental politics seem to lack the human interest that makes traditional accounts of urban politics so fascinating. Certainly, the creation of the revenue bond is not as stirring a story as the political battles that have raged around specific investments such as convention centers. The electorate was not involved in the creation of the revenue bond except as a factor to be excluded.

The tenuous link of intergovernmental politics to traditional democratic politics, however, does not diminish the impact of the former. The decisions made by the intergovernmental style of politics are rarely challenged by traditional political actors. The issues over which territorial politics are fought are rarely on the first page of any newspaper, yet they help define what can be done and by which governments. Finally, it is both significant and troubling that so much of what a government does and will be able to do in the future is shaped by other governments rather than by citizens.

Notes

1. Introduction

1. Jon C. Teaford, "Finis for Tweed and Steffens: Rewriting the History of Urban Rule," *Reviews in American History* 10, no. 4 (December 1982), pp. 137–43 (139).

2. See, for example, Robert Dahl, *Who Governs?* (New Haven: Yale University Press, 1961).

3. Paul E. Peterson, *City Limits* (Chicago: University of Chicago Press, 1981), pp. 3–4. Martin Shefter, *Political Crisis/Fiscal Crisis: The Collapse and Revival of New York City* (New York: Basic Books, 1985), p. 6. Paul Kantor, *The Dependent City Revisited: The Political Economy of Urban Development and Social Policy* (Boulder, Colo.: Westview Press, 1995), p. 5.

4. See, for example, Hendrik Hartog, *Public Property and Private Power: The Corporation of the City of New York in American Law, 1730–1870* (Chapel Hill: University of North Carolina Press, 1983), chap. 14; Gerald E. Frug, "The City as a Legal Concept," *Harvard Law Review* 93, no. 6 (April 1980), pp. 1059–154.

5. Peterson, *City Limits*, p. 133; Annmarie Hauck Walsh, *The Public's Business: The Politics and Practices of Government Corporations* (Cambridge, Mass.: MIT Press, 1978), pp. 1–2. For a discussion of the relationships that may exist between central-city governments and such independent district governments, see Rowan A. Miranda, "Post-Machine Regimes and the Growth of Government: A Fiscal History of the City of Chicago, 1970–1990," *Urban Affairs Quarterly* 28, no. 3 (March 1993), pp. 397–422; Steven P. Erie, "How the Urban West Was Won: The Local State and Economic Growth in Los Angeles, 1880–1932," *Urban Affairs Quarterly* 27, no. 4 (June 1992), pp. 546–48.

6. Peterson, *City Limits*, p. 29; Paul Kantor with Stephen David, *The Dependent City: The Changing Political Economy of Urban America* (Glenview, Ill.: Scott, Foresman, 1988), p. 8. See also Clarence N. Stone, "The Study of the Politics of Urban Development," in *The Politics of Urban Development*, ed. Clarence N. Stone and Heywood T. Sanders (Lawrence: University Press of Kansas, 1987), pp. 3–22.

7. Herman B. Leonard, *Checks Unbalanced: The Quiet Side of Public Spending* (New York: Basic Books, 1986), p. 10.

8. For major studies that do pay attention to authorities, see David C. Perry, "Building the City Through the Back Door: The Politics of Debt, Law, and Public Infrastructure," in *Building the Public City: The Politics, Governance, and Finance of Public Infrastructure,* ed. David C. Perry (London: Sage, 1995), pp. 202–36;

Ester R. Fuchs, *Mayors and Money: Fiscal Policy in New York and Chicago* (Chicago: University of Chicago Press, 1992); Michael N. Danielson and Jameson W. Doig, *New York: The Politics of Urban Regional Development* (Berkeley and Los Angeles: University of California Press, 1982); Walsh, *The Public's Business;* Jameson W. Doig, " 'If I See a Murderous Fellow Sharpening a Knife Cleverly . . .': The Wilsonian Dichotomy and the Public Authority Tradition," *Public Administration Review* 43 (July/August 1983), pp. 292–304; Robert G. Smith, *Public Authorities in Urban Areas* (Washington, D.C.: National Association of Counties Research Foundation, 1969). See also "Symposium on Public Authorities and Public Policy," *Policy Studies Journal* 18, no. 4 (summer 1990), pp. 927–1044; Diana B. Henriques, *The Machinery of Greed: The Abuse of Public Authorities and What to Do About It* (Lexington, Mass.: Lexington Books, 1986); James T. Bennett and Thomas J. DiLorenzo, *Underground Government: The Off-Budget Public Sector* (Washington, D.C.: Cato Institute, 1983); Heywood T. Sanders, "Building the Convention City: Politics, Finance, and Public Investment in Urban America," *Journal of Urban Affairs* 14, no. 2 (1992), pp. 135–59. In the case of Cleveland, Todd Swanstrom points out that "the new growth politics . . . never dominated Cleveland the way it did other cities. . . . Perhaps most important, urban renewal in Cleveland unlike most cities was administered not by an autonomous redevelopment agency but by a department of city government. . . . Many of the problems and delays of urban renewal were brought about by political opposition that found relatively easy expression through Cleveland's ward-based political system." Todd Swanstrom, *The Crisis of Growth Politics: Cleveland, Kucinich, and the Challenge of Urban Populism* (Philadelphia: Temple University Press, 1985), p. 94.

9. Todd Swanstrom refers to A. M. Hillhouse's classic work *Municipal Bonds: A Century of Experience* (New York: Prentice-Hall, 1936) as "one of the best histories of urban growth politics in the United States, albeit from the limited perspective of municipal bond aid to private enterprise." Swanstrom, *The Crisis of Growth Politics,* p. 256.

10. For a discussion of unsavory relationships involved in the financing of public investment by public authorities, see Henriques, *Machinery of Greed,* and also John R. Wilke, "Massachusetts Is Roiled by Bond Scandal," *Wall Street Journal,* July 21, 1993, p. C1. For campaign funding, see, for example, Constance Mitchell and Thomas T. Vogel Jr., "Illegal Payments Mar the Muni Market," *Wall Street Journal,* May 5, 1993, p. C1; Christi Harlan and Thomas T. Vogel Jr., "Bond Group Moves to Curb Political Gifts," *Wall Street Journal,* August 5, 1993, p. C1; Jerry Knight, "Muni Bonds Targeted for Key Reforms," *Washington Post,* September 8, 1993, p. F1; Jonathan Fuerbringer, "Credit Markets: In Shift, Bond Dealers Seek to Halt Political Donations," *New York Times,* October 6, 1993, p. D1; Jonathan Fuerbringer, "Despite Scandal, Politicians Still Want Wall St. Money," *New York Times,* October 14, 1993, p. D1; Thomas T. Vogel Jr. and John Connor, "Muni-Firm Plan Meets Resistance; Political-Donation Limits Spur Protests from State Officials," *Wall Street Journal,* December 13, 1993, p. C1; Thomas T. Vogel Jr., "Politicians Are Mobilizing to Derail Ban on Muni Underwriters' Campaign Gifts," *Wall Street Journal,* December 27, 1993, p. 15; Frank Shafroth, "Proposed

Campaign Finance Regs Would Discriminate Against City Officials," *Nation's Cities Weekly* 17, April 11, 1994, p. 1.

11. Fritz Scharpf has used this term in reference to the interests of the German state governments, the Laender. He argues that the decision-making processes of the German federal system are characterized by the Laenders' attempts to pursue their interests qua governments. Fritz W. Scharpf, "The Joint-Decision Trap: Lessons from German Federalism and European Integration," *Public Administration* 66 (autumn 1988), p. 254.

12. See William H. Riker, *Federalism: Origin, Operation, Significance* (Boston: Little, Brown, 1964); Riker, "Six Books in Search of a Subject—or Does Federalism Exist and Does It Matter?" *Comparative Politics* 2 (1969); Samuel H. Beer, "The Modernization of American Federalism," *Publius: The Journal of Federalism* (1973), pp. 50–95; Deil Wright, *Understanding Intergovernmental Relations* (North Scituate, Mass.: Duxbury Press, 1978); Stephen David and Paul Kantor, "Urban Policy in the Federal System: A Reconceptualization of Federalism," *Polity* 16, no. 2, pp. 284–303.

13. John H. Mollenkopf, *The Contested City* (Princeton: Princeton University Press, 1983), pp. 139–40. See also Amy Bridges, "Winning the West to Municipal Reform," *Urban Affairs Quarterly* 27, no. 4 (June 1992), pp. 494–518.

14. See, for example, Clarence Stone, *Regime Politics* (Lawrence: University Press of Kansas), 1989; Ira Katznelson, *City Trenches: Urban Politics and the Patterning of Class in the United States* (New York: Pantheon Books, 1981); Swanstrom, *The Crisis of Growth Politics;* John Logan and Harvey Molotch, *Urban Fortunes: The Political Economy of Place* (Berkeley and Los Angeles: University of California Press, 1987); Mollenkopf, *The Contested City;* Shefter, *Political Crisis/Fiscal Crisis;* Stephen L. Elkin, *City and Regime in the American Republic* (Chicago: University of Chicago Press, 1987); Clarence N. Stone and Heywood T. Sanders, eds., *The Politics of Urban Development* (Lawrence: University Press of Kansas, 1987); John Logan and Todd Swanstrom, eds., *Beyond the City Limits* (Philadelphia: Temple University Press, 1990); Gregory D. Squires, ed., *Unequal Partnerships* (New Brunswick, N.J.: Rutgers University Press, 1988); Paul Kantor and H. V. Savitch, "Can Politicians Bargain with Business? A Theoretical and Comparative Perspective on Urban Development," *Urban Affairs Quarterly* 29, no. 2 (December 1993), pp. 230–55.

15. Matthew Holden Jr., "The Governance of the Metropolis as a Problem in Diplomacy," *Journal of Politics* 26, no. 3 (August 1964), pp. 627–47 (628). Beer, "Modernization of American Federalism," p. 75.

16. Samuel H. Beer, "The Adoption of General Revenue Sharing: A Case Study in Public Sector Politics," *Public Policy* 24 (1976), pp. 166–71. For a discussion of intergovernmental lobbying, see Donald H. Haider, *When Governments Come to Washington: Governors, Mayors, and Intergovernmental Lobbying* (New York: Free Press, 1974); see also Samuel H. Beer, "Political Overload and Federalism," *Polity* 10, no. 1 (fall 1977), pp. 5–17; Samuel H. Beer, "Federalism, Nationalism, and Democracy in America," *American Political Science Review* 72, no. 1 (March 1978), pp. 9–21.

17. See, for example, Jerome E. Milch, "Influence as Power: French Local Government Reconsidered," *British Journal of Political Science* 4 (April 1974), pp. 139-62; Alberta Sbragia, "Not All Roads Lead to Rome: Local Housing Policy in the Unitary Italian State," *British Journal of Political Science* 9 (July 1979), pp. 315-40. Local governments often have a greater capacity to "sabotage" national policy than do conventional interest groups. Why such behavior should be classified under the term *relations* rather than *politics* is unclear. Having said that, for an excellent study of intergovernmental relations, defined in the administrative sense, see Wright, *Understanding Intergovernmental Relations*.

18. Hartog, *Public Property and Private Power*, pp. 206-07. See also Gerald E. Frug, "Property and Power: Hartog on the Legal History of New York City," *American Bar Foundation Research Journal*, no. 3 (summer 1984), pp. 673-91.

19. Such a view runs counter to Samuel Beer's analysis of the underlying dynamics of American federalism. He argues: "Taking 'ground rules' to mean the juristic protections of federalism, the implication of the analysis in this essay is that the major grounds of centralization and decentralization are to be found not in such 'ground rules' but rather in the forces of economic and political development." Beer, "Modernization of American Federalism."

20. Fuchs, *Mayors and Money*, p. 4.

21. Similarly, state government, at times, has set up local authorities in order to penetrate local policy making and to control it more effectively. See Carolyn Teich Adams, *The Politics of Capital Investment: The Case of Philadelphia* (Albany: State University of New York Press, 1988).

22. Authorities have shown themselves able to carry out new functions as they become needed. Jerry Mitchell points out that authorities concerned with environmental protection are enjoying the fastest rate of growth. Jerry Mitchell, "The Policy Activities of Public Authorities," *Policy Studies Journal* 18, no. 4 (summer 1990), p. 933.

23. Davita Silfen Glasberg, "The Political Economic Power of Finance Capital and Urban Fiscal Crisis: Cleveland's Default, 1978," *Journal of Urban Affairs* 10, no. 1 (1988), pp. 63-76. Adams, *The Politics of Capital Investment*; Elkin, *City and Regime*; Alberta Sbragia, "Politics, Local Government, and the Municipal Bond Market," in *The Municipal Money Chase: The Politics of Local Government Finance*, ed. A. Sbragia (Boulder, Colo.: Westview Press, 1983), pp. 67-112; Shefter, *Political Crisis/Fiscal Crisis* (esp. p. 232). The quotation is from Sbragia, "Politics, Local Government, and the Municipal Bond Market," p. 101.

24. Elkin, *City and Regime*, p. 31. Erie, "How the Urban West Was Won," p. 522.

25. Sbragia, "Politics, Local Government, and the Municipal Bond Market."

26. Shefter, *Political Crisis/Fiscal Crisis*, p. 133.

27. Patricia Giles Leeds, "City Politics and the Market: The Case of New York City's Financing Crisis," in *The Municipal Money Chase: The Politics of Local Government Finance*, ed. Alberta M. Sbragia (Boulder, Colo.: Westview Press, 1983), pp. 113-44.

28. See, for example, Michael Keating, *Comparative Urban Politics: Power and the City in the United States, Canada, Britain, and France* (Aldershot, England:

Edward Elgar, 1991), pp. 68–75; Alberta M. Sbragia, "Cities, Capital, and Banks: The Politics of Debt in the United States, United Kingdom, and France," in *Urban Political Economy,* ed. Kenneth Newton (London: Frances Pinter, 1981), pp. 200–220.

29. Elkin, *City and Regime,* p. 32. British local governments borrow in the capital markets whereas, for example, French and Italian local governments borrow from banks. See Sbragia, "Cities, Capital, and Banks," pp. 200–211; Alberta M. Sbragia, *The Politics of Local Borrowing: A Comparative Analysis,* Studies in Public Policy, no. 37 (Centre for the Study of Public Policy, University of Strathclyde, Glasgow, 1979); Sbragia, "Borrowing to Build: Private Money and Public Welfare," *International Journal of Health Services* 9 (1979), pp. 207–18; Sbragia, *Capital Markets and Central-Local Politics in Britain: The Double Game,* Studies in Public Policy, no. 109 (Centre for the Study of Public Policy, University of Strathclyde, Glasgow, 1983); and Sbragia, "Capital Markets and Central-Local Politics in Britain," *British Journal of Political Science* 16 (July 1986), pp. 311–33. For a good discussion of the general differences between financial systems relying on capital markets and those based on banks, see John Zysman, *Governments, Markets, and Growth: Financial Systems and the Politics of Industrial Change* (Ithaca, N.Y.: Cornell University Press, 1983).

30. See Sbragia, "Capital Markets and Central-Local Politics," pp. 311–33.

31. Arthur F. McEvoy, *The Fisherman's Problem: Ecology and Law in the California Fisheries, 1850–1980* (Cambridge: Cambridge University Press, 1986), p. 13. See Willard Hurst, *Law and Markets in United States History: Different Modes of Bargaining Among Interests* (Madison: University of Wisconsin Press, 1982), and *Law and Social Order in the United States* (Ithaca, N.Y.: Cornell University Press, 1977). See also Robert W. Gordon, "Introduction: J. Willard Hurst and the Common Law Tradition in American Legal Historiography," *Law and Society Review* 10 (1975), pp. 9–56; Harry N. Scheiber, "Public Economic Policy and the American Legal System: Historical Perspectives," *Wisconsin Law Review* 1 (1980), pp. 159–90; Harry N. Scheiber, "At the Borderland of Law and Economic History: The Contributions of Willard Hurst," *American Historical Review* 75, no. 3 (February 1970), pp. 744–56. For a work that moves beyond the analysis of the "Hurst School," see Morton J. Horwitz, *The Transformation of American Law, 1780–1860* (Cambridge: Harvard University Press, 1977).

32. Eric H. Monkkonen, "The Politics of Municipal Indebtedness and Default, 1850–1936," in *The Politics of Urban Fiscal Policy,* ed. Terrence J. McDonald and Sally K. Ward (Beverly Hills: Sage, 1984), pp. 125–59 (134).

33. Peter K. Eisinger, *The Rise of the Entrepreneurial State: State and Local Economic Development Policy in the United States* (Madison: University of Wisconsin Press, 1988).

2. State Governments as Entrepreneurs

1. Although the internal improvements I emphasize are those in the transportation sector, improvements included other forms of capital investment also.

2. Andrew Shonfield, *Modern Capitalism: The Changing Balance of Public and Private Power* (New York and London: Oxford University Press, 1965), pp. 301–02.

3. See Robert Gilpin, *U.S. Power and the Multinational Corporation: The Political Economy of Foreign Direct Investment* (New York: Basic Books, 1975).

4. The notion of a "transportation revolution" comes from an influential book with that title. George Rogers Taylor, *The Transportation Revolution, 1815–1860* (New York: Rinehart and Company, 1951).

5. Carter Goodrich, *Government Promotion of American Canals and Railroads, 1800–1890* (New York: Columbia University Press, 1960), p. 7.

6. Ibid., p. 10. I have relied heavily on this major history of internal improvements.

7. Carter Goodrich, "American Development Policy: The Case of Internal Improvements," *Journal of Economic History* 16, no. 4 (December 1956), pp. 449–60 (452–53). See also Edward C. Kirkland, *Men, Cities, and Transportation: A Study in New England History, 1820–1900* (Cambridge: Harvard University Press, 1948).

8. *Annals of Congress,* 31st Cong., 1st sess., p. 851, cited in Goodrich, *Government Promotion,* p. 9.

9. Alfred D. Chandler Jr., ed., *The Railroads, the Nation's First Big Business: Sources and Readings* (New York: Harcourt, Brace and World, 1965), pp. 43–44. See David Maldwyn Ellis, "The Forfeiture of Railroad Land Grants, 1867–1894," *Mississippi Valley Historical Review* 33 (June 1946), pp. 27–60. For analyses of the federal role in assisting railways, see Lewis H. Haney, *A Congressional History of Railways in the United States* (1908, 1910; reprint, New York: Augustus M. Kelley, 1968); Lloyd Mercer, *Railroads and Land Grant Policy: A Study in Government Intervention* (New York: Academic Press, 1982); R. Carstensen, ed., *The Public Lands: Studies in the History of the Public Domain* (Madison: University of Wisconsin Press, 1963), pp. 121–79. The federal government was also responsible for improvements on navigable waterways. See Albert Lepawsky, "Water Resources and Federalism," *American Political Science Review* 44 (September 1950), pp. 631–49.

10. For a discussion of attempts made to get congressional approval of a stronger federal role in the provision of internal improvements, see Joel H. Silbey, *The Transformation of American Politics, 1840–1860* (Englewood Cliffs, N.J.: Prentice-Hall, 1967), pp. 22–28.

11. Carter Goodrich, "National Planning of Internal Improvements," *Political Science Quarterly* 63, no. 1 (March 1948), pp. 16–44 (26).

12. Goodrich, *Government Promotion,* pp. 46–47. For the War of 1812, see Donald H. Kagin, "Monetary Aspects of the Treasury Notes of the War of 1812," *Journal of Economic History* 44, no. 1 (March 1984), pp. 69–88.

13. Adams quoted in Goodrich, "National Planning of Internal Improvements," pp. 29, 44. Goodrich, *Government Promotion,* p. vii.

14. Louis Hartz, *Economic Policy and Democratic Thought: Pennsylvania, 1776–1860* (Cambridge: Harvard University Press, 1948); Oscar Handlin and Mary Flug Handlin, *A Commonwealth: A Study of the Role of Government in the*

American Economy, Massachusetts, 1774–1861 (New York: New York University Press, 1947); Milton Sydney Heath, "Laissez Faire in Georgia, 1732–1860," *Journal of Economic History* 3 (1943), supplement, pp. 78–100; Carter Goodrich, "The Virginia System of Mixed Enterprise: A Study of State Planning of Internal Improvements," *Political Science Quarterly* 64, no. 3 (September 1949), pp. 355–87, and "Local Government Planning and Internal Improvements," *Political Science Quarterly* 66, no. 3 (September 1951), pp. 411–46.

15. Robert A. Lively, "The American System: A Review Article," *The Business History Review* 29, no. 1 (March 1955), pp. 81–96 (81, 86).

16. G. S. Callender, "The Early Transportation and Banking Enterprises of the States in Relation to the Growth of Corporations," *Quarterly Journal of Economics* 17 (November 1902), pp. 111–62 (113, 161). Andrew Shonfield, *Modern Capitalism: The Changing Balance of Public and Private Power* (Oxford University Press, 1965), p. 303.

17. Harry N. Scheiber, "The Road to *Munn*: Eminent Domain and the Concept of Public Purpose in the State Courts," in *Law in American History*, ed. Donald Fleming and Bernard Bailyn (Boston: Little, Brown, 1971), pp. 329–402. (I have drawn from this major study for my entire discussion of the evolution of eminent domain law at the state level.) For a discussion of how courts assisted entrepreneurs in their handling of nuisance doctrine, see Paul M. Kurtz, "Nineteenth Century Anti-Entrepreneurial Nuisance Injunctions — Avoiding the Chancellor," *William and Mary Law Review* 17, no. 4 (summer 1976), pp. 621–72.

18. Scheiber, "The Road to *Munn*," pp. 332, 363–65 (363); see also Hurst.

19. Quoted in Scheiber, "The Road to *Munn*," p. 380.

20. Herbert Ershkowitz and William G. Shade, "Consensus or Conflict? Political Behavior in the State Legislatures During the Jacksonian Era," *Journal of American History* 58, no. 3 (December 1971), pp. 591–621 (604). See also Scheiber, "At the Borderland of Law and Economic History," p. 753, and Richard L. McCormick, "The Party Period and Public Policy: An Exploratory Hypothesis," *Journal of American History* 66, no. 2 (September 1979), pp. 279–98.

21. Scheiber, *Ohio Canal Era: A Case Study of Government and the Economy, 1820–1861* (Athens: Ohio University Press, 1969), p. xv.

22. Carter Goodrich, "The Revulsion Against Internal Improvements," *Journal of Economic History* 10, no. 2 (November 1950), pp. 145–69 (169); see also Lively, "The American System," and McCormick, "The Party Period and Public Policy," pp. 285–90.

23. Reginald C. McGrane, *The Economic Development of the American Nation*, rev. ed. (New York: Ginn and Company, 1950), p. 187. Goodrich, *Government Promotion*, p. 55.

24. McGrane, *Economic Development of the American Nation*, p. 188; Harold Underwood Faulkner, *American Economic History* (New York: Harper and Brothers, 1924), pp. 320–21.

25. Quotations are from Nathan Miller, *The Enterprise of a Free People: Aspects of Economic Development in New York State During the Canal Period, 1792–1838* (Ithaca, N.Y.: Cornell University Press, 1962), p. 137, and from

McGrane, *Economic Development of the American Nation*, p. 188. See also Roger L. Ransom, "Canals and Development: A Discussion of the Issues," *American Economic Review* 54 (May 1964), pp. 365–76.

26. Taylor, *The Transportation Revolution*, pp. 6–7.

27. Goodrich, *Government Promotion*, pp. 63–64. Hartz, *Economic Policy and Democratic Thought*, p. 11. See also Harvey H. Segal, "Cycles of Canal Construction," in *Canals and American Economic Development*, ed. Carter Goodrich (New York: Columbia University Press, 1961), p. 176.

28. *United States Gazette*, October 18, 1825, quoted in Julius Rubin, "An Imitative Public Improvement: The Pennsylvania Mainline," in Goodrich, *Canals and American Economic Development*, p. 95. Second quotation is from p. 69.

29. McGrane, *Economic Development of the American Nation*, pp. 188–192. Michigan's constitution is cited in Goodrich, *Government Promotion*, p. 144. Scheiber, "Federalism and the American Economic Order, 1789–1910," *Law and Society Review* 10 (fall 1975), pp. 71–72. See also Goodrich, "The Virginia System of Mixed Enterprise," p. 384.

30. Mark W. Summers, *Railroads, Reconstruction, and the Gospel of Prosperity: Aid Under the Radical Republicans, 1865–1877* (Princeton: Princeton University Press, 1984), p. 300.

31. Ershkowitz and Shade, "Consensus or Conflict?" See also McCormick, "The Party Period and Public Policy," p. 287, and Goodrich, *Government Promotion*, p. 266. Ronald Formisano, *The Birth of Mass Political Parties, Michigan, 1837–1861* (Princeton: Princeton University Press, 1971), p. 36. Concerning a later period, James Edward Wright argues that in Colorado, the Democrats and Republicans by the middle 1880s had similar positions concerning federal land reclamation projects. *The Politics of Populism: Dissent in Colorado* (New Haven: Yale University Press, 1974), pp. 64–70.

32. Summers, *Railroads, Reconstruction*, pp. 30, 33–34.

33. McGrane, *Economic Development of the American Nation*, p. 192; A. James Heins, *Constitutional Restrictions Against State Debt* (Madison: University of Wisconsin Press, 1963), p. 5; Reginald C. McGrane, *Foreign Bondholders and American State Debts* (New York: MacMillan, 1935), p. 35.

34. B. U. Ratchford, *American State Debts* (Durham: Duke University Press, 1941), p. 88; Heins, *Constitutional Restrictions*, p. 5.

35. Callender, "Early Transportation and Banking Enterprises," p. 114. On January 1, 1843, the states owed $231 million, whereas cities owed $27 million and the federal government owed a mere $20 million. McGrane, *Foreign Bondholders*, p. 35.

36. Callender, "Early Transportation and Banking Enterprises," pp. 151–52.

37. Ibid., p. 45

38. John W. Million, *State Aid to Railways in Missouri* (Chicago: University of Chicago Press, 1896), p. 8.

39. Miller, *Enterprise of a Free People*, pp. 72, 262.

40. McGrane, *Foreign Bondholders*, p. 7.

41. James C. Riley, *International Government Finance and the Amsterdam*

Capital Market, 1740–1815 (Cambridge: Cambridge University Press, 1980), p. 8; see also pp. 14, 83, 119–25. See also Leland Hamilton Jenks, *The Migration of British Capital to 1875* (London: Thomas Nelson, 1927), pp. 9–14.

42. Jenks, *Migration of British Capital*, pp. 70–72; McGrane, *Foreign Bondholders*, p. 9.

43. D. C. M. Platt, *Foreign Finance in Continental Europe and the United States, 1815–1870: Quantities, Origins, Functions, and Distribution* (London: George Allen and Unwin, 1984), p. 155. Quotation is from McGrane, *Foreign Bondholders*, p. 11.

44. McGrane, *Foreign Bondholders*, p. 8; Jenks, *Migration of British Capital*, pp. 70, 79; Ratchford, *American State Debts*, p. 95.

45. Platt, *Foreign Finance*, appendix 2, p. 191. Overall, foreign capital, while it "speeded up development" was not the most crucial factor in American economic development (ibid., pp. 142, 165). Irving Kravis has argued that foreign capital contributed only 4 percent to American net capital formation between the 1820s and 1860s. Irving B. Kravis, "The Role of Exports in Nineteenth-Century United States Growth," *Economic Development and Cultural Change* (April 1972), p. 403, cited in ibid., p. 141. Whereas foreign capital was not critical in all decades, however, it was critical in the 1830s, when state governments were most aggressively promoting economic development.

46. McGrane, *Foreign Bondholders*, pp. 19–20. Heins, *Constitutional Restrictions*, p. 7.

47. Ratchford, *American State Debts*, p. 93. McGrane, *Foreign Bondholders*, pp. 18–19. Quotation is from Ratchford, *American State Debts*, p. 94.

48. McGrane, *Foreign Bondholders*, p. 19. Ratchford, *American State Debts*, p. 94.

49. The term *repudiation* was first used in 1841 by the governor of Mississippi when he outlined a plan of "repudiating the sale of certain of the state bonds, on account of fraud and illegality." Quoted in Warren M. Persons, *Government Experimentation in Business* (New York: John Wiley, 1934), p. 75.

50. Ratchford, *American State Debts*, p. 97. Persons, *Government Experimentation*, pp. 80–86.

51. McGrane, *Foreign Bondholders*, p. 55.

52. Goodrich, *Government Promotion*, pp. 67–68.

53. Quoted in McGrane, *Foreign Bondholders*, p. 59. The dean was not the only outraged Briton to take pen to paper. Wordsworth wrote a poem entitled "The Pennsylvanians," which gives an idea of the shock the state's default caused British investors.

54. McGrane, *Foreign Bondholders*, pp. 72–81.

55. See Arthur M. Johnson and Barry E. Supple, *Boston Capitalists and Western Railroads: A Study in the Nineteenth-Century Railroad Investment Process* (Cambridge: Harvard University Press, 1967), p. 41. Ratchford, *American State Debts*, p. 134.

56. Ratchford, *American State Debt*, pp. 122–34. See James Neal Primm, *Economic Policy in the Development of a Western State, Missouri, 1820–1860* (Cam-

bridge: Harvard University Press, 1954), pp. 93–113; Milton Sydney Heath, *Constructive Liberalism: The Role of the State in Economic Development in Georgia to 1860* (Cambridge: Harvard University Press, 1954), pp. 276–92; Alfred Glaze Smith Jr., *Economic Readjustment of an Old Cotton State, South Carolina, 1820–1860* (Columbia: University of South Carolina Press, 1958), pp. 174–92; Robert B. Jones, *Tennessee at the Crossroads: The State Debt Controversy, 1870–1883* (Knoxville: University of Tennessee Press, 1977), pp. 3–6; Goodrich, "The Virginia System of Mixed Enterprise."

57. Ratchford, *American State Debts*, pp. 135, 137, 155–61. See also William A. Scott, *The Repudiation of State Debts: A Study in the Financial History of Mississippi, Florida, Alabama, North Carolina, South Carolina, Georgia, Louisiana, Arkansas, Tennessee, Minnesota, Michigan, and Virginia* (New York: Thomas Y. Crowell, 1893).

58. Summers, *Railroads, Reconstruction*, pp. 95, 185, 189–90 (95, 185).

59. Ratchford, *American State Debts*, p. 183, table 14. Summers, *Railroads, Reconstruction*, p. 276.

60. Summers, *Railroads, Reconstruction*, pp. 296–97; Scott, *Repudiation of State Debts*; Ratchford, *American State Debts*, pp. 184–96 (esp. p. 192); McGrane, *Foreign Bondholders*, p. 283.

61. Scott, *Repudiation of State Debts*, pp. 152–61; McGrane, *Foreign Bondholders*, p. 283; James Tice Moore, *Two Paths to the New South: The Virginia Debt Controversy, 1870–1883* (Lexington: The University Press of Kentucky, 1974).

62. For an excellent discussion of the "era of national subsidy," see Goodrich, *Government Promotion*, chap. 5.

63. McGrane, *Foreign Bondholders*, pp. 31–34, 266–69.

64. Platt, *Foreign Finance*, p. 191; McGrane, *Foreign Bondholders*, pp. 35–39.

65. See Goodrich, "The Revulsion Against Internal Improvements," pp. 145–69.

66. Ratchford, *American State Debts*, p. 92. McGrane, *Foreign Bondholders*, pp. 7–8 (8).

67. Quotation is from Hartz, *Economic Policy and Democratic Thought*, p. 124. Daniel W. Lynch, *The Development of State and Local Debt in Kentucky, 1890–1962* (Lexington: Bureau of Business Research, College of Commerce, University of Kentucky, 1966), p. 12; Fletcher M. Green, *Constitutional Development in the South Atlantic States, 1776–1860: A Study in the Evolution of Democracy* (Chapel Hill: University of North Carolina Press, 1930), pp. 272–87, 292–94.

68. Ratchford, *American State Debts*, p. 122.

69. Summers, *Railroads, Reconstruction*, p. 285.

70. Ratchford, *American State Debts*, p. 256.

3. Cities as Investors

1. Harry N. Scheiber, "Urban Rivalry and Internal Improvements in the Old Northwest, 1820–1860," *Ohio History* 71, no. 3 (October 1962), pp. 227–39 (235).

2. Douglas E. Booth, "Transportation, City Building, and Financial Crises— Milwaukee, 1852–1862," *Journal of Urban History* 9, no. 3 (May 1983), pp. 335–63; see also David M. Hecht and Frank L. Mallare, "Wisconsin's Internal Improvements Prohibition: Obsolete in Modern Times?" *Wisconsin Law Review* (March 1961), pp. 294–309 (esp. pp. 294–99).

3. Scheiber, "Urban Rivalry," p. 236.

4. For an interesting discussion of the problems presented for economic growth by the size of the frontier and the distances involved, see Thomas C. Cochran, "The Paradox of American Economic Growth," *Journal of American History* 61 (March 1975), pp. 925–42. For a discussion of rivalry in the West, see Bradford Luckingham, "The American West: An Urban Perspective," *Journal of Urban History* 8, no. 1 (November 1981), pp. 99–105; Lawrence H. Larsen, *The Urban West at the End of the Frontier* (Lawrence: Regents Press of Kansas), 1978; Bradford Luckingham, *The Urban Southwest: A Profile History of Albuquerque, El Paso, Phoenix, Tucson* (University of Texas at El Paso: Texas Western Press, 1982). Cities in the South also competed with one another for railway connections. See Lawrence H. Larsen, *The Rise of the Urban South* (Lexington: The University Press of Kentucky, 1985), chap. 4; Merl E. Reed, *New Orleans and the Railroads: The Struggle for Commercial Empire, 1830–1860* (Baton Rouge: Louisiana State University Press, 1966); Ulrich Bonnell Phillips, *A History of Transportation in the Eastern Cotton Belt to 1860* (New York: Octagon Books, 1968).

5. Wyatt Winton Belcher, *The Economic Rivalry Between St. Louis and Chicago: 1850–1880* (New York: Columbia University Press, 1947), p. 258.

6. See J. Christopher Schnell, "Chicago Versus St. Louis: A Reassessment of the Great Rivalry," *Missouri Historical Review* 71, no. 3 (April 1877), pp. 245–65.

7. Julius Rubin, "Canal or Railroad? Imitation and Innovation in the Response to the Erie Canal in Philadelphia, Baltimore, and Boston," *Transactions of the American Philosophical Society* 51 (November 1961), pt. 7, p. 6.

8. Ibid., pp. 5–106.

9. Ibid., p. 14. Charles N. Glaab and A. Theodore Brown, *A History of Urban America* (London: Macmillan, 1967), p. 132. Richard C. Wade, *The Urban Frontier: The Rise of Western Cities, 1790–1830* (Cambridge: Harvard University Press, 1959), p. 322.

10. Robert R. Dykstra, *The Cattle Towns* (New York: Alfred A. Knopf, 1968), p. 360. Don Harrison Doyle, *The Social Order of a Frontier Community: Jacksonville, Illinois, 1825–1870* (Urbana: University of Illinois Press, 1978), p. 80.

11. Luckingham, *The Urban Southwest*, pp. 9–10. Larsen, *The Urban West*, chap. 1. Quotation is from Erie, "How the Urban West Was Won," pp. 526–27.

12. Scheiber, *Ohio Canal Era*, pp. 95–99; Howard P. Chudacoff, *The Evolution of American Urban Society* (Englewood Cliffs, N.J.: Prentice-Hall, 1975), p. 33; Scheiber, "Urban Rivalry," p. 232.

13. Charles N. Glaab, *Kansas City and the Railroads: Community Policy in the Growth of a Regional Metropolis* (Madison: State Historical Society of Wisconsin, 1962), p. 94; Larsen, *The Urban West*, pp. 100–105. The quotation is from Lela Barnes, ed., "An Editor Looks at Early-Day Kansas: The Letters of Charles Mon-

roe Chase," *Kansas Historical Quarterly* 26 (summer 1960), pp. 115–18, cited in Glaab, *Kansas City and the Railroads,* p. 100.

14. Frederick A. Cleveland and Fred Wilbur Powell, *Railroad Promotion and Capitalization in the United States* (London: Longmans, Green, 1909), pp. 109, 130–31; Carl Abbott, *Boosters and Businessmen: Popular Economic Thought and Urban Growth in the Antebellum Middlewest* (Westport, Conn.: Greenwood, 1981), pp. 100–101.

15. Dykstra, *The Cattle Towns,* pp. 52–53, 360 (52–53).

16. See Bayrd Still, *Milwaukee, the History of a City* (Madison: State Historical Society of Wisconsin, 1948), pp. 342–43; Booth, "Transportation, City Building."

17. Abbott, *Boosters and Businessmen.*

18. Larsen, *The Urban West,* p. 102. Glaab, *Kansas City and the Railroads,* p. 9.

19. In Colorado, localities assisted railways only during Colorado's territorial period. In some states, localities were allowed to help railway companies only as long as the state did. "Alabama, Arkansas, Colorado, Ohio, and Pennsylvania adopted constitutional prohibitions against local aid at the same time as against state aid" (Goodrich, "American Development Policy," p. 453 n. 9). Glaab, *Kansas City and the Railroads,* p. 94.

20. Carter Goodrich, "State In, State Out — A Pattern of Development Policy," *Journal of Economic Issues* 11, no. 4 (December 1968), p. 366. See also Chandler, *The Railroads,* p. 44.

21. Goodrich, *Government Promotion,* pp. 268–71 (271).

22. Albert Fishlow, *American Railroads and the Transformation of the Antebellum Economy* (Cambridge: Harvard University Press, 1965), p. 195. Fishlow goes on to point out that, in the case of intercity competition, the benefits to individual cities, although defensive vis-à-vis other cities, were nonetheless greater than to the macroeconomy, which suffered from overconstruction.

23. This section draws heavily from Goodrich, "Local Government Planning and Internal Improvements," pp. 411–45.

24. George H. Miller, *Railroads and the Granger Laws* (Madison: University of Wisconsin Press, 1971), p. 51. Goodrich, *Government Promotion,* pp. 237–54.

25. Goodrich, *Government Promotion,* pp. 142–44.

26. J. H. Hollander, "The Cincinnati Southern Railway: A Study in Municipal Activity," *Johns Hopkins University Studies in Historical and Political Science,* ed. Herbert B. Adams, I-II (Baltimore: Johns Hopkins Press, 1894), p. 18. My entire discussion of the Cincinnati Southern is based on this classic study of municipal enterprise.

27. Ibid., p. 19.

28. J. A. Burhans, *The Law of Municipal Bonds* (Chicago: S. A. Kean, 1889), pp. 19–22; Hillhouse, *Municipal Bonds,* p. 197; *Reconstruction and Reunion, 1864–1888,* ed. Charles Fairman, vol. 6, pt. 1, *The Oliver Wendell Holmes Devise History of the Supreme Court of the United States,* ed. Paul Freund (New York: Macmillan, 1971), p. 1105.

29. Doyle, *The Social Order of a Frontier Community,* pp. 247–48.

30. The quotation is from Burhans, *Law of Municipal Bonds,* p. 21. Fairman, *Reconstruction and Reunion,* p. 1103.

31. Harry H. Pierce, *Railroads of New York: A Study of Government Aid, 1826–1875* (Cambridge: Harvard University Press, 1953), p. 83. Jon C. Teaford, *The Unheralded Triumph: City Government in America, 1870–1900* (Baltimore: Johns Hopkins University Press, 1984), p. 285.

32. Hillhouse, *Municipal Bonds,* p. 34. Pierce, *Railroads of New York,* p. 84.

33. Gerald D. Nash, *State Government and Economic Development: A History of Administrative Policies in California, 1849–1933* (Institute of Governmental Studies, University of California, 1964), p. 61. Municipalities in Nevada, the territory of New Mexico, and Arizona also gave aid. The quotation is from Hillhouse, *Municipal Bonds,* p. 195.

34. Fishlow, *American Railroads,* pp. 193–95.

35. Ibid., p. 195. The quotation is from Pierce, *Railroads of New York,* p. 21. Cleveland and Powell, *Railroad Promotion,* p. 208.

36. Summers, *Railroads, Reconstruction,* pp. 41–42, 189.

37. Terrence J. McDonald and Sally K. Ward, eds., "Introduction," *The Politics of Urban Fiscal Policy* (Beverly Hills: Sage, 1984), pp. 15, 21, 19. See also Terrence J. McDonald, *The Parameters of Urban Fiscal Policy: Socioeconomic Change and Political Culture in San Francisco, 1860–1906* (Berkeley and Los Angeles: University of California Press, 1986), chap. 1. See Samuel P. Hays, "The Politics of Reform in Municipal Government in the Progressive Era," *Pacific Northwest Quarterly* 55 (1964), pp. 157–69, and "The Changing Political Structure of the City in Industrial America," *Journal of Urban History* 1 (November 1974), pp. 6–38; see also Samuel P. Hays, *American Political History as Social Analysis* (Knoxville: University of Tennessee Press, 1980).

38. Teaford, "Finis for Tweed and Steffens," pp. 137–43.

39. Glaab, *Kansas City and the Railroads,* p. 81. Pierce, *Railroads of New York,* p. 27.

40. Pierce, *Railroads of New York,* p. 55.

41. Ibid., p. 90.

42. Hillhouse, *Municipal Bonds,* p. 167. Goodrich, *Government Promotion,* p. 274. Monkkonen, "Politics of Municipal Indebtedness," pp. 125–60; Hillhouse, *Municipal Bonds,* pp. 161–67.

43. Hillhouse, *Municipal Bonds,* pp. 169, 171–76 (169).

4. The Provision of Services

1. Booth, "Transportation, City Building."

2. Harold L. Platt, *City Building in the New South: The Growth of Public Services in Houston, Texas, 1830–1910* (Philadelphia: Temple University Press, 1983), pp. 10–18.

3. John H. Ellis, "Businessmen and Public Health in the Urban South During the Nineteenth Century: New Orleans, Memphis, and Atlanta: Conclusion," *Bulletin of the History of Medicine* 44, no. 4 (July/August 1970), pp. 346–71 (366). See

also Stuart Galshoff, "Triumph and Failure: The American Response to the Urban Water Supply Problem, *1860–1923*," in *Pollution and Reform in American Cities, 1870–1930*, ed. Martin V. Melosi (Austin: University of Texas, 1980), pp. 35–58.

4. Hillhouse, *Municipal Bonds*, 89–91.

5. McDonald, *Parameters of Urban Fiscal Policy*, p. 126 (see also chap. 5).

6. Eric H. Monkkonen, *America Becomes Urban: The Development of U.S. Cities and Towns, 1780–1980* (Berkeley and Los Angeles: University of California Press, 1988), pp. 105, 108 (105).

7. Teaford, *Unheralded Triumph*, p. 217. See also Jameson W. Doig, "Politics and the Engineering Mind: Ammann and the Hidden Story of the George Washington Bridge," in Perry, *Building the Public City*, pp. 21–70.

8. Teaford, *Unheralded Triumph*, p. 221.

9. Ibid., pp. 222, 280 (280).

10. Blaine A. Brownell and David R. Goldfield, eds., *The City in Southern History: The Growth of Urban Civilization in the South* (Port Washington, N.Y.: Kennikat Press, 1977), pp. 110, 119. See also Larsen, *The Rise of the Urban South*, chap. 6. For Houston, see Larsen, *The Rise of the Urban South*, p. 125, and Platt, *City Building in the New South*, pp. 67ff, 197–99.

11. Galshoff, "Triumph and Failure," p. 50.

12. Monkkonen, *America Becomes Urban*, p. 176 (see also chap. 7).

13. Joel A. Tarr, "The Separate Versus Combined Sewer Problem: A Case Study in Urban Technology Design Choice," *Journal of Urban History* 5, no. 3 (May 1979), pp. 308–39. Joel A. Tarr and Francis Clay McMichael, "Decisions About Wastewater Technology, 1850–1932," *Journal of Water Resources Planning and Management Division, Proceedings of the American Society of Civil Engineers* 103 (May 1977), pp. 47–61 (49), and "Historic Turning Points in Municipal Water Supply and Wastewater Disposal, 1850–1932," *Civil Engineering* (October 1977), pp. 82–83.

14. Tarr and McMichael, "Decisions About Wastewater Technology," p. 50. Teaford, *Unheralded Triumph*, p. 222.

15. Tarr and McMichael use this term in "Decisions About Wastewater Technology," p. 48.

16. See, for example, Larsen, *The Rise of the Urban South*, p. 124.

17. Tarr and McMichael, "Decisions About Wastewater Technology," pp. 47–61 (51). For France, see Gabriel Dupuy and Joel A. Tarr, "Sewers and Cities: France and the United States Compared," *Journal of the Environmental Engineering Division, Proceedings of the American Society of Civil Engineering* 108 (April 1982), pp. 327–37.

18. See Stanley K. Schultz and Clay McShane, "To Engineer the Metropolis: Sewers, Sanitation, and City Planning in Late Nineteenth-Century America," *Journal of American History* 65, no. 2 (September 1978), pp. 389–411 (esp. p. 393).

19. Tarr and McMichael, "Historic Turning Points," p. 83. For discussions of the debate over the type of sewer system to build, see the above Tarr and McMichael articles, plus Joel A. Tarr and Francis C. McMichael, "Water and Wastes: A History," *Water Spectrum* 10, no. 4 (fall 1978), pp. 18–25, and Tarr, "Separate Versus

Combined Sewer Problem," pp. 308–39. A city's response to the technical argument over the kind of sewer to build would have consequences over a century later. Cities that had built combined, rather than separate, sewers for storm water and wastewater would find it difficult to respond to later environmental problems. For example, in response to a *New York Times* article accusing New York City of continuing to allow sewer overflows to pollute beaches, the Commissioner for the Department of Environmental Protection wrote the following:

> Combined sewers — and their overflows — are the result of engineering concepts from the heyday of the city's growth after the Civil War. Where feasible, new parts of our system are built as separate sewers. But most of our 6,000 miles of sewers will always carry a combination of sewage and rain water. The challenge is to stop and treat overflows caused by rain. If we installed screens over all outfalls, they would clog instantly in heavy rain and break loose or cause sewers to back up into streets and homes. New storage and treatment facilities are being planned.

Harvey W. Schultz, Commissioner of the Department of Environmental Protection, New York City, Letter to the Editor, *New York Times,* July 24, 1989, p. A16.

20. Tarr and McMichael, "Water and Wastes," p. 21.

21. Louis P. Cain, *Sanitation Strategy for a Lakefront Metropolis: The Case of Chicago* (DeKalb, Ill.: Northern Illinois University Press, 1978), p. 114. By 1928 the per capita cost figures for sewage disposal in Chicago were dramatically higher than for other cities: New York City spent $0.80 on sewage disposal; Chicago spent $46.69; Detroit spent $2.39; Cleveland and Boston spent roughly $11; Milwaukee, which like Chicago treated some of its sewage completely, spent $41.34 (ibid., p. xi).

22. Tarr and McMichael, "Water and Wastes," p. 21.

23. Joel A. Tarr, James McCurley, and Terry F. Yosie, "The Development and Impact of Urban Wastewater Technology: Changing Concepts of Water Quality Control, 1850–1930," in *Pollution and Reform in American Cities, 1870–1930,* ed. Martin V. Melosi (Austin: University of Texas Press, 1980), pp. 71–74; Stanley K. Schultz and Clay McShane, "Pollution and Political Reform in Urban America: The Role of Municipal Engineers, 1840–1920," in Melosi, *Pollution and Reform in American Cities,* p. 162. See also Tarr and McMichael, "Water and Wastes" (I have drawn heavily from this latter study).

The issue of passing costs on to downstream users is still a prevalent one. The Commissioner of the Department of Environmental Protection of New York City quoted above ended his letter by saying, "In the next 10 years, we'll reduce floating debris and other pollutants from the combined sewers we inherited. But the pollutants will invade our waters from other sources until our neighbors make their own strong commitment to a cleaner environment." Harvey W. Schultz, Commissioner of the Department of Environmental Protection, Letter to the Editor, *New York Times,* July 24, 1989, p. A16.

24. Dupuy and Tarr, "Sewers and Cities," p. 331. Harry Granick, *Underneath New York* (New York: Rinehart, 1947), p. 42.

25. Jon C. Teaford, *City and Suburb: The Political Fragmentation of Metropolitan America, 1850–1970* (Baltimore: Johns Hopkins University Press, 1979). I have drawn very heavily from this work for my discussion of annexation and incorporation.

26. Erie, "How the Urban West Was Won," p. 540. Monkkonen, *America Becomes Urban,* p. 214.

27. Teaford, *City and Suburb,* p. 24.

28. Ibid., p. 28.

29. Ibid., p. 6.

30. Ibid., pp. 65, 64 (64).

31. C. K. Yearley, *The Money Machines: The Breakdown and Reform of Governmental and Party Finance in the North, 1860–1920* (Albany: State University of New York Press, 1970), p. 10.

32. Teaford, *Unheralded Triumph,* p. 285.

33. Yearley, *Money Machines,* p. 11.

34. Teaford, *Unheralded Triumph,* pp. 286, 288 (286).

35. Ibid., p. 290.

36. Hillhouse, *Municipal Bonds,* pp. 34–35.

37. Ibid., p. 35.

38. Ibid., pp. 36–37.

39. Ibid., pp. 70–72.

40. Carl V. Harris, *Political Power in Birmingham, 1871–1921* (Knoxville: University of Tennessee Press, 1977), pp. 179–80.

41. Hillhouse, *Municipal Bonds,* pp. 67, 75–79 (67, 75).

42. Ibid., p. 105.

43. Theodore J. Lowi, Foreword, in Elliot J. Feldman and Jerome E. Milch, *Technocracy Versus Democracy: The Comparative Politics of International Airports* (Boston, Mass.: Auburn, 1982), p. xii.

44. For my discussion of the city comptroller, I have relied exclusively on Teaford, *Unheralded Triumph,* pp. 54–61.

45. Cain, *Sanitation Strategy,* p. 134.

46. Schultz and McShane, "To Engineer the Metropolis," p. 397.

47. Teaford, *Unheralded Triumph,* pp. 132–41 (140).

48. Schultz and McShane, "Pollution and Political Reform in Urban America," p. 165; Schultz and McShane, "To Engineer the Metropolis," p. 410.

5. The Institutionalization of Limits

1. Advisory Commission on Intergovernmental Relations, *State Constitutional and Statutory Restrictions on Local Government Debt: A Commission Report* (Washington, D.C., September 1961), Report A-10, p. 21.

2. M. David Gelfand, "Seeking Local Government Financial Integrity Through Debt Ceilings, Tax Limitations, and Expenditure Limits: The New York City Fiscal Crisis, the Taxpayers' Revolt, and Beyond," *Minnesota Law Review* 63 (1979), pp. 545–608 (esp. p. 549). Robert H. Bowmar, "The Anachronism Called Debt

Limitation," *Iowa Law Review* 52, no. 5 (April 1967), pp. 863–900 (esp. p. 865). Lane Lancaster, *State Supervision of Municipal Indebtedness* (Philadelphia: Westbrook, 1923), p. 24.

3. See Sbragia, "Cities, Capital, and Banks," pp. 200–220; Sbragia, "Capital Markets and Central-Local Politics," pp. 311–33; Sbragia, "Public-Sector Politics, Capital Markets, and Economic Development: Public Investment in Great Britain and the United States," in *Subnational Politics in the 1980s: Organization, Reorganization, and Economic Development,* ed. Louis A. Picard and Raphael Zariski (New York: Praeger, 1987), pp. 161–77; and Sbragia, *The Politics of Public Investment: An Anglo-American Comparison,* Studies in Public Policy, no. 139 (Centre for the Study of Public Policy, University of Strathclyde, 1985).

4. Lancaster, *State Supervision of Municipal Indebtedness,* p. 24.

5. Ibid. *Preserving the Federal-State-Local Partnership: The Role of Tax-Exempt Financing,* Report to Congressman Beryl F. Anthony Jr. (Washington, D.C.: October 1989), p. 6 (hereafter referred to as the Anthony Commission on Public Finance).

6. C. Dickerman Williams and Peter R. Nehemkis Jr., "Municipal Improvements as Affected by Constitutional Debt Limitations," *Columbia Law Review* 37, no. 2 (February 1937), p. 181 n. 18.

7. Royal S. Van de Woestyne, *State Control of Local Finance in Massachusetts* (Cambridge: Harvard University Press, 1935), pp. 29–30.

8. Williams and Nehemkis, "Municipal Improvements," p. 178 n. 2. Advisory Commission on Intergovernmental Relations, *State Constitutional and Statutory Restrictions,* p. 91. Williams and Nehemkis, "Municipal Improvements," pp. 180–82. Teaford, *Unheralded Triumph,* pp. 287–88. Van de Woestyne, *State Control of Local Finance,* pp. 28–29.

9. Christine Meisner Rosen, *The Limits of Power: Great Fires and the Process of City Growth in America* (Cambridge: Cambridge University Press, 1986), p. 123. Maureen A. Flanagan, *Charter Reform in Chicago* (Carbondale, Ill.: Southern Illinois University Press, 1987), p. 26. Heywood T. Sanders, "Politics, Public Finance, and the Implementation of the 1909 Plan for Chicago, or Daniel Burnham Meets 'Hinky Dink' and Bill Thompson" (Paper presented at the annual meeting of the Urban Affairs Association, Cleveland, Ohio, April 30, 1992), p. 6. For a discussion of the effort in 1908 to change the debt limit, see Flanagan, *Charter Reform in Chicago,* pp. 141–45.

10. Erie, "How the Urban West Was Won," pp. 523 (539, 540).

11. Lancaster, *State Supervision of Municipal Indebtedness,* pp. 36–37. The quotation is from Gelfand, "Seeking Local Government Financial Integrity," p. 551.

12. Paul Barrett, *The Automobile and Urban Transit: The Formation of Public Policy in Chicago, 1900–1930* (Philadelphia: Temple University Press, 1983), p. 146. Sanders, "Politics, Public Finance, and the Implementation of the 1909 Plan for Chicago." Erie, "How the Urban West Was Won," p. 546. The quotation is from Sanders, "Building the Convention City," p. 139.

13. Richard Hayes, *Understanding San Francisco's Budget: How City Hall Spends Your Money and What You Can Do About It* (San Francisco: San Fran-

cisco Study Center and the Youth Project, 1973), p. 86. Sanders, "Building the Convention City," pp. 140–41.

14. For an interesting discussion of the process by which states increased their administrative supervision of cities, see Jon C. Teaford, "State Administrative Agencies and the Cities, 1890–1920," *American Journal of Legal History* 25 (1981), pp. 225–48. In the general area of finance, cities were subjected to more than debt limits and referenda requirements. Teaford outlines how, in the area of finance, state administrative control was increased through the use of state auditors and accountants, for example, as well as through the imposition of standardized municipal accounting procedures. See also Dale Pointius, *State Supervision of Local Government: Its Development in Massachusetts* (Washington, D.C.: American Council on Public Affairs, 1942), esp. pp. 113–14; Schuyler C. Wallace, *State Administrative Supervision over Cities in the United States* (New York: Columbia University Press, 1928), esp. pp. 96–100; Van de Woestyne, *State Control of Local Finance* (esp. pp. 28–31).

15. Frug, "The City as a Legal Concept," pp. 1059–154 (1077). My discussion of the city as a corporate entity is based heavily on Frug's article.

16. Ibid., pp. 1083, 1081.

17. Ibid., p. 1100. For an excellent case study of how the public/private distinction evolved, see Hartog, *Public Property and Private Power*. For a discussion of the courts' contemporary manipulation of the public/private distinction, see Frug, "Property and Power."

18. Kenneth Fox, *Better City Government: Innovation in American Urban Politics, 1850–1937* (Philadelphia: Temple University Press, 1977), p. 30.

19. Frug, "The City as a Legal Concept," p. 1108; Howard Lee McBain, *The Law and the Practice of Municipal Home Rule* (New York: Columbia University Press, 1916), p. 6.

20. Hartog, *Public Property and Private Power*, pp. 221–22.

21. Ibid., p. 224.

22. Fairman, *Reconstruction and Reunion*, pp. 1102–03.

23. Dillon, *Treatise on the Law of Municipal Corporations* (1st ed., 1872), chap. 1, para. 9 at 21, quoted in Frug, "The City as a Legal Concept," p. 1110.

24. Dillon supported greater local self-determination in the fifth edition of his *Treatise*, published in 1911. In 1897, Dillon (along with Louis Brandeis) was named as an alternate member of the Municipal Program Committee. That committee produced a document arguing for a strong variant of "home rule." See Fox, *Better City Government*, pp. 56–59, 85.

25. Teaford, *Unheralded Triumph*, p. 104.

26. Albert Lepawsky, *Home Rule for Metropolitan Chicago* (Chicago: University of Chicago Press, 1935), p. 176.

27. Fairman, *Reconstruction and Reunion*, p. 919. I have relied heavily on this study for my discussion of the legal evolution of the municipal bond market.

28. Fairman, *Reconstruction and Reunion*, p. 918. Charles W. McCurdy, "Justice Field and the Jurisprudence of Government-Business Relations: Some Parameters of Laissez-Faire Constitutionalism, 1863–1897," *Journal of American History* 61 (March 1975), p. 983.

29. Charles Warren, *The Supreme Court in United States History*, vol. 2, *1836–1918* (rev. ed., Boston: Little, Brown, 1926), p. 532 n. 1.

30. McCurdy, "Justice Field," p. 972.

31. See Miller, *Railroads and the Granger Laws*, and Chandler, *The Railroads*, p. 186. The first quotation is from Warren, *The Supreme Court, 1836–1918*, p. 579; the second quotation is from McCurdy, "Justice Field," p. 998.

32. Fairman, *Reconstruction and Reunion*, p. 919; McCurdy, "Justice Field," p. 984; Fairman, *Reconstruction and Reunion*, p. 932.

33. Fairman, *Reconstruction and Reunion*, p. 919.

34. Ibid., p. 926.

35. McCurdy, "Justice Field," p. 983.

36. Hillhouse, *Municipal Bonds*, p. 161; Fairman, *Reconstruction and Reunion*, p. 935.

37. Fairman, *Reconstruction and Reunion*, p. 937.

38. Ibid., pp. 970, 984–85 (970).

39. Hillhouse, *Municipal Bonds*, pp. 162–63.

40. Quoted in Breck P. McAllister, "Public Purpose in Taxation," *California Law Review* 18 (November 1929), pp. 137–254 (141).

41. Ibid., p. 143.

42. Ibid., pp. 144, 146, 148 n. 40 (146).

43. Sidney Fine, *Laissez Faire and the General-Welfare State: A Study of Conflict in American Thought, 1865–1901* (Ann Arbor: University of Michigan Press, 1956), pp. 136, 140, 134.

44. Quoted in Fairman, *Reconstruction and Reunion*, p. 1102.

45. Ibid., p. 1105. See also Fine, *Laissez Faire*, pp. 130–38.

46. Fairman, *Reconstruction and Reunion*, p. 1105; Arthur P. Roy, "State Constitutional Provisions Prohibiting the Loaning of Credit to Private Enterprise — A Suggested Analysis," *The University of Colorado Law Review* 41 (1969), p. 138.

47. Justice Miller quoted first in Fairman, *Reconstruction and Reunion*, p. 1068; then in McCurdy, "Justice Field," p. 985.

48. Fairman, *Reconstruction and Reunion*, pp. 932–33, 1057.

49. Platt, *City Building in the New South*, p. 37.

50. Burhans, *Law of Municipal Bonds*, p. 3. Along similar lines, Warren argues that the consistent position of the Court in favor of the holders of railway bonds and against repudiation "had an inestimable effect . . . in restoring confidence in a class of securities which were an indispensable factor in the development of municipal and industrial enterprises." Warren, *The Supreme Court, 1836–1918*, p. 531.

51. Teaford, *Unheralded Triumph*, p. 289.

52. Justice Nelson quoted in McCurdy, "Justice Field," p. 985.

6. Circumvention by Law and Market

1. Williams and Nehemkis, "Municipal Improvements," p. 182. Leonard Owens Rea, "The Financial History of Baltimore, 1900–1926," *Johns Hopkins University Studies in Historical and Political Science* 47 (Baltimore: Johns Hopkins Press, 1929), p. 97.

2. Cited by Williams and Nehemkis, "Municipal Improvements," p. 184. See also John F. Fowler Jr., *Revenue Bonds: The Nature, Uses, and Distribution of Fully Self-Liquidating Public Loans* (New York: Harper, 1938), p. 49. For a more contemporary version of the same story, see Gelfand, "Seeking Local Government Financial Integrity," p. 559.

3. William J. Shultz and M. R. Caine, *Financial Development of the United States* (New York: Prentice-Hall, 1937), p. 479. Lancaster, *State Supervision of Municipal Indebtedness*, p. 12. Shultz and Caine, *Financial Development of the United States*, p. 627.

4. George W. Edwards, *The Evolution of Finance Capitalism* (New York: Longmans, Green, 1938), p. 256, table 28. These figures exclude counties, towns, villages, and school districts. Edwards finds that "the net debt of all municipalities rose from $3,476,000 in 1912 to $15,216,000 in 1932" (p. 257).

5. See for example Platt, *City Building in the New South*, p. 179. The quotation is from Rosen, *Limits of Power*, p. 123.

6. Cited in Lancaster, *State Supervision of Municipal Indebtedness*, p. 7 n. 1.

7. Williams and Nehemkis, "Municipal Improvements," p. 183. See also Yin Ch'u Ma, *The Finances of the City of New York* (New York: AMS Press, 1968), pp. 173–74; Lancaster, *State Supervision of Municipal Indebtedness*, p. 67.

8. Such circumvention has also characterized state governments. See Alan Walter Steiss, *Local Government Finance: Capital Facilities Planning and Debt Administration* (Lexington, Mass.: Lexington Books, 1975), p. 74.

9. The federal judiciary was also critical in shaping the federal regulatory system. For a discussion of how the Supreme Court undermined the power and influence of the Interstate Commerce Commission at the turn of the twentieth century, see Harold Underwood Faulkner, *The Decline of Laissez Faire: 1897–1917*, vol. 7, *The Economic History of the United States* (White Plains, N.Y.: M. E. Sharpe, 1951), pp. 188–91; and Kermit L. Hall, *The Magic Mirror: Law in American History* (Oxford: Oxford University Press, 1989), p. 235.

10. The capital market has been used in other ways as well to circumvent debt limits, and the courts have also been involved in such usage. Such usage, however, has not structurally affected the system of local capital finance and therefore is not discussed here. See Jon Magnusson, "Lease-Financing by Municipal Corporations as a Way Around Debt Limitations," *George Washington Law Review* 25, no. 3 (March 1957), pp. 377–96; and F. Glenn Nichols, "Debt Limitations and the Bona Fide Long-Term Lease with an Option to Purchase: Another Look at Lord Coke," *The Urban Lawyer* 9, no. 2 (spring 1977), pp. 403–20.

11. This period of restructuring has received increasing attention from business historians. Alfred Chandler's work in particular sparked a wave of studies of the restructuring of the American economy. See Alfred D. Chandler Jr., "The Beginnings of 'Big Business' in American Industry," *Business History Review* 33 (spring 1959), pp. 1–31; Chandler, "The Large Industrial Corporation and the Making of the Modern American Economy," in *Institutions in Modern America: Innovation in Structure and Progress,* ed. Stephen E. Ambrose (Baltimore: Johns Hopkins University Press, 1967); and Chandler, *The Visible Hand: The Managerial Revolu-*

tion in American Business (Cambridge: Harvard University Press, 1977); Alfred D. Chandler Jr. and Herman Daems, eds., *Managerial Hierarchies: Comparative Perspectives on the Rise of the Modern Industrial Enterprise* (Cambridge: Harvard University Press, 1980); Naomi R. Lamoreaux, *The Great Merger Movement in American Business, 1895–1904* (Cambridge: Cambridge University Press, 1985); Lance Davis, "The Capital Markets and Industrial Concentration: The U.S. and U.K., a Comparative Study," *Economic History Review,* 2d ser. 19 (August 1966), pp. 255–72; Martin J. Sklar, *The Corporate Reconstruction of American Capitalism, 1890–1916: The Market, the Law, and Politics* (Cambridge: Cambridge University Press, 1988); James Livingston, *Origins of the Federal Reserve System: Money, Class, and Corporate Capitalism, 1890–1913* (Ithaca, N.Y.: Cornell University Press, 1986); Gerald Berk, "Corporate Liberalism Reconsidered: A Review Essay," *Journal of Policy History* 3, no. 1 (1991), pp. 70–84; Thomas K. McCraw, ed., *Regulation in Perspective: Historical Essays* (Cambridge: Harvard University Press, 1981).

12. See Samuel P. Hays, "Politics of Reform in Municipal Government in the Progressive Era," in *Social Change and Urban Politics: Readings,* ed. Daniel N. Gordon (Englewood Cliffs, N.J.: Prentice-Hall, 1973), pp. 107–27; Hays, "Changing Political Structure of the City"; Dennis Judd, *The Politics of American Cities: Private Power and Public Policy,* 2d ed. (Boston: Little, Brown, 1984), pp. 102–03.

13. Sklar, *Corporate Reconstruction of American Capitalism.*

14. Richard Franklin Bensel, *Yankee Leviathan: The Origins of Central State Authority in America, 1859–1877* (Cambridge: Cambridge University Press, 1990), p. 252. James D. Savage, *Balanced Budgets and American Politics* (Ithaca, N.Y.: Cornell University Press, 1988), p. 136.

15. Vincent P. Carosso, *Investment Banking in America: A History* (Cambridge: Harvard University Press, 1970), p. 30. Edwards, *Evolution of Finance Capitalism,* p. 162. Carosso, *Investment Banking in America,* p. 79.

16. Sklar, *Corporate Reconstruction of American Capitalism,* pp. 49, 50.

17. Berk, "Corporate Liberalism Reconsidered," p. 74 (this article is an intriguing review of Sklar's *Corporate Reconstruction of American Capitalism*).

18. Hillhouse, *Municipal Bonds,* p. 31. Carosso, *Investment Banking in America.*

19. Barrie A. Wigmore, *The Crash and Its Aftermath: A History of Securities Markets in the United States, 1929–1933* (Westport, Conn.: Greenwood Press, 1985), p. 110. Frank J. Fabozzi, Sylvan G. Feldstein, Irving M. Pollack, and Frank G. Zarb, eds., *The Municipal Bond Handbook* (Homewood, Ill.: Dow Jones-Irwin, 1983), vol. 1, p. vii.

20. Edwards, *Evolution of Finance Capitalism,* pp. 149, 187 (187). Wigmore, *The Crash,* p. 110.

21. Hillhouse, *Municipal Bonds,* pp. 45–46.

22. Public Securities Association, *Fundamentals of Municipal Bonds,* rev. ed. (New York, 1981), p. 7.

23. The battle over a national income tax was one of the longest of any in the

realm of economic policy. Although an income tax had been approved in the last years of the Civil War, it was terminated in 1872. "In the twenty years thereafter, 66 separate bills were introduced to establish a peacetime Federal income tax of one sort or another. In every case, they were introduced by Western or Southern congressmen and died in committee." Paul Studenski and Herman E. Krooss, *Financial History of the United States: Fiscal, Monetary, Banking, and Tariff, Including Financial Administration and State and Local Finance,* 2d ed. (New York: McGraw Hill, 1963), p. 222. It was not until 1913 that a tax finally became law. Savage points out that the politics of the income tax were inextricably tied to the politics of the tariff; it is for that reason that the 1894 tax was included in a bill dealing with the tariff.

24. Anthony Commission on Public Finance, *Preserving the Federal-State-Local Partnership,* p. 11.

25. Studenski and Krooss, *Financial History of the United States,* pp. 223–24, 272. Laurence S. Knappen, *Revenue Bonds and the Investor* (New York: Prentice-Hall, 1939), pp. 109–13. Public Securities Association, *Fundamentals of Municipal Bonds* (1981), p. 7.

26. Anthony Commission on Public Finance Report, p. 6.

27. Carosso, *Investment Banking in America,* p. 394 n. 62. The quotation is from Wigmore, *The Crash,* p. 511.

28. Fowler, *Revenue Bonds,* p. 52.

29. Maxine Virtue, "The Public Use of Private Capital: A Discussion of Problems Related to Municipal Bond Financing," *Virginia Law Review* 35, no. 3 (April 1949), pp. 285–95 (290–91). There are also so-called double-barreled securities. These are bonds "payable from revenues of certain facilities [which] are also secured by the full faith, credit, and taxing power of the issuer." Such bonds are considered general-obligation bonds because of the ultimate commitment of the taxing power. Ronald David Greenberg, "Municipal Securities: Some Basic Principles and Practices," *Urban Lawyer* 9, no. 2 (spring 1977), pp. 338–63 (342).

30. Victor Rosewater, *Special Assessments: A Study in Municipal Finance,* 2d ed. (New York: Columbia University Press, 1898), pp. 24–25, 32–33.

31. Bowmar, "The Anachronism Called Debt Limitation," p. 873.

32. Hillhouse, *Municipal Bonds,* pp. 73, 106–14.

33. See Williams and Nehemkis, "Municipal Improvements," pp. 187–88.

34. Fowler, *Revenue Bonds,* pp. 8–9.

35. Knappen, *Revenue Bonds,* p. 87. Knappen points out that at least one investment bank "depends on its corporate department rather than its municipal purchasing department to investigate, purchase, and 'set up' its revenue bond issues" (ibid., p. 83).

36. Ibid., pp. 81–83 (82–83). Investment bankers in Chicago seem to be have developed a particular expertise in such bonds (p. 137).

37. Fowler, *Revenue Bonds,* pp. 44, 43. See also Joseph D. McGoldrick, *Law and Practice of Municipal Home Rule, 1916–1930* (New York: Columbia University Press, 1933).

38. For Spokane, see Knappen, *Revenue Bonds,* pp. 9–10.

39. Both quotations are from ibid., p. 9.

40. Knappen, *Revenue Bonds*, p. 11.

41. Knappen, *Revenue Bonds*, pp. 10–12. Quotation is from Fowler, *Revenue Bonds*, p. 22. Knappen, *Revenue Bonds*, p. 13.

42. Fowler, *Revenue Bonds*, pp. 24, 28 (24).

43. Knappen, *Revenue Bonds*, p. 18; Fowler, *Revenue Bonds*, p. 54 (quotation from pp. 28–29); Perry, "Building the City Through the Back Door," pp. 210–16.

44. Williams and Nehemkis, "Municipal Improvements," pp. 186–87. Fowler, *Revenue Bonds*, pp. 50, 168, 167.

45. Knappen, *Revenue Bonds*, p. 50.

46. Using the assessed value of real estate as the basis for limits, however, was not as effective as might have been imagined. For example, New York's Tax Law was amended in 1899 so that the legal definition of the term *real estate* expanded to include "special franchises." The debt limit was therefore effectively increased by an amount equivalent to the assessed value of such franchises. Williams and Nehemkis, "Municipal Improvements," p. 182, n. 26.

47. Bowmar, "The Anachronism Called Debt Limitation," p. 867.

48. See, for example, Virtue, "The Public Use of Private Capital," pp. 294–95; Dennis J. Heil, "Another Day Older and Deeper in Debt: Debt Limitation, the Broad Special Fund Doctrine, and WPPSS 4 and 5," *University of Puget Sound Law Review* 7, no. 1 (fall 1983), pp. 94ff.

49. Gelfand, "Seeking Local Government Financial Integrity," p. 550.

50. Heil, "Another Day Older and Deeper in Debt," p. 93.

51. Ibid., p. 87.

52. Information on Ogden City, Utah, is from E. H. Foley Jr., "Some Recent Developments in the Law Relating to Municipal Financing of Public Works," *Fordham Law Review* 4, no. 1 (January 1935), pp. 13–34 (32).

53. See Williams and Nehemkis, "Municipal Improvements," pp. 192–97; Comment, "The Judicial Demise of State Constitutional Debt Limitations," *Iowa Law Review* 56, no. 3 (February 1971), pp. 648–51; Heil, "Another Day Older and Deeper in Debt," pp. 87–89; and Virtue, "The Public Use of Private Capital," pp. 285–95.

54. In the case of state borrowing, some courts began to use the very existence of a special fund as an indication that debt was not being incurred, even if such a fund were being fed by excise taxes. E. H. Foley Jr., writing in 1937, pointed out the elasticity given by some state courts to the idea of a special fund when the term was applied to state debt:

> It is important to bear in mind that not every obligation payable from a special fund involves the application of the so-called special fund doctrine. . . . Although it is perhaps natural for courts in reaching a new result or extending an existing principle to use the phrases mentioned in the precedents relied upon, confusion has undoubtedly resulted from the use of the terms 'special fund' and 'special fund doctrine' with reference to any obligations payable from a special fund regardless of the sources of the moneys paid into the special fund. The generally accepted special fund doctrine . . . covers only those

cases in which obligations issued for a project are made payable from the fees imposed in connection with the project and from no other source. Obligations payable from an excise tax or from any other special source of state revenue would be payable from a special fund, but they would not be the type of obligation which comes within the compass of the special fund doctrine.

E. H. Foley Jr., "Low-Rent Housing and State Financing," *University of Pennsylvania Law Review* 85, no. 3 (January 1937), pp. 239–60 (248).

55. Wiliams and Nehemkis, pp. 190–91.

56. See Martin J. Schiesl, *The Politics of Efficiency: Municipal Administration and Reform in America, 1800–1920* (Berkeley and Los Angeles: University of California, 1977), pp. 83–87, 158; Platt, *City Building in the New South*, pp. 121–215 (212).

57. Schultz and McShane, "To Engineer the Metropolis," pp. 390–93. See also Carl D. Thompson, *Public Ownership: A Survey of Public Enterprises, Municipal, State, and Federal, in the United States and Elsewhere* (New York: Thomas Y. Crowell Company, 1925), p. 215. Thompson, *Public Ownership*, pp. 205, 269, 271.

58. Williams and Nehemkis, "Municipal Improvements," p. 190 n. 68. See also John A. Fairlie, *Municipal Administration* (New York: MacMillan, 1910), pp. 275–85. See Platt, *City Building in the New South*; Schiesl, *Politics of Efficiency*. E. H. Foley Jr., "Revenue Financing of Public Enterprise," *Michigan Law Review* 35, no. 1 (November 1936), pp. 1–43 (4). Thompson, *Public Ownership*, p. 290.

59. Lawrence L. Durisch, "Publicly Owned Utilities and the Problem of Municipal Debt Limits," *Michigan Law Review* 31, no. 4 (February 1933), pp. 503–11 (esp. p. 506); Lawrence L. Durisch, "Municipal Debt Limits and the Financing of Publicly Owned Utilities," *National Municipal Review* 20 (August 1931), pp. 460–65; Williams and Nehemkis, "Municipal Improvements," p. 191.

60. Rosen, *Limits of Power*, p. 54.

61. Durisch, "Publicly Owned Utilities," p. 511.

62. Fowler, *Revenue Bonds*, pp. 4–5.

63. Hillhouse, *Municipal Bonds*, pp. 4, 6, 7.

64. Edwards, *Evolution of Finance Capitalism*, pp. 255–57. Quotations are from Hillhouse, *Municipal Bonds*, pp. 22, 17.

65. Edwards, *Evolution of Finance Capitalism*, p. 257. The quotation is from Wigmore, *The Crash*, p. 511.

66. Wigmore, *The Crash*, p. 513.

67. Ibid., p. 514.

68. See Mark I. Gelfand, *A Nation of Cities: The Federal Government and Urban America, 1933–1965* (New York: Oxford University Press, 1975), pp. 31–35, for a discussion of the politics of relief aid in Detroit. Hillhouse, *Municipal Bonds*, pp. 22–23, 26.

69. Gelfand, *Nation of Cities*, p. 39.

70. James S. Olson, *Saving Capitalism: The Reconstruction Finance Corporation and the New Deal, 1933–1940* (Princeton: Princeton University Press, 1988), p. 19.

71. Jordon A. Schwarz, *The Interregnum of Despair: Hoover, Congress, and the Depression* (Urbana, Ill.: University of Illinois Press, 1970), p. 162.

72. Olson, *Saving Capitalism*, p. 21.

73. Knappen, *Revenue Bonds*, pp. 172–75, 179–80.

74. See James T. Patterson, *The New Deal and the States: Federalism in Transition* (Princeton: Princeton University Press, 1969), pp. 50–85; Josephine Brown, *Public Relief, 1929–1939* (New York: H. Holt and Company, 1940). Gelfand, *Nation of Cities*, pp. 40–46 (41).

75. Gelfand, *Nation of Cities*, p. 47; Knappen, *Revenue Bonds*, p. 187. Roosevelt, however, was unsympathetic to mayors' pleas for help with their debt burdens. See Gelfand, *Nation of Cities*, pp. 49–59. For a discussion of the credit woes of major cities, see William C. Beyer, "Financial Dictators Replace Political Boss," *National Municipal Review* 22, no. 4 (April 1933) and no. 5 (May 1933).

76. Olson, *Saving Capitalism*, p. 45.

77. Knappen, *Revenue Bonds*, pp. 180–81. Total PWA expenditures, including grants and loans for federal and non-federal projects, totaled $4.8 billion in the period between 1933 and 1939. Knappen, *Revenue Bonds*, pp. 183, 216. The amount of federal money spent on infrastructure was considerable. As Mollenkopf points out, PWA expenditures represented "an unprecedented federal contribution to local infrastructure." Furthermore, funds spent by the Works Progress Administration, created in 1935, also "significantly helped to renew the infrastructure of the major cities." Mollenkopf, *The Contested City*, pp. 65, 67.

78. Gelfand, *Nation of Cities*, p. 48.

79. Williams and Nehemkis, "Municipal Improvements," p. 192. Wylie Kilpatrick, "Federal Regulation of Local Debt," *National Municipal Review* 26, no. 6 (June 1937), pp. 283–98 (290); Knappen, *Revenue Bonds*, table 9, p. 200.

80. Knappen, *Revenue Bonds*, table 11, p. 205. The PWA did not use revenue bonds in its housing program. However, when its housing responsibilities were transferred to the U.S. Housing Authority on September 1, 1937, revenue bonds "are the only type of obligation that is being accepted. . . . [T]he Authority may lend only to a municipality, county, state or other public body, such as a local housing authority" (ibid., p. 217).

81. Quotation is from ibid., p. 13. Foley, "Recent Developments in the Law," p. 15.

82. Kilpatrick, "Federal Regulation of Local Debt," p. 290; Foley, "Recent Developments in the Law," p. 27. Fowler, *Revenue Bonds*, p. 55.

83. Foley, "Recent Developments in the Law," pp. 27–32. Fowler, *Revenue Bonds*, p. 7.

84. Fowler, *Revenue Bonds*, pp. 11–14 (11).

85. Foley, "Recent Developments in the Law," p. 33.

7. Circumvention by Law and Government

1. Smith, *Public Authorities in Urban Areas*, p. 3. See also Jerome J. Shestack, "The Public Authority," *University of Pennsylvania Law Review* 105, no. 4 (February 1957), pp. 553–69 (esp. p. 555).

2. Council of State Governments, *Public Authorities in the States: A Report to the Governors' Conference* (Chicago, 1953), p. 5. Thus, revenue bonds can be viewed as authorities' "calling cards." Henriques, *Machinery of Greed,* p. 6.

3. See Advisory Commission on Intergovernmental Relations, *State Constitutional and Statutory Restrictions,* pp. 53–62; Advisory Commission on Intergovernmental Relations, *The Problem of Special Districts in American Government* (Washington, D.C., May 1964), Report A-22, p. 32.

4. Doig, " 'If I See a Murderous Fellow,' " pp. 292–304.

5. Harry B. Strickland, *Inside the Trojan Horse* (Clarks Summit, Pa.: Logo Publishing and Research, 1969), p. 17. George G. Sause and Andrew S. Bullis, *Municipal Authorities: The Pennsylvania Experience* (Harrisburg, Pa.: Commonwealth of Pennsylvania, Department of Internal Affairs, 1962), p. 3.

6. Henriques, *Machinery of Greed,* pp. 5–6. Ronald Smothers, "Now Atlanta Begins Going for its Gold," *New York Times,* September 20, 1990, p. B9.

7. Mortimer S. Edelstein, "The Authority Plan — Tool of Modern Government," *Cornell Law Quarterly* 28, no. 2 (January 1943), pp. 177–91 (187).

8. See, for example, Mollenkopf, *The Contested City;* Danielson and Doig, *New York;* Adams, *The Politics of Capital Investment;* Peterson, *City Limits,* chap. 7; Fuchs, *Mayors and Money;* Mitchell, "The Policy Activities of Public Authorities."

9. See Bennett and DiLorenzo, *Underground Government;* Henriques, *Machinery of Greed.*

10. Jameson W. Doig, *Metropolitan Transportation Politics and the New York Region* (New York: Columbia University Press, 1966), p. 7.

11. See Smith, *Public Authorities in Urban Areas,* and Fuchs, *Mayors and Money,* p. 199. Still another variant is "the holding company" authority. See the Council of State Governments, *State Public Authorities* (Chicago, July 1970), pp. 14–15.

12. Quotations are from William J. Quirk and Leon E. Wein, "A Short Constitutional History of Entities Commonly Known as Authorities," *Cornell Law Review* 56, no. 4 (April 1971), pp. 521–97 (571, 567).

13. Shestack, "The Public Authority," p. 567. Quirk and Wein, "A Short Constitutional History," p. 597.

14. Robert A. Caro, *The Power Broker: Robert Moses and the Fall of New York* (New York: Alfred A. Knopf, 1974), pp. 19, 15. Danielson and Doig, *New York,* pp. 183, 184 (184).

15. Pennsylvania Economy League, *A Review of Philadelphia's Authorities,* Report no. 566 (October 1989), p. 57. See also p. 3.

16. Caro, *The Power Broker,* p. 617.

17. Ibid., p. 624.

18. Ibid., pp. 626, 624.

19. Sause and Bullis, *Municipal Authorities,* p. 13.

20. Danielson and Doig, *New York,* p. 162. For a discussion of how the pressures on authorities in New York City differ from the pressures on the city's line agencies, see Wallace S. Sayre and Herbert Kaufman, *Governing New York City: Politics in the Metropolis* (New York: Norton, 1960), pp. 328–37.

21. Danielson and Doig, *New York,* p. 334. See also Jameson W. Doig, "To Claim the Seas and the Skies: Austin Tobin and the Port of New York Authority," in *Leadership and Innovation: A Biographical Perspective on Entrepreneurs in Government,* ed. Jameson W. Doig and Erwin C. Hargrove (Baltimore: Johns Hopkins Press, 1987), pp. 124–73.

22. See, among many others, Mollenkopf, *The Contested City,* chap. 5. Jameson W. Doig, "Coalition-Building by a Regional Agency: Austin Tobin and the Port of New York Authority," in Stone and Sanders, *Politics of Urban Development,* pp. 73–104; Caro, *The Power Broker,* pp. 984–1002.

23. Walsh, *The Public's Business,* pp. 3–4.

24. Ibid., p. 4.

25. Ibid., pp. 353–55 (for a general discussion of the difficulties involved in identifying and counting public authorities, see the appendix). Mitchell, "The Policy Activities of Public Authorities," pp. 929–30. Dennis Zimmerman, *The Private Use of Tax-Exempt Bonds: Controlling Public Subsidy of Private Activity* (Washington, D.C.: The Urban Institute Press, 1991), p. 63.

26. Robert G. Smith, *Public Authorities, Special Districts, and Local Government* (Washington, D.C.: National Association of Counties Research Foundation, 1964), p. 22. See also Walsh, *The Public's Business,* pp. 4–5.

27. For the Pennsylvania Turnpike Commission, see Nathaniel Stone Preston, *The Use and Control of Public Authorities in American State and Local Government,* Ph.D. diss., Princeton University, 1960, p. 20. Mitchell, "The Policy Activities of Public Authorities," p. 930; Walsh, *The Public's Business;* Doig, " 'If I See a Murderous Fellow.' "

28. The Census Bureau defines special districts thus: "In order to be classified as a special district government rather than a subordinate agency, an entity must possess three attributes — existence as an organized entity, governmental character, and substantial autonomy." Bureau of the Census, *1982 Census of Governments,* vol. 4, *Government Finances, No. 2, Finances of Special Districts* (Washington, D.C.: U.S. Government Printing Office, March 1984), p. vi.

The conventional distinction between special districts and public authorities is based on their degree of formal independence from their parent governments. Walsh, however, criticizes the way independence is measured:

> The error is rooted in the originally confused concept of "autonomy" promoted by the academic writers on special districts. Continuing the confusion, John C. Bollens, the author of a classic work on the subject[,] ... declared that authorities are more dependent on parent governments than special districts are. Official definitions continue to use tax powers as a measure of fiscal independence; access to private money markets and to revenue-producing monopoly services is nowhere recognized as a source of independent financial power. An appointed governing board — even with long and staggered terms — is considered an indicator of administrative dependence.

Walsh, *The Public's Business,* p. 355. For our purposes, we are interested in all authorities (organizations with corporate status) that rely on revenue-bond financing and that are insulated from the electorate regardless of whether official definitions would classify them as special districts or as dependencies of a general-purpose government. Their finances and their link to voters is of interest in this study.

29. For a discussion of special districts, see John C. Bollens, *Special District Governments in the United States* (Berkeley and Los Angeles: University of California Press, 1961); Robert B. Hawkins Jr., *Self Government by District: Myth and Reality* (Stanford: Hoover Institution Press, 1976); Advisory Commission on Intergovernmental Relations, *The Problem of Special Districts in American Government;* Smith, *Public Authorities, Special Districts, and Local Government;* Virginia Marion Perrenod, *Special Districts, Special Purposes: Fringe Governments and Urban Problems in the Houston Area* (College Station: Texas A&M Press, 1984); William H. Cape, Leon B. Graves, Burton M. Michaels, *Government by Special Districts* (Governmental Research Center, The University of Kansas, 1969); Susan MacManus, "Special District Governments: A Note on Their Use as Property Tax Relief Mechanisms in the 1970s," *Journal of Politics* 43, no. 4 (November 1981), pp. 1207–14; Douglas R. Porter, Ben C. Lin, and Richard B. Peiser, *Special Districts: A Useful Technique for Financing Infrastructure* (Washington, D.C.: Urban Land Institute, 1987); Advisory Commission on Intergovernmental Relations, *The Organization of Local Public Economies* (Washington, D.C., December 1987), Report A-109.

30. Authorities are very diverse, and this diversity cannot be dealt with adequately in this study but needs to be researched in more depth. For an overview of such diversity, see Preston, *The Use and Control of Public Authorities* (esp. chap. 3). For an overview of how authorities in the New York region differ from each other in terms of formal independence from parent governments and in their financial base, see Danielson and Doig, *New York,* pp. 156–57.

31. Robert G. Smith, *Ad Hoc Governments: Special Purpose Transportation Authorities in Britain and the United States* (Beverly Hills: Sage, 1974), pp. 43–44. State laws determine the extent to which a revenue bond can be repaid from earmarked tax revenue without having the bond become a general-obligation bond under state law. See Dillon, Read, and Company, Inc., *Infrastructure Financing: An Overview* (Dillon, Read, 1983), pp. 18–19.

Smith argues that the predecessors to the current county and local public authorities were the "special municipal corporations" that were formed long before the Port of New York Authority was established in 1920. Smith concludes that these "early municipal corporations had attributes . . . of both the special districts and the public authorities of today." Smith, *Public Authorities, Special Districts, and Local Government,* p. 11. Regarding municipal corporations, Smith cites Charles Kettleborough, "Special Municipal Corporations," *American Political Science Review* 8 (November 1914), pp. 614–21.

32. Salaries paid by authorities are typically higher than those paid by state or municipal governments, and the argument is made that such a policy allows authorities to "hire the best" and "compete with the private sector." In 1988, Governor Cuomo of New York made a political issue of the fact that salaries paid by

authorities in New York were higher than those paid by the state government. The public affairs director for the Port Authority of New York and New Jersey earned $134,966 whereas Governor Cuomo's press secretary was paid $92,000; the Port Authority's executive director earned $170,000 whereas Governor Cuomo earned $130,000. Jeffrey Schmalz, "Cuomo Pushes Challenge to Salaries at Authorities," *New York Times,* February 7, 1988, p. 42. Even those authorities that follow civil service regulations typically do not follow the salary schedules of their parent governments.

33. For an overview of the reasons for creating public authorities, see Shestack, "The Public Authority."

34. Temporary State Commission on Coordination of State Activities, *Staff Report on Public Authorities Under New York State* (Albany: Williams Press, 1956), p. 44.

35. Cited in Tom Barnes, "Water Tax Hike Irks DePasquale," *Pittsburgh Post-Gazette,* February 28, 1987, p. 6.; Barnes, "City Water Authority Hopes to Hold Rate Increase in Line," *Pittsburgh Post-Gazette,* October 15, 1988, p. 5.

36. Virginia Linn, "Foerster Doubts Need for New Agency," *Pittsburgh Post-Gazette,* July 16, 1988, p. 1.

37. Virginia Linn, "Airport to Spur Jobs for 17,600," *Pittsburgh Post-Gazette,* July 15, 1988, p. 1.

38. Smith, *Ad Hoc Governments,* pp. 117–18.

39. See, for example, Walsh, *The Public's Business,* pp. 22–24; William E. Mitchell, *The Effectiveness of Debt Limits on State and Local Government Borrowing* (New York University, Graduate School of Business Administration, Institute of Finance, Bulletin no. 45, October 1967); Smith, *Public Authorities, Special Districts, and Local Government,* p. 192; Edelstein, "The Authority Plan," pp. 177–84; Harold F. Alderfer, "Is 'Authority' Financing the Answer?" *The American City* (February 1955), pp. 115–16; Peter R. Nehemkis Jr., "The Public Authority: Some Legal and Practical Aspects," *Yale Law Review* 47, no. 1 (November 1937), pp. 14–33; Advisory Commission on Intergovernmental Relations, *State Constitutional and Statutory Restrictions,* pp. 53–62; Temporary State Commission on Coordination of State Activities, *Staff Report on Public Authorities,* pp. 46–49; Gelfand, "Seeking Local Government Financial Integrity," pp. 560–67; Williams and Nehemkis, "Municipal Improvements"; Hillhouse, *Municipal Bonds,* p. 481; Heins, *Constitutional Restrictions,* pp. 13–19.

40. Sbragia, *The Politics of Local Borrowing,* p. 13.

41. Foley, "Revenue Financing of Public Enterprise," p. 2. However, Bollens found that more than a third of nonschool special districts had no taxing authority. Bollens, *Special District Governments,* p. 42.

42. Bollens, *Special District Governments,* p. 43.

43. See Tina V. Weintraub and James D. Patterson, *The "Authority" in Pennsylvania: Pro and Con* (Philadelphia: Bureau of Municipal Research of Philadelphia, May 1949), p. 3; Horace A. Davis, "Borrowing Machines," *National Municipal Review* 24, no. 6 (June 1935), pp. 328–34.

44. Doig, " 'If I See a Murderous Fellow.' "

45. Ibid., p. 295. The quotation is from Shestack, "The Public Authority," p. 555.

46. Sause and Bullis, *Municipal Authorities*, p. 5. Pennsylvania Economy League, *Review of Philadelphia's Authorities*, pp. 8, vii (vii). Sause and Bullis, *Municipal Authorities*, p. 8.

47. Strickland, *Inside the Trojan Horse*, pp. 30–31. The quotation is from Sause and Bullis, *Municipal Authorities*, p. 8.

48. Weintraub and Patterson, *The "Authority" in Pennsylvania*, p. 4. See also Raymond J. Saffeldt and Kenneth Unger, "Pennsylvania's Capital Budgeting System," *State Government* 58, no. 3 (February 1985), pp. 119–21.

49. Pennsylvania Economy League, *Review of Philadelphia's Authorities*, pp. 56–57. For a discussion of how the debt limit affected the politics of capital investment in Philadelphia, see Adams, *The Politics of Capital Investment*, chap.6.

50. See, for example, Shestack, "The Public Authority," pp. 560–62.

51. The quotation is from Pennsylvania Economy League, Eastern Division, *Philadelphia's Debt Limit: A Restraint on Debt or an Obstacle to Growth?* Report no. 531 (April 1988), p. x. See also Roger J. Vaughan, "Rebuilding America: Financing Public Works in the 1980s," in *Rebuilding America's Infrastructure: An Agenda for the 1980s,* ed. Michael Barker (Durham: Duke University Press, 1984), p. 181.

52. John Incorvaia, "Brevard County, Florida: Case Study in an Issuer's Willingness to Pay Its Obligation," *Moody's Municipal Issues* 9, no. 1 (April 1992), p. 3.

53. Edelstein, "The Authority Plan," p. 178.

54. Council of State Governments, *Public Authorities in the States*, p. 26.

55. Smith, *Ad Hoc Governments*, pp. 108–09.

56. Foley, "Revenue Financing of Public Enterprise," pp. 22–23. Foley, "Recent Developments in the Law," pp. 14–18. Smith, *Ad Hoc Governments*, p. 110.

57. Council of State Governments, *Public Authorities in the States*, pp. 27, 29, 34.

58. Mollenkopf, *The Contested City*, p. 65. Foley, "Low-Rent Housing and State Financing," pp. 251–57.

59. Bollens, *Special District Governments*, pp. 121, 119 (119).

60. Ibid., pp. 121–24. For a discussion of the politics of the Housing Act of 1949, see Gelfand, *Nation of Cities*, pp. 105–56.

61. Greenberg, "Municipal Securities," pp. 345–46.

62. Gelfand, *Nation of Cities*, pp. 209–10, 211–12.

63. Temporary State Commission on Coordination of State Activities, *Staff Report on Public Authorities*, p. 51; quoted in Smith, *Ad Hoc Governments*, p. 122.

64. Mollenkopf, *The Contested City*, p. 65.

65. Smith, *Ad Hoc Governments*, p. 121.

66. "President Seeks Tax Immunity End by a 'Simple Law,'" *New York Times,* January 18, 1939, p. 1.

67. My account of Austin Tobin's role in the fight to protect the tax exemption is drawn from Doig, "To Claim the Seas and the Skies," pp. 135–37.

68. Ibid., p. 137.

69. Ibid., p. 135.

70. C. Robert Morris Jr., "Evading Debt Limitations with Public Building Authorities: The Costly Subversion of State Constitutions," *Yale Law Journal* 68, no. 2 (December 1958), pp. 234–68 (239).

71. Ibid., p. 234. Other devices — which do not necessarily involve an authority — have been developed since then. See, for example, Nichols, "Debt Limitations," pp. 363–403.

72. Magnusson, "Lease-Financing by Municipal Corporations," p. 377.

73. Strickland, *Inside the Trojan Horse,* p. 62.

74. Ibid., p. 67. Morris, "Evading Debt Limitations," p. 236 n. 5.

75. Walsh, *The Public's Business,* pp. 122, 126 (122).

76. Pennsylvania Economy League, *Review of Philadelphia's Authorities,* p. 27.

8. Local Entrepreneurship via Tax Exemption

1. Dennis R. Judd and David Brian Robertson, "Urban Revitalization in the United States: Prisoner of the Federal System," in *Regenerating the Cities: The U.K. Crisis and the U.S. Experience,* ed. Michael Parkinson, Bernard Foley, and Dennis R. Judd (Glenview, Ill.: Scott, Foresman, 1989), p. 9.

2. The Tax Reform Act of 1986 came during a period of severe reductions in federal aid to localities. As the General Accounting Office (GAO) pointed out:

In the 1980s . . . federal budget priorities favored defense and entitlement program spending over programs for housing, economic development, and infrastructure. Since the latter kinds of programs were predominantly federal-local, aid to localities declined between 1978 and 1988, when measured in constant dollars. As a percentage share of total municipal revenues, federal assistance dropped 62 percent from 1980 to 1988. As a percentage share of total county revenues, federal aid dropped 73 percent over the same period. . . . General Revenue Sharing was the most visible, but by no means the only, program cut."

U.S. General Accounting Office (GAO), *Distressed Communities: Capital Investments Were Postponed in Texas as Local Economies Weakened,* Report to the Chairman, Committee on Finance, U.S. Senate, February 1991, p. 12.

3. Council of State Governments, *Public Authorities in the States,* p. 28. Smith, *Public Authorities, Special Districts, and Local Government,* p. ix. Bollens, *Special District Governments,* pp. 122–23. Council of State Governments, *Public Authorities in the States,* pp. 29, 98–99.

4. John E. Petersen, "The Municipal Bond Market: Recent Changes and Future Prospects" (unpublished paper, Government Finance Research Center, Municipal Finance Officers Association, 13 February 1981), p. 8. See also Sbragia, "Politics, Local Government, and the Municipal Bond Market," p. 68.

5. *New York's Local Industrial Development Agencies, a Closer Look: An Interim Report of the New York State Legislative Commission on State-Local Relations* (September 1989), p. 2. Walsh, *The Public's Business,* p. 133.

6. Sbragia, "Politics, Local Government, and the Municipal Bond Market," p. 68. See also Mitchell, "The Policy Activities of Public Authorities," p. 928.

7. Smith, *Ad Hoc Governments*, pp. 114–15; Mitchell, "The Policy Activities of Public Authorities," p. 930; Walsh, *The Public's Business,* 1978.

8. Although defaults on municipal bonds are rare, those bonds issued by authorities more frequently default than general-obligation bonds, which are backed by the full faith and credit of the issuer, typically a general-purpose government or a special district with taxing authority. (If an issuer is unable to pay interest or principal when due, a bond is said to have defaulted. "Technical" defaults occur if the payment is only late or if it is paid from a reserve fund.)

Revenue bonds defaulted more often, with bonds issued for traditional purposes such as water supply systems, sewers, or housing for the elderly defaulting much less often than those issued for private purposes. It is not surprising, given the link between authorities and revenue bonds, that the ACIR found defaulting revenue bonds "were issued by special districts or statutory authorities rather than units of general-purpose government such as cities and counties." Advisory Commission on Intergovernmental Relations (ACIR), *Bankruptcies, Defaults, and Other Local Government Financial Emergencies* (Washington, D.C., March 1985), pp. 20–21.

9. The quotation is from Government Finance Research Center of the Municipal Finance Officers Association, *Building Prosperity: Financing Public Infrastructure for Economic Development* (Washington, D.C., 1983), p. 42. The information for this paragraph is taken from Public Securities Association, *Fundamentals of Municipal Bonds,* 3d ed. (New York, 1987), p. 57; ACIR, *Strengthening the Federal Revenue System: Implications for State and Local Taxing and Borrowing* (Washington, D.C., October 1984), p. 122; John E. Petersen, *Tax-Exempts and Tax Reform: Assessing the Consequences of the Tax Reform Act of 1986 for the Municipal Securities Market* (Government Finance Research Center of the Government Finance Officers Association and the Academy for State and Local Government, research report, February 1987), p. 1.3; Walsh, *The Public's Business,* pp. 60–61.

10. ACIR, *Strengthening the Federal Revenue System,* p. 123. The quotation is from Public Securities Association, *Fundamentals of Municipal Bonds* (1987), p. 57.

11. U.S. General Accounting Office (GAO), *Trends and Changes in the Municipal Bond Market as They Relate to Financing State and Local Public Infrastructure,* GAO/PAD-83–46, September 12, 1983, pp. 14, 15 (15).

12. George E. Peterson, "Capital Spending and Capital Obsolescence: The Outlook for Cities," in *The Fiscal Outlook for Cities: Implications of a National Urban Policy,* ed. Roy Bahl (Syracuse, N.Y.: Syracuse University Press, 1978), p. 59.

13. ACIR, *Strengthening the Federal Revenue System,* p. 122. Zimmerman, *The Private Use of Tax-Exempt Bonds,* p. 339. ACIR, *Strengthening the Federal Revenue System,* p. 122.

14. John E. Petersen, "Recent Developments in Tax-Exempt Bond Markets" (unpublished paper, Government Finance Research Center, Government Finance Officers Association, April 15, 1985), pp. 2.6–2.7. See also Ronald Forbes, Philip

Fischer, and John Petersen, "Recent Trends in Municipal Revenue Bond Financing," in *Efficiency in the Municipal Bond Market: The Use of Tax Exempt Financing for "Private" Purposes,* ed. George G. Kaufman (Greenwich: Conn.: JAI Press, 1981), p. 161.

15. For overviews of the post–World War II municipal bond market, see Walsh, *The Public's Business,* chap. 3; Zimmerman, *The Private Use of Tax-Exempt Bonds,* chap. 4; Robert Lamb and Stephen P. Rappaport, *Municipal Bonds: The Comprehensive Review of Tax-Exempt Securities and Public Finance* (New York: McGraw-Hill, 1980); Ronald W. Forbes and John E. Petersen, "Background Paper," in *Building a Broader Market: Report of the Twentieth Century Fund Task Force on the Municipal Bond Market* (New York: McGraw-Hill, 1976); Forbes and Petersen, *The Rating Game: Report of the Twentieth Century Fund Task Force on Municipal Bond Credit Ratings* (New York: The Twentieth Century Fund, 1974); ACIR, *Understanding the Market for State and Local Debt* (Washington, D.C., May 1976); John E. Petersen, "State and Local Government Debt Policy and Management," in *Essays in Public Finance and Financial Management: State and Local Perspectives,* ed. John E. Petersen and Catherine Lavigne Spain (Chatham, N.J.: Chatham House, 1978); Public Securities Association, *Fundamentals of Municipal Bonds* (1987); Sbragia, "Politics, Local Government, and the Municipal Bond Market," pp. 67–112; Alberta M. Sbragia, "Finance Capital and the City," in *Cities in Stress: A Look at the Urban Crisis,* ed. Mark Gottdiener (Beverly Hills: Sage, 1986).

16. Public Securities Association, *Fundamentals of Municipal Bonds* (1987), p. 2. Petersen, *Tax-Exempts and Tax Reform,* p. 1.2; Dennis Zimmerman, "The Intergovernmental Struggle over Tax-Exempt Bond Reform," in *Intergovernmental Fiscal Relations in an Era of New Federalism,* ed. Michael Bell (Greenwich, Conn.: JAI Press, 1988), p. 102.

17. ACIR, *Strengthening the Federal Revenue System,* p. 117. Public Securities Association, *Fundamentals of Municipal Bonds* (1981), p. 52.

18. John Illyes, *Tax-Exempt Municipal Leases: Certificates of Participation, Nonappropriation Outs* (Nuveen Research, John Nuveen and Co. Inc., Investment Bankers, April 1987), p. 1 (quotation is from the Introduction).

19. Ibid., p. 3. See also Congressional Budget Office, "Trends in Municipal Leasing," *Municipal Finance Journal* 4, no. 3 (summer 1983), pp. 239–49; Frieda K. Wallison, "Tax-Exempt Lease Financing Gains Attention as Economic Conditions Change," in *Creative Capital Financing for State and Local Governments,* ed. John E. Petersen and Wesley C. Hough (Government Finance Research Center, Municipal Finance Officers Association, 1983), pp. 177–82; Greg Eden, "The Tax-Exempt Municipal Lease," in Petersen and Hough, *Creative Capital Financing,* pp. 183–91. In 1991, Standard and Poor's Corporation rated $7.3 billion in leases. "U.S. Supreme Court Declines Appeal of Virginia Lease Case," *Public Finance Digest* (Government Finance Group Inc., A Legg Mason Company, Arlington, Virginia, June 1992), p. 1.

See also Moody's Investors Service, "Moody's Views on Lease Rental Debt," *Moody's Municipal Issues* 6, no. 1 (March 1989), p. 1; Naomi Caiden and Jeffrey I. Chapman, "Constraint and Uncertainty: Budgeting in California," *Public Budgeting and Finance* (winter 1982), pp. 111–29 (esp. pp. 124–25); Randy Hamilton, "The World Turned Upside Down: The Contemporary Revolution in State and Local Government Financing," *Public Administration Review* 43, no. 1 (January/February 1983), pp. 22–31.

20. See, for example, Congressional Budget Office, *Federal Support of U.S. Business*, January 1984.

21. See, for example, Peter J. Bearse, ed., *Mobilizing Capital: Program Innovation and the Changing Public/Private Interface in Development Finance* (New York: Elsevier, 1982).

22. See Congressional Budget Office, *Loan Guarantees: Current Concerns and Alternatives for Control* (January 1979); Clifford M. Hardin and Arthur T. Denzau, *The Unrestrained Growth of Federal Credit Programs* (Center for the Study of American Business, Washington University, St. Louis, Publication no. 45, December 1981). See also Sbragia, *The Politics of Public Investment*.

23. GAO, *Trends and Changes in the Municipal Bond Market*, p. 15.

24. Petersen, *Tax-Exempts and Tax Reform*, p. 2.1.

25. ACIR, *Strengthening the Federal Revenue System*, p. 118. "Background," *Trends in Municipal Financing and the Use of Tax-Exempt Bonds to Finance Private Activities*, Hearing before the Committee on Ways and Means, House of Representatives, 98th Cong., 1st sess., June 15, 16, 1983, p. 1.

26. Leonard, *Checks Unbalanced*, p. 155; Petersen, *Tax-Exempts and Tax Reform*, p. 1.3.

27. Forbes, Fischer, and Petersen, "Recent Trends in Municipal Revenue Bond Financing," p. 155.

28. Peterson, "Capital Spending and Capital Obsolescence," p. 53. GAO, *Trends and Changes in the Municipal Bond Market*, p. ii.

29. Department of the Treasury, *Treasury Report on Private Purpose Tax-Exempt Bond Activity During Calendar Year 1983* (Office of Tax Analysis, March 28, 1984), p. 1. In 1984 the equivalent figure was 62 percent. Reported in *Alliance: The Newsletter for State and Local Government Finance* 1, no. 3 (April 1985), p. 3.

30. Letter to Senator Alfonse M. D'Amato, April 15, 1985.

31. Phil Clark and Tom Neubig, "Private Activity Tax-Exempt Bonds, 1983," *Statistics of Income Bulletin, Internal Revenue Service* (summer 1984), pp. 97–107 (97).

32. Clark and Neubig, "Private Activity Tax-Exempt Bonds," p. 103. John E. Petersen, "Infrastructure Financing: Examining the Record and Considering the Options," in *Public Infrastructure Planning and Management*, ed. Jay M. Stein (Beverly Hills: Sage, 1988), p. 107.

33. Alan B. Lechner, *Industrial Aid Financing* (New York City: Goodbody and Company, 1965), p. 1.

34. Joint Committee Print, *Trends in the Use of Tax-Exempt Bonds to Finance Private Activities, Including a Description of H.R. 1176 and H.R. 1635*, Prepared by the Staff of the Joint Committee on Taxation, Scheduled for a Hearing before the Committee on Ways and Means, House of Representatives, 98th Cong., 1st

sess., June 15, 16, 1983, published June 13, 1983 (Washington, D.C.: Government Printing Office, 1983), p. 4.

35. Congressional Budget Office, *Small Issue Industrial Revenue Bonds* (Washington, D.C.: U.S. Government Printing Office, April 1981), p. 1.

36. Alexandra Peers, "Corporate-Bond Storm Flood into 'Munis'," *Wall Street Journal,* November 23, 1988, p. C1.

37. Congressional Budget Office, *Small Issue Industrial Revenue Bonds,* p. 1.

38. Lamb and Rappaport, *Municipal Bonds,* p. 221; Government Finance Research Center, *Building Prosperity,* p. 29.

39. Lechner, *Industrial Aid Financing,* pp. 3–4.

40. ACIR, *Industrial Development Bond Financing* (Washington, D.C., June 1963), Report A-18, pp. 5–6. Congressional Budget Office, *Small Issue Industrial Revenue Bonds,* p. xii.

41. Walsh, *The Public's Business,* p. 324. Eisinger, *The Rise of the Entrepreneurial State,* p. 159.

42. Walsh, *The Public's Business,* pp. 324–25.

43. Congressman Byrnes quoted in Council of Industrial Development Bond Issuers, *Small Issue Industrial Development Bonds and the U.S. Economy* (March 1986), p. 143. *Industrial Development Bond Financing,* p. 15.

44. Congressional Budget Office, *Small Issue Industrial Revenue Bonds,* p. xii. George E. Peterson and Brian Cooper, *Tax-Exempt Financing of Housing Investment* (Washington, D.C.: The Urban Institute, 1979), p. 168.

45. Congressional Budget Office, *Small Issue Industrial Revenue Bonds,* pp. xii–xiii.

46. Ibid., pp. 47, 13–14.

47. Clark and Neubig, "Private Activity Tax-Exempt Bonds," p. 101.

48. Congressional Budget Office, *Small Issue Industrial Revenue Bonds,* pp. 29, 88.

49. Ibid., pp. 31–32. See also Gregory D. Squires, "Industrial Revenue Bonds and the Deindustrialization of America," *Urbanism Past and Present* 9, no. 17 (winter/spring 1984), pp. 1–9; Thomas S. Moore and Gregory D. Squires, "Public Policy and Private Benefits: The Case of Industrial Revenue Bonds," in *Business Elites and Urban Development: Case Studies and Critical Perspectives,* ed. Scott Cummings (Albany, N.Y.: State University of New York Press, 1988), pp. 97–117; Thomas A. Pascarella and Richard D. Raymond, "Buying Bonds for Business: An Evaluation of the Industrial Revenue Bond Program," *Urban Affairs Quarterly* (September 1982), pp. 73–89.

For a good overview of the debates and arguments about IRBs, see Matthew R. Marlin, "Industrial Development Bonds at Fifty: A Golden Anniversary Review," *Economic Development Quarterly* 1, no. 4 (November 1987), pp. 391–410; Dennis Zimmerman, "Federal Tax Policy, IDBs, and the Market for State and Local Bonds," *National Tax Journal* (September 1984), pp. 411–20 (esp. pp. 411–13). For an overview of the criticisms of IDBs before they were restricted in 1968, see Lechner, *Industrial Aid Financing,* chap. 5.

50. Moore and Squires, "Public Policy and Private Benefits," p. 101.

51. Congressman Rostenkowski quoted in Committee on Ways and Means, *Trends in Municipal Financing*, p. 4. K-Mart example is from Congressional Budget Office, *Small Issue Industrial Revenue Bonds*, p. 23.

52. Council of Industrial Development Bond Issuers, *Small Issue Industrial Development Bonds*, pp. 5–8.

53. Bruce F. Davie, "A Congressional View of Tax-Exempt Bonds — With Alarm?" in *Efficiency in the Municipal Bond Market: The Use of Tax Exempt Financing for "Private" Purposes*, ed. George G. Kaufman (Greenwich, Conn.: JAI Press, 1981), pp. 43–49 (44).

54. Joint Committee Print, *Trends in the Use of Tax-Exempt Bonds*, pp. 7, 36; Joan Pryde, "The Ongoing Battle: Almost Seventy Years of Assaults on Tax-Exempt Municipals," *The Bond Buyer: 100 Anniversary Edition* (1991), p. 89; Zimmerman, "Federal Tax Policy," pp. 411–20.

55. Ballard, Spahr, Andrews, and Ingersoll, *Tax-Free Bonds Today: 1984 Tax Law Changes* (Washington D.C.: Packard Press, 1984).

56. ACIR, *Strengthening the Federal Revenue System*, pp. 117, 119. Lamb and Rappaport, *Municipal Bonds*, p. 221. George E. Peterson and Harvey Galper, "Tax Exempt Financing of Private Industry's Pollution Control Investment," *Public Policy* 23, no. 1 (winter 1975), p. 82. See also Lamb and Rappaport, *Municipal Bonds*, pp. 225–26.

57. Congressional Budget Office, *Tax-Exempt Bonds for Single-Family Housing: A Study*, prepared for the Subcommittee on the City of the Committee on Banking, Finance, and Urban Affairs, House of Representatives, 96th Cong., 1st sess. (Washington, D.C.: U.S. Government Printing Office, April 1979), p. 41 n. 5.

58. Both quotes are from Walsh, *The Public's Business*, p. 151. Walsh's study is especially good in its analysis of the independent role of the financial community in shaping the use of the revenue bond.

59. The first quotation is from Peterson and Galper, "Tax Exempt Financing of Private Industry's Pollution Control Investment," p. 83. Walsh, *The Public's Business*, p. 151; Alice M. Rivlin, "CBO's Position on Tax-Exempt Financing for Private Activities," *Municipal Finance Journal* 4, no. 4 (1983), p. 306. The second quotation is from Rivlin, "CBO's Position," p. 307.

60. Forbes, Fischer, and Petersen, "Recent Trends in Municipal Revenue Bond Financing," pp. 156–57, table 3. Congressional Budget Office, *Tax-Exempt Bonds for Single-Family Housing*, p. 41 n. 5.

61. Walsh, *The Public's Business*, p. 152.

62. Public Securities Association, *Fundamentals of Municipal Bonds* (1981), p. 21. Petersen, *Tax-Exempts and Tax Reform*, fig. 6. See also Leonard, *Checks Unbalanced*, p. 155.

63. Leonard, *Checks Unbalanced*, pp. 162–63.

64. George E. Peterson, John A. Tuccillo, and John C. Weicher, "The Impact of Local Mortgage Revenue Bonds on Securities, Markets, and Housing Policy Objectives," in *Efficiency in the Municipal Bond Market: The Use of Tax Exempt Financing for "Private" Purposes*, ed. George G. Kaufman (Greenwich, Conn.: JAI Press, 1981), p. 52.

65. Congressional Budget Office, *Tax-Exempt Bonds for Single-Family Housing,* p. 3 n. 2.

66. Peterson and Cooper, *Tax-Exempt Financing of Housing Investment,* p. 29, table 7.

67. The quotation is from Sbragia, "Politics, Local Government, and the Municipal Bond Market," p. 93. Congressional Budget Office, *Tax-Exempt Bonds for Single-Family Housing,* p. 31 n. 21.

68. Peterson and Cooper, *Tax-Exempt Financing of Housing Investment,* p. 27.

69. Peterson, Tuccillo, and Weicher, "The Impact of Local Mortgage Revenue Bonds," p. 74. Congressional Budget Office, *Tax-Exempt Bonds for Single-Family Housing.*

70. Both quotations are from Peterson and Cooper, *Tax-Exempt Financing of Housing Investment,* p. 164.

71. Ibid., p. ix. George C. Kaufman, "Preface," in *Efficiency in the Municipal Bond Market: The Use of Tax Exempt Financing for "Private" Purposes,* ed. George C. Kaufman (Greenwich, Conn.: JAI Press, 1981), p. xii. ACIR, *Strengthening the Federal Revenue System,* p. 118, table 6-2.

72. Congressional Budget Office, *The Mortgage Subsidy Bond Tax Act of 1980: Experience Under the Permanent Rules* (Staff working paper, March 1982), p. xiii. The quotation is from pp. 35-36.

73. Ibid., pp. xiv-xv.

74. "Deficit Reduction Bill Extends Mortgage, Housing Programs," *Public Finance Network News* (August 1993), p. 1.

75. Sam Spatter, "Low-Income Families Get State, Local Housing Funds," *Pittsburgh Press,* March 20, 1988, p. G8.

76. GAO, *Home Ownership: Mortgage Bonds Are Costly and Provide Little Assistance to Those in Need,* GAO/RCED-88-111, March 1988, p. 5.

77. Committee on Ways and Means, *Trends in Municipal Financing,* p. 177.

78. Ibid., p. 642 (for an excellent summary of the arguments to be made against the widespread use of IDBs, see the association's statement, pp. 638-42).

79. Sbragia, *The Politics of Public Investment,* p. 20. See, for example, the testimony of the then Lieutenant Governor John Kerry of Massachusetts, a liberal Democrat, to the House of Representatives Committee on Ways and Means, *Trends in Municipal Financing,* pp. 181-84, 203-04.

80. Patrick Healy, "Further Comments on Proposed Capital Financing Alternatives," *Tax Policy* 37 (January/February 1970), pp. 1-12 (8-9); see also Sbragia, *The Politics of Local Borrowing.*

9. Washington Takes Control

1. The epigraph is from former IRS Commissioner Sheldon Cohen, quoted in Jeffrey H. Birnbaum and Alan S. Murray, *Showdown at Gucci Gulch: Lawmakers, Lobbyists, and the Unlikely Triumph of Tax Reform* (New York: Random House, 1987), p. 289.

2. James L. Rowe Jr., "Municipal Bond Market Sinks: Investors Panic over

Proposed Tax Change in Senate Finance Committee," *Washington Post,* March 20, 1986, pp. E1, E6.

3. Public Securities Association, *Fundamentals of Municipal Bonds* (1981), p. 7.

4. Ibid., pp. 7–8. Cathie Eitelberg, "Putting Down Grassroots: A National Strategy to Save Tax-Exempt Bonds," *Government Finance Review* (February 1989), p. 30.

5. See Zimmerman, *The Private Use of Tax-Exempt Bonds,* pp. 176–77. I have drawn liberally from Zimmerman's study. (I am not discussing all the changes in the tax code as they affect tax-exempt borrowing. For example, I am not considering the alternative minimum tax nor how changes in tax burden affect the attractiveness of municipal bonds to various types of investors.)

6. Petersen, *Tax-Exempts and Tax Reform,* p. 1.10.

7. For an overview of such restrictions, see Zimmerman, *The Private Use of Tax-Exempt Bonds,* pp. 177, 200–206, which provides an excellent overview of many of the themes developed in this chapter.

8. Zimmerman, *The Private Use of Tax-Exempt Bonds,* p. 186. Petersen, *Tax-Exempts and Tax Reform,* p. 1.9.

9. Petersen, *Tax-Exempts and Tax Reform,* p. 1.1, and executive summary.

10. D. William Graham, Paul L. Shinn, and John E. Petersen, *State Revolving Fund Under Tax Reform,* Council of Infrastructure Financing Authorities, Monograph no. 2, June 1989, p. 4. This chapter analyzes only selected aspects of private-activity bonds (those related to public purpose and to volume caps) and does so in a way designed to be comprehensible for the non-specialist reader. For excellent and much more specialized analyses of the various ways tax legislation has affected the municipal bond market, see Zimmerman, *The Private Use of Tax-Exempt Bonds* (esp. chap. 11) and Petersen, *Tax-Exempts and Tax Reform.*

11. Arthur Andersen and Company, *Tax Reform 1986: Analysis and Planning* (Chicago: Arthur Andersen, 1986), pp. 3–4, quoted in Timothy J. Conlan, Margaret T. Wrightson, and David R. Beam, *Taxing Choices: The Politics of Tax Reform* (Washington, D.C.: Congressional Quarterly Press, 1990), p. 2. Albert R. Hunt, the Washington bureau chief of the *Wall Street Journal* argued that, "in the history of the Republic, very few pieces of legislation have more profoundly affected so many Americans," in the Introduction to Birnbaum and Murray, *Showdown at Gucci Gulch,* p. xi.

12. For a general overview of how Congress defined the term *public purpose* in the period 1968–1989, see Zimmerman, *The Private Use of Tax-Exempt Bonds,* pp. 178–91.

13. "Private Activity Bond Volume for 1989," *Government Finance Review* (February 1989), p. 5; Robert L. Bland and Li-Khan Chen, "Taxable Municipal Bonds: State and Local Governments Confront the Tax-Exempt Limitation Movement," *Public Administration Review* (January/February 1990), pp. 42–48 (44).

14. "Private Activity Bond Volume for 1989," *Government Finance Review* (February 1989), p. 5.

15. Graham, Shinn, and Petersen, *State Revolving Funds,* p. 10.

16. See Petersen, *Tax-Exempts and Tax Reform*, pp. 2.3, 2.4. The following information is drawn from his study, pp. 2.3, 2.4, A2, A3. See also D. William Graham and Paul L. Shinn, *Federal Tax Policy and Infrastructure Financing*, A Report to the Office of Technology Assessment, U.S. Congress, Government Finance Research Center, September 13, 1990, pp. II.6–II.14.

17. Graham and Shinn, *Federal Tax Policy and Infrastructure Financing*, p. III.11.

18. See Petersen, *Tax-Exempts and Tax Reform*, p. 2.2.

19. Graham and Shinn, *Federal Tax Policy and Infrastructure Financing*, p. I.9.

20. *New York's Local Industrial Development Agencies*, p. 23.

21. See Bland and Chen, "Taxable Municipal Bonds," p. 43, table 1, for 1983 figures.

22. Congressman Rostenkowski cited in Committee on Ways and Means, *Trends in Municipal Financing*, pp. 1–2. See also Sbragia, *The Politics of Public Investment*.

23. Birnbaum and Murray, *Showdown at Gucci Gulch*, p. 138.

24. Mary L. Williams and Cynthia Saltzman, "The Impact of County Mortgage Programs on County Net Revenues," *State and Local Government Review* (winter 1991), p. 24.

25. "President Seeks Tax Immunity End by a 'Simple Law,'" *New York Times*, January 18, 1939, pp. 1, 4 (1). See also John Keohane, "The Federal Government and State/Local Government Securities: A Short History of Reciprocal Immunity," *Government Finance Review* (June 1988), pp. 7–11.

26. Conlan, Wrightson, and Beam, *Taxing Choices*, p. 60.

27. Birnbaum and Murray, *Showdown at Gucci Gulch*, p. 137.

28. Ibid., p. 138.

29. Ibid., pp. 138–39.

30. Conlan, Wrightson, and Beam, *Taxing Choices*, pp. 118–19.

31. Birnbaum and Murray, *Showdown at Gucci Gulch*, pp. 225–26.

32. Ibid., p. 242.

33. John E. Petersen, "Innovations in Tax-Exempt Instruments and Transactions," *National Tax Journal* 44 (1991), p. 12 n. 5; Daphne A. Kenyon, "Effects of Federal Volume Caps on State and Local Borrowing," *Tax Journal* 44 (1991), p. 81. Municipal bonds issued by housing and hospital corporations are private-activity bonds but are not subject to the unified volume cap.

34. Guy Land, "IDB Program Has Strong Support," *Public Finance Network News* (July/August 1991), p. 4.

35. Graham and Shinn, *Federal Tax Policy and Infrastructure Financing*, p. I.11. Nearly all federal spending for infrastructure is directed toward highways and airports and is funded by the highway and airport trust funds, which rely on user charges. Ibid., p. IV.6.

36. Petersen, "Innovations in Tax-Exempt Instruments," p. 24.

37. Testimony of Jeffrey S. Green on behalf of the Government Finance Officers Association, *State and Local Governments Under Stress: The Role of the Capital Markets*, Hearings before the Subcommittee on Securities of the Committee on

Banking, Housing, and Urban Affairs, U.S. Senate, 102d Cong., 1st sess., March 13, April 24, 1991, p. 203.

38. John Cranford, "Finance: Muni Bond Forecast Sunny . . . For Now," *Governing* (June 1992), p. 70.

39. Graham and Shinn, *Federal Tax Policy and Infrastructure Financing,* pp. II.7, II.9.

40. Petersen, "Infrastructure Financing," p. 113.

41. Lawrence W. Pierce, "Tax-Exempt Financing for Convention Centers," *Government Finance Review* (December 1988), pp. 40–43 (40). For a discussion of how industrial-development agencies are adapting to the limits on tax-exempt financing imposed by Congress, see *New York's Local Industrial Development Agencies*. For a general overview of creative ways to use the municipal bond market, see Rodd Zolkos, "A Guide to Muni Bond Deals of the Year," *Governing* 7 (June 1994), pp. 59–68.

42. Zimmerman, *The Private Use of Tax-Exempt Bonds,* pp. 305, 321. Kenyon, "Effects of Federal Volume Caps on State and Local Borrowing," p. 90. "Washington Outlook," *Governing* (June 1992), p. 73.

43. For a discussion of New York's system for allocating the volume cap, see *New York's Local Industrial Development Agencies,* pp. 27–31.

44. Zimmerman, *The Private Use of Tax-Exempt Bonds,* pp. 296, 322 (296). For an overview of various states' priorities, see pp. 297–301.

45. To put the *South Carolina* decision in context, see William C. Mathewson, "A New Bridge to Cross: The Doctrine of Inverse Federalism," *Detroit College of Law Review* (winter 1989), pp. 1315–50. See also Martha Derthick, "Preserving Federalism: Congress, the States, and the Supreme Court," *Brookings Review* (winter/spring 1986), pp. 32–37. Margaret T. Wrightson, "The Road to *South Carolina:* Intergovernmental Tax Immunity and the Constitutional Status of Federalism," *Publius: The Journal of Federalism* (summer 1989), pp. 39–55 (39).

46. Brief of the Government Finance Officers Association, as Amicus Curiae in Support of Plaintiffs, State of South Carolina, Plaintiff, National Governors' Association, Plaintiff in *Intervention v. James A. Baker III,* Defendant, p. 29.

47. Wrightson, "The Road to *South Carolina,*" p. 42. For some of the issues raised by *Garcia,* see Derthick, "Preserving Federalism," pp. 32–37; A. E. Dick Howard, "*Garcia:* Of Federalism and Constitutional Values," *Publius: The Journal of Federalism* (summer 1986), pp. 17–31.

48. George Elser, "South Carolina v. Baker—Bad News from the Supreme Court," *Government Finance Review* (June 1988), pp. 34–35. For an overview of the development of the theory of intergovernmental tax immunity, see George Elser, "After South Carolina," *Municipal Finance Journal* 10, no. 1 (winter 1989), pp. 7–21 (8–13).

49. Wrightson, "The Road to *South Carolina,*" pp. 51–52.

50. To get a sense of some of these changes involving so-called technicalities, see Lester T. Wood III, "Investing Bond Proceeds and the Arbitrage Rebate Requirements," *Government Finance Review* (February 1990), pp. 19–22; Patrick C. Glisson, "The Gas Tax: Robbing Peter . . . ," *Government Finance Review* (April 1988),

p. 3; "GFOA Offers Suggestions to Simplify the Federal Tax Code," *Government Finance Review* (June 1990), pp. 26–27; Betsy Dotson and Catherine L. Spain, "Bond Allocation Practices: How Issuers Treat Commingled Investments and Project Expenditures," *Government Finance Review* (October 1990), pp. 41–42.

51. Anthony cited in Penelope Lemov, "Working Smarter: The Tax-Exempt Bond Lobby Wins Three Big Ones," *Governing* (January 1990), pp. 21–26 (26).

52. "President's Budget: Bad News for Bonds," *Public Finance Network News* (March/April 1991), pp. 4, 6. Lemov, "Working Smarter," p. 26. The quotation is from "Caucus Formed to Address Public Finance," *Public Finance Network News* (November/December 1991), p. 1.

53. See, for example, the statement of Joseph M. Giglio, chairman, Private Sector Advisory Panel on Infrastructure Financing; the statement by Benjamin M. Rawls on behalf of the Private Sector Advisory Panel on Infrastructure Financing; the statement of Representative John Bragg, National Conference of State Legislatures; the statement of Andrew O'Rourke on behalf of the National Association of Counties; the statement of Kyle C. Testerman, Mayor, City of Knoxville, Tennessee, all in *Comprehensive Tax Reform,* Hearings before the Committee on Ways and Means, House of Representatives, 99th Cong., 1st sess., on The President's Tax Proposals to the Congress for Fairness, Growth and Simplicity, Part 6 of 9, July 11, 12, and 17, 1985, Serial 99–46. Although the Treasury proposals were made somewhat less restrictive in the Tax Reform Act of 1986, public-private partnerships were still hurt.

For a discussion of the issues surrounding tax-exempt financing and public-private partnerships in the provision of infrastructure, see Kevin Quinn and Myron Olstein, "Privatization: Public/Private Partnerships Provide Essential Services," in *Public/Private Partnerships: Financing a Commonwealth,* ed. Barbara Weiss (Washington, D.C.: Government Finance Research Center, Government Finance Officers Association, 1985), pp. 67–82; Eugene Carlson, "Treasury's Proposal Threatens Cities' Garbage-Disposal Plans," *Wall Street Journal,* January 8, 1985, p. 37; Dennis Melamed, "As the Feds Bow Out, Communities Seek New Ways to Pay for Clean Water," *Governing* (July 1990), pp. 19–23; John G. Heilman and Gerald W. Johnson, "System and Process in Capital-Intensive Privatization: A Comparative Case Study of Municipal Wastewater Treatment Works," *Policy Studies Review* 8, no. 3 (spring 1989), pp. 549–72; International City Management Association, "Making Environmental Partnerships Work," *MIS Report* 22, no. 9 (September 1990).

54. "Guarini Prepares Environmental Infrastructure Facilities Bill," *Public Finance Network News* (March/April 1991), p. 5; James Smith, "Two Infrastructure Proposals Under Congressional Review," *Public Finance Network News* (May/June 1991), p. 5.

55. Elser, "After South Carolina," p. 16.

56. Jeffrey Esser, "Tax Exemption After South Carolina," *Government Finance Review* (October 1988), p. 3.

57. See, for example, Michael A. Pagano and Richard J. T. Moore, *Cities and Fiscal Choices: A New Model of Urban Public Investment* (Durham: Duke Univer-

sity Press, 1985), pp. 86–90; Larry E. Huckins and George S. Tolley, "Investments in Local Infrastructure," in *Urban Policy Analysis: Directions for Future Research*, ed. Terry Nichols Clark (Beverly Hills: Sage, 1981), pp. 123–32; Government Finance Research Center, *Building Prosperity*. For an early book that sounded the warning that infrastructure was a major problem, see Pat Choate and Susan Walter, *America in Ruins: The Decaying Infrastructure* (Durham: Duke University Press, 1983).

58. "Donnelly Wants to Tax Muni Bond Interest," *Public Finance Network News* (March/April 1991), p. 3.

59. Network members include the GFOA, Airports Operators Council International, American Association of Port Authorities, Association of Metropolitan Sewerage Agencies, Council of Infrastructure Financing Authorities, Water Pollution Control Federation, Council of State Governments, Council of Industrial Development Bond Issuers, American Public Transit Association, American Public Gas Association, American Public Works Association, and the International Bridge, Tunnel, and Turnpike Association.

60. *Public Finance Network*, January 27, 1992.

61. Eitelberg, "Putting Down Grassroots," p. 30.

62. Lemov, "Working Smarter," p. 24.

63. Quoted in Eitelberg, "Putting Down Grassroots," p. 31.

64. *Public Finance Network News* (May/June 1991), p. 2.

65. Ibid.

66. Joanne Field, "Public Finance Network Celebrates First Anniversary," *Government Finance Review* (December 1989), pp. 28–29.

67. Lobbyist cited in Lemov, "Working Smarter," p. 23.

68. Ibid.

10. Conclusion

1. Scharpf, "The Joint-Decision Trap," p. 242.

Bibliography

Abbott, Carl. *Boosters and Businessmen: Popular Economic Thought and Urban Growth in the Antebellum Middlewest.* Westport, Conn.: Greenwood, 1981.

Advisory Commission on Intergovernmental Relations (ACIR). *Bankruptcies, Defaults, and Other Local Government Financial Emergencies.* Washington, D.C.: March 1985.

———. *Industrial Development Bond Financing.* Report A-18. Washington, D.C.: June 1963.

———. *The Organization of Local Public Economies.* Report A-109. Washington, D.C.: December 1987.

———. *The Problem of Special Districts in American Government.* Report A-22. Washington, D.C.: May 1964.

———. *State Constitutional and Statutory Restrictions on Local Government Debt: A Commission Report.* Report A-10. Washington, D.C.: September 1961.

———. *Strengthening the Federal Revenue System: Implications for State and Local Taxing and Borrowing.* Washington, D.C.: October 1984.

———. *Understanding the Market for State and Local Debt.* Washington, D.C.: May 1976.

Adams, Carolyn Teich. *The Politics of Capital Investment: The Case of Philadelphia.* Albany: State University of New York Press, 1988.

Alderfer, Harold F. "Is 'Authority' Financing the Answer?" *The American City* (February 1955).

Ballard, Spahr, Andrews, and Ingersoll. *Tax-Free Bonds Today: 1984 Tax Law Changes.* Washington D.C.: Packard Press, 1984.

Barnes, Lela, ed. "An Editor Looks at Early-Day Kansas: The Letters of Charles Monroe Chase." *Kansas Historical Quarterly* 26 (summer 1960).

Barnes, Tom. "City Water Authority Hopes to Hold Rate Increase in Line." *Pittsburgh Post-Gazette,* October 15, 1988.

———. "Water Tax Hike Irks DePasquale." *Pittsburgh Post-Gazette,* February 28, 1987.

Barrett, Paul. *The Automobile and Urban Transit: The Formation of Public Policy in Chicago, 1900–1930.* Philadelphia: Temple University Press, 1983.

Bearse, Peter J. ed. *Mobilizing Capital: Program Innovation and the Changing Public/Private Interface in Development Finance.* New York: Elsevier, 1982.

Beer, Samuel H. "The Adoption of General Revenue Sharing: A Case Study in Public Sector Politics." *Public Policy* 24 (1976), pp. 166–71.

——. "Federalism, Nationalism, and Democracy in America." *American Political Science Review* 72 (March 1978), pp. 9–21.

——. "The Modernization of American Federalism." *Publius: The Journal of Federalism* (1973), pp. 50–95.

——. "Political Overload and Federalism." *Polity* 10 (fall 1977), pp. 5–17.

Belcher, Wyatt Winton. *The Economic Rivalry Between St. Louis and Chicago: 1850–1880.* New York: Columbia University Press, 1947.

Bennett, James T., and Thomas J. DiLorenzo. *Underground Government: The Off-Budget Public Sector.* Washington, D.C.: Cato Institute, 1983.

Bensel, Richard Franklin. *Yankee Leviathan: The Origins of Central State Authority in America, 1859–1877.* Cambridge: Cambridge University Press, 1990.

Berk, Gerald. "Corporate Liberalism Reconsidered: A Review Essay." *Journal of Policy History* 3 (1991), pp. 70–84.

Beyer, William C. "Financial Dictators Replace Political Boss." *National Municipal Review* 22, no. 4 (April 1933) and no. 5 (May 1933).

Birnbaum, Jeffrey H., and Alan S. Murray. *Showdown at Gucci Gulch: Lawmakers, Lobbyists, and the Unlikely Triumph of Tax Reform.* New York: Random House, 1987.

Bland, Robert L., and Li-Khan Chen. "Taxable Municipal Bonds: State and Local Governments Confront the Tax-Exempt Limitation Movement." *Public Administration Review* (January/February 1990).

Bollens, John C. *Special District Governments in the United States.* Berkeley and Los Angeles: University of California Press, 1961.

Booth, Douglas E. "Transportation, City Building, and Financial Crises — Milwaukee, 1852–1862." *Journal of Urban History* 9 (May 1983), pp. 335–63.

Bowmar, Robert H. "The Anachronism Called Debt Limitation." *Iowa Law Review* 52 (April 1967), pp. 863–900.

Bridges, Amy. "Winning the West to Municipal Reform." *Urban Affairs Quarterly* 27 (June 1992), pp. 494–518.

Brown, Josephine. *Public Relief, 1929–1939.* New York: H. Holt and Company, 1940.

Brownell, Blaine A., and David R. Goldfield, eds. *The City in Southern History: The Growth of Urban Civilization in the South.* Port Washington, N.Y.: Kennikat Press, 1977.

Bureau of the Census. *1982 Census of Governments.* Vol. 4, *Government Finances, No. 2, Finances of Special Districts.* Washington, D.C.: U.S. Government Printing Office. March 1984.

Burhans, J. A. *The Law of Municipal Bonds.* Chicago: S. A. Kean, 1889.

Caiden, Naomi, and Jeffrey I. Chapman. "Constraint and Uncertainty: Budgeting in California." *Public Budgeting and Finance* (winter 1982), pp. 111–29.

Cain, Louis P. *Sanitation Strategy for a Lakefront Metropolis: The Case of Chicago.* DeKalb, Ill.: Northern Illinois University Press, 1978.

Callender, G. S. "The Early Transportation and Banking Enterprises of the States in Relation to the Growth of Corporations." *Quarterly Journal of Economics* 17 (November 1902), pp. 111–62.

Cape, William H., Leon B. Graves, and Burton M. Michaels. *Government by Special Districts*. Government Research Center, The University of Kansas, 1969.

Carlson, Eugene. "Treasury's Proposal Threatens Cities' Garbage-Disposal Plans." *Wall Street Journal*, January 8, 1985.

Caro, Robert A. *The Power Broker: Robert Moses and the Fall of New York*. New York: Alfred A. Knopf, 1974.

Carosso, Vincent P. *Investment Banking in America: A History*. Cambridge: Harvard University Press, 1970.

Carstensen, R., ed. *The Public Lands: Studies in the History of the Public Domain*. Madison: University of Wisconsin Press, 1963.

"Caucus Formed to Address Public Finance." *Public Finance Network News* (November/December 1991).

Chandler, Alfred D. Jr. "The Beginnings of 'Big Business' in American Industry." *Business History Review* 33 (spring 1959), pp. 1–31.

———. "The Large Industrial Corporation and the Making of the Modern American Economy." In *Institutions in Modern America: Innovation in Structure and Progress*, ed. Stephen E. Ambrose. Baltimore: Johns Hopkins University Press, 1967.

———. *The Visible Hand: The Managerial Revolution in American Business*. Cambridge: Harvard University Press, 1977.

Chandler, Alfred D. Jr., ed. *The Railroads, the Nation's First Big Business: Sources and Readings*. New York: Harcourt, Brace and World, 1965.

Chandler, Alfred D. Jr., and Herman Daems, eds. *Managerial Hierarchies: Comparative Perspectives on the Rise of the Modern Industrial Enterprise*. Cambridge: Harvard University Press, 1980.

Choate, Pat, and Susan Walter. *America in Ruins: The Decaying Infrastructure*. Durham: Duke University Press, 1983.

Chudacoff, Howard P. *The Evolution of American Urban Society*. Englewood Cliffs, N.J.: Prentice-Hall, 1975.

Clark, Phil, and Tom Neubig. "Private Activity Tax-Exempt Bonds, 1983." *Statistics of Income Bulletin, Internal Revenue Service* (summer 1984), pp. 97–107.

Cleveland, Frederick A., and Fred Wilbur Powell. *Railroad Promotion and Capitalization in the United States*. London: Longmans, Green, 1909.

Cochran, Thomas C. "The Paradox of American Economic Growth." *Journal of American History* 61 (March 1975), pp. 925–42.

Comment. "The Judicial Demise of State Constitutional Debt Limitations." *Iowa Law Review* 56 (February 1971), pp. 648–51.

Conlan, Timothy J., Margaret T. Wrightson, and David R. Beam. *Taxing Choices: The Politics of Tax Reform*. Washington, D.C.: Congressional Quarterly Press, 1990.

Council of Industrial Development Bond Issuers. *Small Issue Industrial Development Bonds and the U.S. Economy*. March 1986.

Council of State Governments. *Public Authorities in the States: A Report to the Governors' Conference*. Chicago, 1953.

———. *State Public Authorities*. Chicago, July 1970.

Cranford, John. "Finance: Muni Bond Forecast Sunny . . . For Now." *Governing* (June 1992).

Dahl, Robert. *Who Governs?* New Haven: Yale University Press, 1961.

Danielson, Michael N., and Jameson W. Doig. *New York: The Politics of Urban Regional Development*. Berkeley and Los Angeles: University of California Press, 1982.

David, Stephen, and Paul Kantor. "Urban Policy in the Federal System: A Reconceptualization of Federalism." *Polity* 16, no. 2, pp. 284–303.

Davie, Bruce F. "A Congressional View of Tax-Exempt Bonds — With Alarm?" In *Efficiency in the Municipal Bond Market: The Use of Tax Exempt Financing for "Private" Purposes*, ed. George G. Kaufman. Greenwich, Conn.: JAI Press, 1981.

Davis, Horace A. "Borrowing Machines." *National Municipal Review* 24 (June 1935), pp. 328–34.

Davis, Lance. "The Capital Markets and Industrial Concentration: The U.S. and U.K., a Comparative Study." *Economic History Review*, 2d ser. 19 (August 1966), pp. 255–72.

"Deficit Reduction Bill Extends Mortgage, Housing Programs." *Public Finance Network News* (August 1993).

Derthick, Martha. "Preserving Federalism: Congress, the States, and the Supreme Court." *Brookings Review* (winter/spring 1986), pp. 32–37.

Dillon, Read, and Company, Inc. *Infrastructure Financing: An Overview*. Dillon, Read, 1983.

Doig, Jameson W. "Coalition-Building by a Regional Agency: Austin Tobin and the Port of New York Authority." In *The Politics of Urban Development*, ed. Clarence N. Stone and Heywood T. Sanders. Lawrence: University Press of Kansas, 1987.

——. " 'If I See a Murderous Fellow Sharpening a Knife Cleverly . . .': The Wilsonian Dichotomy and the Public Authority Tradition." *Public Administration Review* 43 (July/August 1983), pp. 292–304.

——. *Metropolitan Transportation Politics and the New York Region*. New York: Columbia University Press, 1966.

——. "Politics and the Engineering Mind: Ammann and the Hidden Story of the George Washington Bridge." In *Building the Public City: The Politics, Governance, and Finance of Public Infrastructure*, ed. David C. Perry. London: Sage, 1995.

——. "To Claim the Seas and the Skies: Austin Tobin and the Port of New York Authority." In *Leadership and Innovation: A Biographical Perspective on Entrepreneurs in Government*, ed. Jameson W. Doig and Erwin C. Hargrove. Baltimore: Johns Hopkins Press, 1987.

"Donnelly Wants to Tax Muni Bond Interest." *Public Finance Network News* (March/April 1991).

Dotson, Betsy, and Catherine L. Spain. "Bond Allocation Practices: How Issuers Treat Commingled Investments and Project Expenditures." *Government Finance Review* (October 1990).

Doyle, Don Harrison. *The Social Order of a Frontier Community: Jacksonville, Illinois, 1825–1870.* Urbana: University of Illinois Press, 1978.

Dupuy, Gabriel, and Joel A. Tarr. "Sewers and Cities: France and the United States Compared." *Journal of the Environmental Engineering Division, Proceedings of the American Society of Civil Engineering* 108 (April 1982), pp. 327–37.

Durisch, Lawrence L. "Municipal Debt Limits and the Financing of Publicly Owned Utilities." *National Municipal Review* 20 (August 1931), pp. 460–65.

——. "Publicly Owned Utilities and the Problem of Municipal Debt Limits." *Michigan Law Review* 31 (February 1933), pp. 503–11.

Dykstra, Robert R. *The Cattle Towns.* New York: Alfred A. Knopf, 1968.

Edelstein, Mortimer S. "The Authority Plan — Tool of Modern Government." *Cornell Law Quarterly* 28 (January 1943), pp. 177–91.

Eden, Greg. "The Tax-Exempt Municipal Lease." In *Creative Capital Financing for State and Local Governments,* ed. John E. Petersen and Wesley C. Hough. Government Finance Research Center, Municipal Finance Officers Association, 1983.

Edwards, George W. *The Evolution of Finance Capitalism.* New York: Longmans, Green, 1938.

Eisinger, Peter K. *The Rise of the Entrepreneurial State: State and Local Economic Development Policy in the United States.* Madison: University of Wisconsin Press, 1988.

Eitelberg, Cathie. "Putting Down Grassroots: A National Strategy to Save Tax-Exempt Bonds." *Government Finance Review* (February 1989).

Elkin, Stephen L. *City and Regime in the American Republic.* Chicago: University of Chicago Press, 1987.

Ellis, David Maldwyn. "The Forfeiture of Railroad Land Grants, 1867–1894." *Mississippi Valley Historical Review* 33 (June 1946), pp. 27–60.

Ellis, John H. "Businessmen and Public Health in the Urban South During the Nineteenth Century: New Orleans, Memphis, and Atlanta: Conclusion." *Bulletin of the History of Medicine* 44 (July/August 1970), pp. 346–71.

Elser, George. "After South Carolina." *Municipal Finance Journal* 10 (winter 1989), pp. 7–21.

——. "South Carolina v. Baker — Bad News from the Supreme Court." *Government Finance Review* (June 1988).

Erie, Steven P. "How the Urban West Was Won: The Local State and Economic Growth in Los Angeles, 1880–1932." *Urban Affairs Quarterly* 27 (June 1992).

Ershkowitz, Herbert, and William G. Shade. "Consensus or Conflict? Political Behavior in the State Legislatures During the Jacksonian Era." *Journal of American History* 58 (December 1971), pp. 591–621.

Esser, Jeffrey. "Tax Exemption After South Carolina." *Government Finance Review* (October 1988).

Fabozzi, Frank J., Sylvan G. Feldstein, Irving M. Pollack, and Frank G. Zarb, eds. *The Municipal Bond Handbook.* Homewoood, Ill.: Dow Jones-Irwin, 1983.

Fairlie, John A. *Municipal Administration.* New York: MacMillan, 1910.

Fairman, Charles, ed. *Reconstruction and Reunion, 1864–1888.* Vol. 6, pt. 1, *The*

Oliver Wendell Holmes Devise History of the Supreme Court of the United States, ed. Paul Freund. New York: Macmillan, 1971.

Faulkner, Harold Underwood. *American Economic History.* New York: Harper and Brothers, 1924.

——. *The Decline of Laissez Faire: 1897–1917.* Vol. 7, *The Economic History of the United States.* White Plains, N.Y.: M. E. Sharpe, 1951.

Field, Joanne. "Public Finance Network Celebrates First Anniversary." *Government Finance Review* (December 1989).

Fine, Sidney. *Laissez Faire and the General-Welfare State: A Study of Conflict in American Thought, 1865–1901.* Ann Arbor: University of Michigan Press, 1956.

Fishlow, Albert. *American Railroads and the Transformation of the Antebellum Economy.* Cambridge: Harvard University Press, 1965.

Flanagan, Maureen A. *Charter Reform in Chicago.* Carbondale, Ill.: Southern Illinois University Press, 1987.

Foley, E. H. Jr. "Low-Rent Housing and State Financing." *University of Pennsylvania Law Review* 85 (January 1937), pp. 239–60.

——. "Revenue Financing of Public Enterprise." *Michigan Law Review* 35 (November 1936), pp. 1–43.

——. "Some Recent Developments in the Law Relating to Municipal Financing of Public Works." *Fordham Law Review* 4 (January 1935), pp. 13–34.

Forbes, Ronald W., and John E. Petersen. "Background Paper." In *Building a Broader Market: Report of the Twentieth Century Fund Task Force on the Municipal Bond Market.* New York: McGraw-Hill, 1976.

——. *The Rating Game: Report of the Twentieth Century Fund Task Force on Municipal Bond Credit Ratings.* New York: The Twentieth Century Fund, 1974.

Forbes, Ronald, Philip Fischer, and John Petersen. "Recent Trends in Municipal Revenue Bond Financing." In *Efficiency in the Municipal Bond Market: The Use of Tax Exempt Financing for "Private" Purposes,* ed. George G. Kaufman. Greenwich: Conn.: JAI Press, 1981.

Formisano, Ronald. *The Birth of Mass Political Parties, Michigan, 1837–1861.* Princeton: Princeton University Press, 1971.

Fowler, John F. Jr. *Revenue Bonds: The Nature, Uses, and Distribution of Fully Self-Liquidating Public Loans.* New York: Harper, 1938.

Fox, Kenneth. *Better City Government: Innovation in American Urban Politics, 1850–1937.* Philadelphia: Temple University Press, 1977.

Frug, Gerald E. "The City as a Legal Concept." *Harvard Law Review* 93 (April 1980), pp. 1059–154.

——. "Property and Power: Hartog on the Legal History of New York City." *American Bar Foundation Research Journal,* no. 3 (summer 1984), pp. 673–91.

Fuchs, Ester R. *Mayors and Money: Fiscal Policy in New York and Chicago.* Chicago: University of Chicago Press, 1992.

Fuerbringer, Jonathan. "Credit Markets: In Shift, Bond Dealers Seek to Halt Political Donations." *New York Times,* October 6, 1993.

———. "Despite Scandal, Politicians Still Want Wall St. Money." *New York Times,* October 14, 1993.

Galshoff, Stuart. "Triumph and Failure: The American Response to the Urban Water Supply Problem, 1860–1923." In *Pollution and Reform in American Cities, 1870–1930,* ed. Martin V. Melosi. Austin: University of Texas, 1980.

GAO. See U.S. General Accounting Office (GAO).

Gelfand, M. David. "Seeking Local Government Financial Integrity Through Debt Ceilings, Tax Limitations, and Expenditure Limits: The New York City Fiscal Crisis, the Taxpayers' Revolt, and Beyond." *Minnesota Law Review* 63 (1979), pp. 545–608.

Gelfand, Mark I. *A Nation of Cities: The Federal Government and Urban America, 1933–1965.* New York: Oxford University Press, 1975.

"GFOA Offers Suggestions to Simplify the Federal Tax Code." *Government Finance Review* (June 1990).

Gilpin, Robert. *U.S. Power and the Multinational Corporation: The Political Economy of Foreign Direct Investment.* New York: Basic Books, 1975.

Glaab, Charles N. *Kansas City and the Railroads: Community Policy in the Growth of a Regional Metropolis.* Madison: State Historical Society of Wisconsin, 1962.

Glaab, Charles N., and A. Theodore Brown. *A History of Urban America.* London: Macmillan, 1967.

Glasberg, Davita Silfen. "The Political Economic Power of Finance Capital and Urban Fiscal Crisis: Cleveland's Default, 1978." *Journal of Urban Affairs* 10, no. 1 (1988), pp. 63–76.

Glisson, Patrick C. "The Gas Tax: Robbing Peter. . . ." *Government Finance Review* (April 1988).

Goodrich, Carter. "American Development Policy: The Case of Internal Improvements." *Journal of Economic History* 16 (December 1956), pp. 449–60.

———. *Government Promotion of American Canals and Railroads, 1800–1890.* New York: Columbia University Press, 1960.

———. "Local Government Planning and Internal Improvements." *Political Science Quarterly* 66 (September 1951), pp. 411–46.

———. "National Planning of Internal Improvements." *Political Science Quarterly* 63 (March 1948), pp. 16–44.

———. "The Revulsion Against Internal Improvements." *Journal of Economic History* 10 (November 1950), pp. 145–69.

———. "State In, State Out — A Pattern of Development Policy." *Journal of Economic Issues* 11 (December 1968).

———. "The Virginia System of Mixed Enterprise: A Study of State Planning of Internal Improvements." *Political Science Quarterly* 64 (September 1949), pp. 355–87.

Goodrich, Carter, ed. *Canals and American Economic Development.* New York: Columbia University Press, 1961.

Gordon, Robert W. "Introduction: J. Willard Hurst and the Common Law Tradition in American Legal Historiography." *Law and Society Review* 10 (1975), pp. 9–56.

Government Finance Research Center. *Building Prosperity: Financing Public Infrastructure for Economic Development.* Washington, D.C.: Municipal Finance Officers Association, 1983.

Graham, D. William, Paul L. Shinn, and John E. Petersen. *State Revolving Funds Financing.* A Report to the Office of Technology Assessment, U.S. Congress, Government Finance Research Center. September 13, 1990.

Graham, D. William, Paul L. Shinn, and John E. Petersen. *State Revolving Fund Under Tax Reform.* Council of Infrastructure Financing Authorities. Monograph no. 2, June 1989.

Granick, Harry. *Underneath New York.* New York: Rinehart, 1947.

Green, Fletcher M. *Constitutional Development in the South Atlantic States, 1776–1860: A Study in the Evolution of Democracy.* Chapel Hill: University of North Carolina Press, 1930.

Greenberg, Ronald David. "Municipal Securities: Some Basic Principles and Practices." *Urban Lawyer* 9 (spring 1977), pp. 338–63.

"Guarini Prepares Environmental Infrastructure Facilities Bill." *Public Finance Network News* (March/April 1991).

Haider, Donald H. *When Governments Come to Washington: Governors, Mayors, and Intergovernmental Lobbying.* New York: Free Press, 1974.

Hall, Kermit L. *The Magic Mirror: Law in American History.* Oxford: Oxford University Press, 1989.

Hamilton, Randy. "The World Turned Upside Down: The Contemporary Revolution in State and Local Government Financing." *Public Administration Review* 43 (January/February 1983), pp. 22–31.

Handlin, Oscar, and Mary Flug Handlin. *A Commonwealth: A Study of the Role of Government in the American Economy, Massachusetts, 1774–1861.* New York: New York University Press, 1947.

Haney, Lewis H. *A Congressional History of Railways in the United States.* 1908, 1910. Reprint, New York: Augustus M. Kelley, 1968.

Hardin, Clifford M., and Arthur T. Denzau. *The Unrestrained Growth of Federal Credit Programs.* Center for the Study of American Business, Washington University, St. Louis. Publication no. 45, December 1981.

Harlan, Christi, and Thomas T. Vogel Jr. "Bond Group Moves to Curb Political Gifts." *Wall Street Journal,* August 5, 1993.

Harris, Carl V. *Political Power in Birmingham, 1871–1921.* Knoxville: University of Tennessee Press, 1977.

Hartog, Hendrik. *Public Property and Private Power: The Corporation of the City of New York in American Law, 1730–1870.* Chapel Hill: University of North Carolina Press, 1983.

Hartz, Louis. *Economic Policy and Democratic Thought: Pennsylvania, 1776–1860.* Cambridge: Harvard University Press, 1948.

Hawkins, Robert B. Jr. *Self Government by District: Myth and Reality.* Stanford: Hoover Institution Press, 1976.

Hayes, Richard. *Understanding San Francisco's Budget: How City Hall Spends Your Money and What You Can Do About It.* San Francisco: San Francisco Study Center and the Youth Project, 1973.

Hays, Samuel P. *American Political History as Social Analysis.* Knoxville: University of Tennessee Press, 1980.

———. "The Changing Political Structure of the City in Industrial America." *Journal of Urban History* 1 (November 1974), pp. 6–38.

———. "Politics of Reform in Municipal Government in the Progressive Era." In *Social Change and Urban Politics: Readings,* ed. Daniel N. Gordon. Englewood Cliffs, N.J.: Prentice-Hall, 1973.

———. "The Politics of Reform in Municipal Government in the Progressive Era." *Pacific Northwest Quarterly* 55 (1964).

Healy, Patrick. "Further Comments on Proposed Capital Financing Alternatives." *Tax Policy* 37 (January/February 1970), pp. 1–12.

Heath, Milton Sydney. *Constructive Liberalism: The Role of the State in Economic Development in Georgia to 1860.* Cambridge: Harvard University Press, 1954.

———. "Laissez Faire in Georgia, 1732–1860." *Journal of Economic History* 3 (1943), supplement, pp. 78–100.

Hecht, David M., and Frank L. Mallare. "Wisconsin's Internal Improvements Prohibition: Obsolete in Modern Times?" *Wisconsin Law Review* (March 1961), pp. 294–309.

Heil, Dennis J. "Another Day Older and Deeper in Debt: Debt Limitation, the Broad Special Fund Doctrine, and WPPSS 4 and 5." *University of Puget Sound Law Review* 7 (fall 1983).

Heilman, John G., and Gerald W. Johnson. "System and Process in Capital-Intensive Privatization: A Comparative Case Study of Municipal Wastewater Treatment Works." *Policy Studies Review* 8 (spring 1989), pp. 549–72.

Heins, A. James. *Constitutional Restrictions Against State Debt.* Madison: University of Wisconsin Press, 1963.

Henriques, Diana B. *The Machinery of Greed: The Abuse of Public Authorities and What to Do About It.* Lexington, Mass.: Lexington Books, 1986.

Hillhouse, A. M. *Municipal Bonds: A Century of Experience.* New York: Prentice-Hall, 1936.

Holden, Matthew Jr. "The Governance of the Metropolis as a Problem in Diplomacy." *Journal of Politics* 26 (August 1964), pp. 627–47.

Hollander, J. H. "The Cincinnati Southern Railway: A Study in Municipal Activity." In *Johns Hopkins University Studies in Historical and Political Science,* ed. Herbert B. Adams, I-II. Baltimore: Johns Hopkins Press, 1894.

Horwitz, Morton J. *The Transformation of American Law, 1780–1860.* Cambridge: Harvard University Press, 1977.

Howard, A. E. Dick. "*Garcia:* Of Federalism and Constitutional Values." *Publius: The Journal of Federalism* (summer 1986), pp. 17–31.

Huckins, Larry E., and George S. Tolley. "Investments in Local Infrastructure." In *Urban Policy Analysis: Directions for Future Research,* ed. Terry Nichols Clark. Beverly Hills: Sage, 1981.

Hurst, Willard. *Law and Markets in United States History: Different Modes of Bargaining Among Interests.* Madison: University of Wisconsin Press, 1982.

———. *Law and Social Order in the United States.* Ithaca, N.Y.: Cornell University Press, 1977.

Illyes, John. *Tax-Exempt Municipal Leases: Certificates of Participation, Nonappropriation Outs.* Nuveen Research, John Nuveen and Co. Inc., Investment Bankers. April 1987.

Incorvaia, John. "Brevard County, Florida: Case Study in an Issuer's Willingness to Pay Its Obligation." *Moody's Municipal Issues* 9 (April 1992).

International City Management Association. "Making Environmental Partnerships Work." *MIS Report* 22 (September 1990).

Jenks, Leland Hamilton. *The Migration of British Capital to 1875.* London: Thomas Nelson, 1927.

Johnson, Arthur M., and Barry E. Supple. *Boston Capitalists and Western Railroads: A Study in the Nineteenth-Century Railroad Investment Process.* Cambridge: Harvard University Press, 1967.

Jones, Robert B. *Tennessee at the Crossroads: The State Debt Controversy, 1870–1883.* Knoxville: University of Tennessee Press, 1977.

Judd, Dennis. *The Politics of American Cities: Private Power and Public Policy.* 2d ed. Boston: Little, Brown, 1984.

Judd, Dennis R., and David Brian Robertson. "Urban Revitalization in the United States: Prisoner of the Federal System." In *Regenerating the Cities: The U.K. Crisis and the U.S. Experience,* ed. Michael Parkinson, Bernard Foley, and Dennis R. Judd. Glenview, Ill.: Scott, Foresman, 1989.

Kagin, Donald H. "Monetary Aspects of the Treasury Notes of the War of 1812." *Journal of Economic History* 44 (March 1984).

Kantor, Paul. *The Dependent City Revisited: The Political Economy of Urban Development and Social Policy.* Boulder, Colo.: Westview Press, 1995.

Kantor, Paul, and H. V. Savitch. "Can Politicians Bargain with Business? A Theoretical and Comparative Perspective on Urban Development." *Urban Affairs Quarterly* 29 (December 1993), pp. 230–55.

Kantor, Paul, with Stephen David. *The Dependent City: The Changing Political Economy of Urban America.* Glenview, Ill.: Scott, Foresman, 1988.

Katznelson, Ira. *City Trenches: Urban Politics and the Patterning of Class in the United States.* New York: Pantheon Books, 1981.

Kaufman, George C. Preface to *Efficiency in the Municipal Bond Market: The Use of Tax Exempt Financing for "Private" Purposes,* ed. George C. Kaufman. Greenwich, Conn.: JAI Press, 1981.

Keating, Michael. *Comparative Urban Politics: Power and the City in the United States, Canada, Britain, and France.* Aldershot, England: Edward Elgar, 1991.

Kenyon, Daphne A. "Effects of Federal Volume Caps on State and Local Borrowing." *Tax Journal* 44 (1991).

Keohane, John. "The Federal Government and State/Local Government Securities: A Short History of Reciprocal Immunity." *Government Finance Review* (June 1988).

Kettleborough, Charles. "Special Municipal Corporations." *American Political Science Review* 8 (November 1914), pp. 614–21.

Kilpatrick, Wylie. "Federal Regulation of Local Debt." *National Municipal Review* 26 (June 1937), pp. 283–98.

Kirkland, Edward C. *Men, Cities, and Transportation: A Study in New England History, 1820–1900.* Cambridge: Harvard University Press, 1948.

Knappen, Laurence S. *Revenue Bonds and the Investor.* New York: Prentice-Hall, 1939.

Knight, Jerry. "Muni Bonds Targeted for Key Reforms." *Washington Post,* September 8, 1993.

Kravis, Irving B. "The Role of Exports in Nineteenth-Century United States Growth." *Economic Development and Cultural Change* (April 1972).

Kurtz, Paul M. "Nineteenth Century Anti-Entrepreneurial Nuisance Injunctions — Avoiding the Chancellor." *William and Mary Law Review* 17 (summer 1976), pp. 621–72.

Lamb, Robert, and Stephen P. Rappaport. *Municipal Bonds: The Comprehensive Review of Tax-Exempt Securities and Public Finance.* New York: McGraw-Hill, 1980.

Lamoreaux, Naomi R. *The Great Merger Movement in American Business, 1895–1904.* Cambridge: Cambridge University Press, 1985.

Lancaster, Lane. *State Supervision of Municipal Indebtedness.* Philadelphia: Westbrook, 1923.

Land, Guy. "IDB Program Has Strong Support." *Public Finance Network News* (July/August 1991).

Larsen, Lawrence H. *The Rise of the Urban South.* Lexington: The University Press of Kentucky, 1985.

———. *The Urban West at the End of the Frontier.* Lawrence: Regents Press of Kansas, 1978.

Lechner, Alan B. *Industrial Aid Financing.* New York City: Goodbody and Company, 1965.

Leeds, Patricia Giles. "City Politics and the Market: The Case of New York City's Financing Crisis." In *The Municipal Money Chase: The Politics of Local Government Finance,* ed. Alberta M. Sbragia. Boulder, Colo.: Westview Press, 1983.

Lemov, Penelope. "Working Smarter: The Tax-Exempt Bond Lobby Wins Three Big Ones." *Governing* (January 1990), pp. 21–26.

Leonard, Herman B. *Checks Unbalanced: The Quiet Side of Public Spending.* New York: Basic Books, 1986.

Lepawsky, Albert. *Home Rule for Metropolitan Chicago.* Chicago: University of Chicago Press, 1935.

———. "Water Resources and Federalism." *American Political Science Review* 44 (September 1950), pp. 631–49.

Linn, Virginia. "Airport to Spur Jobs for 17,600." *Pittsburgh Post-Gazette,* July 15, 1988.

———. "Foerster Doubts Need for New Agency." *Pittsburgh Post-Gazette,* July 16, 1988.

Lively, Robert A. "The American System: A Review Article." *The Business History Review* 29 (March 1955), pp. 81–96.

Livingston, James. *Origins of the Federal Reserve System: Money, Class, and Corporate Capitalism, 1890–1913.* Ithaca, N.Y.: Cornell University Press, 1986.

Logan, John, and Harvey Molotch. *Urban Fortunes: The Political Economy of Place.* Berkeley and Los Angeles: University of California Press, 1987.

Logan, John, and Todd Swanstrom, eds. *Beyond the City Limits.* Philadelphia: Temple University Press, 1990.

Lowi, Theodore J. Foreword to *Technocracy Versus Democracy: The Comparative Politics of International Airports,* by Elliot J. Feldman and Jerome E. Milch. Boston, Mass.: Auburn, 1982.

Luckingham, Bradford. "The American West: An Urban Perspective." *Journal of Urban History* 8 (November 1981), pp. 99–105.

———. *The Urban Southwest: A Profile History of Albuquerque, El Paso, Phoenix, Tucson.* University of Texas at El Paso: Texas Western Press, 1982.

Lynch, Daniel W. *The Development of State and Local Debt in Kentucky, 1890–1962.* Lexington: Bureau of Business Research, College of Commerce, University of Kentucky, 1966.

MacManus, Susan. "Special District Governments: A Note on Their Use as Property Tax Relief Mechanisms in the 1970s." *Journal of Politics* 43 (November 1981), pp. 1207–14.

Magnusson, Jon. "Lease-Financing by Municipal Corporations as a Way Around Debt Limitations." *George Washington Law Review* 25 (March 1957), pp. 377–96.

Marlin, Matthew R. "Industrial Development Bonds at Fifty: A Golden Anniversary Review." *Economic Development Quarterly* 1 (November 1987), pp. 391–410.

Mathewson, William C. "A New Bridge to Cross: The Doctrine of Inverse Federalism." *Detroit College of Law Review* (winter 1989), pp. 1315–50.

McAllister, Breck P. "Public Purpose in Taxation." *California Law Review* 18 (November 1929), pp. 137–254.

McBain, Howard Lee. *The Law and the Practice of Municipal Home Rule.* New York: Columbia University Press, 1916.

McCormick, Richard L. "The Party Period and Public Policy: An Exploratory Hypothesis." *Journal of American History* 66 (September 1979), pp. 279–98.

McCraw, Thomas K., ed. *Regulation in Perspective: Historical Essays.* Cambridge: Harvard University Press, 1981.

McCurdy, Charles W. "Justice Field and the Jurisprudence of Government-Business Relations: Some Parameters of Laissez-Faire Constitutionalism, 1863–1897." *Journal of American History* 61 (March 1975).

McDonald, Terrence J. *The Parameters of Urban Fiscal Policy: Socioeconomic Change and Political Culture in San Francisco, 1860–1906.* Berkeley and Los Angeles: University of California Press, 1986.

McDonald, Terrence J., and Sally K. Ward, eds. *The Politics of Urban Fiscal Policy.* Beverly Hills: Sage, 1984.

McEvoy, Arthur F. *The Fisherman's Problem: Ecology and Law in the California Fisheries, 1850–1980.* Cambridge: Cambridge University Press, 1986.

McGoldrick, Joseph D. *Law and Practice of Municipal Home Rule, 1916–1930.* New York: Columbia University Press, 1933.

McGrane, Reginald C. *The Economic Development of the American Nation.* Rev. ed., New York: Ginn and Company, 1950.

———. *Foreign Bondholders and American State Debts.* New York: MacMillan, 1935.

Melamed, Dennis. "As the Feds Bow Out, Communities Seek New Ways to Pay for Clean Water." *Governing* (July 1990).

Melosi, Martin V., ed. *Pollution and Reform in American Cities, 1870–1930.* Austin: University of Texas, 1980.

Mercer, Lloyd. *Railroads and Land Grant Policy: A Study in Government Intervention.* New York: Academic Press, 1982.

Milch, Jerome E. "Influence as Power: French Local Government Reconsidered." *British Journal of Political Science* 4 (April 1974).

Miller, George H. *Railroads and the Granger Laws.* Madison: University of Wisconsin Press, 1971.

Miller, Nathan. *The Enterprise of a Free People: Aspects of Economic Development in New York State During the Canal Period, 1792–1838.* Ithaca, N.Y.: Cornell University Press, 1962.

Million, John W. *State Aid to Railways in Missouri.* Chicago: University of Chicago Press, 1896.

Miranda, Rowan A. "Post-Machine Regimes and the Growth of Government: A Fiscal History of the City of Chicago, 1970–1990." *Urban Affairs Quarterly* 28 (March 1993), pp. 397–422.

Mitchell, Constance, and Thomas T. Vogel Jr. "Illegal Payments Mar the Muni Market." *Wall Street Journal,* May 5, 1993.

Mitchell, Jerry. "The Policy Activities of Public Authorities." *Policy Studies Journal* 18 (summer 1990).

Mitchell, William E. *The Effectiveness of Debt Limits on State and Local Government Borrowing.* New York University, Graduate School of Business Administration, Institute of Finance. Bulletin no. 45, October 1967.

Mollenkopf, John H. *The Contested City.* Princeton: Princeton University Press, 1983.

Monkkonen, Eric H. *America Becomes Urban: The Development of U.S. Cities and Towns, 1780–1980.* Berkeley and Los Angeles: University of California Press, 1988.

———. "The Politics of Municipal Indebtedness and Default, 1850–1936." In *The Politics of Urban Fiscal Policy,* ed. Terrence J. McDonald and Sally K. Ward. Beverly Hills: Sage, 1984.

Moody's Investors Service. "Moody's Views on Lease Rental Debt." *Moody's Municipal Issues* 6 (March 1989).

Moore, James Tice. *Two Paths to the New South: The Virginia Debt Controversy, 1870–1883.* Lexington: The University Press of Kentucky, 1974.

Moore, Thomas S., and Gregory D. Squires. "Public Policy and Private Benefits: The Case of Industrial Revenue Bonds." In *Business Elites and Urban Development: Case Studies and Critical Perspectives,* ed. Scott Cummings. Albany, N.Y.: State University of New York Press, 1988.

Morris, C. Robert Jr. "Evading Debt Limitations with Public Building Authorities: The Costly Subversion of State Constitutions." *Yale Law Journal* 68 (December 1958), pp. 234–68.

Nash, Gerald D. *State Government and Economic Development: A History of Administrative Policies in California, 1849–1933.* Institute of Governmental Studies, University of California, 1964.

Nehemkis, Peter R. Jr. "The Public Authority: Some Legal and Practical Aspects." *Yale Law Review* 47 (November 1937), pp. 14–33.

New York's Local Industrial Development Agencies, a Closer Look: An Interim Report of the New York State Legislative Commission on State-Local Relations. September 1989.

Nichols, F. Glenn. "Debt Limitations and the Bona Fide Long-Term Lease with an Option to Purchase: Another Look at Lord Coke." *The Urban Lawyer* 9 (spring 1977), pp. 403–20.

Olson, James S. *Saving Capitalism: The Reconstruction Finance Corporation and the New Deal, 1933–1940.* Princeton: Princeton University Press, 1988.

Pagano, Michael A., and Richard J. T. Moore. *Cities and Fiscal Choices: A New Model of Urban Public Investment.* Durham: Duke University Press, 1985.

Pascarella, Thomas A., and Richard D. Raymond. "Buying Bonds for Business: An Evaluation of the Industrial Revenue Bond Program." *Urban Affairs Quarterly* (September 1982), pp. 73–89.

Patterson, James T. *The New Deal and the States: Federalism in Transition.* Princeton: Princeton University Press, 1969.

Peers, Alexandra. "Corporate-Bond Storm Flood into 'Munis'." *Wall Street Journal,* November 23, 1988.

Pennsylvania Economy League. *A Review of Philadelphia's Authorities.* Report no. 566. October 1989.

Pennsylvania Economy League, Eastern Division. *Philadelphia's Debt Limit: A Restraint on Debt or an Obstacle to Growth?* Report no. 531. April 1988.

Perrenod, Virginia Marion. *Special Districts, Special Purposes: Fringe Governments and Urban Problems in the Houston Area.* College Station: Texas A&M Press, 1984.

Perry, David C. "Building the City Through the Back Door: The Politics of Debt, Law, and Public Infrastructure." In *Building the Public City: The Politics, Governance, and Finance of Public Infrastructure,* ed. David C. Perry. London: Sage, 1995.

Perry, David C., ed. *Building the Public City: The Politics, Governance, and Finance of Public Infrastructure.* London: Sage, 1995.

Persons, Warren M. *Government Experimentation in Business.* New York: John Wiley, 1934.

Petersen, John E. "Infrastructure Financing: Examining the Record and Considering the Options." In *Public Infrastructure Planning and Management,* ed. Jay M. Stein. Beverly Hills: Sage, 1988.

———. "Innovations in Tax-Exempt Instruments and Transactions." *National Tax Journal* 44 (1991).

———. "The Municipal Bond Market: Recent Changes and Future Prospects."

Unpublished paper. Government Finance Research Center, Municipal Finance Officers Association, February 13, 1981.

———. "Recent Developments in Tax-Exempt Bond Markets." Unpublished paper. Government Finance Research Center, Government Finance Officers Association, April 15, 1985.

———. "State and Local Government Debt Policy and Management." In *Essays in Public Finance and Financial Management: State and Local Perspectives,* ed. John E. Petersen and Catherine Lavigne Spain. Chatham, N.J.: Chatham House, 1978.

———. *Tax-Exempts and Tax Reform: Assessing the Consequences of the Tax Reform Act of 1986 for the Municipal Securities Market.* Research report. Government Finance Research Center of the Government Finance Officers Association and the Academy for State and Local Government. February 1987.

Petersen, John E., and Wesley C. Hough, ed. *Creative Capital Financing for State and Local Governments.* Government Finance Research Center, Municipal Finance Officers Association, 1983.

Peterson, George E. "Capital Spending and Capital Obsolescence: The Outlook for Cities." In *The Fiscal Outlook for Cities: Implications of a National Urban Policy,* ed. Roy Bahl. Syracuse, N.Y.: Syracuse University Press, 1978.

Peterson, George E., and Brian Cooper. *Tax-Exempt Financing of Housing Investment.* Washington, D.C.: The Urban Institute, 1979.

Peterson, George E., and Harvey Galper. "Tax Exempt Financing of Private Industry's Pollution Control Investment." *Public Policy* 23 (winter 1975).

Peterson, George E., John A. Tuccillo, and John C. Weicher. "The Impact of Local Mortgage Revenue Bonds on Securities, Markets, and Housing Policy Objectives." In *Efficiency in the Municipal Bond Market: The Use of Tax Exempt Financing for "Private" Purposes,* ed. George G. Kaufman. Greenwich, Conn.: JAI Press, 1981.

Peterson, Paul E. *City Limits.* Chicago: University of Chicago Press, 1981.

Phillips, Ulrich Bonnell. *A History of Transportation in the Eastern Cotton Belt to 1860.* New York: Octagon Books, 1968.

Pierce, Harry H. *Railroads of New York: A Study of Government Aid, 1826–1875.* Cambridge: Harvard University Press, 1953.

Pierce, Lawrence W. "Tax-Exempt Financing for Convention Centers." *Government Finance Review* (December 1988).

Platt, D. C. M. *Foreign Finance in Continental Europe and the United States, 1815–1870: Quantities, Origins, Functions, and Distribution.* London: George Allen and Unwin, 1984.

Platt, Harold L. *City Building in the New South: The Growth of Public Services in Houston, Texas, 1830–1910.* Philadelphia: Temple University Press, 1983.

Pointius, Dale. *State Supervision of Local Government: Its Development in Massachusetts.* Washington, D.C.: American Council on Public Affairs, 1942.

Porter, Douglas R., Ben C. Lin, and Richard B. Peiser. *Special Districts: A Useful Technique for Financing Infrastructure.* Washington, D.C.: Urban Land Institute, 1987.

Preserving the Federal-State-Local Partnership: The Role of Tax-Exempt Financ-

ing. Report to Congressman Beryl F. Anthony Jr. Washington, D.C.: October 1989.

"President's Budget: Bad News for Bonds." *Public Finance Network News* (March/April 1991).

"President Seeks Tax Immunity End by a 'Simple Law'." *New York Times,* January 18, 1939.

Preston, Nathaniel Stone. *The Use and Control of Public Authorities in American State and Local Government.* Ph.D. dissertation, Princeton University, 1960.

Primm, James Neal. *Economic Policy in the Development of a Western State, Missouri, 1820–1860.* Cambridge: Harvard University Press, 1954.

"Private Activity Bond Volume for 1989." *Government Finance Review* (February 1989).

Pryde, Joan. "The Ongoing Battle: Almost Seventy Years of Assaults on Tax-Exempt Municipals." *The Bond Buyer: 100 Anniversary Edition* (1991).

Public Securities Association. *Fundamentals of Municipal Bonds.* Rev. ed., New York, 1981.

———. *Fundamentals of Municipal Bonds.* 3d ed. New York, 1987.

Quinn, Kevin, and Myron Olstein. "Privatization: Public/Private Partnerships Provide Essential Services." In *Public/Private Partnerships: Financing a Commonwealth,* ed. Barbara Weiss. Washington, D.C.: Government Finance Research Center, Government Finance Officers Association, 1985.

Quirk, William J., and Leon E. Wein. "A Short Constitutional History of Entities Commonly Known as Authorities." *Cornell Law Review* 56 (April 1971).

Ransom, Roger L. "Canals and Development: A Discussion of the Issues." *American Economic Review* 54 (May 1964).

Ratchford, B. U. *American State Debts.* Durham: Duke University Press, 1941.

Rea, Leonard Owens. "The Financial History of Baltimore, 1900–1926." *Johns Hopkins University Studies in Historical and Political Science* 47. Baltimore: Johns Hopkins Press, 1929.

Reed, Merl E. *New Orleans and the Railroads: The Struggle for Commercial Empire, 1830–1860.* Baton Rouge: Louisiana State University Press, 1966.

Riker, William H. *Federalism: Origin, Operation, Significance.* Boston: Little, Brown, 1964.

———. "Six Books in Search of a Subject — or Does Federalism Exist and Does It Matter?" *Comparative Politics* 2 (1969).

Riley, James C. *International Government Finance and the Amsterdam Capital Market, 1740–1815.* Cambridge: Cambridge University Press, 1980.

Rivlin, Alice M. "CBO's Position on Tax-Exempt Financing for Private Activities." *Municipal Finance Journal* 4 (1983).

Rosen, Christine Meisner. *The Limits of Power: Great Fires and the Process of City Growth in America.* Cambridge: Cambridge University Press, 1986.

Rosewater, Victor. *Special Assessments: A Study in Municipal Finance.* 2d ed. New York: Columbia University Press, 1898.

Rowe, James L. Jr. "Municipal Bond Market Sinks: Investors Panic over Proposed Tax Change in Senate Finance Committee." *Washington Post,* March 20, 1986.

Roy, Arthur P. "State Constitutional Provisions Prohibiting the Loaning of Credit to Private Enterprise—A Suggested Analysis." *The University of Colorado Law Review* 41 (1969).

Rubin, Julius. "Canal or Railroad? Imitation and Innovation in the Response to the Erie Canal in Philadelphia, Baltimore, and Boston." *Transactions of the American Philosophical Society* 51 (November 1961).

——. "An Imitative Public Improvement: The Pennsylvania Mainline." In *Canals and American Economic Development,* ed. Carter Goodrich. New York: Columbia University Press, 1961.

Saffeldt, Raymond J., and Kenneth Unger. "Pennsylvania's Capital Budgeting System." *State Government* 58 (February 1985).

Sanders, Heywood T. "Building the Convention City: Politics, Finance, and Public Investment in Urban America." *Journal of Urban Affairs* 14 (1992), pp. 135–59.

——. "Politics, Public Finance, and the Implementation of the 1909 Plan for Chicago, or Daniel Burnham Meets 'Hinky Dink' and Bill Thompson." Paper presented at the annual meeting of the Urban Affairs Association, Cleveland, Ohio, April 30, 1992.

Sause, George G., and Andrew S. Bullis. *Municipal Authorities: The Pennsylvania Experience.* Harrisburg, Pa.: Commonwealth of Pennsylvania, Department of Internal Affairs, 1962.

Savage, James D. *Balanced Budgets and American Politics.* Ithaca, N.Y.: Cornell University Press, 1988.

Sayre, Wallace S., and Herbert Kaufman. *Governing New York City: Politics in the Metropolis.* New York: Norton, 1960.

Sbragia, Alberta M. "Borrowing to Build: Private Money and Public Welfare." *International Journal of Health Services* 9 (1979), pp. 207–18.

——. "Capital Markets and Central-Local Politics in Britain." *British Journal of Political Science* 16 (July 1986), pp. 311–33.

——. *Capital Markets and Central-Local Politics in Britain: The Double Game.* Studies in Public Policy, no. 109. Centre for the Study of Public Policy, University of Strathclyde, Glasgow. 1983.

——. "Cities, Capital, and Banks: The Politics of Debt in the United States, United Kingdom, and France." In *Urban Political Economy,* ed. Kenneth Newton. London: Frances Pinter, 1981.

——. "Finance Capital and the City." In *Cities in Stress: A Look at the Urban Crisis,* ed. Mark Gottdiener. Beverly Hills: Sage, 1986.

——. "Not All Roads Lead to Rome: Local Housing Policy in the Unitary Italian State." *British Journal of Political Science* 9 (July 1979), pp. 315–40.

——. "Politics, Local Government, and the Municipal Bond Market." In *The Municipal Money Chase: The Politics of Local Government Finance,* ed. A. Sbragia. Boulder, Colo.: Westview Press, 1983.

——. *The Politics of Local Borrowing: A Comparative Analysis.* Studies in Public Policy, no. 37. Centre for the Study of Public Policy, University of Strathclyde, Glasgow, 1979.

———. *The Politics of Public Investment: An Anglo-American Comparison.* Studies in Public Policy, no. 139. Centre for the Study of Public Policy, University of Strathclyde, 1985.

———. "Public-Sector Politics, Capital Markets, and Economic Development: Public Investment in Great Britain and the United States." In *Subnational Politics in the 1980s: Organization, Reorganization, and Economic Development,* ed. Louis A. Picard and Raphael Zariski. New York: Praeger, 1987.

Scharpf, Fritz W. "The Joint-Decision Trap: Lessons from German Federalism and European Integration." *Public Administration* 66 (autumn 1988).

Schefter, Martin. *Political Crisis/Fiscal Crisis: The Collapse and Revival of New York City.* New York: Basic Books, 1985.

Scheiber, Harry N. "At the Borderland of Law and Economic History: The Contributions of Willard Hurst." *American Historical Review* 75 (February 1970), pp. 744–56.

———. "Federalism and the American Economic Order, 1789–1910." *Law and Society Review* 10 (fall 1975), pp. 57–118.

———. *Ohio Canal Era: A Case Study of Government and the Economy, 1820–1861.* Athens: Ohio University Press, 1969.

———. "Public Economic Policy and the American Legal System: Historical Perspectives." *Wisconsin Law Review* 1 (1980), pp. 159–90.

———. "The Road to *Munn:* Eminent Domain and the Concept of Public Purpose in the State Courts." In *Law in American History,* ed. Donald Fleming and Bernard Bailyn. Boston: Little, Brown, 1971.

———. "Urban Rivalry and Internal Improvements in the Old Northwest, 1820–1860." *Ohio History* 71 (October 1962), pp. 227–39.

Schiesl, Martin J. *The Politics of Efficiency: Municipal Administration and Reform in America, 1800–1920.* Berkeley and Los Angeles: University of California, 1977.

Schmalz, Jeffrey. "Cuomo Pushes Challenge to Salaries at Authorities." *New York Times,* February 7, 1988.

Schnell, J. Christopher. "Chicago Versus St. Louis: A Reassessment of the Great Rivalry." *Missouri Historical Review* 71 (April 1877), pp. 245–65.

Schultz, Harvey W. Commissioner of the Department of Environmental Protection, New York City, Letter to the Editor. *New York Times,* July 24, 1989.

Schultz, Stanley K., and Clay McShane. "To Engineer the Metropolis: Sewers, Sanitation, and City Planning in Late Nineteenth-Century America." *Journal of American History* 65 (September 1978), pp. 389–411.

———. "Pollution and Political Reform in Urban America: The Role of Municipal Engineers, 1840–1920." In *Pollution and Reform in American Cities, 1870–1930,* ed. Martin V. Melosi. Austin: University of Texas, 1980.

Schwarz, Jordon A. *The Interregnum of Despair: Hoover, Congress, and the Depression.* Urbana, Ill.: University of Illinois Press, 1970.

Scott, William A. *The Repudiation of State Debts: A Study in the Financial History of Mississippi, Florida, Alabama, North Carolina, South Carolina, Georgia, Louisiana, Arkansas, Tennessee, Minnesota, Michigan, and Virginia.* New York: Thomas Y. Crowell, 1893.

Segal, Harvey H. "Cycles of Canal Construction." In *Canals and American Economic Development,* ed. Carter Goodrich. New York: Columbia University Press, 1961.

Shafroth, Frank. "Proposed Campaign Finance Regs Would Discriminate Against City Officials." *Nation's Cities Weekly,* April 11, 1994.

Shestack, Jerome J. "The Public Authority." *University of Pennsylvania Law Review* 105 (February 1957), pp. 553–69.

Shonfield, Andrew. *Modern Capitalism: The Changing Balance of Public and Private Power.* Oxford University Press, 1965.

Shultz, William J., and M. R. Caine. *Financial Development of the United States.* New York: Prentice-Hall, 1937.

Silbey, Joel H. *The Transformation of American Politics, 1840–1860.* Englewood Cliffs, N.J.: Prentice-Hall, 1967.

Sklar, Martin J. *The Corporate Reconstruction of American Capitalism, 1890–1916: The Market, the Law, and Politics.* Cambridge: Cambridge University Press, 1988.

Smith, Alfred Glaze Jr. *Economic Readjustment of an Old Cotton State, South Carolina, 1820–1860.* Columbia: University of South Carolina Press, 1958.

Smith, James. "Two Infrastructure Proposals Under Congressional Review." *Public Finance Network News.* May/June 1991.

Smith, Robert G. *Ad Hoc Governments: Special Purpose Transportation Authorities in Britain and the United States.* Beverly Hills: Sage, 1974.

———. *Public Authorities in Urban Areas.* Washington, D.C.: National Association of Counties Research Foundation, 1969.

———. *Public Authorities, Special Districts, and Local Government.* Washington, D.C.: National Association of Counties Research Foundation, 1964.

Smothers, Ronald. "Now Atlanta Begins Going for its Gold." *New York Times,* September 20, 1990.

Spatter, Sam. "Low-Income Families Get State, Local Housing Funds." *Pittsburgh Press,* March 20, 1988.

Squires, Gregory D. "Industrial Revenue Bonds and the Deindustrialization of America." *Urbanism Past and Present* 9 (winter/spring 1984), pp. 1–9.

Squires, Gregory D., ed. *Unequal Partnerships.* New Brunswick, N.J.: Rutgers University Press, 1988.

State and Local Governments Under Stress: The Role of the Capital Markets. Hearings before the Subcommittee on Securities of the Committee on Banking, Housing, and Urban Affairs. U.S. Senate, 102d Cong., 1st sess., March 13, April 24, 1991.

Steiss, Alan Walter. *Local Government Finance: Capital Facilities Planning and Debt Administration.* Lexington, Mass.: Lexington Books, 1975.

Still, Bayrd. *Milwaukee, the History of a City.* Madison: State Historical Society of Wisconsin, 1948.

Stone, Clarence N. *Regime Politics.* Lawrence: University Press of Kansas, 1989.

———. "The Study of the Politics of Urban Development." In *The Politics of Urban Development,* ed. Clarence N. Stone and Heywood T. Sanders. Lawrence: University Press of Kansas, 1987.

Stone, Clarence N., and Heywood T. Sanders, eds. *The Politics of Urban Development*. Lawrence: University Press of Kansas, 1987.

Strickland, Harry B. *Inside the Trojan Horse*. Clarks Summit, Pa.: Logo Publishing and Research, 1969.

Studenski, Paul, and Herman E. Krooss. *Financial History of the United States: Fiscal, Monetary, Banking, and Tariff, Including Financial Administration and State and Local Finance*. 2d ed. New York: McGraw Hill, 1963.

Summers, Mark W. *Railroads, Reconstruction, and the Gospel of Prosperity: Aid Under the Radical Republicans, 1865–1877*. Princeton: Princeton University Press, 1984.

Swanstrom, Todd. *The Crisis of Growth Politics: Cleveland, Kucinich, and the Challenge of Urban Populism*. Philadelphia: Temple University Press, 1985.

"Symposium on Public Authorities and Public Policy." *Policy Studies Journal* 18 (summer 1990), pp. 927–1044.

Tarr, Joel A. "The Separate Versus Combined Sewer Problem: A Case Study in Urban Technology Design Choice." *Journal of Urban History* 5 (May 1979), pp. 308–39.

Tarr, Joel A., and Francis Clay McMichael. "Decisions About Wastewater Technology, 1850–1932." *Journal of Water Resources Planning and Management Division, Proceedings of the American Society of Civil Engineers* 103 (May 1977), pp. 47–61.

——. "Historic Turning Points in Municipal Water Supply and Wastewater Disposal, 1850–1932." *Civil Engineering* (October 1977).

——. "Water and Wastes: A History." *Water Spectrum* 10 (fall 1978), pp. 18–25.

Tarr, Joel A., James McCurley, and Terry F. Yosie. "The Development and Impact of Urban Wastewater Technology: Changing Concepts of Water Quality Control, 1850–1930." In *Pollution and Reform in American Cities, 1870–1930*, ed. Martin V. Melosi. Austin: University of Texas Press, 1980.

Taylor, George Rogers. *The Transportation Revolution, 1815–1860*. New York: Rinehart and Company, 1951.

Teaford, Jon C. *City and Suburb: The Political Fragmentation of Metropolitan America, 1850–1970*. Baltimore: Johns Hopkins University Press, 1979.

——. "Finis for Tweed and Steffens: Rewriting the History of Urban Rule." *Reviews in American History* 10 (December 1982), pp. 137–43.

——. "State Administrative Agencies and the Cities, 1890–1920." *American Journal of Legal History* 25 (1981), pp. 225–48.

——. *The Unheralded Triumph: City Government in America, 1870–1900*. Baltimore: Johns Hopkins University Press, 1984.

Temporary State Commission on Coordination of State Activities. *Staff Report on Public Authorities Under New York State*. Albany: Williams Press, 1956.

Thompson, Carl D. *Public Ownership: A Survey of Public Enterprises, Municipal, State, and Federal, in the United States and Elsewhere*. New York: Thomas Y. Crowell Company, 1925.

U.S. General Accounting Office (GAO). *Distressed Communities: Capital Invest-*

ments Were Postponed in Texas as Local Economies Weakened. Report to the Chairman, Committee on Finance, U.S. Senate, February 1991.

———. *Home Ownership: Mortgage Bonds Are Costly and Provide Little Assistance to Those in Need.* GAO/RCED-88-111, March 1988.

———. *Trends and Changes in the Municipal Bond Market as They Relate to Financing State and Local Public Infrastructure.* GAO/PAD-83-46, September 12, 1983.

U.S. Congress. Congressional Budget Office. *Federal Support of U.S. Business.* January 1984.

———. *Loan Guarantees: Current Concerns and Alternatives for Control.* January 1979.

———. *The Mortgage Subsidy Bond Tax Act of 1980: Experience Under the Permanent Rules.* Staff working paper, March 1982.

———. *Small Issue Industrial Revenue Bonds.* Washington, D.C.: U.S. Government Printing Office, April 1981.

———. *Tax-Exempt Bonds for Single-Family Housing: A Study.* Prepared for the Subcommittee on the City of the Committee on Banking, Finance, and Urban Affairs, House of Representatives, 96th Cong., 1st sess. Washington, D.C.: U.S. Government Printing Office, April 1979.

———. "Trends in Municipal Leasing." *Municipal Finance Journal* 4 (summer 1983), pp. 239-49.

U.S. Congress. House of Representatives. "Background." *Trends in Municipal Financing and the Use of Tax-Exempt Bonds to Finance Private Activities.* Hearing before the Committee on Ways and Means, 98th Cong., 1st sess. June 15, 16, 1983.

———. *Comprehensive Tax Reform.* Hearings before the Committee on Ways and Means, 99th Cong., 1st sess., on The President's Tax Proposals to the Congress for Fairness, Growth and Simplicity, Part 6 of 9. July 11, 12, and 17, 1985, Serial 99-46.

———. Joint Committee Print. *Trends in the Use of Tax-Exempt Bonds to Finance Private Activities, Including a Description of H.R. 1176 and H.R. 1635.* Prepared by the Staff of the Joint Committee on Taxation, Scheduled for a Hearing before the Committee on Ways and Means, 98th Cong., 1st sess., June 15, 16, 1983, published June 13, 1983. Washington, D.C.: Government Printing Office, 1983.

U.S. Government. Department of the Treasury. *Treasury Report on Private Purpose Tax-Exempt Bond Activity During Calendar Year 1983.* Office of Tax Analysis, March 28, 1984.

"U.S. Supreme Court Declines Appeal of Virginia Lease Case." *Public Finance Digest.* Government Finance Group Inc., A Legg Mason Company, Arlington, Virginia (June 1992).

Van de Woestyne, Royal S. *State Control of Local Finance in Massachusetts.* Cambridge: Harvard University Press, 1935.

Vaughan, Roger J. "Rebuilding America: Financing Public Works in the 1980s." In

Rebuilding America's Infrastructure: An Agenda for the 1980s, ed. Michael Barker. Durham: Duke University Press, 1984.

Virtue, Maxine. "The Public Use of Private Capital: A Discussion of Problems Related to Municipal Bond Financing." *Virginia Law Review* 35 (April 1949), pp. 285–95.

Vogel, Thomas T. Jr. "Politicians Are Mobilizing to Derail Ban on Muni Underwriters' Campaign Gifts." *Wall Street Journal,* December 27, 1993.

Vogel, Thomas T. Jr., and John Connor. "Muni-Firm Plan Meets Resistance; Political-Donation Limits Spur Protests from State Officials." *Wall Street Journal,* December 13, 1993.

Wade, Richard C. *The Urban Frontier: The Rise of Western Cities, 1790–1830.* Cambridge: Harvard University Press, 1959.

Wallace, Schuyler C. *State Administrative Supervision over Cities in the United States.* New York: Columbia University Press, 1928.

Wallison, Frieda K. "Tax-Exempt Lease Financing Gains Attention as Economic Conditions Change." In *Creative Capital Financing for State and Local Governments,* ed. John E. Petersen and Wesley C. Hough. Government Finance Research Center, Municipal Finance Officers Association, 1983.

Walsh, Annmarie Hauck. *The Public's Business: The Politics and Practices of Government Corporations.* Cambridge, Mass.: MIT Press, 1978.

Warren, Charles. *The Supreme Court in United States History.* Vol. 2, *1836–1918.* Rev. ed., Boston: Little, Brown, 1926.

"Washington Outlook." *Governing* (June 1992).

Weintraub, Tina V., and James D. Patterson. *The "Authority" in Pennsylvania: Pro and Con.* Philadelphia: Bureau of Municipal Research of Philadelphia, May 1949.

Wigmore, Barrie A. *The Crash and Its Aftermath: A History of Securities Markets in the United States, 1929–1933.* Westport, Conn.: Greenwood Press, 1985.

Wilke, John R. "Massachusetts Is Roiled by Bond Scandal." *Wall Street Journal,* July 21, 1993.

Williams, C. Dickerman, and Peter R. Nehemkis Jr. "Municipal Improvements as Affected by Constitutional Debt Limitations." *Columbia Law Review* 37 (February 1937).

Williams, Mary L., and Cynthia Saltzman. "The Impact of County Mortgage Programs on County Net Revenues." *State and Local Government Review* (winter 1991).

Wood, Lester T. III. "Investing Bond Proceeds and the Arbitrage Rebate Requirements." *Government Finance Review* (February 1990), pp. 19–22.

Wright, Deil. *Understanding Intergovernmental Relations.* North Scituate, Mass.: Duxbury Press, 1978.

Wright, James Edward. *The Politics of Populism: Dissent in Colorado.* New Haven: Yale University Press, 1974.

Wrightson, Margaret T. "The Road to *South Carolina:* Intergovernmental Tax Immunity and the Constitutional Status of Federalism." *Publius: The Journal of Federalism* (summer 1989), pp. 39–55.

Yearley, C. K. *The Money Machines: The Breakdown and Reform of Governmental and Party Finance in the North, 1860–1920*. Albany: State University of New York Press, 1970.

Yin Ch'u Ma. *The Finances of the City of New York*. New York: AMS Press, 1968.

Zimmerman, Dennis. "Federal Tax Policy, IDBs, and the Market for State and Local Bonds." *National Tax Journal* (September 1984), pp. 411–20.

———. "The Intergovernmental Struggle over Tax-Exempt Bond Reform." In *Intergovernmental Fiscal Relations in an Era of New Federalism,* ed. Michael Bell. Greenwich, Conn.: JAI Press, 1988.

———. *The Private Use of Tax-Exempt Bonds: Controlling Public Subsidy of Private Activity*. Washington, D.C.: The Urban Institute Press, 1991.

Zolkos, Rodd. "A Guide to Muni Bond Deals of the Year." *Governing* 7 (June 1994), pp. 59–68.

Zysman, John. *Governments, Markets, and Growth: Financial Systems and the Politics of Industrial Change*. Ithaca, N.Y.: Cornell University Press, 1983.

Index

MFM